International Political Economy Series

The global political economy is in flux as a series of cumulative crises impacts its organization and governance. The IPE series has tracked its development in both analysis and structure over the last three decades. It has always had a concentration on the global South. Now the South increasingly challenges the North as the centre of development, also reflected in a growing number of submissions and publications on indebted Eurozone economies in Southern Europe. An indispensable resource for scholars and researchers, the series examines a variety of capitalisms and connections by focusing on emerging economies, companies and sectors, debates and policies. It informs diverse policy communities as the established trans-Atlantic North declines and 'the rest', especially the BRICS, rise.

More information about this series at
http://www.springer.com/series/13996

Abel Polese • Colin C. Williams • Ioana A. Horodnic • Predrag Bejakovic
Editors

The Informal Economy in Global Perspective

Varieties of Governance

palgrave
macmillan

Editors
Abel Polese
Dublin City University, School of Law and Government, Dublin, Ireland

University of Sheffield, Management School, Sheffield, United Kingdom

Tallinn University of Technology
Tallinn School of Law, Tallinn, Estonia

Colin C. Williams
University of Sheffield
Management School
Sheffield, United Kingdom

Predrag Bejakovic
Institute of Public Finance
Zagreb, Croatia

Ioana A. Horodnic
Alexandru Ioan Cuza University of Iaşi
Faculty of Economics and Business Administration, Iaşi, Romania

International Political Economy Series
ISBN 978-3-319-40930-6 ISBN 978-3-319-40931-3 (eBook)
DOI 10.1007/978-3-319-40931-3

Library of Congress Control Number: 2016963252

Printed on acid-free paper

This Palgrave Macmillan imprint is published by Springer Nature
The registered company is Springer International Publishing AG
The registered company address is: Gewerbestrasse 11, 6330 Cham, Switzerland

Acknowledgements

The idea for this book has been in the air for some time. As often happens, having an idea is easy. But turning that idea into something concrete takes much more. We have to thank the European Commission's Framework 7 Industry-Academia Partnerships Programme (IAPP) under grant no. 611259 entitled 'Out of the shadows: developing capacities and capabilities for tackling undeclared work' (GREY) for allowing the editors and the authors to work together to this volume. The initial shaping of the book emerged at the summer school 'Multiple moralities and shadow economies in post-socialism: debating positive and negative incentives to tackle the informal economy' that was hosted by the Institute of Public Finance in Zagreb.

We would like to thank the participants of the summer school for the thought-provoking discussions that allowed authors and editors to put their ideas into better shape and fine-tune the concept of this book. A special thanks goes to the authors who ended up contributing to the volume for their valuable work and capacity to keep up with our comments.

Not all the chapters are directly derived from the summer school and we are grateful to those authors who joined the project at a later stage, since their contributions have made the book even more "global" (and this was especially welcome given the title of the volume).

We are also grateful to the series editor, Tim Shaw, who has encouraged us from the very early stages of the project and provided advice throughout the whole process. Tim was one of the greatest discoveries of the past months and our dinner together in Boston is still very alive in our memories. Judith Allan is also to be thanked for coaching us into the publication process and patiently sending (and resending) all the documents and instructions needed.

In the course of this project we have greatly benefited from the support and friendship of a large number of colleagues and friends. The list is long and we are confident they all know about our debt of gratitude. Our thoughts go to all the marvellous people we have had the honour to meet and that have encouraged us to go on with this project, supporting us during all the different stages and inspiring us throughout the whole process, and in general throughout our long-term commitment to the study of informality. If, after many years, we continue working in academia, is because of the chance to do something fun and useful while meeting such a variety of interesting and amicable colleagues, who often end up turning into friends.

Contents

Acronyms

AFD	Agence Française de Développement
AGPC	Bolaven Plateau Coffee Producers Cooperative
ATJ	Alter Trade Japan, Inc.
BaC	Business against Corruption
BEEPS	Business Environment and Enterprise Performance Survey
CAP	Common Agricultural Policy
CCP	Chinese Communist Party
CDM	Cash-Deposit Method
CEE	Central and Eastern Europe
DIY	Do It Yourself
DLM	Dual Labor Market
ECM	Error-Correction Model
EHFCN	European Healthcare Fraud and Corruption Network
EMIMIC	Error Correction Multiple Indicators and Multiple Causes
ENOE	National Occupational and Employment Survey
ENOE	Mexico's National Survey of Occupation and Employment
ETF	European Training Foundation
EU	European Union
EUROSTAT	Statistical Office of the European Communities
FAO	Food and Agriculture Organization of the United Nations
GDP	Gross Domestic Product
GP	General Practitioner
GPRTU	Ghana Private Roads Transport Union

GRA	Ghana Revenue Authority
GRP	Gross Regional Product
GTUC	Ghana Trade Union Congress
HRM	Human Resources Management
ICA	Investment Climate Assessment
ICAC	Independent Commission Against Corruption
ICLS	International Conference of Labour Statisticians
ILO	The International Labour Organization
INEGI	Instituto Nacional de Estadística y Geografía
IPF	The Institutional Possibility Frontier
ISTAT	Italian National Statistical Institute
JCFC	Jhai Coffee Farmer's Cooperative
LCA	Lao Coffee Association
LFS	Labour Force Survey
LPRP	Lao People's Revolutionary Party
MIMIC	Multiple Indicators-Multiple Causes
NAFDAC	Nigerian National Agency for Food and Drug Administration and Control
NGO	Non-Governmental Organization
NOE	Non Observed Economy
OECD	Organisation for Economic Co-operation and Development
OIT	Organización Internacional del Trabajo
OLS	Ordinary Least Squares
PDR	People's Democratic Republic
PG	Production Groups
RLI	Rate of Labor Informality
ROSSTAT	The Russian Federal Statistical Service
SEM	Structural Equation Model
SME	Small and Medium Scale Enterprises
SSA	Sub-Saharan Africa
SSSU	State Statistics Service of Ukraine
TS	Tax Stamp
UAH	Ukrainian Hryvnia
UK	United Kingdom
ULMS	Ukrainian Longitudinal Monitoring Survey
UN	United Nations
UNDP	United Nations Development Programme

UNECE	United Nations Economic Commission for Europe
UNIDO	United Nations Industrial Development Organization
UNIWA	Union of Informal Workers Association
UNODC	United Nations Office on Drugs and Crime
USA	United States of America
USSR	Union of Soviet Socialist Republics
VIT	Vehicle Income Tax

Contributors

Philippe Adair Ph.D. in Economics and Ph.D. in Sociology, has over 100 publications to his name. His research topics are labour economics (the informal economy) and finance (small businesses funding and micro-finance), both in developing and developed countries. His area of expertise focuses on the MENA region, especially North Africa. He is a member of the ERUDITE research team and is currently a Ph.D. supervisor.

Kwame Adom is a Lecturer in Marketing and Entrepreneurship at the University of Ghana Business School. His research interests are in the informal economy and entrepreneurship in the global south and draw on experiences from Africa, specifically Ghana, to inform theoretical developments in entrepreneurship dynamics, motives of informal workers, social entrepreneurship and the relationship between formal and the informal economy and socioeconomic development. These interests lie at the union of a variety of disciplines including anthropology, business/management, economics, philosophy and sociology.

Predrag Bejakovic took his doctorate at the Economics Faculty in Zagreb, and now works in the Institute of Public Finance, Zagreb. He has taken part in a number of projects, such as the Underground Economy in the Republic of Croatia, the Development of the Tax Administration in Croatia and Pensions Reform and a Sustainable Budget of the Institute of Public Finance, and the Employment Policy Programme of the Government of the Republic of Croatia. Currently he is participating in the European Commission Project led by the Croatian Science Foundation 6558 Business and Personal Insolvency – the Ways to Overcame Excessive

Indebtedness and is the team leader for Croatia for the Seventh Framework Programme, "The People Programme – IAPP". He publishes in scientific and professional journals and is the author and the editor of a number of books on the economy, public finance, the underground economy, the pension system and labour economics.

Nancy Claire Benjamin gained a Ph.D. in economics from UC Berkeley, and then worked as an Assistant Professor at Syracuse University, in the Asia Department of the International Monetary Fund, the Research Department of the US International Trade Commission, and published on resource-rich countries, the impact of trade policy on productivity and growth, nontariff barriers, and on trade in services. At the World Bank, she has worked on West African and Middle Eastern countries, focusing on public expenditures, growth, governance and informality, as well as the regulation of multi-country infrastructure.

Ramon A. Castillo Ponce is professor and researcher in the Department of Economics and International Relations at the Universidad Autónoma de Baja California, Mexico and the Department of Economics and Statistics at the California State University, Los Angeles. He holds a Ph.D. in economics from the University of California, Irvine and specializes in applied time series econometrics and industrial organization. He is a member of the Mexican National System of Researchers under the Mexican National Bureau of Science and Technology. Castillo Ponce teaches microeconomic theory, industrial organization and econometrics at the undergraduate and graduate levels.

Wim Groot has been Professor of Health Economics since 1998 and Professor of Evidence Based Education since 2008 at Maastricht University. He is scientific director of the Top Institute Evidence Based Education Research and of the Teachers Academy of Maastricht University. His research interests are in the field of health economics and economics of education. As from 2016, he is an elected member of the Supervisory Board of the Patientfederation NPCF.

Fatou Gueye is Assistant Professor of Economics at the University Cheikh Anta Diop (UCAD- Dakar, Senegal). She has been at the forefront of recent research undertaken by UCAD on the informal sector in West and Central Africa. She has also conducted research on various topics of development.

Sabina Hodzic is Assistant Professor and Head of the Department of Public Finance at the University of Rijeka, Faculty of Tourism and Hospitality Management (Croatia). Her main field of research is public finance and current taxation issues. She lectures on public finance and international taxation and is the author of several papers published in academic journals.

Adrian V. Horodnic is an Assistant Professor of Ethics and Health Economics at Grigore T. Popa University of Medicine and Pharmacy in Romania. His current research interests include issues related to informal payments in healthcare, informal economy, chronic care model and health disparities.

Ioana A. Horodnicis an Assistant Professor in the Faculty of Economics and Business Administration at the Alexandru Ioan Cuza University of Iasi in Romania. Previously she was a post-doctoral researcher at the Romanian Academy. Her current research interests are in the informal sector and academic performance, subjects on which she has published about 25 peer-reviewed articles.

Abbas Khandan gained a Ph.D. in Economics from the University of Siena (Italy) in 2014. Since then, he has been a lecturer in several universities in Iran. His fields of specialization are public choice and public finance, social security and pensions. He has published, in English and Persian, several articles on the informal economy, lobbying and bribery, social security and pension finance.

Rogelio Varela Llamas is Professor and Researcher in the Department of Economics and International Relations at the Universidad Autónoma de Baja California, Mexico. He is a member of the Mexican National System of Researchers under the Mexican National Bureau of Science and Technology. His research focuses on the labor market and economic development. He currently teaches multivariate statistical analysis and econometrics in the MA programme in economic sciences.

Ahmadou Aly Mbaye is Professor of Economics at the University Cheikh Anta Diop (Dakar, Senegal). He has served until recently as the Dean of the faculty of Economics and management at Cheikh anta DIOP University (UCAD). He holds a Doctorate in Development Economics from the University of Clermont Ferrand (France) and has held several international academic positions, including as a Fulbright Professor at Swarthmore and George Washington University, a Cornell Visiting Professorship at Swarthmore College, and research visiting scholar at the research department of the World Bank. He has several publications in the area of development economics, and on Africa. He has also served as a consultant for many international organizations such as UNCTAD, World Trade Organization, the Food and Agriculture Organization of the United Nations, the World Bank, UNECA, West African Economic and Monetary Union), and the Senegalese government.

Arihiro Minoo is an Assistant Professor of Cultural Anthropology at Toyo University, Japan. His research topic is the impact of Fair Trade on coffee farmers in Lao PDR. His research interests include the emergence of counterpublic spheres in rural areas, the moral economy of middlemen and farmers, and the global economy.

Oksana Nezhyvenko is a Lecturer and Researcher at the National University of Kyiv-Mohyla Academy. With a Ph.D. in Economics, her research area focuses on labour market (informal employment) and the shadow economy. Her area of expertise is Eastern Europe and transition countries. She is a member of the ERUDITE research team (France, UPEC) and the Laboratory of Financial and Economic Research (Ukraine, NaUKMA).

Juan Manuel Ocegueda Hernandez is Professor and Researcher in the Department of Economics and International Relations at the Universidad Autónoma de Baja California, Mexico (UABC). He obtained his doctoral degree from Universidad Nacional Autónoma de México. A member of the Mexican National System of Researchers under the Mexican National Bureau of Science and Technology, he has published a number of research papers and books on regional development and economic growth. He teaches macroeconomics and economic growth theory in the MA and Doctoral programs in economic sciences at UABC.

Liviu Oprea is an Associate Professor of Bioethics and Behavioural Sciences at Grigore T. Popa University of Medicine and Pharmacy in Romania. He has a Ph.D. from University of Adelaide. His research interests are in doctor–-patient relationships, ethical issues in primary care, public health ethics and informal payments.

Milena Pavlova is Associate Professor of Health Economics at the Department of Health Services Research, Faculty of Health, Medicine and

Life Sciences, Maastricht University. Her research focuses on the financing of the health care sector, including formal and informal patient payments, as well as stated preference approaches, such as willingness-to-pay methods. She is Section Editor at the impact factor journal BMC Health Services Research.

Abel Polese is a scholar and development worker dividing his time between Europe, the former USSR and Southeast Asia. He has previously worked as a policy analyst for the European Commission (DG Research) and as a consultant for Austrian and Finnish Agencies for Erasmus+; Estonian Research Council; Rustaveli Foundation; SALTO; YouthForum; WAGGGS; UNOPS. His project "Sustainable Development in Cultural Diversity" received the Global Education Award from the Council of Europe in 2011. He is a member of the Global Young Academy, gathering scholars from around the world active in research policy and dialogue with non-academic institutions and has been a visiting fellow at the University of Toronto, Harvard, Renmin (China), Tbilisi (Georgia), JNU and Tezpur (India), Corvinus (Hungary), Cagliari (Italy) and the Moscow Higher School of Economics. His most recent work, co-edited with Jeremy Morris, debates the modes and forms of informality in the post-socialist world: *Informal Economies in Post-Socialist Spaces: Practices, Institutions and Networks* (Palgrave, 2015).

Lela Rekhviashvili is a post-doctoral researcher for the project on fluid mobilities for cities in transformation: spatial dynamics of marshrutkas in Central Asia and Caucasus at Leibniz Institute for Regional Geography. She has been visiting doctoral fellow at the Leibniz Institute for Regional Geography and a research fellow at the Center for Social Sciences. Lela's publications focus on urban informality, commodification of public spaces, internal displacement. Her broad research interests include: political economy, informal economic practices, post-socialist transformation, social movements, and urban reconfiguration.

Michael Rochlitz is Assistant Professor in the Faculty of Politics, at the Higher School of Economics in Moscow, Russia. He holds a Ph.D. from IMT Lucca, Italy. His research focuses on the political economy of state–business relations in Russia and China, authoritarian politics, the role of propaganda and collective action, as well as questions related to bureaucratic incentives and economic growth.

Julia Schipperges is Alumna of Program Health Policy Innovation and Management, Faculty of Health, Medicine and Life Sciences, Maastricht University. She has done internships at various organizations including Städtische Kliniken Mönchengladbach, LVR Klinik Viersen and EHFCN – European Healthcare Fraud & Corruption Network. Currently she is Customer Service Representative at Medtronic.

Tetiana Stepurko is Assistant Professor at the School of Public Health, National University of 'Kyiv-Mohyla Academy' in Kiev, Ukraine. She is also Head of Master Program at the School of Public Health, and Member of the Organizational Committee of Summer School Administration in Changed Health care System in Ukraine. She has broad research interests covering topics from sociology to health economics, including informal patient payments in post-communist context. She is Associate Editor at the impact factor journal BMC Health Services Research.

Diana Traikova is a trained agricultural economist. She is a post-doctoral researcher at the Leibniz Institute of Agricultural Development in Transitional Economies, where she deals with rural development issues. Her current research interests include rural entrepreneurship, corruption and informality in transition countries.

Paul Vincke is the Managing Director of EHFCN – European Healthcare Fraud & Corruption Network located in Brussels. He is also the Director of Staff at the Service of Medical Evaluation and Control of the National Institute for Health and Disability Insurance in Belgium. He is expert in personnel management, finance, healthcare fraud, waste and corruption.

Marius Wamsiedel is a Ph.D. candidate in Sociology at the University of Hong Kong. His doctoral project examines the social categorization of patients at emergency departments in Romania. He is also interested in post-socialist informal practices, public secrets and Romani studies.

Colin C. Williams is Professor of Public Policy in the Management School at the University of Sheffield, UK. His research interests are in production and consumption in the informal economy, subjects on which he has published some 25 books and 390 journal articles over the past 25 years.

Jingqing Yang is Senior Lecturer in China Studies at the University of Technology Sydney, Australia. His research interests cover social history of Chinese healthcare system, health professions and health reforms.

Adriana Zait is full professor at Alexandru Ioan Cuza University of Iaşi, Romania, Department of Management, Marketing and Business Administration. With a Ph.D. in Econometrics, she is doctoral thesis coordinator in the field of Marketing. She has significant international experience, for example as Visiting Professor in Austria, France, Germany, Ireland, Italy and Spain. In 2002 she was awarded the Petre S. Aurelian Prize from the Romanian Academy for the book *Economic Equilibrium or Disequilibrium?*. She has also been director of the research department, project director and team member in research projects on subjects related to economic convergence, intercultural management, academic marketing, research productivity and entrepreneurship.

List of Figures

List of Tables

Introduction: Informal Economies as Varieties of Governance

Abel Polese, Colin C. Williams, Ioana A. Horodnic, and Predrag Bejakovic

The growing body of research on informality, that has its origins in the work of Hart (1973) in Ghana, and which has resulted in a burgeoning literature comprising thousands of new articles ever year, has moved in recent years a long way from the monodisciplinary approach and lack of dialogue between disciplines that conventionally plagued the study of the informal sector. Initially approached from the perspectives of economic anthropology (1973) and labour studies (ILO 1972) that dealt, respectively, with informal economy and informal labour, studies on informality have increasingly broadened in terms of disciplines and geographical scope.

A. Polese (✉)
Tallinn University and Tallinn University of Technology,
Tallinn, Estonia

C.C. Williams
University of Sheffield, Sheffield, UK

I.A. Horodnic
Faculty of Economics and Business Administration, Alexandru Ioan Cuza
University of Iași, Iași, Romania
e-mail: ursachi_ioana_alexandra@yahoo.com

P. Bejakovic
Institute of Public Finance, Zagreb, Croatia

A. Polese et al. (eds.), *The Informal Economy in Global Perspective*, International Political Economy Series,
DOI 10.1007/978-3-319-40931-3_1

Drawing from a range of diverse theoretical approaches, recent scholarship on informality, informal practices, diverse and shadow economy have tended to agree on two major points. First, informality is—although in different forms and affecting different areas of a state's competence—present both in the global North and global South. Second, informality is not necessarily a transitory phenomenon nor it is limited to sweatshops and is not used only by the poor and marginalised. Starting from Gibson-Graham's seminal work contending that capitalism is not the only way (Gibson-Graham 1996, 2008), several works have been informing the creation of the understanding of diverse economies and, subsequently, the rediscovery of anarchism in geography (White and Williams 2014). This is a tendency that may be seen as stretching the literature on informal welfare and practices (Polese et al. 2014, 2015) to reject the state as the only provider of services and welfare so as to rediscover the role of human agency (Morris and Polese 2015) and mechanisms and practices that are not informed by the state or its institutions.

Recent tendencies on informality have gone beyond both a mere economic view and, building on Granovetter's early works (1984), rediscovered its interconnection with social phenomena (Gudeman 2001; Yelcin-Hackman 2014). The outcome has been a proposal for a more holistic interpretation of the meaning of informality and its influence in various spheres of life (Helmke and Levitsky 2004; Isaacs 2011; Ledeneva 1998, 2013; Misztal 2000; Morris 2011). The contemporary literature has also grown partially away from the original understanding that informality is premised on mostly a monetary logic (Gudeman 2001; Parry and Bloch 1989; Williams 2005) and there has also been recognition that it permeates societies in not only the global South but also the global North. In addition, whilst class and social status may influence the way informal practices are conceived and perpetuated, it has been shown that informal transactions exist among all segments of a society as well as winners and losers of transitions (Morris 2012; Morris and Polese 2014).

The above debates have also informed policy recommendations and policymaking in the field of fighting informal and shadow economies, policies that have gradually become more pragmatic and directed towards formalisation (Williams and Onoshchenko 2015). After the failures of zero-tolerance punitive approaches, a growing number of countries have concentrated on incentives to invite people "out of the shadow". This shift is explained in part by a growing number of studies which point to informality as a phenomenon covering a wide range of (economic, social and political) practices, far from being relegated to sweatshops and small-scale, ad hoc economic transactions. Instead, it is a global phenomenon penetrating all aspects of public life rather than being limited to the poor and marginalised (Maloney 2004; Misztal 2000). Informality is present everywhere, but in different forms and, whilst limited in some areas, cannot be liquidated as it is an integral part of state-citizen interactions and even state activity and (Polese 2015).

Informality and Governance

What is the relationship between an informal transaction that is often performed by two individuals, and state policies? We start here from Scott's understanding of infrapolitics (2012) to suggest that a particular action, performed by a substantial number of people, can have an effect on state policies. It is the aggregate of informal practices or transactions that feeds the very life of informal or shadow economies. Instead of looking normatively at informal transactions as a way to engage with illegal practices, they can be regarded as an act of insubordination, a rejection of state rule or acceptance that the state should be governing a particular aspect of the societal life (Polese 2016).

At this point, an overview of the genesis of informal transactions can help to better explain this approach. When a new informal practice is born, only a few people in a society use it so that, unless it is particularly visible or perceived as dangerous, the state is either unaware of it or simply ignores it. The cost of repression of a practice performed by a limited minority is too high and its social and political relevance too low to invest in tacking it. With time, however, a growing number of people might find the new practice useful or convenient. Should this happen, the number of people engaging with the sort of transaction increases. If the number of people adopting this new practice does not pose a threat to the state or its society, that is if the socio-economic damage stemming from it is limited, the informal practice is likely to remain tolerated. However, once it comes to be perceived as socially or economically dangerous, intervention will be needed and the state will have to choose between several options.

A first possibility is institutionalisation of the practice. There are cases where a state has "bought" a practice, formalised the marked and gained profit from it. The most recent case has been the legalisation of the use of marijuana in some US states. In such a situation, institutions are now saving on repression costs while generating income from sale of a product that circulated illegally, or informally, until very recently. A second possibility is attempting repression of the practice. This is, in principle, a risk. If the state does not identify proper (positive and negative) incentives, the practice is likely to continue and citizens might even assert their rights with regards to those practices or challenge the state and its competencies.

A sub-variation of the above situation is when a state succeeds in liquidating the practice and limits it to an extent that becomes irrelevant socially or economically. However, this exposes the state to the risk of failure. If the practice has become so embedded in society that it turns out to be impossible to eradicate it, a split of power might occur. Some citizens might unite into an institution or a group and challenge the state. There are many possible outcomes but reorganisation of groups into informal, non-state structures might bring one to the creation of insurgent governance structures (Kevlihan 2013).

In the past ten years, there have been several names and approaches used to describe political phenomena that originate beyond the state level and use institutions other than the official ones. However, the boundary between unorganised and organised dissidence has started being explored only recently. Interestingly enough, a number of relevant observations has been drawn from literature on rebel, insurgent and real governance (Péclard and Mechoulan 2015). As Tilly noticed "even in zones of civil war and widespread brawling, most people most of the time are interacting in nonviolent ways" (Tilly 2003, p. 12). This approach has paved the way to the study of what is now called "real governance" that, in an attempt to go beyond a normative understanding of power, is intended to explore the actors that participate in the construction of the policy processes of a given territory (Boege et al. 2009; Hagmann and Péclard 2010; Meagher 2012; Menkhaus 2008; Titeca and De Herdt 2011). It has been noticed that insurgent organisations or governments, in order to survive, need to transform the power of violence into legitimate domination (Schlichte 2009), provide a series of services and support to the citizens they intend to attract and ultimately gain legitimacy from the same people they are trying to hijack into a new administrative unit (Mampilly 2011). Rebel organisations might want, as a major strategy, to try and win the support of local populations and thus adapt to local beliefs, educate them or at least convince them to take the rebels' side (Kasfir 2005, p. 281). However, this is, in many respects, what any young or new state would have to do to secure support; Olson (1993) noted that rebel organisations' goals have a tendency to overlap with the ones of embryonic states. In fact, insurgent and rebel governance, it has been argued, has a tendency to replicate the phases and approaches that led to the formation of a state (Mampilly 2011; Olson 1993; Tilly 1990).

Informal economies are an act of deliberate, if unorganised, non-compliance. They may be distinct from rebel and insurgent governance in that the people who engage with them are not necessarily interested in finding a group identity or refer to a central leader. But it is possible that they are two sides of the same coin or that can be considered two positions on the same spectrum of non-state governance (Polese and Kevlihan 2015). On the one extreme we have informal practices, individual-centred, unorganised and socially irrelevant, in the very beginning at least. These practices can become more and more popular and spread across a given population. They are initially perceived as a survival strategy but are also a way to deny or challenge the role of the state at a given moment, or the right of a state to regulate a particular aspect of its social or economic life. It is possible to hypothesise the existence of a tipping point after which a leader emerge, a collective consciousness spreads and people become aware of being part of a larger movement. After all, all relevant social movements have lived through a tipping point, passing from virtually unknown to nationally or internationally recognised. Where were the (anti-austerity movement) *indignados* before 2011? Or the Polish Solidarity movement before 1980? The fact that they were not as famous or widely visible as they would become does not deny their existence before.

We tend to ignore phenomena until they make it into the headlines (Hobsbawm and Ranger [1968] 2014) but this does not mean that they do not exist. Engaging with research on informality means to study phenomena that are not immediately visible, perceived or sufficiently loud. It is an exploration of what have been defined as "invisible" phenomena (Polese 2016) on which data-gathering is more difficult than in other cases but that can help a better understanding of the society we inhabit. This book is an attempt to explore the invisible world of informality, to understand its role in a spectrum of governance approaches that includes the economy, the social and the legal structure of a country.

Structure of the Book and Overview of the Chapters

This book is composed of three main parts: theoretical and methodological dilemmas in the study of informal economies, informal economies in a European context and informal economies in a world context. The first part explores the methodological approaches used and usable to measure informal economies and the theoretical foundations of these approaches. Needless to say, our argument that there are many ways informality manifests itself is also our limit, as in no way can we claim to provide an exhaustive overview on the variety of approaches used to measure informality. However, the general message of this part is that measurement of informality is an ongoing process and that scientific creativity can be used to increase and improve the ways informality is dealt with.

Part one commences with a theoretical discussion, starting from an empirical case from Georgia, on the understandings and perceptions of informal economies. In her chapter, Lela Rekhviashvili discusses two contrasting, namely formalist and substantivist, interpretations of the second economy in Soviet Georgia and shows that the formalist interpretation fails to comprehend societal resistance against well-implemented market-enhancing reforms in post-revolution (2003) Georgia. Lack of explanations for this puzzling development is related to the failure of existing theories to offer consistent interpretation of socialist and post-socialist informality. Analysing the literature on post-Soviet informality, namely new institutionalist economics (formalist perspective) and economic sociology (embeddedness perspective), the chapter argues that a Polanyian substantivist reading of informality is the only one that warns of the market's propensity to undermine existing social and cultural institutions, and hence impose significant social costs on societies. Only this perspective allows one to establish continuity in interpreting socialist and post-socialist informality, explaining resistance against institutional reform in Georgia.

The third chapter, by Abbas Khandan, is an attempt to empirically test the effect of government interventions on the size of the informal economy, using an EMIMIC model with data of Iran as a case study for the sample period 1972–2013. The authors demonstrate that formal and informal economy share common long-run trends, but in the short run they are substitutes. In the long run government interventions based on legalist views are the main motivation to hide. This confirms that informal economy is the result of government's invisible hand. In the short run, however, higher per capita income and unemployment insurance mediate and decrease the informal economy to levels lower than the long-run trend. In addition, an index of the size of Iran's informal economy is estimated for long and short runs. The historical trend of the index show that the revolution of 1979, the Iran–Iraq war and the current sanctions have increased significantly the size of informal economy relative to GDP.

The third contribution provides us with a further methodological approach to measure the size of the shadow economy. In particular, Sabina Hodzic, estimates the size of Croatian shadow economy in the period 2008–2014 and provides insights regarding the time periods when the shadow economy in Croatia reached the highest level. The results show that the Croatian government needs to implement various sets of measures, especially structural reforms and also to continue the development of the judiciary, taking actions to improve its independence, reviewing the principles of financial support for law enforcement and providing measures to improve their wages.

The following chapter, by Oksana Nezhyvenko and Philippe Adair, introduces the study of informal employment and presents the current state of informal employment in Ukraine according to standards of the International Labour Organisation (ILO) and paying detailed attention to distribution across and within four categories of workers: formal employees and self-employed as well as informal employees and self-employed. Using the data from the Ukrainian Longitudinal Monitoring Survey (ULMS) for 2007, the authors design a Mincer earnings distribution function in order to investigate the factors that determine the income of individuals. The results reveal that human capital theory proves robust in as much as educational attainment is a major explanatory factor for formal workers, although it is not as robust regarding informal workers.

Measuring informality, however, is not only a matter of figures. Our idea is that, while numbers can give us an idea of the width of the phenomenon, its profundity can only be understood through in-depth qualitative studies. This is why part one ends with Marius Wamsiedel's chapter arguing that a methodological framework for the study of open secrecy is needed. His contribution explores voluntary concealment of the nature of proceedings jointly performed by members of a social order with a vested interest in protecting the current state of affairs. After discussing the ambiguity inherent in open secrets, the chapter focuses on the "rear-mirror methodology" proposed by Ledeneva (2011) and extends it to the ethnographic inquiry. The chapter argues in favour of a flexible approach to fieldwork and recommends that researchers adopt the status of partial insider and the role of naïve newcomer, maintain rapport with but also distance from participants, and regard as meaningful the apparent incongruities between data generated through casual talk and data obtained via formal interviews.

The second part of the book explores informality in a European context. Given the efforts of the EU to tackle informal labour and informal transactions in general, there is a growing body of literature on Europe-related informality. This section is intended to engage with this while providing some more original empirical material and reflections on the topic.

The first contribution of this part by Colin C. Williams and Ioana A. Horodnic, explores the validity of institutional theory in the informal economy context. Drawing upon evidence from 1,027 face-to-face interviews conducted in Romania during 2013, this chapter reveals that participation in the informal economy arises when there is asymmetry between the norms, values and beliefs of citizens (informal institutions) and the codified laws and regulations (formal institutions), and that tackling the informal economy thus needs to focus upon changing not only informal institutions but also formal institutions in order to reduce this institutional asymmetry. How to achieve this in post-communist societies is then discussed.

Informality has its specificities depending on the context, making the study of rural areas particularly interesting. Diana Traikova's contribution focuses on the pulse of the rural economy, which is known to be a slower one. The chapter explains how remoteness, dependency on agriculture, high unemployment, lower purchase power, deteriorating infrastructure and depopulation pose great challenges for rural development and describes how after the fall of the communist regime many countries lost sight of the rural economy, and often not more than a local administration, maybe a public local school and a post office remained in rural villages. This contribution seeks to better understand the rural manifestations of informal business activities considering that job creation was left to private initiative and became closely linked to the wide practice of informality.

The following chapter, by Adrian V. Horodnic, Colin C. Williams, Abel Polese, Adriana Zait and Liviu Oprea explores the prevalence of informal payments in public healthcare services in Greece. To evaluate the relationship between extra payments or valuable gifts (apart from official fees) and the level of acceptability of corruption, as well as the socio-spatial variations in the tendency to offer informal payments, data from a 2013

Eurobarometer survey is reported. Using logistic regression analysis, the finding is that patients with a high acceptability of corruption, those considering corruption as a very widespread phenomenon and those located in rural areas are more likely to offer, apart from official fees, extra payments or valuable gifts for healthcare services. The chapter concludes by discussing the health policy implications.

The last chapter shows the relationship between business, shadow economies and unorthodox governance in the context of contemporary Russia. Michael Rochlitz explores if the violent pressure on business influences the decision of firms to stay in the informal economy. Using evidence from Russian regions, this chapter shows that the result might depend on the type of violence. Physical violence in a given region is positively correlated with the number of people working outside the corporate sector, but negatively with the degree of competition from the informal sector. On the other hand, insecure property rights for entrepreneurs and investors increase the amount of competition from the informal economy. These findings are consistent with a theory where firms seek the protection of the formal economy against different types of physical violence in regions with decentralised predation, but hide in the informal economy against predatory state officials and corporate raiders in regions where predation is centralised.

The third and last part of the book is an exploration of informality beyond the European context and starts with a chapter by Rogelio Varela Llamas, Ramón A. Castillo Ponce and Juan Manuel Ocegueda Hernández which analyses labour informality in Mexico. To that end, the authors provide a discussion of different theoretical approaches to explaining the phenomenon and conduct an empirical exercise using data from the National Occupational and Employment Survey for the first quarter of 2015. The results suggest that the probability of becoming an informal worker decreases as individuals acquire more education or live in urban areas. Women are more likely to join the informal labour market relative to men. Searching for additional employment also increases the probability of entering informality.

The next contribution, by Ahmadou Aly Mbaye, Nancy Claire Benjamin and Fatou Gueye, investigates the complex relationship between formal and informal firms in Francophone Africa, using Dakar and Cotonou as the main case studies. Their chapter explores the relations between formal and informal firms and how this affects value chains, employment and productivity and reveals that some are sectors mainly characterised by competition between formal and informal segments, while others are engaged in more trade and outsourcing, although mainly for marketing rather than for production. The implications of these types of relations for the productivity of formal firms are also examined in the chapter.

Jingqing Yang's chapter explores the informal payment that patients offer to public doctors under the table. It is an illegitimate practice that has been endemic in the Chinese healthcare system for decades. This chapter examines two market mechanisms that have been used to combat informal payments, namely, internal competition and differential pricing. It reveals that due to market failures, especially information asymmetry and imperfect competition, internal competition, which is embedded in the scheme of "patients choose doctors", pushed up the demand for the services of elite practitioners and led to the concentration of informal payments in their hands. Differential pricing, which is embraced under the name of "operation by nomination" and is explicitly intended to formalise informal payments, faced the same problem—concentration of informal payments in the hands of senior surgeons. Furthermore, it exacerbated health inequality and subverted the government's ideological commitment to social justice. Both market mechanisms did not achieve the purpose of controlling informal payments and have been abandoned either by hospitals or by the government. The chapter tentatively concludes that due to market failures, the market is not likely to be a solution to informal payments.

As we suggested in the beginning, informality plays a role that goes well beyond economic governance and Arihiro Minoo's study is an interesting case. His contribution examines the mechanisms and conditions of the emergence of a counterpublic sphere through describing the features of the connections possessed by a coffee farmers' cooperative in two different but interrelated dimensions: the transformation of connections inside the cooperative and the construction of connections outside the cooperative. Minoo's chapter presents a case study in Lao PDR, and reveals that the distrust among the farmers has affected the mechanism of the exclusion of members, on the one hand, and the cooperatives have acquired political power in order to effect the functioning of such mechanisms through connection with external organisations. In this process, the exclusion of members might occur in contrast to the openness of the members which is often referred as an ideal of the counterpublic sphere.

The binary of formal–informal is further explored in Kwame Adom's chapter on formalisation of entrepreneurship in the informal economy in sub-Saharan Africa. Using Ghana as case study, the author critically evaluates the role of formal institutions in formalising entrepreneurship in the informal economy in Ghana. The chapter finds that not only are formal institutions seen as strategic leaders in formalising informal entrepreneurship but they are also perceived as enemies of formalisation since they profit from the current bureaucratic impediments as informal entrepreneurs try to formalise their operations. The chapter concludes that if true formalisation is ever to see the light of day then government policy must be focused on deregulating the formal economy since the real issue is not so much informality but overregulation by formal institutions. There is a need to streamline the bureaucratic processes relevant to making the formalisation dream a reality.

The last chapter concludes our exploration of informality around the world with a discussion of the link between corruption and informality worldwide. Julia Schipperges, Milena Pavlova, Tetiana Stepurko, Paul Vincke and Wim Groot examine the effect of bribery, kickbacks, collusion and favouritism in public procurements. In healthcare, these informal practices—often labelled as "corruption"—may have consequences ranging from financial losses to higher morbidity and mortality rates. Corruption is generally seen as socially undesirable, and most informal practices in public procurement indeed fit the definition of corruption, for example bribery and kickbacks. However, other informal practices, such as collusion and favouritism, are less tangible and sometimes it is arguable whether they can in fact be called corruption. They have also received less attention. In this chapter, the authors follow a normative vision and present a review of evidence on corruption in public procurements of medical devices and pharmaceuticals based on a document analysis focusing specifically on the forms of corruption in public procurements. This review shows that the most common corruptive practice in procurements of medical devices and pharmaceuticals, which has been reported in the documents, is bribery. The chapter argues that e-procurements can play an important role in dealing with this problem as they can improve transparency, integrity and accountability and also suggests that further research on the use of e-procurements is needed for a better understanding of the context-specific informal practices in health and its sub-sectors, including public procurements.

References

Boege, V., Brown, M. A., Clements, K. P., & Nolan, A. (2009). On hybrid political orders and emerging states: What is failing–states in the global south or research and politics in the West? *Berghof Handbook for Conflict Transformation Dialogue Series, 8*, 15–35.

Gibson-Graham, J. K. (1996). *The end of capitalism (as we knew it): A feminist critique of political economy*. Oxford/Cambridge: Blackwell Publishers.

Gibson-Graham, J. K. (2008). Diverse economies: Performative practices for "other worlds". *Progress in Human Geography, 32*(5), 613–632.

Granovetter, M. (1984). Economic actions and social structures: The problem of embeddedness. *American Journal of Sociology, 91*(3), 481–510.

Gudeman, S. (2001). *The anthropology of economy: Community, market and culture*. Malden/Oxford: Blackwell Publishers.

Hagmann, T., & Péclard, D. (2010). Negotiating statehood: Dynamics of power and domination in Africa. *Development and Change, 41*(4), 539–562.

Hart, K. (1973). Informal income opportunities and urban employment in Ghana. *Journal of Modern African Studies, 11*(1), 61–89.

Helmke, G., & Levitsky, S. (2004). Informal institutions and comparative politics: A research agenda. *Perspectives on Politics, 2*(4), 725–740.

Hobsbawm, E., & Rudé, G. (2014). *Captain swing*. London: Verso Books.

ILO. (1972). *Employment, incomes and equality: A strategy for increasing productive employment in Kenya*. Geneva: ILO.

Isaacs, R. (2011). *Party system formation in Kazakhstan: Between formal and informal politics*. London: Routledge.

Kasfir, N. (2005). Guerrillas and civilian participation: The national resistance army in Uganda, 1981–86. *The Journal of Modern African Studies, 43*(2), 271–296.

Kevlihan, R. (2013). *Aid, insurgencies and conflict transformation, when greed is good*. New York: Routledge.

Ledeneva, A. (1998). *Russia's economy of favours: "Blat", networking and informal exchange*. Cambridge: Cambridge University Press.

Ledeneva, A. (2011). Open secrets and knowing smiles. *East European Politics & Societies, 25*(4), 720–736.

Ledeneva, A. (2013). *Can Russia modernise: Sistema, power networks and informal governance*. Cambridge: Cambridge University Press.

Maloney, W. (2004). Informality revisited. *World Development, 32*(7), 1159–1178.

Mampilly, Z. (2011). *Rebel rulers: Insurgent governance and civilian life during war*. New York: Cornell University Press.

Meagher, K. (2012). The strength of weak states? Non-state security forces and hybrid governance in Africa. *Development and Change, 43*(5), 1073–1101.

Menkhaus, K. (2008). The rise of a mediated state in northern Kenya: The Wajir story and its implications for state-building. *Afrika Focus, 21*(2), 23–38.

Misztal, B. A. (2000). *Informality: Social theory and contemporary practice.* London: Routledge.

Morris, J. (2011). Socially embedded workers at the nexus of diverse work in Russia: An ethnography of blue-collar informalization. *International Journal of Sociology and Social Policy, 31*(11/12), 619–631.

Morris, J. (2012). Unruly entrepreneurs: Russian worker responses to insecure formal employment. *Global Labour Journal, 3*(2), 217–236.

Morris, J., & Polese, A. (Eds.). (2014). *The informal post-socialist economy: Embedded practices and livelihoods.* London/New York: Routledge.

Morris, J., & Polese, A. (2015). Quo Vadis informality? In J. Morris & A. Polese (Eds.), *Informal economies in post-socialist spaces: Practices, institutions and networks.* London: Palgrave.

Olson, M. (1993). Dictatorship, democracy, and development. *The American Political Science Review, 87*(3), 567–576.

Parry, J., & Bloch, M. (Eds.). (1989). *Money and the morality of exchange.* Cambridge: Cambridge University Press.

Péclard, D., & Mechoulan, D. (2015). *Rebel governance and the politics of Civil War* (Working Paper), Swiss Peace Foundation.

Polese, A. (2015). Informality crusades: Why informal practices are stigmatized, fought and allowed in different contexts according to an apparently unintelligible logic. *Caucasus Social Science Review, 2*(1), 1–26.

Polese, A. (2016). *Limits of a state: How informality replaces, renegotiates and reshapes governance in post-soviet spaces.* Stuttgart: Ibidem Verlag.

Polese, A., & Kevlihan, R. (2015). *Locating insurgency, informality and social movements on a spectrum: Is there a theory linking them all? In 9th Pan-European Conference on International Relations, September, Giardini Naxos, Sicily, Italy.*

Polese, A., Morris, J., Kovacs, B., & Harboe, I. (2014). Welfare states' in Central and Eastern Europe: Where informality fits in. *Journal of Contemporary European Studies, 22*(2), 184–198.

Polese, A., Morris, J., & Kovacs, B. (2015). The failure and future of the welfare state in post-socialism. *Journal of Eurasian Studies, 6*(1), 1–5.

Schlichte, K. (2009). With the state against the state? The formation of armed groups. *Contemporary Security Policy, 30*(2), 246–264.

Scott, J. C. (2012). *Two cheers for anarchism: Six easy pieces on autonomy, dignity, and meaningful work and play.* Princeton: Princeton University Press.

Tilly, C. (1990). *Capital, coercion and European states.* Cambridge, MA: Basil Blackwell.

Tilly, C. (2003). *The politics of collective violence.* Cambridge: Cambridge University Press.

Titeca, K., & De Herdt, T. (2011). Real governance beyond the 'failed state': Negotiating education in the Democratic Republic of the Congo. *African Affairs, 110*(439), 213–231.

White, R., & Williams, C. (2014). Anarchist economic practices in a 'capitalist' society: Some implications for organisation and the future of work. *Ephemera, 14*(1), 951–975.

Williams, C. C. (2005). *A commodified world? Mapping the limits of capitalism.* London: Zed.

Williams, C. C., & Onoshchenko, O. (2015). Evaluating the validity of the contrasting theoretical perspectives towards the informal economy in Ukraine. In *Informal economies in post-socialist spaces* (pp. 25–50). London: Palgrave Macmillan.

Yalçın-Heckmann, L. (2014). Informal economy writ large and small: From Azerbaijani herb traders to Moscow shop owners. In J. Morris & A. Polese (Eds.), *The informal post-socialist economy: Embedded practices and livelihoods.* London/New York: Routledge.

Why Read Informality in a Substantivist Manner? On the Embeddedness of the Soviet Second Economy

Lela Rekhviashvili

Good Socialist and Bad Post-Socialist Informality

The Rose Revolution of 2003 in Georgia was a reaction against both the socialist past and the corruption and informality prevalent in the 1990s. The fight that the United National Movement under president Saakashvili waged against corruption and informality, even if empowered by popular support initially, faced social resistance from various groups, and led to the reproduction and diversification of informal practices over time (Polese et al., forthcoming). The social claims of the loss (Frederiksen 2013), exclusion and marginalisation (Curro 2015; Rekhviashvili 2015) seem particularly challenging for the dominant theoretical perspectives on informality, given that the institutional changes received much acclaim (Engvall 2012; Kupatadze 2012; The World Bank 2012). Once more, it seemed that the Western best practices were emulated successfully, but it was the irrationality of the actors and the overwhelming influence of "sticky" cultural norms that hindered the actors from perceiving the opportunities offered by redesigned institutional structures. Such a development seems quite difficult for the dominant perspectives on informality. From the dominant

L. Rekhviashvili (✉)
Leibniz Institute for Regional Geography, Leipzig, Germany
e-mail: l_rekhviashvili@ifl-leipzig.de

A. Polese et al. (eds.), *The Informal Economy in Global Perspective*, International Political Economy Series,
DOI 10.1007/978-3-319-40931-3_2

new institutionalist perspective, informal entrepreneurial practices under socialism were seen as efficiency-enhancing acts, and actors relying on these practices were seen as rational rent-seeking individuals (Levy 2007). Paradoxically, these rational actors succeeded in perceiving deficiencies in the socialist system, but failed to perceive the opportunities offered by an institutionally embedded market economy. The difficulty of interpreting the case of Georgia, I suggest, is intertwined with a much broader challenge in the informality literature, and its inability to offer consistent accounts of informality in socialist and post-socialist times.

Throughout the last two decades, a large, diverse and interdisciplinary literature has dealt with the question of the prevalent and increasing informalisation of social, political and economic life in transitioning societies in particular (Karjanen 2014; Morris and Polese 2014a, 2015; Rodgers and Williams 2009; Williams 2005, 2004) as well as, more generally, in the global North and South (De Soto 1989; Gibson-Graham 2008; Guha-Khasnobis et al. 2006; Haldar and Stiglitz 2013; Helmke and Levitsky 2004). Literature aimed at understanding the post-socialist transformation has faced an intriguing challenge and exhibited a still unresolved contradiction while interpreting the (dis)continuity of informal practices throughout and after the socialist period. To date, the explanations which ascribe the prevalence of informality in socialist times to the deficiency of socialist institutions (Kornai 1992; Ledeneva 1998; Verdery 1999) remain unchallenged. From such a perspective, rational, efficiency-maximising individuals escaped restrictive and deficient socialist institutions and elaborated practices and spaces for underground, unregulated, market-based exchange. After the transition, however, these agents and their informal practices came to be portrayed in an increasingly negative light (Johnson et al. 1998, 1997; Rose 1998). Moreover, informal practices were often seen as one of the many unfortunate legacies of socialism. The same practices that were praised for being entrepreneurial and emancipatory under socialism were later portrayed as parasitic practices undermining nationwide economic performance and state capacities in different post-socialist states. This paradox is captured by Tatjana Thelen in her article "Shortage, fussy property, and other dead ends in anthropological analysis of (post)socialism". Criticising anthropological analysis of (post)socialism, Thelen observes the process of "othering" socialist and post-socialist societies in the Western academic accounts.

> In socialist countries, the "other" institutional world was encountered by actors marked by their fundamental "sameness"... While institutions were aligned with those of the West after socialism, it is now the actors who seem increasingly different (Thelen 2011, pp. 48–51).

In this chapter, I take on the concerns explicated by Thelen, and suggest ways to overcome this paradox of inconsistent interpretations. In doing so, I also illustrate the policy and theoretical relevance of aligning the interpretations of socialist and post-socialist informality. I take the literature on informality in Soviet and post-Soviet Georgia as a case study, focusing particularly on substantivist and formalist interpretations of the Soviet second economy there. I show how these two different types of readings of informality can help or hamper our capacity to interpret the post-Soviet (formal and informal) institutional transformation in Georgia.

In what follows, I first identify the causes for the inconsistency in the interpretation of socialist and post-socialist informality, relying on and elaborating the problem of identification suggested by Thelen. Here I propose that explicit or implicit influences of neo-institutionalist (or new institutionalist) thought have led to theoretically inconsistent readings of informality. Moreover, I argue that current attempts at overcoming such inconsistencies that rely on the Granovetterian conception of embeddedness are insufficient to achieve those aims. Secondly, I suggest a theoretical solution to the puzzle arguing in favour of the substantivist reading of the socialist second economy. Here I elaborate the importance of redefining the concept of embeddedness for interpreting socialist and post-socialist economies. In particular, I demonstrate the analytical power of a Polanyian definition of embeddedness over the conceptions offered by new economic sociologists. Thirdly, I demonstrate the relevance of such a theoretical exercise on the example of the readings of the second economy in Soviet Georgia. I show how the substantivist reading of informality helps us establish continuity in interpreting socialist and post-socialist informality and to understand the challenges of institutional transformation in post-Soviet Georgia. Finally, I summarise the chapter and emphasise the current theoretical as well as political relevance of the proposed argument.

How Formalist Readings of Informality Prevail

To understand the challenges of interpreting Soviet and post-Soviet informality in a consistent manner, I suggest we need to step back and recall a long forgotten debate about formalist and substantivist readings of the economy. On one side of this debate, economic anthropologists have defended the classical economist's propositions about the universality of human rationality and profit-seeking motivation. Others, namely substantivists, contending the economistic reading of social organisation, argued that the economy was commonly embedded in social and cultural institutions of respective societies and that the subjection of social life to economic rationales was a historically unique characteristic of capitalism (Bohannan and Dalton 1965; Dalton 1968; Herskovits 1952). Even the most vigorous executions of unregulated market dominance have failed to materialise, as social forces always mount a strike back to subject the economy to social and political needs—or to re-embed the economy (Polanyi 1968, 1957).

Although this debate was defining for the field of economic anthropology, and influenced a range of other disciplines (political economy and economic sociology to name a couple), since the 1970s the debate has lost relevance, and is hardly ever now recalled in the literature on informality (Fehlings 2017, forthcoming). While not that many anthropologists were left defending the formalist position, even the economists and political economists started challenging the classical and neoclassical economist position, articulating the importance of social, cultural and political institutions for economic life (Booth 2011; North 1995; Rodrik 2004; Sokoloff 2000). The resulting field of new institutional economics then turned out to be one of the most vocal critics of neoclassical economic thought, as well as neoliberal policy agenda. Reckoning the similarities between liberal economic thought and a vast share of the new institutionalist literature, primarily the rational choice new institutionalism, the new economic sociologists, most importantly Mark Grannovetter (Granovetter 1985; Granovetter and Swedberg 1992), have challenged this school of thought, emphasising the social embeddedness of economic action. Granovetter's infamous assertion that economic actors' "purposive actions are instead embedded in concrete, ongoing systems of social relations" (Granovetter 1985, p. 487), has largely refocused the research agenda away from the formalist versus substantivist debate and towards understanding how exactly the economy is embedded in social relations. Doing so, Granovetter blamed the new institutionalist school in proposing an *undersocialised* version of how social relations and networks influence economic action. He also distanced his theory of embeddedness from substantivist thought, arguing that economic anthropologists and sociologists of his time proposed an *oversocialised* conception of human behaviour.

The reason I offer a brief detour into what Beckert has called "The great transformation of embededdness" (Beckert 2007), is that I believe the two schools of thought, the new institutional economics and new economic sociology, have been definitive for thinking on informality in the post-Soviet region. Unfortunately, as I will argue, neither of these schools of thought enabled the literature on informality to avoid theoretical pitfalls. Thelen, whose masterful detection of the paradoxical and inconsistent readings of socialism and post-socialism inspires this chapter, explicitly identifies the overwhelming influence of new institutionalist thought as a core reason leading anthropological accounts of (post)socialism to dead ends, and to the incapacity of this literature to contribute to discipline-wide debates.

> The absence of concepts of anthropological origin alongside the adoption of neo-institutionalist ideas had a decisive influence on how scholars interpreted the changes that occurred after 1989. Although explicit neo-institutionalist approaches are rare, almost all anthropological contributions to the study of post-socialism pay tribute to Kornai's ideas about the socialist economy of shortage. Their origin in neo-institutionalist economics is, however, often left unaddressed. Some authors may even be unaware of it (Thelen 2011, p. 49).

The new institutionalist thought entered the literature on informality often in an implicit way, through the back door. Kornaj's interpretation of socialist informality as a response to the economy of shortages was reflected in sociological explorations of informality (Ledeneva 1998). Similarly, De Soto's claims that informality is a reaction to inconsistent regulations, corruption and high taxes has often prevailed in not only cross-country comparatives (Abdih and Medina 2013; Johnson et al. 1998; Piculescu and Hibbs 2005; Schneider et al. 2010), but also in ethnographic in-depth studies of post-socialist informality (Ledeneva 2009; Nasritdinov et al. 2010; Roti 2014). The problem in buying into the new institutionalist arguments is that they indeed depict an undersocialised version of economic life in general and of informal practices in particular. This perspective is rooted in a belief that informal institutions and economic practices are designed to enable economic exchange. In the absence of a third party (state) enforcement, these institutions ensure that the economic interests of individuals are realised (Becker 2004; De Soto 2000; Johnson et al. 1998; Loayza 1999; North 1995, 1981). In doing so, this literature assigns a narrow instrumental meaning to informal practices and institutions, and dismisses the possibility that reproduction of these practices is important for non-economic reasons, primarily for providing continuity for culturally specific ways of social integration, for asserting pre-existing (versus instrumental) social bonds and mutuality. To illustrate this point, let me recall Gudeman's discussion concerning the new institutionalist conceptualisation of norms and institutions:

> New institutionalists try to show how social relationships, norms, and their changes can be modelled as outcomes of calculative reason. Social bonds, in this view, are not always frictions or inefficiencies to be eliminated in modernization, because these ties can be efficient in an historical context ... But there is an elision in their model, for new institutionalists are explaining only the uses, predications, or spillovers of existent mutuality. By presuming that individuals are self-interested, which leads to contextually efficient institutions, new institutionalists fail to account for the prior, necessary presence of relationships that constitutes these persons-in-community (Gudeman 2009, p. 18).

In summary then, the new institutionalist perspective has largely represented a modified but still quite orthodox formalist way of interpreting economic life. What I find even more concerning is that the attempts to overcome the implicit or explicit influences of new institutionalist thought have so far come only halfway, and have failed in critically and straightforwardly engaging with such influences. Recent literature on post-socialist informality has indeed challenged the primacy of economistic and profit-seeking reasoning of individuals, asserting that informal economic practices are socially and culturally embedded phenomena (Morris 2011; Morris and Polese 2014a, 2015; Williams, 2005). This literature has also emphasised the role of informality for bottom-up welfare provisioning (Morris and Polese 2016; Polese et al. 2014) and paid attention to the non-capitalist nature of a range of informal practices (Smith and Rochovská 2007; Smith and Stenning 2006; Stenning et al. 2010; Williams 2004).

The problem with the recent literature on embedded informal practices is, I suggest, twofold. First, this literature does not articulate what the empirical findings about the embeddedness of informality imply in relation to new institutionalist thought. Hence, at best, this literature leaves the new institutionalist remedies and advocacy for the security of property rights, contract enforcement, reduction of taxes and regulations, unchallenged. At worst, it explicitly cites the champions of new institutionalist thought, such as De Soto, and implicitly reproduces the perception of choices between formality and informality as a matter of cost–benefit calculation.

> In the end, the amount of money paid in "gifts", and the time spent on walking the tightrope between legality and illegality might be higher than the costs of staying legal in the long run (Polese 2014, p. 97).

The second challenge is that, employing Granovetter's definition of embeddedness, this literature fails to explain how exactly embeddedness of informal practices matters analytically if we assume that all economies at all times are socially embedded. Critical accounts of Granovetter's (re) definition of embeddedness criticise "the great transformation of embeddedness" for stretching the scope of the concept so much that it became meaningless (Beckert 2007; Machado 2011). This challenge is even more acute when we use this conception in relation to informality. What differentiates informal practices from any other practices in case ongoing social relations similarly influence all economic exchange? Do we, in such a case, simply abandon the difference between formal and informal practices, or do we abandon embeddedness as a descriptive, differentiating tool, given that it is assumed to be universally present?

Substantivist Readings of Markets and Embeddedness

Despite the renewed interest in the legacies of the substantivist works, especially of the works by Karl Polanyi (Burawoy 1999; Gudeman 2009; Hann and Hart 2009; Machado 2011), the conceptual tools offered by this school of thought have not yet entered the ongoing debates about post-Soviet informality. As mentioned above, I posit that the substantivist reading of (post-)Soviet economies can overcome the two challenges of the literature on informality. First, its inability to critically re-evaluate the instrumental reading of informal practices and institutions as suggested by the new institutionalists. Second, its inability to elaborate the concept of embeddedness to make it analytically useful for understanding informality. From a substantivist point of entry, one cannot take the existence of a market economy or the assumptions about human behaviour for granted. Such readings demand the identifying of specific institutional patterns that shape social and economic interactions, such as market, reciprocity, redistribution and household economy. Doing so, we can distinguish between (1) the existence of commodity markets that do not dominate socio-economic organisation overall, but coexist with other forms of integration, (2) the existence of an unregulated market economy as a dominant mode of integration and movements and (3) practices that try to re-embed the market economy by defending and elaborating social regulations (Dalton 1968; Polanyi 1968, 1957).

In contrast to both the new institutionalists as well as the new economic sociologists, the substantivist reading of the economy has crucial advantages. Such a reading emphasises tangible and specific social and economic costs of establishing a market economy, by illustrating that deepening marketisation is only possible at the cost of subverting and undermining pre-existing social norms and regulations. This aspect is largely absent from the discussion of the new institutionalist as well as new economic sociologist's readings of markets and embeddedness. The new institutionalists see markets as the most efficient systems of allocation, best fitting to the human desires. New economic sociologists on the other hand, see markets as already socially embedded, and thus are not concerned by the costs of marketisation or by the processes that lead to embeddedness of markets.

Subverting the new institutionalist claims, the substantivist readings and empirical evidence illustrate that historically the economy has been socially and culturally embedded. Instead of being a universal form of organisation, best designed to fit human nature, the emergence of a market economy has been a result of intentional, state-supported and often violent (Graeber 2011) imposition of market-supporting institutions. The process of subjecting resources and socio-economic life to the market demand and supply principle is an intentional process, supported by specific actors, interests, practices and institutions. In contrast to the definition of embeddedness offered by new economic sociologists, the substantivist reading of markets and embeddedness emphasizes tension, conflict and the role of intentional, collective action. The attempts of re-embedding markets—subjecting them to social and political needs and logic—is an intentional process and often a collective struggle, not simply the nature of things and an inevitability of the influence of social networks on economic interactions.

Substantivist Contributions to Understanding (Post-)Soviet Informality

In the substantivist reading of markets and informality, I suggest that the contradictory readings of socialist and post-socialist informality would not be so sharp or would not occur at all. First, the substantivist reading would immediately cast a doubt on the claim that the Soviet second markets resembled free-spirited unregulated markets. Overall, market-enhancing institutions did not dominate the socialist economies; hence, commodity markets were relatively marginal to the socio-economic life of respective societies. Without having state-supported market institutions in place, substantivists would observe what kind of social regulations shaped Soviet commodity markets. In other words, substantivists would focus on embeddedness of the informal/second economy throughout the socialist period too. Secondly, the substantivist reading would not expect that the transition to a market economy would be a harmonious process. Even if actors found it convenient to take part in commodity exchanges during socialism, the subjection of core productive resources, such as land labour and money, would genuinely and principally alter pre-existing formal and informal institutional patterns. Even for those actors specifically involved in Soviet second economic activities, the transition and establishment of key market institutions would be a painful rupture, rather than an emancipatory and natural process. Hence, the actors would resist changes precisely because marketisation threatened such practices and culturally embedded norms. Finally, the reproduction of the embedded forms of economic activity would not be seen as an irrational submissiveness to cultural norms, as an actor's inability to appreciate the opportunities offered by the collapse of socialism and emergence of market-enhancing institutions. Nor would it be seen as simply a reaction to wrongly institutionalised markets during the transition. Instead, the conflict between new market rules and socially embedded norms, and the intentionality of attempts at re-embedding economic life in social regulations, would be observed.

In such a reading, the paradox postulating that informally operating actors were profit seeking and rational during socialism, but turned out to be overtly influenced by wrong (and irrational) cultural "sticky" norms, would not occur. On the one hand, a substantivist reading (in contrast to the new institutionalists) would attend to social and cultural embeddedness already in the socialist period. On the other hand, such a reading (in contrast to new economic sociologists) would not take continuity in embeddedness of economic practices for granted. Conversely, it would focus on intentionality of the attempts of re-embedding economic life, and reinvention of informal practices in the face of new institutional patterns emerging due to marketisation. To illustrate the point, below I offer an overview of a formalist and a substantivist reading of the Georgian second economy.

Reading the "Second Economy" in Soviet Georgia

By the 1970s, the Georgian Soviet republic was one of the most corrupt republics, with the largest share (over 25 % of GNP) of it being the second economy (Mars and Altman 1983). At the same time, the living standards of the Georgian population were believed to be one of the highest among the Soviet republics. Those few accounts explaining this high prevalence of the informal economy in Soviet Georgia in the 1960s and 1970s approximate to what would be a formalist and a substantivist reading of economic practices. On the one hand, Levy describes corruption, that enabled the functioning of black markets, as efficiency-enhancing practice (Levy 2007). On the other hand, Mars and Altman explain the prevalence of the informal economy through analysing the distinctive cultural features of Georgian society (Mars and Altman 1983).

The emergence of corruption and rent-seeking behaviour in Georgia was a response to the inefficiencies of a centrally planned economy and constant shortages in goods and services, from Levy's perspective. Relying on extensive anecdotal evidence from his childhood years spent in Georgia, Levy offers a rich and detailed account on the diversity of informal practices that enabled the functioning of black markets in Georgia. He describes how the traders in the bazaars and nearby shops inflated the official prices of goods. They bribed the printing presses to print price tags with inflated prices, and bribed police officers to turn a blind eye to the inflated prices. For the goods in high demand, the traders created artificial shortages, insisting they did not have the right size/amount of the requested goods, compelling customers to offer a higher price for them. In addition to inflating official prices through various means, the production of "counterfeit merchandise" was also common. Many of the Soviet enterprises underreported the amount of production and sold goods on the black market. From Levy's point of view, the primary driver of all these illegal transactions was the rent-seeking motives of the engaged actors. The main function of the black market was to introduce market incentives, thus overcoming the rigidities of the centrally planned economy, increasing the output and overall enhancing the overall efficiency of the economy: "Indeed, Georgian economy had prospered and Georgians were enjoying a relatively high standard of living in comparison to the rest of the Soviet Union, at least in part, thanks to the 'free market institutions' that Georgians were able to establish and promote" (Levy 2007, p. 443).

Levy's reading of the Soviet "second economy" approximates to the new institutionalist interpretations that also explain informality by referring to the shortages and deficiencies of the Soviet economy.[1] The problem with this interpretation arises when it is faced with the persistence of corruption as well as diversity of informal economic practices long after the collapse of the Soviet Union. The same practices that were seen as unregulated market exchanges, under the post-Soviet period came to hinder the advancement of the market economy. Commonly, there are two answers offered to explain the paradox stemming from the formalist interpretation. One is evoked by Levy himself: "it should be noted that the corruption in Georgia likely has socio-cultural roots as well. For example, the corruption seems to persist even in contemporary Georgia despite the process of large-scale privatization and other free market reforms implemented by Georgia's current reform-minded government" (Levy 2007, p. 426). This way, the persistence of these practices is explained by the socio-cultural roots of these practices. This interpretation can in fact be supported by the new institutionalist analysis of path dependency of informal institutions which might persist even after they are no longer efficient (North 1995). Yet another new institutionalist explanation of the persistence of informality would refer to the weakness of the post-Soviet states that failed to put in place market-supporting institutions, thus informal markets continued existing and imposing high transaction costs over the economy. Put another way, the "second economy" was efficient relative to the socialist economy, but remained inefficient relative to a well-functioning market economy.

What seems odd with this explanation is that the socio-cultural roots of informality become a primary explanatory variable under post-socialism, yet they are hardly seen as important during the socialist period. While under socialism institutions were seen as deficient and actors were seen as rational; during post-socialism the institutions became similar to capitalist institutions, but this time, the actors appeared to be heavily influenced by socio-cultural norms incompatible with market rationality (Thelen 2011). This paradox would not arise if we considered the Polanyian distinction between the existence of markets and a market economy. Markets have existed throughout history and in many economies, but commonly it was dismissed that: first, they were not the central or dominant mode of integration prior to the capitalist era, and secondly, they were often strictly regulated according to the norms and social institutions of the respective societies (Polanyi 1957). The portrayal of Soviet black markets as "free market institutions" ignores that markets were not central to the Soviet economy in general, and where they existed beyond the purview of the state, they were embedded in dense networks and socio-cultural institutions of the societies.

Interestingly, Levy himself gives hints on the informal norms and regulations that were shaping black markets in Georgia: "Various types of profit-sharing mechanisms that the Georgians have developed were designed in such a way that all participants had incentives to follow the unwritten rules. The system worked precisely because everybody benefited from it and nobody had an incentive to disrupt its smooth functioning" (Levy 2007, p. 444). In other words, the black market was embedded in the informal/alternative redistributive networks that operated based on unwritten but well-enforced rules. The importance of the networks and cultural norms becomes apparent in the substantivist reading of Georgia's second economy by Mars and Altman.[2]

Describing the core cultural values of Georgian society is the starting point for Mars and Altman. They characterise Georgian society as part of the Mediterranean and Latin cultures, emphasising the importance of descent and family membership: "When an individual's acts are evaluated, this is done in the context of an assessment – and of continual reassessment – of his family and honour. The same assessments, through less pronounced, apply also to associates and to friends" (Mars and Altman 1983, p. 548). Describing the cornerstones of Georgian "honour and shame" society, they underline the importance of asserting masculinity as understood in Georgian culture, as a perpetual struggle to prove oneself as a worthy and honoured man. Networks are seen as the "backbone" of the second economy, as these networks define an individual's access to different resources and even their occupational choices. Networks rely on trust relations, trustworthiness being the basis of one's honour. Georgian culture is portrayed as encouraging competition and, what Mars and Altman call, "reckless" risk taking. Taking business-related risks, drinking and eating out with friends, dressing up well, displaying and sharing resources are all part of performing identities and reaffirming honour and respectability. Mars and Altman even see a kind of "entrepreneurial spirit" in Georgian culture, but they carefully highlight the cultural specificity of this "spirit": "Those are entrepreneurs of a different mould from those traditionally associated with Western Capitalism – with the development of thrift and with Weberian ideas of deferred gratification: these are gambling entrepreneurs concerned to spend and display" (Mars and Altman 1983, p. 550).

Success of informal and illegal operations is, in turn, to a big extent defined by actors' embeddedness in social networks and kinship ties. Trust enables the actors to borrow money, exchange goods and raise huge sums in case they face unexpected failures. The reciprocal obligations of the network members are coercive—all the members are expected to keep up with the rules of the game and their failure to do so can come at high social cost.

In contrast with the formalist view of the second economy, the interpretation given by Mars and Altman reveals two important commonly under-emphasized aspects of Soviet Georgia's second economy. First, in this interpretation culture is not merely a supportive condition for the operation of rational actors but the very basis of economic exchange. The motivation of the actors is rather shaped by the urge to improve their social standing and successfully perform manliness, trustworthiness and honour. The success of establishing oneself as an honourable member of society in turn defines not only personal attributes, but the reputation and standing of the family and respective peer networks. Secondly, this value system stresses the importance of reciprocity and alternative/parallel redistribution, placing the actor's will and ability to share his/her profits and resources as an ultimate proof of successful performance of identity. This type of socially embedded economy cannot simply be seen as an economy that imposes high transaction costs on actors due to its informal character and the costliness of enforcement. To be sure, the enforcement in itself does not seem excessively costly due to high levels of institutionalisation of norms inside the informal networks. In contrast, the norms in themselves are costly, as they demand that the individuals share resources with kin and peer networks. Just as Polanyi describes, the interdependency that characterises reciprocal exchanges highlights social motives of economic actors. The above described norms, unlike the ones assumed under a market economy (Streeck 2011), impose a "roof" to the profit maximising behaviour, and ensure relative social security of the various network members.

Understanding the Reaction Against Marketisation in Post-Revolution Georgia

As explained in the introduction, a team of Georgian reformists have enabled market-enhancing institutions with vigour since the mid-2000s. If in the case of many other post-Soviet countries, the new institutionalist/formalist interpretations could blame the weakness of state institutions for prevalent informality, in Georgia such an explanation seems highly implausible. The resistance that followed the institutionalisation of the market economy seems incomprehensible if we accept Levy's interpretation of Soviet Georgia's second economy and formalist readings of the economy in general. If Georgian society was already flexible, profit-seeking and entrepreneurial throughout socialism, then the marketisation process of the 2000s should have come as a blessing. For Levy, like for any other formalist interpreter of informality, the networks were there to functionally enable the economic exchange of self-interested actors. Once the state stepped in and created institutional support for such exchange, the informal context must have lost its relevance. This kind of formalist thinking indeed underlined the modernisation project and institutional reform in post-revolution Georgia (Rekhviashvili 2013). As president Saakashvili postulated, the state was there to ensure equal treatment of citizens and fair competition. Citizens would find ways of enjoying such an opportunity independently:

> No single state body will treat you badly. The rest is up to people.
>
> The government is not able to feed its citizens the way they were fed, and everybody has to accept this fact, since it's a normal market relationship. The important thing is that if somebody believes in their own power, in their own talent, if they think they are stronger than others and can go forward, then they should compete in free competition. (The Administration of The President of Georgia, Press Office, Annual Report, 2005, cited in Rekhviashvili 2013).

To the surprise of the Georgian reformers, as well as the supporters of Georgia's marketisation reforms, the social groups that should have benefited from the reforms the most, such as informal traders and small size entrepreneurs, saw their productivity and income declining (Rudaz 2012). Moreover, informally self-employed traders mounted collective struggles against the changes, devised various tactics for subverting new reforms and showed strong preference for informal trade (Khutsishvili 2012; Rekhviashvili 2015). Besides the traders, Georgian labour unions, and different opposition movements continuously challenged the changes, primarily emphasising the social costs of the marketisation project (Bagnardi 2015; Jones 2012; Muskhelishvili 2011; Muskhelishvili and Jorjoliani 2009).

If we take seriously the reading of Georgia's second economy as described by Mars and Altman, we can easily decode the reasons behind the resistance. Mars and Altman's insistence on understanding the cultural bases and specificities of entrepreneurial activities in socialist Georgia, and their emphasis on reciprocal and redistributive social networks, allows us to move beyond the assumption of the universality of market-likeness of economic practices. From this reading, the socially embedded and regulated market-based exchange in the socialist period is not necessarily compatible with or easily transformable into a self-regulated market economy. The modernisation project introduced and cemented new patterns of economic relations, articulated the division between private and public property, and subjected the access to productive resources to market-exchange rules. Even if commodity trade was familiar to the economic actors, deepened commodification of land, labour and money, was not. Hence, it is no surprise that the commodification of productive resources and subsequent loosening of the role of social networks was contested in post-revolutionary Georgia. For Mars and Altman, the function of networks was much more complex than just "greasing the wheels of commerce" (Huntington 1968). Informal practices and institutions were intertwined with cultural, symbolic and social meanings and functions. This is why, as the administrative reforms made informality irrelevant for dealing with (previously) dysfunctional state bureaucracy since the mid-2000s, informal practices persisted as a coping mechanism and a way of sustaining social safety nets (Aliyev 2014).

In summary, formalist interpretations are unfit to grasp this reproduction of informal practices and societal resistance in the face of marketisation. However, comprehending these processes seems impossible based on Granovetter's definition of embeddedness too. Much like the formalists, Granovetter's vision of embeddedness of the economy avoids focusing on the disembedding propensity of marketisation. Hence, it does not presuppose either that marketisation can challenge the existing embeddedness of the economy and compromises the social security of different social groups, or that retaining and regaining embeddedness requires purposive action, and is achieved often through conflict and struggle. The substantivist reading of the Georgian case illustrates that informal practices do not simply reproduce themselves because they are culturally embedded and because this condition is universal/transcends different modes of socio-economic integration. Conversely, informal practices reproduce and diversify precisely because marketisation is capable of marginalising embedded norms and institutions. Such a process can have very tangible social consequences, such as the impoverishment, rising inequality (Gugushvili 2014) and marginalisation of various social groups (Curro 2015; Frederiksen 2013), as observed in the Georgian case. In turn, these social groups purposefully and intentionally resist marketisation and strive for it to be re-embedded. The re-embedding of the economy, however, does not have to be an informal process. When states recognise the costs of marketisation, they can also formally institutionalise protective measures. The emergence of welfare states is widely cited as a case of re-embedding market economies (Bohle and Greskovits 2012; Dalton 1968; Streeck 2011). In the Georgian case, the informal character of the resistance can be seen as related to the Georgian government's unwillingness to recognise the social costs of marketisation, to facilitate adjustment to such a process and offer social security guarantees (Baumann 2010; Gugushvili 2014).

Political and Theoretical Implications of the Substantivist Reading

Unlike the formalists, who assume the universality of market rules, and the new economic sociologists, who insist on the universality of social embeddedness of economic action, the substantivist reading allows us to pay attention to conflicts and tension between markets and embeddedness and the purposeful action behind both marketisation and embedding. On a theoretical level, the substantivist reading is capable of overcoming the inconsistency in reading socialist and post-socialist informality, detected by Tatyana Thelen. It also unravels the reasons behind the resistance towards market-enhancing regulations in post-revolution Georgia. The substantivist reading of the socialist second economy in Georgia reveals tight social regulation and the cultural embeddedness of the commodity market exchange. Hence, it comes as no surprise that new market institutions were often found alien and threatening under post-socialism. This position does not assume, like the Granovetterian conception of embeddedness, that markets are always embedded. Primarily, when the market becomes the dominant form of economic exchange, production and allocation, it threatens and undermines social regulations (Williams 2005). The impacted actors then rely on long-lasting informal norms but also newly elaborated informal practices to reclaim the control over economic exchange and social reproduction. Ultimately, Granovetter is right to note that it is hard to find an entirely disembedded economy in practice. What this position fails to recognise is the conflict, struggle and reinvention of social relations and economic practices necessary in order to achieve re-embedding.

When thinking of policymaking in transitional contexts, both positions seem dangerous. The formalist one would assert that well-designed market institutions do not require social regulation and embedding. New economic sociologists would claim that they are embedded by default. The substantivist reading is the only one that warns of the market's propensity to undermine existing social and cultural institutions, and hence impose significant social costs on societies. On the policy level then, this position would suggest intentional facilitation of adjustment to a market economy, provision of social security, a gradual approach and careful consideration of the resisting voices. This can and often does mean recognition of the cultural, social and symbolic significance of certain informal practices and acknowledgement of their legitimacy for social and political life.

Notes

1. For the original accounts on understanding the socialist economy as an "economy of shortages" see Janos Kornai (1992).
2. This piece was published by Mars and Altman in 1983, based on the method that they refer to as "retrospective reconstruction". As the opportunity of making direct observations on informal economic practices in Soviet Georgia was restricted, the authors conducted an ethnographic study with Georgian Jews in Israel. The authors were aware that Georgian Jews could not be seen as culturally synonymous with the Georgian majority, but as the Georgian Jewish population was well integrated into the society, they rightfully consider their findings to be generalisable to the non-Jewish population of Georgia. The narratives that the Georgian Jewish respondents recall from the period of their stay in Georgia also confirm that the practices they describe were not constrained to the Georgian Jewish population, but rather characterised the rest of the society as well.

References

Abdih, M. Y., & Medina, L. (2013). *Measuring the informal economy in the caucasus and central Asia* (IMF Working paper no. 13/137). International Monetary Fund.

Aliyev, H. (2014). The effects of the saakashvili era reforms on informal practices in the republic of Georgia. *Studies of Transition States and Societies, 6*.

Bagnardi, F. (2015). *The changing pattern of social dialogue in Europe and the influence of ILO and EU: Georgian tripartism*. CSSR 2.

Baumann, E. (2010). *Post-soviet Georgia: The rocky path towards modern social protection*. Presented at the social policy and the global crisis, the network for European social policy analysis ESPANET, Budapest, 1–21.

Becker, K. F. (2004). *The informal economy* (fact finding study no. SIDA3630en). Sida department for infrastructure and economic co-operation.

Beckert, J. (2007). *The great transformation of embeddedness – Karl Polanyi and the new economic sociology* (MPIfG Discussion paper no. 1/07). Max Planck institute for the study of societies.

Bohannan, P., & Dalton, G. (Eds.). (1965). *Markets in Africa, Northwestern University (Evanston, Ill.) African studies*. Garden City: Doubleday & Co.

Bohle, D., & Greskovits, B. (2012). *Capitalist diversity on Europe's periphery, Cornell studies in political economy*. Ithaca: Cornell University Press.

Booth, D. (2011). Aid, institutions and governance: What have we learned? *Development Policy Review, 29*, s5–s26. doi:10.1111/j.1467-7679.2011.00518.x.

Burawoy, M. (1999). *The great involution: Russia's response to the market*. Chicago: University of Chicago Press.

Curro, C. (2015). Davabirzhaot! Conflicting claims on public space in Tbilisi between transparency and opaqueness. *International Journal of Sociology and Social Policy, 35*, 497–512. doi:10.1108/IJSSP-12-2014-0122.

Dalton, G. (1968). *Introduction, in: Primitive, archaic, and modern economies: Essays of KarlPolanyi*. Garden City: Doubleday, p. ix–xlvi.

De Soto, H. (1989). *The other path: The invisible revolution in the third world* (1st ed.). New York: Harper & Row.

De Soto, H. (2000). *The mystery of capital: Why capitalism triumphs in the West and fails everywhere else*. New York: Basic Books.

Engvall, J. (2012). *Against the grain: How Georgia fought corruption and what it means, silk road paper*. Central Asia-Caucasus Institute and Silk Road studies program.

Frederiksen, M. D. (2013). Good hearts or big bellies: Dzmak'atsoba and images of masculinity in the republic of Georgia. In V. Amit & N. Dyck (Eds.), *Young men in uncertain times* (pp. 165–187). New York/Oxford: Berghahn Books.

Gibson-Graham, J. K. (2008). Diverse economies: Performative practices for other worlds. *Progress in Human Geography, 32*, 613–632. doi:10.1177/0309132508090821.

Graeber, D. (2011). *Debt: the first 5,000 years*. Brooklyn: Melville House.

Granovetter, M. (1985). Economic action and social structure: The problem of embeddedness. *American Journal of Sociology, 91*, 481–510.

Granovetter, M., & Swedberg, R. (Eds.). (1992). *The sociology of economic life*. Boulder: Westview Press.

Gudeman, S. (2009). Necessity or contingency: Mutuality and market. In C. M. Hann & K. Hart (Eds.), *Market and society: The great transformation today* (pp. 17–37). Cambridge/New York: Cambridge University Press.

Gugushvili, D. (2014). *Do the benefits of growth trickle-down to Georgia's poor? A case for a strong welfare system* (PhD in Social Policy). Kent, United Kingdom, University of Kent.

Guha-Khasnobis, B., Kanbur, R., & Ostrom, E. (2006). Beyond formality and informality. In B. Guha-Khasnobis, R. Kanbur, & E. Ostrom (Eds.), *Linking the formal and informal economy* (pp. 1–29). Oxford: Oxford University Press.

Haldar, A., & Stiglitz, J. E. (2013). Analyzing legal formality and informality: Lessons from land titling and microfinance programs1. In D. Kennedy & J. E. Stiglitz (Eds.), *Law and economics with Chinese characteristics* (pp. 112–148). Oxford: Oxford University Press.

Hann, C. M., & Hart, K. (Eds.). (2009). *Market and society: The great transformation today.* Cambridge/New York: Cambridge University Press.

Helmke, G., & Levitsky, S. (2004). *Informal institutions and comparative politics: A research agenda.* Perspectives on politics null (pp. 725–740). doi: 10.1017/S1537592704040472.

Herskovits, M. J. (1952). *Economic anthropology: A study in comparative economics.* New York: Alfred A. Knopf.

Huntington, S. P. (1968). *Political order in changing societies.* New Haven: Yale University Press.

Johnson, S., Kaufman, D., & Shleifer, A. (1997). The unofficial economy in transition. *Brookings Papers on Economic Activity, 28*, 159–240.

Johnson, S., Kaufmann, D., & Zoido-Lobaton, P. (1998). Regulatory discretion and the unofficial economy. *American Economic Review, 88*, 387–392.

Jones, S. F. (2012). Reflections on the rose revolution. *European Security, 21*, 5–15. doi:10.1080/09662839.2012.656596.

Karjanen, D. (2014). When is an illicit taxi driver more than a taxi driver? Case studies from transit and trucking in post-socialist Slovakia. In J. Morris & A. Polese (Eds.), *The informal post-socialist economy: Embedded practices and livelihoods* (Routledge Contemporary Russia and Eastern Europe Series) (pp. 102–118). New York: Routledge.

Khutsishvili, K. (2012). Bazaar culture in Georgia: Case of Tbilisi. In M. Krebs & M. Pilz (Eds.), *Die Postsowjetische Stadt: Urbane Aushandlungsprozesse Im Südkaukasus* (pp. 41–52). Berlin: Panama Verlag.

Kornai, J. (1992). *The socialist system: The political economy of communism.* Oxford: Clarendon Press.

Kupatadze, A. (2012). Explaining Georgia's anti-corruption drive. *European Security, 21*, 16–36. doi:10.1080/09662839.2012.656597.

Ledeneva, A. (1998). *Russia's economy of favours: Blat, networking, and informal exchanges, Cambridge Russian, soviet and post-soviet studies.* New York: Cambridge University Press.

Ledeneva, A. (2009). From Russia with "blat": Can informal networks help modernize Russia? *Social Research, 76*, 257–288.

Levy, D. (2007). Price adjustment under the table: Evidence on efficiency-enhancing corruption. *European Journal of Political Economy, 23*, 423–447. doi:10.1016/j.ejpoleco.2007.01.001.

Loayza, N. (1999). *The economics of the informal sector: A simple model and some empirical evidence from Latin America* (Policy research working papers), The World Bank.

Machado, N. M. C. (2011). Karl Polanyi and the new economic sociology: Notes on the concept of (dis)embeddedness. *RCCS Annual Review*. A selection from the Portuguese journal Revista Crítica de Ciências Sociais.

Mars, G., & Altman, Y. (1983). The cultural bases of soviet Georgia's second economy. *Soviet Studies, 35*, 546–560.

Morris, J. (2011). Socially embedded workers at the nexus of diverse work in Russia. *International Journal of Sociology and Social Policy, 31*, 619–631. doi:10.1108/01443331111177832.

Morris, J., & Polese, A. (Eds.). (2014a). *The informal post-socialist economy: Embedded practices and livelihoods* (Routledge contemporary Russia and Eastern Europe series). New York: Routledge.

Morris, J., & Polese, A. (2016). Informal health and education sector payments in Russian and Ukrainian cities: Structuring welfare from below. *European Urban and Regional Studies.*July 2016 vol. 23 no. 3 481–496.(http://eur.sagepub.com/content/23/3/481)

Morris, J., & Polese, A. (Eds.). (2015). *Informal economies in post-socialist spaces: Practices, institutions and networks*. New York: Palgrave Macmillan.

Muskhelishvili, M. (2011). *Social dialogue in Georgia. Friedrich-Ebert-Stiftung*. Tbilisi.

Muskhelishvili, M., & Jorjoliani, G. (2009). Georgia's ongoing struggle for a better future continued: Democracy promotion through civil society development. *Democratization, 16*, 682–708. doi:10.1080/13510340903083000.

Nasritdinov, E., Rayapova, R., Kholmatova, N., Damirbek kyzy, E., & Igoshina, N. (2010). *Informal economy and social vulnerability in Kyrgyzstan and Tajikistan*. Social Research Center at American University of Central Asia and HelpAge International, Bishkek.

North, D. C. (1981). *Structure and change in economic history* (1st ed.). New York: Norton.

North, D. C. (1995). *Institutions, institutional change, and economic performance, The Political economy of institutions and decisions*. Cambridge: Cambridge University Press.

Piculescu, V., & Hibbs, J. (2005). *Institutions, corruption and tax evasion in the unofficial economy* (Report).

Polanyi, K. (1957). *The great transformation, Beacon paperbacks*. Boston: Beacon Press.

Polanyi, K. (1968). *Primitive, archaic, and modern economies: Essays of KarlPolanyi*. Garden City: Doubleday.

Polese, A. (2014). Drinking with Vova: An individual entrepreneur between illegality and informality. In J. Morris & A. Polese (Eds.), *The informal post-socialist economy: Embedded practices and livelihoods* (Routledge Contemporary Russia and Eastern Europe Series) (pp. 85–101). New York: Routledge.

Polese, A., Morris, J., Kovács, B., & Harboe, I. (2014). "Welfare states" and social policies in Eastern Europe and the former USSR: Where informality fits in? *Journal of Contemporary European Studies, 22*, 184–198. doi:10.1080/14782804.2014.902368.

Rekhviashvili, L. (2013). Development and the role of the state: Visions of post-revolutionary Georgian government. *Caucasus Social Science Review, 1*, 1–20.

Rekhviashvili, L. (2015). Marketization and the public-private divide. *International Journal of Sociology and Social Policy, 35*, 478–496. doi:10.1108/IJSSP-10-2014-0091.

Rodgers, P., & Williams, C. (2009). Guest editors' introduction. *International Journal of Sociology, 39*, 3–11. doi:10.2753/IJS0020-7659390200.

Rodrik, D. (2004). *Institutions and economic performance – getting institutions right* (CESifo DICE report 2), p. 10–15.

Rose, R. (1998). *Getting things done in an anti-modern society: Social capital networks in Russia* (Working paper no. 6). Social Capital Initiative. Washington, DC: The World Bank.

Roti, M. (2014). *Spheres of semi-legality: Discourse, media and informal economic practices in St. Petersburg, Russia (2000–Present)*. WSU Dissertations, Wayne State University Dissertations – Digital Commons.

Rudaz. (2012). Entrepreneurship in Georgia. *The Caucasus Analytical Digest, 45*, 2–6.

Schneider, F., Buehn, A., & Montenegro, C. E. (2010). *Shadow economies all over the world: New estimates for 162 countries from 1999 to 2007* (Policy research working paper series no. 5356). The World Bank.

Smith, A., & Rochovská, A. (2007). Domesticating neo-liberalism: Everyday lives and the geographies of post-socialist transformations. *Geoforum, Theme Issue: Geographies of Generosity, 38*, 1163–1178. doi:10.1016/j.geoforum.2007.03.003.

Smith, A., & Stenning, A. (2006). Beyond household economies: Articulations and spaces of economic practice in postsocialism. *Progress in Human Geography, 30*, 190–213. doi:10.1191/0309132506ph601oa.

Sokoloff, K. L. (2000). *History lessons: Institutions, factor endowments, and paths of development in the new world* [WWW document].

Stenning, A., Smith, A., Rochovská, A., & Świątek, D. (2010). *Domesticating neo-liberalism: Spaces of economic practice and social reproduction in post-socialist cities* (1st ed.). Malden: Wiley-Blackwell.

Streeck, W. (2011). *Taking capitalism seriously: Towards an institutionalist approach to contemporary political economy* [WWW document].

The World Bank. (2012). *Fighting corruption in public services, directions in development – general.* The World Bank.

Thelen, T. (2011). Shortage, fuzzy property and other dead ends in the anthropological analysis of (post)socialism. *Critique of Anthropology, 31*, 43–61. doi:10.1177/0308275X10393436.

Verdery, K. (1999). Fuzzy property: Rights, power, and identity in Transylvania's decollectivization. In M. Burawoy & K. Verdery (Eds.), *Uncertain transition: Ethnographies of change in the postsocialist world* (pp. 53–82). Lanham: Rowman and Littlefield Publishers.

Williams, C. (2004). The myth of marketization: An evaluation of the persistence of non-market activities in advanced economies. *International Sociology, 19*, 437–449. doi:10.1177/0268580904047366.

Williams, C. (2005). Unraveling the meanings of underground work. *Review of Social Economy, 63*, 1–18.

Informal Economy: The Invisible Hand of Government

Abbas Khandan

Introduction

The informal economy embraces a broad range of essentially different activities which are undertaken for different reasons. At one extreme, there are goods like narcotics which are illegal in production, distribution and consumption. But not all informal activities are illegal. A big part of the informal economy consists of ordinary goods or activities hidden from government. Hiding may serve either as an active strategy complementary to corruption and rent seeking, or as a passive rent-avoidance strategy to escape from a government captured by influence groups. The shadow or gray color of these activities places them in the middle of the spectrum. At the other end, there are activities not hidden but which remain unobserved either due to government failures in registration and control of the economy or because of the underdeveloped and small scale of these irregular activities, like peddlers and travelling vendors.

The informal economy contributes a considerable and growing share of gross domestic product (GDP) in a large number of countries. Schneider (2007) reports that in Georgia, Azerbaijan, Ukraine, Bolivia, Peru, Thailand

A. Khandan (✉)
Lecturer at Ferdowsi University of Mashhad, Mashhad, Iran
e-mail: khandan.abbas@gmail.com; khandan@unisi.it

A. Polese et al. (eds.), *The Informal Economy in Global Perspective*, International Political Economy Series,
DOI 10.1007/978-3-319-40931-3_3

and Nigeria, the size of the informal economy accounts for more than half of their entire GDP. Numerous studies have tried to explain the prevalence of the informal economy and its growth. The literature can mainly be divided into two theories. The first theory, based on the International Labor Office's report (1972), considers the informal economy as a separate market in which poor people work only to survive. This theory, which is known as "dual labor market" (DLM) or "labor market segmentation", studies the effect of immigration, citizenship, gender, education and other sources of discrimination on workers' allocation between formal and informal sectors.

According to this theory, the informal economy grows when the formal economy fails to create adequate jobs to absorb all labor force. Most of the studies remain mainly descriptive, focusing on the characteristics and distinctions of different segments and mobility between the two sectors (Hudson et al. 2012; Lang and Manove 2006; Pagés and Stampini 2009). The DLM theory concerns the quality of informal jobs and wellbeing of people who are forced to work informally. This theory recommends policies that increase productivity in the informal economy (Fields 2004; Kantor et al. 2006; Lehmann and Pignatti 2008; Tiwari et al. 2002). DLM is helpful in understanding formal and informal economies' competition in absorbing workers and the effect of the macroeconomic situation on production factors' substitution between the two sectors. But it does not explain the illicit incentives involved in many illegal and hidden activities.

Although activities in the informal economy occur for different reasons and cannot be treated equally, there is always something in common: the invisible hand of government. Illegal goods like narcotics and prostitution are hidden because the government has decided to fight them. Government is the one which draws the boundary between legal and illegal goods. For example, alcohol and marijuana are permitted in some countries and are forbidden in some others. At the other extreme, where economic activities remain unobserved due to their small scale and failure in registration, the role of government is also profound. Governments traditionally have the duty of protecting property rights and preparing the environment for private businesses. In an uncontrolled and chaotic atmosphere, production takes place at low levels of organization with little or no division between labor and capital, and work relations are based on occasional jobs, kinship or personal relations.

Although government's active role is necessary to control the informal activities of the two extremes, namely the illegal economy and irregular production, the shadow economy in between takes place because of government overregulation. The idea of hiding in response to an overregulated formal economy is based on the writings of famous Peruvian economist Hernando De Soto. According to his theory known as the legalist's view, "small-, medium-, and micro-enterprises can transgress government regulation and bureaucracy, with lower costs and higher wealth creation by moving their activities to the informal sector" (De Soto 1989). Government interventions are the main reason for entrepreneurs to hide; they prefer to operate in the informal economy when it is impossible to comply with the bureaucratic procedures and enforcements of the government. Deregulation and liberalization are the main policy recommendations of this approach (Centeno and Portes 2006; Chaudhuri 2003; Maiti and Marjit 2008).

This short chapter tries to explain the growth and development of the informal economy. The main focus is on macroeconomic reasons and government's role. The next section tries to clarify the invisible hand of government on the informal economy. It is devoted to the effect of public policies and regulations on firms' incentives and their choice between the formal and informal economy. After understanding the motivations behind hidden activities and the role of government in shaping these illicit incentives, the third section uses both DLM and legalist's views to explain the causes of the informal economy and its indicators or consequences. For the empirical analysis, Iran is selected as a case study. Drawing on the model, the section entitled"Informal Economy: Long-Run Trend and Short-Run Deviations" then reports the results and determines the influencing factors on both long-run development and short-run fluctuations of the informal economy. The section "Iran's Informal Economy: Looking Back at Historical Events" looks back at history with the purpose of studying the effect of some important incidents like the Islamic revolution of 1979, the Iran–Iraq war and recent sanctions on the informal economy of Iran.

Government's Intervention and the Informal Economy

Governments consider themselves as having a regulatory role in the economy. The literature is full of pros and cons for this. Regulation is necessary for protecting public interests and resolving externalities, but the problem comes up when government is captured by interest groups. Interest groups try to influence public decisions. These rent-seeking firms persuade government to regulate and control markets in favor of them rather than the public. On the other hand, weak firms search for ways to escape from these restricting rules and interventions of government. These rent-avoidance firms, taking into account the costs and benefits of compliance, decide whether to act formally or to bring their production underground. Overregulation brings forth corruption and rent seeking and, as a result, increases the size of informal economy. Therefore, although beneficial, regulation of markets by government bears some costs. The optimal size of government can be shown in the Fig. 1, which is derived from Djankov et al. (2003).

Social loss due to disorder in an unregulated economy is shown on vertical axis. In a society without government, property rights would be expropriated by organized crime groups. In such a lawless economy, due to the unsecure environment private enterprises run at small scales and work relations are based on kinship. On the other hand, in an overregulated economy, private businesses try to hide themselves from state expropriation or influence groups dominate the government. Hidden enterprises are also smaller than optimal size and work relations are based on occasional jobs without formal contracts. The social loss due to overregulation is shown on the horizontal axis.

The total loss function is a weighted average of the loss due to disorder and overregulation. Assuming equal weights, the isocost line is a 45 falling line depicted by dashes in the figure above. Moving on this isocost line, the total loss remains unchanged but the combination alters between private or state expropriations. The objective is to minimize the total loss. But the minimization is constrained to the institutional capacity of societies.

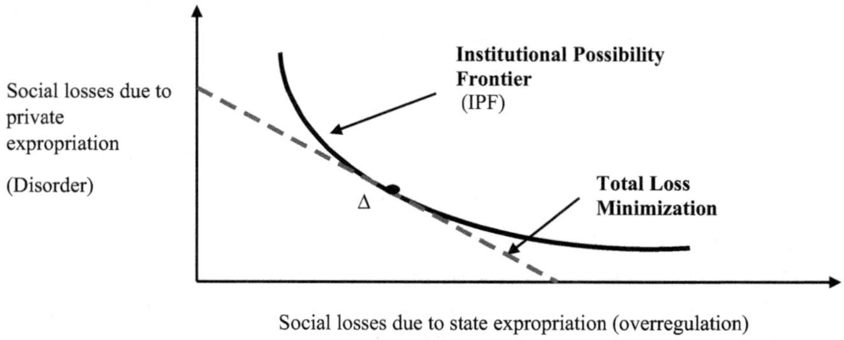

Fig. 1 The optimal size of government

The institutional possibility frontier (IPF) shows various combinations of social and regulatory institutions that protect property rights necessary for a prosperous economy. The location of the IPF is contingent on social capital and culture. The slope of the IPF line shows the trade-off between social and regulatory institutions in the protection of property rights. The vertical slopes at the ends show that although the two institutions may substitute each other to some extent, both are necessary.

At point A, where the isocost line is tangent to the IPF, government is of optimal size. In an unregulated market, private expropriation spreads and, thus, property rights may be protected only by social institutions. In order to protect themselves, private businesses run at under optimal scales and rely on work relations based on kinship. Therefore, the illegal economy and irregular production, the two extreme types of informal activities, proliferate. Moving from point A along the IPF line toward overregulation also increases social loss. Overregulation means that property rights would be broken by the state or powerful influence groups. As a result, the shadow activities of the informal economy increase rapidly as businesses try to hide to reduce compliance costs. Point A shows the optimal size of government where total social loss is minimized.

The optimal size of government corresponds to an optimal tax rate. While a level of taxation is necessary to run the public sector, increasing the tax rate to greater than the optimal point make firms hide from government by going underground. This argument results in a new Laffer curve. Figure 2 shows the relation between the public sector, informal and formal economies. There is an optimal size of government at which the informal economy is minimized.

Informal Economy: The Empirical Analysis[1]

The informal economy includes a broad range of activities which are undertaken for different reasons. The different motivations for these various activities make it impossible to put all them into an ambiguous general class and treat them equally. This study focuses on evaluating the causes and size of informal activities which have been concealed for economic reasons. In other words, illegal goods and irregular productions are set aside. Narrowing the scope of our research has two main advantages. First, we are able to do an accurate investigation on a precise subject and, second, since these activities are hidden for economic reasons, we are able to elucidate the role played by government. The study also narrows down its

Fig. 2 The relation between public sector, formal and informal economies

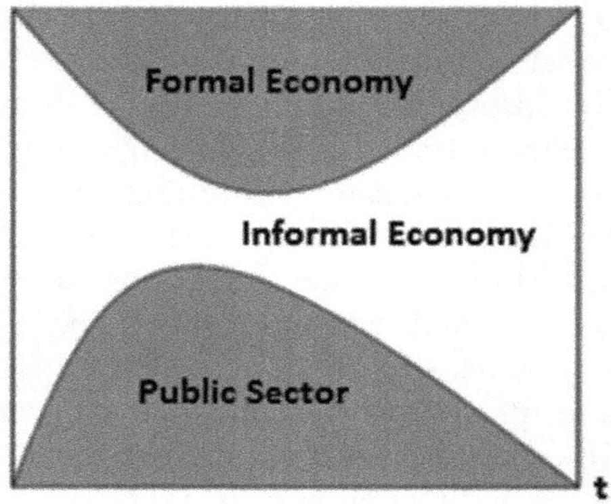

scope by deliberately ignoring illegal trade, simply because these activities with different indicators and causes need separate treatment.

A model approach is applied to track the extension of the informal economy through multiple indicators and multiple causes. This approach is based on the latent variable theory and uses structural equation models (SEMs) for estimation. One of the most practical linear structural models is the multiple indicators multiple causes (MIMIC) model. It consists of two parts: "the measurement equations", linking the latent variables to observed indicators, and "the structural equations", showing the causal relationships between the latent and observed variables. Using the arguments of previous section, Fig. 3, known as "path diagram", is drawn to illustrate different indicators and causes of the informal economy.

To track changes in the size of the informal economy's GDP, the coverage rate of social security insurance and employment are used as indicators. In the short run and at a given level of economic endowments, the informal economy acts as substitute for the formal economy. Lower levels of formal economy mean more inputs have been absorbed in the informal sector, or "the lower level of formal economy means the fewer possibilities people have to earn money, and then they have higher motivation to go to informal economy" (Buehn and Schneider 2008, p. 13). Therefore, in the short run a negative relation between the two forms of economy is expected (Buehn and Schneider 2008; Loayza 1996; Schneider and Enste 2000). However, in the long run the informal economy and GDP are complementary and share common trends, assuming that favorable economic conditions do not divide them.

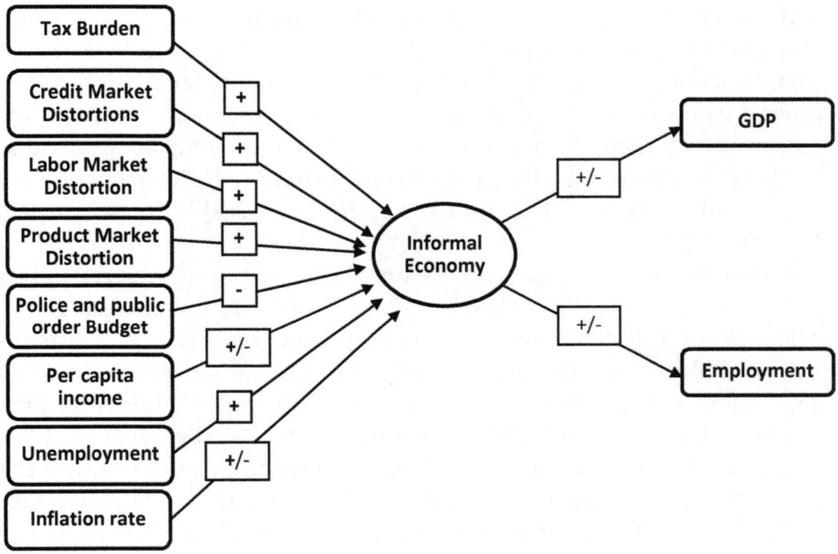

Fig. 3 The informal economy, its causes and indicators

The same reason applies to the labor market. Employment and number of workers covered by mandatory social security insurance characterize formal labor market. In the short run, formal and informal labor markets are substitutes for one another. If more laborers work in one market, then fewer work in the other one. However, since formal and informal economies are complementary in the long run, a positive relation between the two is expected.

The second part of the model is the structural equation, which incorporates causes of the latent variable, the informal economy. In the literature, these causes can be divided into two groups. The first group, based on the legalist's view, contains mainly economic and pecuniary reasons behind engaging in hidden activities. Avoiding taxes or all other burdensome government regulations are major reasons for operating informally (Schneider and Enste 2000; Torgler and Schneider 2007). We expect a positive relation between tax burdens and the size of the informal economy. In developing countries, however, the influence of other government interventions seems to be more significant simply because their severity is much stronger (Loayza et al. 2005; Schneider and Enste 2000). For example, government interventions in credit markets may result in diversion of loans toward the black market or unproductive businesses (Evrensel 2009; Straub 2005); or higher interventions in the labor market may impose excessive costs to firms and motivate them to act informally. Other interventions in product markets like price controls increase firms' costs and, thus, affect positively the size of the informal economy (Chong et al. 2008; Dinkelman and Ranchhod 2011).

Nevertheless, informal firms are unable to use public services such as police or public subsidies (Johnson et al. 1998; Schneider et al. 2010). The risk of expropriation is a major problem of acting informally. Informal firms operate suboptimally due to fear of being detected. The uncertainty increases the costs of financing for informal firms (Antunes and Cavalcant 2007; Blackburn et al. 2012; Ellul et al. 2011; Straub 2005). Higher government expenditures on police means that property rights are protected better in the formal economy. Therefore, police budget is expected to have a negative relation with the size of the informal economy.

The second group of causes includes the undesirable macroeconomic situation mentioned in the DLM theory. Lower per capita income representing poverty is expected to increase the size of the informal economy (Gibson 2005; Kim 2005). Higher per capita income, however, as an indicator of higher purchasing power, may push up demand for both formal and informal economies in the long run. Summing up, with an increase in the per capita income, a positive relation in the long run and negative in the short run is expected. A high unemployment rate, another sign of a poor macroeconomic situation, means that the formal labor market was not able to absorb all of the labor force. Therefore, these jobless workers are compelled to act informally. Finally, the effect of inflation on the size of the informal economy is somehow ambiguous. A higher inflation rate causes the informal economy to grow because it intensifies inequality, indicates an unstable macroeconomic situation and decreases the quality of economic institutions. However, as a counter argument, some scholars have emphasized that "since inflationary pressure lowers nominal tax burdens, we expect inflation to have a negative impact on the amount of both shadow economic and DIY (Do It Yourself) activities" (Buehn et al. 2009, p. 19).

Data and Pre-Estimation Analysis

In order to analyze the effect of government regulations and burdensome interventions on the size of the informal economy, Iran seems to be a good case study. Iran, with a population of 78 million and a GDP of about US$1280 billion in 2014 (current US dollars, Purchasing Price Parity) is the biggest economy among oil-exporting countries in the Persian Gulf region and the second largest in the Middle East. Thirty-five % of GDP is spent by the government on the public budget, which substantiates the fact that the government has an important role in this economy; this ratio will be about 60 % if one also considers the budget of state-owned companies. Income obtained from oil export provides enough resources for these huge public expenditures and enables the government to intervene in different markets. These interventions placed Iran as the 171st free economy in the world according to The Heritage Foundation 2012 index of economic freedom. Iran, moreover, was under tough international sanctions. Although sanctions were imposed on international trade and finance, it is very likely that Iran's domestic economy have also been impacted and the size of informal economy has increased.

Data are collected from the sample period 1972–2013. Distortion indices in credit, labor and product markets are obtained by principal component analysis, represented with details in the Appendix I. Before estimation, two points need to be clarified. First is that the result of MIMIC models is an index because the latent variable has no origin or unit of measurement. Therefore, latent variables can be measured only relative to another variable by fixing the coefficient of one of the indicators. The second point is that because some economic variables are not stationary, application of this model to time series analysis might be problematic. Granger and Weiss (1983) demonstrated that it is quite possible for integrated variables to have stationary linear combinations. These linear combinations, known as cointegration vectors, are considered as the long-run equilibrium. Deviations from this equilibrium are reconstructed by the error correction model (ECM). Buehn and Schneider (2008) combined the MIMIC model with the cointegration vectors and ECM models, and developed a new model called the "EMIMIC model". These long-run equilibriums are modeled as below. Appendix II describes the technical part of the estimation.

$$GDP = a_1 \times tax\,burden + a_2 \times creditmarket$$
$$distortions + a_3 \times labormarketdistortions +$$
$$a_4 \times productmarketdistortions +$$
$$a_5 \times governmentexpenditure +$$
$$a_6 \times per\,capitaincome +$$
$$a_7 \times unemployment + a_8 \times inflation + u_1$$

$$Employment = a_1 \times tax\,burden + a_2 \times creditmarket$$
$$distortions + a_3 \times labormarketdistortions$$
$$+a_4 \times productmarketdistortions +$$
$$a_5 \times governmentexpenditure + a_6 \times per\,capitaincome$$
$$+a_7 \times unemployment + a_8 \times inflation + u_2$$

$$Insurance = a_1 \times tax\,burden + a_2 \times creditmarket$$
$$distortions + a_3 \times labormarketdistortions +$$
$$a_4 \times productmarketdistortions +$$
$$a_5 \times governmentexpenditure +$$
$$a_6 \times per\,capitaincome +$$
$$a_7 \times unemployment + a_8 \times inflation + u_3$$

Informal Economy: Long-Run Trends and Short-Run Deviations

The model introduced in previous section is estimated here and the results are presented in Table 1. The long-run model shows the cointegrated vectors. The three indicators are positively correlated with latent informal economy in the long run. The coefficient of GDP is set equal to one with the purpose to give the latent variable the same origin and unit of measurement. The reason for setting the coefficient equal to one in the long run and minus one in the short run is because we expect these two variables to be complementary in the long run and substitute in the short run. The two other indicators are highly significant.

Among the causes represented in the structural equation, tax burden is not significant both in the long and short run. The explanation for this is that in developing countries the discretionary application of the tax system seems to be more burdensome than the tax rates. A high level of regulatory

Table 1 Long-run and short-run coefficients

	Variables	*Long-run*	*Short-run*
Indicators	GDP	1	−1
	Employment	1.4	−0.23
		(0.166)***	(0.07)***
	Insurance	1.24	−0.083
		(0.14)***	(0.04)***
Causes	Tax burden	−0.017	−0.01
		(0.031)	(0.028)
	Credit distortion	0.15	0.098
		(0.05)***	(0.028)***
	Labor distortion	0.497	0.12
		(0.062)***	(0.064)*
	Product distortion	0.132	0.086
		(0.04)***	(0.052)*
	Police budget	0.059	0.042
		(0.038)	(0.039)
	Capita income	0.31	−0.64
		(0.07)***	(0.075)***
	Unemployment	0.008	0.022
		(0.034)	(0.032)
	Inflation	−0.046	−0.009
		(0.052)	(0.042)
	Error		−6.67
			(1.91)***

discretion helps create the potential for corruption and drives firms into the unofficial economy (Johnson et al. 1998, p. 1). Moreover, keeping in mind the fact that the complexity of the tax system, tax exemptions and other factors are not considered in this model, the result is not surprising since the tax rate in Iran is very low, about 6 % of GDP.

The results show that in contrast to indirect regulation through taxation, direct interventions are very destructive and have effects on formal actions of firms both in the long and short run. The positive and significant effect was expected because government interventions in the credit, market making access to loans difficult, or raising incentives for rent seeking and corruption, spoil formal firms' advantages in external financing. Therefore, the positive coefficient shows that government interventions in the credit market motivate firms to become informal. The effect of interventions in the product market is also significant. It shows that government interventions such as price controls motivate firms to become informal.

The coefficients of labor market distortions are more significant and greater. This shows that interventions in the labor market are more burdensome than other public regulations. Minimum wages and laws limiting firms' power to hire and fire encourage employment of informal laborers. In the short run, however, the effect is less significant. It seems that in the short run these interventions, for example higher unemployment insurance or higher minimum wage, give unemployed workers the possibility of being unemployed for a longer time and reduce workers' vulnerability against the possibility of being laid off. Considering this contrasting effect, now it is less likely that unemployed workers, or those fired by the firm due to the huge costs imposed by government intervention, will immediately approach the informal job market. In other words, in the short run this conflicting effect based on DLM theory counteracts the detrimental effect of government interventions.

The next variable is government expenditures on police and public order. Since informal firms are unable to use some public goods, police budget is expected to have a negative relationship with the size of the informal economy. The coefficients, however, both in the long run and short run are not significant. This unexpected result has occurred for two reasons. The first reason is that efficiency matters more than the budget expended. The second explanation is that police, especially in Iran, tend to combat public order crimes rather than facing up to corruption and corporate or economic crimes. The police endeavor has reduced the risk of expropriation for both formal and informal economic activities.

The next variable, per capita income, has a positive relationship with the informal economy in the long run. It shows the suitable situation to be indiscriminate for both formal and informal economies to prosper. In the short run, however, as was expected, per capita income and informal economy are correlated negatively. These results confirm the dualist view that higher per capita income and lower poverty bring down the size of the informal economy. Other variables, unemployment and inflation, are insignificant both in the long and short run. The reason is that in the sample period Iran never experienced low unemployment and low inflation. Figure 4 presents the unstable macroeconomic situation of Iran over the previous four decades.

Generally, it seems that in the long run the legalist's view dominates. Variables such as government interventions significantly motivate firms to hide. The main conclusion, thus, is that the informal economy is the result of the government's invisible hand in markets. In the short run, however,

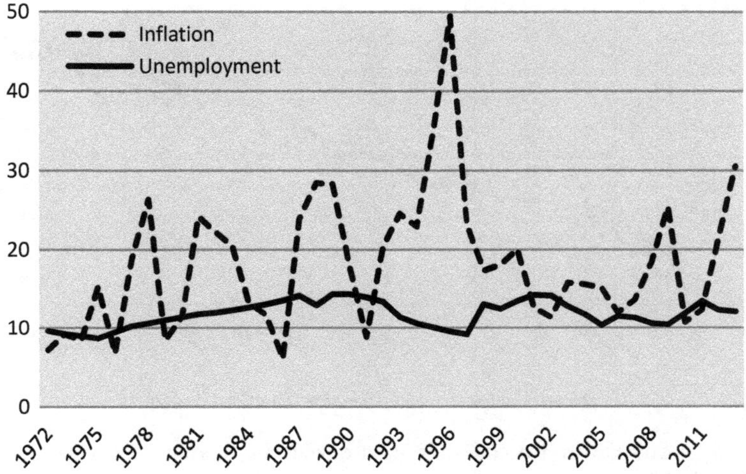

Fig. 4 Inflation and unemployment in Iran

the dualist view mediates. Higher per capita income and unemployment insurance improve the welfare of poor and unemployed workers and decrease the informal economy to levels lower than the long-run trend. The ordinal index of Iran's informal economy is illustrated in Fig. 5. According to this, the real index of Iran's informal economy increased by more than five times over the previous four decades. The unstable macroeconomic situation and poverty has steepened the trend, raising number of laborers ready to accept low quality jobs.

Iran's Informal Economy: Looking Back at Historical Events

The index obtained in the previous section shows the increasing pattern of Iran's informal economy and the effect of determining factors in the long and short run. The index would be more revealing if it is compared with GDP or the real size of the economy. For this purpose, the real GDP (constant price of 1997) was converted to an index by setting the base year as one. The index of the informal economy was also adapted to start from one. Then, the index of the informal economy was divided by the GDP index to see the relative trends. Figure 6 illustrates the relative index of Iran's informal economy. It would be more interesting if we knew

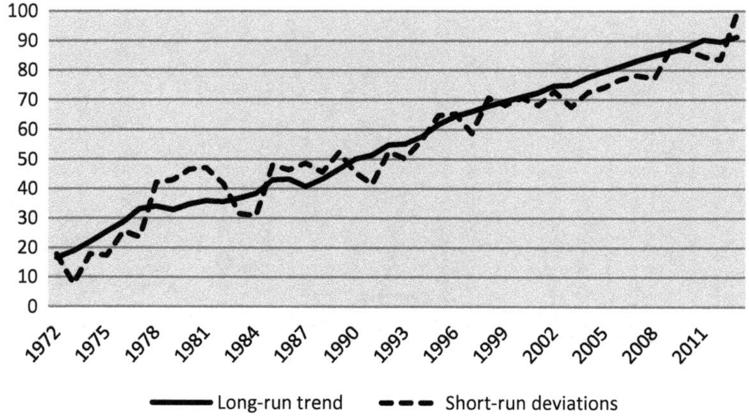

Fig. 5 Long-run trend and short-run deviations of Iran's informal economy (1972–2013)

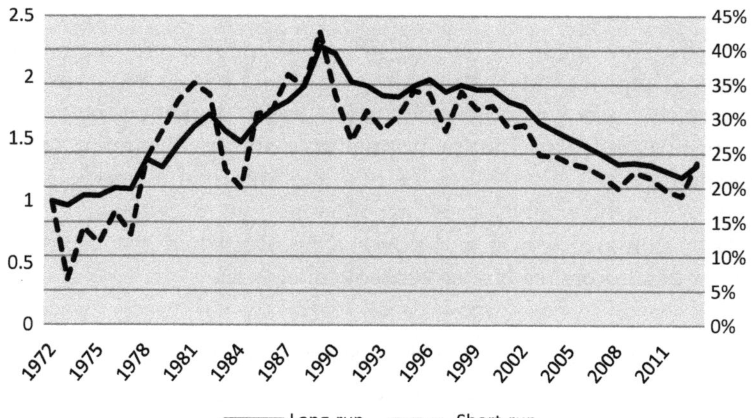

Fig. 6 The relative index of Iran's informal economy in the long run and short run

the magnitude, but the MIMIC approach provides only an index. To resolve this problem, the index can be calibrated using other estimations. Schneider (2007) estimated the size of informal economy for Iran and some other countries. Taking his estimation, 20.2 % of GDP for the year 2007 as the base year, the size of Iran's informal economy relative to GDP is shown by the second axis.

This section uses historical events to explain the trend of Iran's informal economy and its fluctuations in previous decades. The first period separated by the black line and numbered as one in the figure corresponds to the Islamic revolution of 1979. The chaos and confusion of the revolution increased the relative size of informal economy from 13.4 to 30% of GDP in 1980. The next period, indicated by two, refers to the Iran–Iraq war. The relative size during the war increased from 30 to 39.7% of GDP in 1989. Together, the size of Iran's informal economy relative to GDP tripled after the revolution and the war. This is a huge increase, showing the unstable economic and political situation of Iran in that period.

After the war, the country gradually recovered. The relative size of the informal economy returned to the situation it was in before the revolution. The trend over these 20 years was not the same. The great and continuous fall in the relative size happened from 2000 to 2008 mainly due to the high growth of the formal economy. In that period, not only did the relative index decrease, Fig. 6, but also the short-run index fell below the long-run trend, Fig. 5. This means that the economy was thriving through creating enough decent jobs to stop the growth of the informal economy.

The sanctions—the last important event—is separated as the fourth period. Since 2012, severe sanctions imposed on Iran have increased the size of the informal economy. This increase happened in the real index and its relative size to the GDP. These sanctions, preventing merchandise trade and financial transactions by Iran with other countries, increased illegal transactions and the informal economy. The relative size increased from 17.4 % in 2012 to 21.9 % of GDP in 2013.

Conclusion

Informal economic activities, which are not observed and controlled by government, contribute to a considerable and growing share of gross domestic product (GDP) in a large number of countries. These include a broad range of essentially different activities which occur for different reasons and cannot be treated equally. However, the invisible hand of government can be traced in all such activities. Illegal goods are hidden because government has decided to fight them. Irregular production takes place when the government fails on his classic duties i.e. protection of property rights and preparing the environment for private business. In an uncontrolled and chaotic stmospheres, work relations will be based on occasional jobs, kinship and personal relations. In contrast, shadow economy takes place not because of non-presence of government but due to its overreagulation. Government interventions are the main reason for entrepreneurs to hide.

This chapter reveals the invisible hand of government. It studies the effect of public policies and regulations on firms' individual incentives and their choice between the formal and informal economy. Iran has been selected for this purpose. The reason is that Iran is a big economy in the Persian Gulf region characterized with huge public expenditures and direct government interventions. Iran, moreover, was under tough international sanctions which make it an interesting case of study. The MIMIC model was used to estimate the size of informal economy. Time series data for 1972–2013 were employed and both the long-run trend and short-run deviation were estimated.

The formal and informal economy share common long-run trends. But in the short run, the formal and informal economies compete to absorb a greater share of the labor force. Investigating the causes of the informal economy shows that, in general, the legalist view dominates in the long run, confirming that the informal economy is the result of government's invisible hand in markets. In the short run, however, the dualist view mediates. The MIMIC model provides an index of the size of the latent variable, the informal economy.

The long-run trends and short-run fluctuation of the index were investigated both in level and relative to GDP. The real index of Iran's informal economy has increased five-fold in the last four decades. Comparing it with the formal economy, the GDP reveals interesting historical coincidences. The rise in the size of Iran's informal economy relative to GDP may be attributed to three periods. In the ten years during the Islamic revolution and the war between Iran and Iraq, the size of the informal economy increased from 12.2 % of the formal economy to 39.7 %. The recent sanctions were also impactful. Severe sanctions imposed since 2012 increased the relative size of informal economy from 17.4 % of GDP to 21.9 % one year later.

Note

1. The analysis presented here is based on a previous paper of mine (Khandan and Nili 2014). For a more detailed discussion read the paper, however, this section provides an updated analysis for a longer time period.

Appendix I

Government Interventions' Indices

Principal component analysis (PCA) is used to deal with the various dimensions of government actions. Government intervention in three main markets, credit, labor and product markets, are investigated. Original variables used in PCA are presented in Table 2. The data are collected from the Central Bank of Iran for the sample period (1972/73–2013/14).

Appendix II

Testing the Existence of Cointegration Vectors

The first step is to test which variables are not stationary. Integrated variables can be specified through the augmented Dickey-Fuller unit root test. Number of lag variables included has been chosen using Akaike information criterion indices. As it is shown in Table 3 most of the variables are I(1) but the conclusions for some of the variables are not direct. For inflation and tax burden, the result depends on the inclusion of trend in the regression. Since assuming a trend for these two variables is not plausible, it can be expected that the two variables are stationary. Empirical tests also indicate that trend is not significant in either case. Then cointegration between I(1) variables should be tested. Engle and Granger's (1987) two-step approach is used for this purpose. The variables are cointegrated only if their linear combination and their residuals are stationary. Therefore, the

Table 2 Original variables used in PCA modeling for different market distortions

Credit market distortions	*Labor market distortions*	*Product market distortions*
Share of obligatory credit facilities[a]	Ratio of minimum wage to average wage	Relative price of industrial goods to CPI
Share of public sector from disbursed facilities	Ratio of the unemployment insurance to average wage	
Negative real interest rate	Dummy variable representing quality of labor law	

[a]The government to support infrastructural sectors, create jobs and achieve other social goals, has obliged its state-run banks to pay obligatory facilities

Table 3 Dickey-Fuller unit root test and integration

Variables	*Level*			*First difference*			*Integration*
	Constant & trend	*Constant*	*None*	*Constant & trend*	*Constant*	*None*	
	−3.54	*−2.96*	*−1.95*	*−3.54*	*−2.96*	*−1.95*	
GDP	−1.94	−0.42	0.58	−4.16	−4.05	−3.95	I(1)
Employment	−2.284	−1.21	1.17	−3.44	−3.27	−1.533	I(1)
Tax burden	−3.25	−3.28	−1.68	−7.24	−7.3	−7.37	I(0)
Credit distortion	−2.72	−2.8	−0.97	−5.55	−5.59	−5.64	I(1)
Labor distortion	−1.99	−0.83	1.06	−8.13	−8.24	−7.86	I(1)
Product distortion	−2.14	−2.75	−0.53	−4.39	−3.98	−4	I(1)
Police budget	−2.13	−2.14	−0.76	−2.9	−2.99	−3.07	I(1)
Capita income	−1.9	−1.5	−0.54	−3.08	−3	−3.05	I(1)
Unemployment	−2.4	−2.52	−0.78	−5.92	−5.94	−5.99	I(1)
Inflation	−3.05	−3.08	−0.79	−6.6	−6.7	−6.78	I(0)

Table 4 Dickey-Fuller unit root test of residuals

Variables	*Number of lags*	*No trend & no constant*	*Integration*
		−1.95	
e(Employment)	0	−3.41	I(0)
e(GDP)	2	−3.41	I(0)
e(Insurance)	0	−4.79	I(0)
e(Structural)	0	−4.76	I(0)

same unit root test should be done, but this time for residuals of estimated reduced form equations. The residuals are tested for unit root and the results are shown in Table 4. Accordingly, the residuals are stationary and, thus, variables in the structural equations are cointegrated.

References

Antunes, A. R., & Cavalcanti, T. V. (2007). Startup cost, limited enforcement, and the hidden economy. *European Economic Review, 51*(1), 203–204.

Blackburn, K., Bose, N., & Capasso, S. (2012). Tax evasion, the underground economy and financial development. *Journal of Economic Behavior and Organization, 83*(2), 243–253.

Buehn, A., & Schneider, F. (2008). *MIMIC models, co-integration and error correction: The shadow economies in France and the UK* (IZA discussion paper No. 3306).

Buehn, A., Karmann, A., & Schneider, F. (2009). Shadow economy and do-it-yourself activities: The German case. *Journal of Institutional and Theoretical Economics, 165*(4), 701–722.

Centeno, M. A., & Portes, A. (2006). The informal economy in the shadow of the state. In P. Fernandez-Kelly & J. Shefner (Eds.), *Out of the shadows: Political action and the informal economy in Latin America* (pp. 23–49). Pennsylvania: The Pennsylvania State University Press.

Chaudhuri, S. (2003). How and how far to liberalize a developing economy with informal sector and factor market distortions. *The Journal of International Trade & Economic Development, 12*(4), 403–428.

Chong, A., Galdo, J., & Saavedra, J. (2008). Informality and productivity in the labor market in Peru. *Journal of Economic Policy Reform, 11*(4), 229–245.

De Soto, H. (1989). *The other path: The invisible revolution in the third world.* New York: Harper and Row.

Dinkelman, T., & Ranchhod, V. (2011). *Evidence on the impact of minimum wage laws in an informal sector: Domestic workers in South Africa* (CEPR discussion paper No. DP8682).

Djankov, S., Glaeser, E., La Porta, R., Lopez-de-Silanes, F., & Shleifler, A. (2003). *The new comparative economics.* Journal of Comparative Economics, 31(4), 595–619.

Ellul, A., Jappelli, T., Pagano, M., & Panunzi, F. (2011). *Transparency, tax pressure and access to finance* (ECGI – Finance working paper No. 332).

Engle, R. F., & Granger, C. W. J. (1987). Co-integration and error correction: Representation, estimation, and testing. *Econometrica, 55*(2), 251–276.

Evrensel, A. Y. (2009). Differences in bank regulations: The role of governance and corruption. *Journal of Economic Policy Reform, 12*(2), 91–110.

Fields, G. S. (2004). *A guide to multisector labor market models.* Cornell University ILR School (Working paper no. 86).

Gibson, B. (2005). The transition to a globalized economy: Poverty, human capital and the informal sector in a structuralist CGE model. *Journal of Development Economics, 78*(1), 60–94.

Granger, C. W. J., & Weiss, A. A. (1983). Time series analysis of error-correcting models. In S. Karlin (Ed.), *Studies in econometrics, time series, and multivariate statistics* (pp. 255–278). New York: Academic Press.

Hudson, J., Williams, C. C., Orvisk, M., & Nadin, S. (2012). Evaluating the impact of the informal economy on businesses in South East Europe: Some lessons from the 2009 World Bank enterprise survey. *South East European Journal of Economics and Business, 7*(1), 99–110.

International Labour Office. (1972). *Employment, incomes and equality: A strategy for increasing productive employment in Kenya* (pp. 223–232). Geneva: International Labour Office.

Johnson, S., Kaufmann, D., & Zoido-Lobatón, P. (1998). Regulatory discretion and the unofficial economy. *American Economic Review, 88*(2), 387–392.

Kantor, P., Rani, U., & Unni, J. (2006). Decent work deficits in informal economy: Case of Surat. *Economic and Political Weekly, 41*(21), 2089–2097.

Khandan, A., & Nili, M. (2014). Government interventions and the size of the informal economy. The case of Iran (1971–2007). *Journal of Economic Policy Reform, 17.*

Kim, B. Y. (2005). Poverty and informal economy participation: Evidence from Romania. *Economics of Transition, 13*(1), 163–185.

Lang, K., & Manove, M. (2006). *Education and labor-market discrimination* (NBER working paper No. 12257).

Lehmann, H., & Pignatti, N. (2008). *Informal employment relationships and labor market segmentation in transition economies: Evidence from Ukraine* (IZA working paper No. 3269).

Loayza, N. V. (1996). The economics of the informal sector: A simple model and some empirical evidence from Latin America. *Carnegie-Rochester Conference Series on Public Policy, 45*(1), 129–162.

Loayza, N. V., Oviedo, A. M. & Serven, L. (2005). *The impact of regulation on growth and informality cross-country evidence* (World Bank policy research working paper No. 3623).

Maiti, D., & Marjit, S. (2008). Trade liberalization, production organization and informal sector of the developing countries. *Journal of International Trade & Economic Development, 17*(3), 453–461.

Pagés, C., & Stampini, M. (2009). No education, no good jobs? Evidence on the relationship between education and labor market segmentation. *Journal of Comparative Economics, 37.*

Schneider, F. (2007). Shadow economies and corruption all over the world: New estimates for 145 countries. *Economics: The Open Access Open Assessment E-Journal, 1*(9), 1–66.

Schneider, F., & Enste, D. H. (2000). Shadow economies: Size, causes, and consequences. *Journal of Economic Literature, 38*(1), 77–114.

Schneider, F., Buehn, A., & Montenegro, C. E. (2010). *Shadow economies all over the world: New estimates for 162 countries from 1999 to 2007* (World Bank policy research working paper No. 5356).

Straub, S. (2005). Informal sector: The credit market channel. *Journal of Development Economics, 78*(2), 299–321.

Tiwari, P., Kawakami, T., & Doi, M. (2002). Dual labor markets and trade reform in China. *Journal of Economic Policy Reform, 5*(2), 101–113.

Torgler, B., & Schneider, F. (2007). *Shadow economy, tax morale, governance and institutional quality: A panel analysis* (CESifo working paper No. 1923).

Estimating the Size of the Croatian Shadow Economy: A Labour Approach

Sabina Hodzic

Introduction

In all countries of the world, the shadow economy is a hot topic. Croatia is no exception. Since Croatia is a country in transition, numerous elements exist that support the existence of the shadow economy. Some of these elements include inefficiency in privatisation, non-existent industrial policy, frequent changes of laws and ordinances, lenient criminal measures for combating illegal activities and so forth. It is characteristic of countries in transition to achieve a faster and more successful transition due to higher rates of economic growth, lower unemployment rates and faster development of the private sector. A lack of democratic, economic and regulatory institutions leads to corruption, lobbying and different forms of informal work. There are numerous factors that affect the growth of the shadow economy in countries in transition. Vehovec (2002), North (1997) and Kaufmann and Kaliberda (1996) claim these are political repression, an inadequate legal system, high tax burdens, macroeconomic instability and the culture of non-payment. Vehovec

S. Hodzic (✉)
University of Rijeka, Faculty of Tourism and Hospitality Management, Opatija, Croatia
e-mail: sabinah@fthm.hr

A. Polese et al. (eds.), *The Informal Economy in Global Perspective*, International Political Economy Series,
DOI 10.1007/978-3-319-40931-3_4

(2002) and North (1997) also list the following factors: non-functioning of property rights, high entrepreneurial risk and high transaction costs. The World Bank (2001) claims these are large-scale legislative and regulatory changes, massive redistribution of national wealth, lack or inefficiency of institutions of public control. Meanwhile, Bejakovic (2002) lists the following factors: lack of democratic, economic and regulatory institutions, lack of tax-paying experience, discretionary rights of public servants and state prodigality.

In 2004, the Croatian government adopted a plan of short-term and long-term measures for combating the shadow economy which were carried out until 2007. Therefore, the Ministry of Finance of the Republic of Croatia continued with the consistent supervisory activities in its scope, particularly in cooperation with the Tax Administration and the Customs Administration. These activities mainly refer to increased supervision of fiscalisation and value-added taxes as well as supervision and detection of illegal activities in the field of transport of excise goods, performance of unregistered activities, residence tax and vessel control. Taxpayers whose goods and services are paid in cash are under supervision. Special attention is given to supervision on the Adriatic coast and in the city of Zagreb.

The aim of this chapter is to use a labour approach to estimate the size of the shadow economy in Croatia in the period 2008–2014. The empirical approach is based on methodology used by Svec (2009) and Crnkovic-Pozaic (1997) for Croatia and Nastav and Bojnec (2007) for Slovenia. For the purposes of this chapter, the shadow economy is defined as paid work which is legal in all respects other than it is not declared to authorities for tax, social security or labour law purposes (Aliyev 2015; Boels 2014; European Commission 2007; OECD 2012; Polese and Rodgers 2011; Williams and Franic 2015; Williams et al. 2014).

The remainder of the chapter is organised as follows: section two presents a literature review, section three describes the methodology of the paper, section four describes the data analysis and results, while the final section concludes and provides recommendations for future research.

Literature Review

A universal definition of the shadow economy does not exist; therefore, different authors offer different definitions. For example, Feige (1979) very simply defined the shadow economy as all economic activities which have not been registered or calculated. Depending on the compliance with the rules and on the legality of economic transactions, Karajic (2002) differentiates between *official economy* and *shadow economy*; depending on the impact of national legislation, he differentiates between *uncorrupted* and *corrupt* official economy, with the shadow economy pertaining to the latter category along with *fictive* and *criminal* economy. Schneider and Enste (2000) define the shadow economy as a set of economic activities that contribute to the official gross domestic product, but are not registered. In its handbook "Measuring the Non-Observed Economy", Organisation for Economic Co-operation and Development (OECD) (2002) introduced the notion of non-observed economy. This framework was developed by the Italian National Statistical Institute (ISTAT); it divides non-observed economy into underground, informal and illegal production which is later divided again according to the type of cause. Therefore, ISTAT distinguishes between seven types of non-observed activities marked as T1–T7 (they were later on modified to N1–N7; the classification is commonly used by Eurostat and OECD). These seven types of non-observed economy are: N1—Producer should have registered (underground producer), N2—Illegal producer that fails to register, N3—Producer is not obliged to register, N4—Registered legal person is not included in statistics, N5—Registered entrepreneur is not included in statistics, N6—Misreporting by the producer and N7—Statistical deficiencies in the data.

Activities covered by the notion of the unofficial economy are activities which are not registered in official national statistics or have not been recorded by tax authorities (Greenfield 1993; Tanzi 1983; Thomas 1992). This phenomenon can be found in every political, social and economic system, as well as in all stages of development and is of various levels of intensity. As such, it has both positive and negative effects on the economy. A positive effect would be activating the working-age population, otherwise left unused, while a negative effect would be the evasion of paying taxes and contributions, which leads to the reduction of national revenues. By using the MIMIC method (multiple indicators multiple causes), Schneider (2011) found that the shadow economy in Croatia in 2007 amounted to 30.4 % of gross domestic product, which makes Croatia, apart from Bulgaria, the country with the highest rate of shadow economy in all EU-27 member states.

According to Williams et al. (2014), Croatia has one of the largest undeclared economies in South-Eastern Europe. Rubic (2013) and Williams (2014) examine the results of direct surveys, while Galic-Nagyszombaty (2012), Klaric (2011), Ott (2002) and Schneider (2013) examine indirect measurement methods and also find similar results. Williams and Franic (2015) found that "undeclared economy is equivalent to around a quarter of the total gross domestic product and employment in Croatia" (p. 19). Schneider (2013) estimates that undeclared work in 2013 in Croatia was equivalent to 28.4 % of gross domestic product and Williams (2014) estimates that the share of employment in the undeclared economy in 2013 in Croatia was 22.7 %.

Baric and Williams (2013) found that the "undeclared economy in Croatia is equivalent to 30.4 per cent of gross domestic product, and as such, is larger than in all EU-27 Member States with the exception of Bulgaria. It is most concentrated in agriculture and allied trades, followed by manufacturing and retailing" (p. 27).

In a project, the Institute of Public Finance (1996) found that the share of the unofficial economy in the Republic of Croatia amounted to at least 25 % of gross domestic product. The project also showed that economic policies must be focused on combating the unofficial economy through a reduction of taxes and customs fees, and a selective reduction of regulations and the role of the public sector in the economy. Research done by the Institute of Public Finance (2002) within the above project led to measures being determined for reducing the unofficial economy within the framework of general institutional measures, measures in the privatisation process, measures in the pension system and other measures within the tax system and system for stimulating employment. In its project (2005), the Institute of Economics found that the share of shadow economy in selected EU-10 and Central and Eastern European (CEE) countries shows that Albania has the highest rate of shadow economy with as much as 31.4 % of the gross domestic product, followed by Lithuania and Macedonia (18.9 % and 17.2 % respectively). Croatia showed the highest rate of shadow economy in hotels and restaurants (30.02 %), real estate and business services (29.9 %) and construction (23.6 %). Researchers from the Institute of Economics in Zagreb (Lovrincevic et al. 2002) and Mikulic and Galic-Nagyszombaty (2013) published research papers showing the level of the unofficial economy in Croatia according to activities and individual manifestations (N1–N7), but also the determinants for the development of the unofficial economy as well as the link between the unofficial and official economy. The papers cover the period up to 2009; however, the professional community has not provided any estimates covering more recent years that would enable the assessment of the effects of long-term recession on the unofficial economy as well as the impact of changes in the tax system (lower rates for hotels and restaurants and the effect of fiscalisation).

The following methods were used to measure the shadow economy in Croatia: national accounts discrepancy method (Madzarevic-Sujster and Mikulic 2002); monetary method and electricity consumption method (Jankov 1997; Sosic and Faulend 2002); Eurostat method (Lovrincevic et al. 2002); estimation of tax evasion method (Madzarevic-Sujster 2002); socio-cultural dimension of informal economy (Stulhofer and Rimac 2002) and labour approach method (Crnkovic-Pozaic 1997; Svec 2009).

Jankov (1997) examined the behaviour of certain basic explanatory monetary variables in the period 1992–1996 and found that they point to a possible growth of the unofficial economy: nominal and real cash increased more quickly than other monetary aggregates, and there was a great increase of taxes, for example, the share of tax revenue in the gross domestic product increased around 10 %.

By applying a labour approach, Crnkovic-Pozaic (1997) found that the share of persons employed in the unofficial economy increased from 6.42 % in 1992 to 16.42 % in 1993, and in 1994 up to 19.3 % of the active population. After that, the share decreased below the level from 1993 (15.3 %). The author also deemed that the growth of the unofficial economy was a consequence of a series of bankruptcies from 1991 to 1993 and the inability of the private sector to provide a sufficient number of jobs in the official economy.

According to Madzarevic-Sujster and Mikulic (2002), "the average level of shadow economy in the period 1990–1995 amounted to 25.4 per cent, while in the period (1996–2000) there was a significant decrease of shadow economy to an average of 10.4 per cent. The first period (1990–1995) is characterized by economic activities in war; the second period (1996–2000) is characterized by the stabilisation of the political and economic situation in which the ethical and legal systems grew stonger" (p. 47).

Based on their analysis, Sosic and Faulend (2002) found that results based on evaluations of foreign cash in circulation in Croatia showed a growing tendency in unofficial economy as well as in traditional monetary methods.

Using the Eurostat method, Lovrincevic et al. (2002) found that the entire shadow economy of the Republic of Croatia is 11.1 % of official gross value added calculated by basic prices, or 8.9 % of the official gross domestic product, which along with added value by basic prices also includes all taxes and subsidies on products which are not arranged by activities but are shown at the level of national economy.

Madzarevic-Sujster (2002) examines a separate analysis of the evasion of individual direct and indirect taxes for the period 1994–2000. Two estimates have been obtained: the lower estimate of tax evasion that approximately keeps up with the trend in the share of the unofficial economy in gross domestic product and that amounts to around 5.5 % of gross domestic product; and the upper assessment which partially shadows the movements in the increase or decrease in the tax burden on the economy and that considerably decreases after 1998, with a reduction in the taxation of labour from about 11 to 7.5 % of gross domestic product in 2000.

Stulhofer and Rimac (2002) point out that in 1995 and 1999 the level of opportunism decreased with respect to both the intensity and the distribution. They also examined a theoretical model in which the level of opportunism reflects the moral costs related to participants in the underground economy; the decrease in the level of opportunism and economic growth in the post-war period suggest a moderate reduction in the underground economy in Croatia during the second half of the 1990s (p. 2).

According to Svec (2009), a comparison of the two periods 1991–1996 and 2001–2007 based on administrative data showed a negative relationship between the activity rates and the estimated values of the shadow economy. The value of the shadow economy in the 1990s amounted to more than 20 %, but that number drastically decreased in the period 2001–2007.

Methodology

The shadow economy can be difficult to quantify because of the complexity of the phenomenon itself. Depending on the analysed period and theoretical assumptions, different assessment methods have been used. The methods can be divided into those with a direct approach and those with an indirect approach. The direct approach encompasses the use of micro approaches, or well-designed surveys and samples based on voluntary responses or tax inspection and other effects for determining compliance with the law. The indirect approach focuses on developing a psychological contact between the state and its citizens to encourage commitment to compliance among citizens and thus greater self-regulation.

The indirect approach, also known as “indicating”, offers four indicators. These are:

1. The currency demand method (Cagan 1958; Gutmann 1977; Tanzi 1983, 1980)
2. The electricity consumption method—two indicators: Kaufmann-Kaliberda method (1996) and Lackó method (Lackó 1998, 1996).

3. The multiple indicators multiple causes (MIMIC) method (Frey and Weck-Hannemann 1984; Giles et al. 1999; Schneider 1997, 1994; Thomas 1992).

According to Nastav and Bojnec (2007), the three main groups of methods to quantify the size of the shadow economy can be identified as *direct methods*, *indirect methods* and *modelling*.

In this chapter the labour approach is used because it belongs to indirect methods and relies in the difference between real and registered use of labour.

Davidescu (2014) considers that "the labour approach method is one of the indirect methods and is meaningful only if the changes in official population activity rates are caused by factors related to the shadow economy. The advantages of this method are data availability and simplicity. The disadvantage is the fact that the initial value of unofficial employment is always zero" (p. 26). The assumption is not realistic but the method algorithm itself gives such a value. The obstacles of this method are:

- The assumption of the full-time participation of the unemployed in the shadow economy (and that no one with an official job participates (part-time) in the shadow economy) is not properly grounded due to sampling errors, underreporting and the fact that not all of those registered as unemployed according to the Labour Force Survey work full-time in the shadow economy.
- The problem of underreporting of the data to the Labour Force Survey.
- Different data sources on the labour force in the economy are very limited in their consistency: the Labour Force Survey measures employment, whereas the administrative sources usually report jobs.
- The method does not include and measure people with a second job.

According to Svec (2009) and Crnkovic-Pozaic (1997), the activity rate can be defined as a ratio of persons who either are or wish to be economically active, in relation to all persons of working age:

$$Activity\,rate = \left(the\,employed + the\,unemployed\right) / \,persons\,of\,working\,age \quad (1)$$

$$\textit{The employed} + \textit{the unemployed} = \textit{labour force}$$
$$(\textit{total labour supply, total working population, de facto economically active population}) \quad (2)$$

Alternative definition:

$$\textit{Activity rate} = (\textit{the employed} + \textit{the unemployed}) / \textit{total population} \quad (3)$$

The main steps for calculation are:

1. Data on the employed and unemployed should be obtained from the *Statistical Yearbook* of the Croatian Bureau of Statistics and the de facto active population calculated according to the formula (2),
2. Activity rate is to be calculated using formula (1) or (3),
3. The zero activity rate is defined according to formula (1) or (3), in the process of which initial data of the given time series are used. Hypothetically active population for the time period *t* is equal to the period multiplication of the zero activity rate and total population in year *t*,
4. After the values from step 1), 2) and 3) have been calculated, it is possible to calculate the value of those employed in the unofficial economy according to formula (4). The formula served to calculate the so-called hypothetical activity rates which were then compared in each year to the official, de facto activity rates,
5. The share of the employed in the unofficial economy is computed as:

$$\textit{Share of the employed in the unofficial economy} = (\textit{hypothetically active} - \textit{de facto active}) / \textit{de facto active} \quad (4)$$

Data Analysis and Results

The aim of this chapter is to use a labour approach to calculate the value of the shadow economy in Croatia: the method based on historical activity rates (administrative data) using annual data covering the period 2008–2014. Moreover, the chapter also presents a correlation coefficient under the assumption of a regression analysis. The main source of data is the Croatian Bureau of Statistics' *Statistical Yearbook 2008–2014*.

For the calculation of unofficial employment, the following data are needed: population, number of employed and number of unemployed people. Based on that, an algorithm is used to calculate the activity rate, hypothetically active population and the unofficial economy for a certain time series. The results are shown in Table 1.

It can be concluded that in the observed period, there is a significant decrease in the activity rate until 2010, after which growth was achieved. In the period 2008–2010, the de facto active population declined much faster than the total population grew. After 2010, the de facto active population grew and thus the rate grew too, especially after 2011. After 2013, the de facto active population recorded high declines despite European Union accession (after 1 July 2013).

The activity rate is inversely proportional to the estimate of people employed in the unofficial economy. As the activity rate falls, unofficial employment grows. The obtained result is meaningful as the Croatian population switches from the official to unofficial economy. Therefore, the assumption that everybody who leaves the labour force enters the unofficial economy is not entirely correct. There is always a share of the active population that becomes inactive, but this method cannot be used to calculate its percentage.

In the observed period 2009–2014 (the initial year has been ignored, in which the labour approach supposes that the unofficial employment is zero, because the difference between the hypothetically active and de facto active population is zero), by analysing possible correlations between employment in the official economy, unemployment in the official economy and employment in the unofficial economy, a negative significant relationship between official employment and official registered unemployment has been observed. The results are presented in Table 2.

In the Croatian economy, it is realistic to assume that an increase in the number of employed persons in the official economy at the same time decreases the number of registered unemployed persons. The positive relationship between unofficial employment and official employment (0.08) can be explained as follows: persons in official employment are satisfied with their jobs and income and do not think about moving to the shadow economy. Also interesting is the fact that the number of registered unemployed persons decreased over time, especially if we compare 2011 and 2012, but in the official statistics a decrease in the number of employees was recorded in

Table 1 Administrative data from 2008 to 2014 (in thousands)

	2008	*2009*	*2010*	*2011*	*2012*	*2013*	*2014*
Total population	4434,00	4429,00	4418,00	4280,00	4268,00	4256,00	4239,00
Total employed	1554,80	1498,70	1432,40	1411,20	1395,10	1364,00	1342,00
Total unemployed	236,70	263,20	302,40	305,30	324,30	345,11	328,20
De facto active population	1791,50	1761,90	1734,80	1716,50	1719,40	1709,11	1670,20
Activity rate (%)	40,4	39,8	39,3	40,1	40,3	40,2	39,4
Hypothetically active	1791,50	1789,48	1785,04	1729,28	1724,43	1719,58	1712,71
Unofficial employed (%)	0,00	1,57	2,89	0,74	0,29	0,61	2,54

Source: Author's calculation based on data from the *Statistical Yearbook 2008–2014*, Croatian Bureau of Statistics

Table 2 Pearson's correlation coefficients for the period 2008–2014 (administrative data)

Variable	*Correlation coefficient*
Official employment and official unemployment	−0,94
Unofficial employment and official employment	0,08
Unofficial employment and official unemployment	−0,26

Source: Author's calculations

the same period. If we take into consideration the Croatian economy with its slow growth rate of gross domestic product and lack of structural reforms, a possible explanation could be the fact that there are unemployed persons who work in that economy. This also means that a decrease in the number of unemployed persons leads to an increase in unofficial employment, by involving those unemployed in the unofficial sector. This is one of the reasons for the negative correlation between unofficial and official employment.

A comparison of these data with the data presented by Svec (2009), in which the author also analysed the correlation coefficient between official unemployment, official employment and unofficial employment for the period 2002–2007 in Croatia, shows that the results are very similar. Svec also found a negative correlation between official unemployment and official employment (−0.92). What is interesting is the fact that there is a huge difference between unofficial employment and official employment (−0.74) which is negative compared to my results, while the difference between unofficial employment and official unemployment (0.41) was positive, as opposed to my results which gave a negative correlation coefficient (−0.26).

All correlation coefficients in this chapter are calculated based on the assumption of a regression analysis. In Fig. 1, a correlation between official unemployment and official employment is presented.

The scatter diagram shows a negative statistical relationship. A negative relationship means that the increase of the value of one variable leads to a decrease of the value of the other variable, that is, the decrease of the first variable leads to an increase in the second variable. In our example, this means that official employment increased and official unemployment decreased in the observed period (2008–2014).

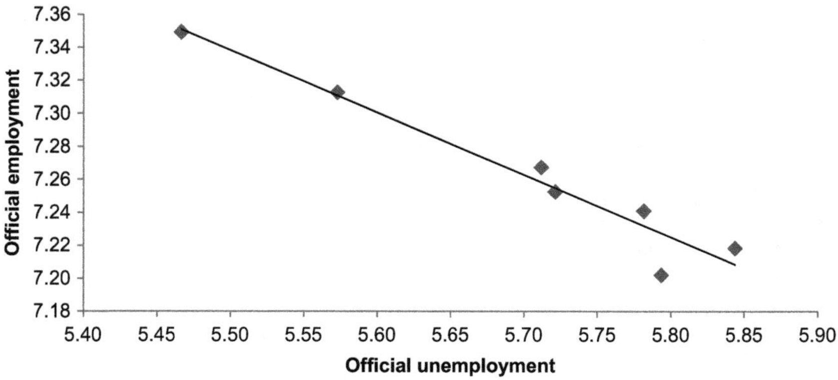

Fig. 1 Correlation between official unemployment and official employment (2009–2014)
(*Source*: Author's calculations)

In Fig. 2, the correlation between unofficial employment and official employment is presented.

This scatter diagram shows a positive statistical relationship. A positive relationship means that as one variable increases so does the other, that is, as one variable decreases so does the other. In our example, that means that official employment and unofficial employment increased in the observed period (2008–2014). In Fig. 3, the correlation between unofficial employment and official unemployment is presented.

The scatter diagram also shows a negative statistical relationship.

Crnkovic-Pozaic's (1997) paper will serve as a basis for explaining the results obtained for the periods 1991–1996 and 2001–2007. The periods 1991–1996 and 2001–2007 show the same trend in activity rates and the unofficial economy. There was a drop in rates in the period 1991–1996 until 1994 when there was a slight increase, which can also be noted in the period 2001–2007. The ratio of the activity rate and unofficial employment is inversely proportional in both periods, which can be explained with the assumption that a part of the active population transferred from the official to the unofficial economy. The same author also calculated the correlation coefficient for all three examples. The correlation between official unemployment and official employment in 1992–1996 was 0.75, while in 2002–2007 it was −0.92. The correlation between unofficial employment and official employment in 1992–1996 was −0.991, while

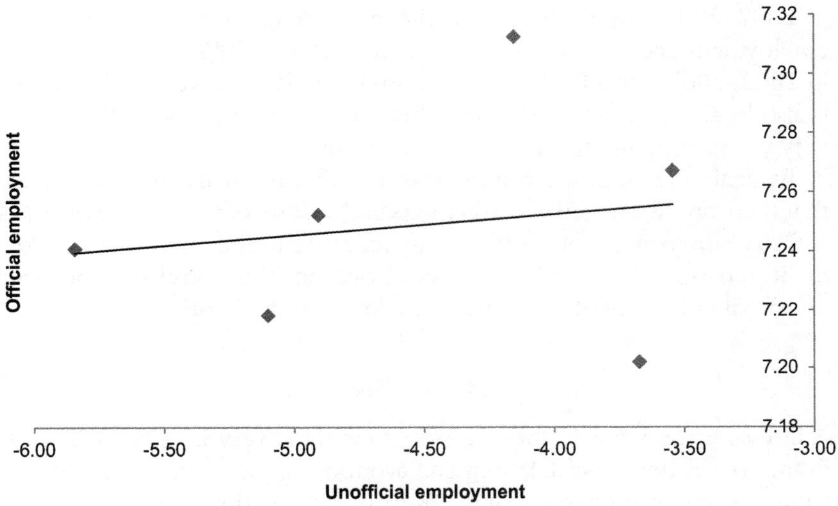

Fig. 2 Correlation between unofficial employment and official employment (2009–2014)
(*Source*: Author's calculations)

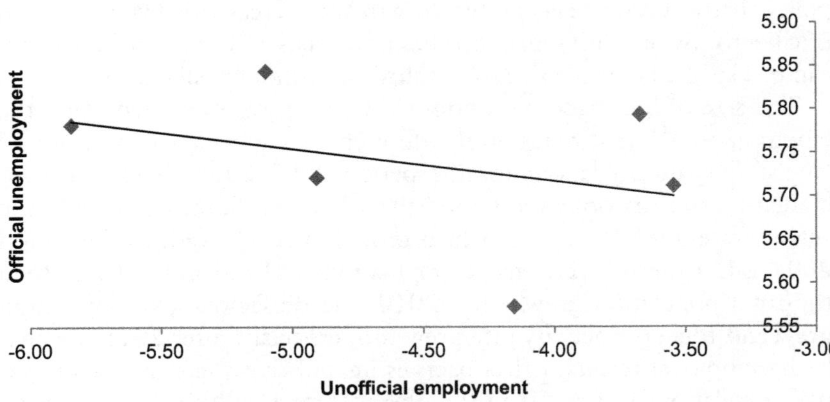

Fig. 3 Correlation between unofficial employment and official unemployment (2009–2014)
(*Source*: Author's calculations)

in 2002–2007 it was −0.74; and the last correlation between unofficial employment and official unemployment in 1992–1996 was −0.82, while in 2002–2007 it was 0.41. The last correlation is negative (−0.82), which is also logical because if members of the workforce lose their official jobs, they will participate in the unofficial economy.

By analysing empirical results from this chapter, it has been estimated that there are two negative correlations in the observed period 2009–2014 (official employment and official unemployment and unofficial employment and official unemployment) and one positive correlation between unofficial employment and official employment in Croatia.

Conclusion

Addressing the issue of the shadow economy is very important because doing so will affect social, labour and economic policies, put an end to disrupted relations in the tax system, improve the functioning of government policies as well as improving living and working conditions of citizens. The main reasons that have affected the growth of the shadow economy in the past decades in Croatia are: the tax policy (with a substantial increase of tax rates), the increasing burden of labour costs, obtaining different social supports, lack of satisfaction with the goals of the government and changes in work ethics. The Croatian government has to lead such an economic policy that will provide economic growth and increase the living standard of citizens. By increasing real incomes of citizens and economic growth it can be expected that the size of the shadow economy will decrease.

The size of the shadow economy in Croatia was estimated using the labour approach that relies on the difference of actual (real) and official (registered) use of labour for the period 2008–2014. It can be concluded that in the observed period there is a significant decrease in the activity rate until 2010, after which growth was achieved. In the period 2008–2010 the de facto active population declined much faster than the total population grew. After 2010, the de facto active population grew and thus, the activity rate grew too, especially after 2011. By analysing empirical results, it has been estimated that there are two negative correlations in Croatia in the observed period 2009–2014 (official employment and official employment, -0.94, and unofficial employment and official unemployment, -0.26) and one positive correlation between unofficial employment and official employment (0.08).

Due to a lack of accurate evidence, the use of the labour approach (only administrative data) is limited for concrete policy measures. Even so, in order to reduce the shadow economy, the Croatian government needs to implement serious measures, especially structural reforms. According to Ott (2002), it is necessary that: laws and regulations are more clear, precise and harmonised; the independence and resources of the courts are reinforced; statistics, organisation and efficiency are improved as well as the expertise and cooperation of state organs; the role of state is reduced; public expenditures are rationalised; the quality of the public sector is improved; the tax burden is reduced; and the possibility of education expanded to all citizens. Croatia cannot fight against the shadow economy in an organised and efficient way while the authorities are not ready to eliminate corruption. In order to improve the quality of the fight against corruption, it is necessary to continue the development of the judiciary, take actions to improve its independence, review the principles of financial support for law enforcement and provide measures to improve their wages.

Thus, further research and detailed, in-depth studies are needed. A recommendation would be to design a special country-based survey for every economic activity, which would result in deeper insights into the true state of the Croatian shadow economy.

References

Aliyev, H. (2015). Post-soviet informality: Towards theory-building. *International Journal of Sociology and Social Policy, 35*(3–4), 121–142.

Baric, M., & Williams, C. C. (2013). Tackling the undeclared economy in Croatia. *South-Eastern Europe Journal of Economics, 1*, 7–36.

Bejakovic, P. (2002). Evazija doprinosa za mirovinsko osiguranje [The evasion of contributions for retirement insurance]. *Financial Theory and Practice, 26*(1), 317–349.

Boels, D. (2014). It's better than stealing: Informal street selling in Brussels. *International Journal of Sociology and Social Policy, 34*(9–10), 670–693.

Cagan, P. (1958). The demand for currency relative to the total money supply. *Journal of Political Economy, 66*(3), 302–328.

Crnkovic-Pozaic, S. (1997). Neslužbeno gospodarstvo mjereno radnom snagom [The unofficial economy measured by labour]. *Financijska praksa, 1–2*, 169–194.

Croatian Bureau of Statistics. *Statistical yearbook 2008–2014*. Zagreb, Croatia.

Davidescu, A. (2014). Estimating the size of Romanian shadow economy. A labour approach. *Journal of Social and Economic Statistics, 3*(1), 25–37.

European Commission. (2007). *Stepping up the fight against undeclared work.* Brussels: European Commission.

Feige, E. (1979). How big is the irregular economy. *Challenge, 22*, 5–13.

Frey, B. S., & Weck-Hanemann, H. (1984). The hidden economy as an "unobserved" variable. *European Economic Review, 26*(1), 33–53.

Galic-Nagyszombaty, A. (2012). Unofficial economy in Croatia: Estimation methods and results. *Ekonomski pregled, 63*, 734–672.

Giles, D. E. A., Linsey, T. M., & Werkneh, G. (1999). *The Canadian underground and measured economie.* Victoria: University of Victoria.

Greenfield, H. (1993). *Invisible, outlawed and untaxed, America's underground economy.* Connecticut: Praeger.

Gutmann, P. M. (1977). The subterranean economy. *Financial Analysts Journal, 34*(1), 24–27.

Institute of Economics. (2005). *Estimating the unofficial economy in Croatia 2003–2004.* Zagreb: Project.

Institute of Public Finance. (1996). *Estimating the unofficial economy in Croatia.* Zagreb: Project.

Institute of Public Finance. (2002). *Estimating the unofficial economy in Croatia.* Zagreb: Project.

Jankov, L. (1997). Monetaristički oblik neslužbenog gospodarstva [Monetary form of unofficial economy]. *Financijska praksa, 1–2*, 157–168.

Karajic, N. (2002). Siromaštvo i neslužbeno gospodarstvo u Hrvatskoj – kvalitativni aspekti [Poverty and the Underground Economy in Croatia – Qualitative Aspects]. *Financial Theory and Practice, 26*(1), 273–299.

Kaufmann, D., & Kaliberda, A. (1996). *Integrating the unofficial economy into the dymanics of post socijalist economies: A framework of analyses and evidence* (Policy research working paper No. 1691). Washington: The World Bank.

Klaric, V. (2011). Estimating the size of non-observed economy in Croatia using the MIMIC approach. *Financial. Theory and Practice, 35*, 59–90.

Lackó, M. (1996). *Hidden economy in East-European countries in international comparison.* Luxembourg: International Institute for Applied Systems.

Lackó, M. (1998). The hidden economies of Visegrad countries in international comparison: A household electricity approach. In L. Halpern & C. H. Wyplosz (Eds.), *Two wards in market economy* (pp. 128–152). Cambridge: Cambridge University Press.

Lovrincevic, Ž., Mikulic, D., & Niksic-Paulic, B. (2002). Pristup službene statistike za procjenu neslužbenog gospodarstva [The official statistics approach to an estimate of the underground economy]. *Financial Theory and Practice, 26*(1), 83–116.

Madzarevic-Sujster, S. (2002). Procjena porezne evazije u Hrvatskoj [An estimate of tax evasion in Croatia]. *Financial Theory and Practice, 26*(1), 117–144.

Madzarevic-Sujster, S., & Mikulic, D. (2002). Procjena neslužbenog gospodarstva sustavom nacionalnih računa [An estimate of the underground economy via the National Accounting System]. *Financial Theory and Practice, 26*(1), 31–56.

Mikulic, D., & Galic-Nagyszombaty, A. (2013). Causes of the unofficial economy in new EU member states. Ekonomska istrazivanja - Economic Research, Vol. Special Issue(1), 29–44. *Ekonomska istrazivanja- Economic Research Special Issue*, 29–44.

Nastav, B., & Bojnec, S. (2007). Shadow economy in Slovenia. The labour approach. *Managing Global Transitions, 5*(2), 193–208.

North, D. C. (1997). *The contribution of the new institutional economics to an understanding of the transition problems* (WIDER annual lecture, No.1). Helsinki: UNU/WIDER.

OECD. (2002). *Measuring the non-observed economy*. Paris.

OECD. (2012). *Reducing opportunities for tax non-compliance in the underground economy*. Paris.

Ott, K. (2002). Neslužbeno gospodarstvo u Republici Hrvatskoj [Unofficial economy in Croatia]. *Financial Theory and Practice, 26*(1), 1–30.

Polese, A., & Rodgers. (2011). Surviving post-socialism: The role of informal economic practices. *International Journal of Sociology and Social Policy, 31*(11–12), 612–618.

Rubic, T. (2013). Afternoon moonlighting- it was a must: The dynamics and paradoxes of the Croatian socialist and post-socijalist labor market. *Narodna umjetnost, 50*(1), 121–145.

Schneider, F. (1994). Can the shadow economy be reduced through major tax reforms? An empirical investigation for Austria. *Supplement to Public Finance/Finances Publiques, 49*(2), 137–152.

Schneider, F. (1997). The shadow economies of Western Europe. *Journal of the Institute of Economic Affairs, 17*(3), 42–48.

Schneider, F. (2011). *Shadow economies in all over the world: New estimates for 162 countries from 1999 to 2007: Handbook on the shadow economy*. Cheltenham: Edward Elgar.

Schneider, F. (2013). *Size and development of the shadow economy of 31 European and 5 other OECD countries from 2003 to 2013: A further decline*. Available from: http://www.econ.jku.at/members/Schneider/files/publications/2013/ShadEcEurope31_Jan2013.pdf. 20 July 2015.

Schneider, F., & Enste, D. (2000). *Shadow economies around the world: Size, causes and consequences* (IMF working paper, No. 26). Washington.

Sosic, V., & Faulend, M. (2002). Dolarizacija i neslužbeno gospodarstvo: slučajni partneri? [Dollarisation and the underground economy: Accidental partners?]. *Financial Theory and Practice, 26*(1), 57–81.

Stulhofer, A., & Rimac, I. (2002). *Opportunism, institutions and moral costs: The socio-cultural dimension of the underground economy in Croatia 1995–1999* (Occasional paper No. 14). Zagreb, Institute of Public Finance.

Svec, M. (2009). Siva ekonomija u Hrvatskoj [Underground economy in Croatia]. *Financial Theory and Practice, 33*(4), 415–444.

Tanzi, V. (1980). The underground economy in the United States: Estimates and implications. *Banca Nazionale del Lavoro, 135*(4), 427–453.

Tanzi, V. (1983). The underground economy. *Finance and Development, 20*(4), 10–13.

Thomas, J. J. (1992). *Informal economic activity*. Ann Arbor: The University of Michigan.

Vehovec, M. (2002). Neslužbeno gospodarstvo i neformalne norme ponašanja: koliko etika u poslovnom ponašanju može pomoći? [The underground economy and informal norms of conduct: How much ethics can help in business conduct]. *Financial Theory and Practice, 26*(1), 229–244.

Williams, C. C. (2014). *Confronting the shadow economy: Evaluating tax compliance and behaviour policies*. Cheltenham: Edward Elgar.

Williams, C. C., & Franic, J. (2015). Tackling the propensity towards undeclared work: Some policy lessons from Croatia. *South East European Journal of Economics and Business, 10*(1), 18–31.

Williams, C. C., Franic, J., & Dzhekova, R. (2014). Explaining and tackling the undeclared economy in Bulgaria: An institutional asymetry perspective. *The South-East European Journal of Economics and Business, 9*(2), 33–45.

World Bank. (2001). *Croatia economic vulnerability and welfare study* (Report No. 22079-HR). Washington.

Informal Employment and Earnings Determination in Ukraine

Oksana Nezhyvenko and Philippe Adair

Introduction

Following almost 25 years of independence, informal employment remains one of the main challenges for Ukraine during its economic transformation period. The transition in Ukraine went through a two-step process, experiencing a severe output decline from 1991 to 1999 and a recovery from 2000 until the 2008 recession. However, real wages lagged behind real GDP from 1992 to 2004. By 2007, GDP had reached 88 % of the 1992 level. However, total employment has not increased substantially since then, approaching about 85.3 % of its 1992 level in 2007 (European Training Foundation (ETF) 2009).

Informal employment in Ukraine has increased dramatically over the period 2000–2007 from 14.8 % up to 22.3 % of total employment for people aged 15–70, namely 4.7 million people. According to Labour Force Survey (LFS) data in 2007, the age groups at the two extremes of the age

O. Nezhyvenko (✉)
National University of Kyiv-Mohyla Academy, Kyiv, Ukraine
e-mail: nezhyvenkoov@ukma.edu.ua

P. Adair
University Paris-Est Creteil, Paris, France
e-mail: adair@u-pec.fr

A. Polese et al. (eds.), *The Informal Economy in Global Perspective*, International Political Economy Series,
DOI 10.1007/978-3-319-40931-3_5

structure (15–19 years and 60–70 years) have larger shares in informal than in formal employment. The incidence of informal employment decreases with educational attainment for both sexes as well as for urban versus rural areas, wherein it is higher (ETF 2009).

In as much as informal employment drives pervasive cash payment to employees, it cheats on fiscal revenue for both the employees and the employers. Tax compliance is a major issue, the lack of which hampers growth and paves the way to bribery. According to a study upon a representative sample (2,082 active private companies for the tax year 2007 and 1,000 active sole proprietors in for tax year 2008), small businesses pay on average the equivalent of an 8 % on their turnover in complying with tax requirements, which is 0.5 % of GDP. One out of four companies used unofficial ways to "solve" tax-related problems. Approximately 18 % of wages and salaries are paid to employees "in an envelope", without taxes or mandatory social contributions, using fictitious companies (which is clearly illegal), engaging individual sole proprietors (International Finance Corporation 2009).

Besides salaried workers, private entrepreneurs ("physical entities") is a legal form of self-employment that amounted to 5.79 % of the registered labour force in 2009 (State Statistics Service of Ukraine (SSSU) 2012).

Ukraine lags behind other transition economies with respect to private sector employment. The privatisation of state-owned enterprises started in 1992 and the creation of private firms brought about dramatic changes in the ownership structure of employment. However, the share of employment in the public sector consisting in both state-owned and municipal organisations was still 51.9 % in 2006, whereas the private sector represented a 48.1 % share. Despite considerable growth in the number of small businesses (up to 50 employees) over the period 1991–2007, the share in total wage employment and in total output were around 18.4 % and 4.4 %, respectively, for 2007 (ETF 2009).

Indeed, informal employment and related cash payment as well as tax evasion fuel an extensive shadow economy or non-observed economy (NOE), which should be accounted for in the GDP. However, figures are controversial (Bochi and Povoroznyk 2014; Ogreba 2012), depending on the various definitions, sources and measurement methods that are used.

Presence of substantive informal employment hinders the economic development of Ukraine and its perception at the international level, being one of the main reasons behind the fluctuating acceptance of Ukraine as

Box 1 How Large Is the So-Called Shadow or Non-Observed Economy in Ukraine?

Comparing the whole spectrum of macro estimates for the year 2000 in descending order, the multiple causes multiple indicators method (MIMIC) ranks first, followed by electricity consumption method (ECM) and cash-deposit method (CDM), whereas NOE ranks last. However, once ECM and CDM estimates are adjusted, they fall below the NOE estimate, respectively 11.8 % and 12.9 % (Feige and Urban 2008). Average measurement over 2000–2007 amounts to 17.6 % of GDP as for NOE (United Nations Economic Commission for Europe (UNECE) 2010) and 49.35 % of GDP as for MIMIC (Schneider et al. 2010), which stands almost three times higher. Furthermore, trends do not match (Table 1).

Is there any best indirect method? All methods provide insights and experience pitfalls (Adair 2012; Feige 2015). Estimates from monetary aggregates (CDM) and electricity consumption methods have little if any theoretical underpinnings and are too crude to capture the various components in the Non Observed Economy that is in accordance with national accounts. On the one hand, national accounts provide the most exhaustive estimate for NOE within a consistent framework, although there are lacunae and some components that may overlap. Estimates are robust but rather conservative in as much as the design for national accounts is scarcely revised, although the data are adjusted. On the other hand, the MIMIC structural equations method provides time series and capture trends, albeit the calibration with the currency demand method overstates the magnitude of the shadow economy.

a trustworthy and honourable economic partner. This is reflected in the consistently low ranking of the country by the Worldwide Governance Indicators, 'Doing Business' report and other independent foreign cross-country comparisons (Shumska and Nezhyvenko 2013). The informal sector poses unfair competition for formal firms. In addition, it can become a source for independent changes in the economy whether procyclical and/or countercyclical, affecting both the direction and strength of economic policy (Ott 2002).

Table 1 Several methods for estimating the NOE in Ukraine (as a percentage of GDP)

	1991 2001	*1999*	*2000*	*2001*	*2002*	*2003*	*2004*	*2005*	*2006*	*2007*	*2008*	*2009*	*2010*	*2011*
NOE			20	16.3	17.7	17.2	18.9	18.1	17.3	15.5	15.1	16.1	16.5	17
MIMIC		52.7	52.2	51.4	50.8	49.7	48.8	47.8	47.3	46.8				
CDM			35.5											
ECM			41.2											

Sources: UNECE (2010) and SSSU (2012) for NOE, Schneider et al. (2010) for MIMIC, Feige and Urban (2008) for CDM and ECM

The informal sector is the main feature of the dynamics of transition. Whether it will have a positive or negative role in the transition depends on the speed with which the government will redefine its role in the market. For these countries, the positive impact that informal employment has had on national welfare was in keeping economies afloat, since the costs of efficient production in the official economy have often increased.

Large informal employment and unbalanced labour markets have serious consequences for the official economy, in as much as there is an impact of human capital availability on the growth rate (Tkachenko and Mosiychuk 2014). Informal employment is low paid and does not provide social protection for the worker from the labour legislation of the country. Moreover, this situation creates barriers to the economic inclusion of certain groups of population.

The social costs of informality—forgone tax revenues, lower productivity and lack of social security coverage—outweigh the potential social benefits such as a social safety net, a trampoline for formal business. Accordingly, effective policies to promote formal employment enhance social welfare (Kuddo and Rutkowski 2011).

Thus, it is worth investigating the determinants of individuals to participate in formal or informal employment according to their characteristics. Thanks to the Ukrainian Longitudinal Monitoring Survey (ULMS) for 2007, we apply a Mincer earnings distribution function in order to determine the factors that influence wages. The next section "Literature Review" provides an extensive literature review on the topic; this is followed by "The Case of Ukraine: Data Sources, Definition, Methodology" then the results and the conclusion.

Literature Review

This chapter stands at the crossroads of two literatures: the literature on informal employment and the literature on the human capital theory. We first present the achievements of Mincer's contribution, followed by its application to various countries as regards informal employment; then we end up with the case of Ukraine.

Mincer (1974) was the first to treat schooling and occupation as investment opportunities. He develops his human capital theory in further works stating that education and training act as a link both for the causes and effects of economic and demographic changes. He proves it by showing that the indexes of human capital (for example, average levels of education) are better correlated with average income levels across countries than measures of physical capital per unit of labour. According to Mincer (1981), the growth of human capital is both a condition and a consequence of economic growth, although the growth of a considerable level of human capital is a lengthy process that involves deep social and cultural changes. Hence, investing in human capital is the main explanatory variable of income distribution and the occupations that require more training are better paid in order to compensate the individuals not only for the direct costs of training, but especially for the postponement of their earning period. Most earnings functions include numerous supplementary variables in addition to the schooling and potential experience terms used by Mincer. These include race, gender, regional dummy categorical variables, health status, ethnicity, marital status, children, union membership, city size and numerous other variables. They serve as exogenous "control variables" (Polachek 2007).

Tansel and Kan (2012) showed that employees in the formal sector in Turkey get higher wages then those from the informal sector, and self-employed are often less paid than other workers. An interesting finding is that the penalty for participating in the informal sector decreases with the level of earnings, so it would be not significant for the upper-tier jobs and may be a larger penalty for lower-tier jobs. Hence, the upper-tier jobs would be better paid, whereas lower-tier jobs experience heavy penalties.

Angel-Urdinola and Tanabe (2012) study informal employment in the Middle East and North Africa region, estimating the impact of human capital. They provide evidence that the sizes of public and agricultural sectors are the main determinants of the informal sector in the region: the bigger the agricultural sector is, the higher the informality will be; and the stronger the public sector is, the smaller will be the informal sector. They document that the youth aged 15–24 years old are more susceptible to participating in informality. By applying Mincer equations, they show that the returns to education in the informal sector are very low, compared to public and private sectors.

Clementi and Giammatteo (2014) used four waves of data from the Participation Labour Unemployment Survey, a database of information on the Italian labour market supply, addressing the question of earnings dispersion thanks to a 'nested' decomposition procedure of the Theil inequality measure. Empirical evidence obtained points to the key role played by the self-employed in shaping labour income inequality, especially at the upper extreme of the earnings distribution, and the emergence of non-standard forms of employment not covered by labour legislation as an important feature of the segmentation of the Italian productive system. Between 2008 and 2010, the self-employed accounted for a definitely lower income share, relative mean and earnings dispersion. Economic downturn may have induced a substitution of non-standard employees with autonomous 'false' positions in order to reduce labour costs.

Gorodnichenko and Sabirianova Peter (2005) used semiparametric decomposition techniques upon the 2003 ULMS for Ukraine to analyse the sources of cross-country differences in returns to schooling by comparing the Mincerian earnings functions. Counterfactual distributions of log wages for university and secondary school graduates in Ukraine use the distributions of Russian characteristics, returns to characteristics and unobservables. Skill–wage inequality in Ukraine did not increase as much over the same period and returns to schooling were among the lowest of the countries of Central and Eastern Europe. The dependent variable is the log of monthly contractual (accrued) wages after taxes at a person's primary job. Using the contractual wage in the earnings functions is preferred over wages received in some short reference period, for example a month, especially during periods of mass wage delays and high volatility in wage payments, which both countries experienced in the 1990s.

Pagés and Stampini (2009) assess labour market segmentation across formal and informal salaried jobs and self-employment in six countries including Ukraine, using the ULMS waves for 2003 and 2004. It looks separately at the markets for skilled and unskilled labour, inquiring if segmentation is an exclusive feature of the latter. Longitudinal data are used to assess wage differentials and mobility patterns across jobs. There is evidence of a formal wage premium relative to informal salaried jobs in the three Latin American countries included, but not in transition economies. There is also evidence of extensive mobility, particularly from informal salaried to formal jobs. These patterns suggest a preference for formal over informal salaried jobs in all countries. In contrast, there is little mobility between self-employment and formal salaried jobs, suggesting the existence of barriers to this type of mobility or a strong assortative matching according to workers' individual preferences. For both wage differentials and mobility, there is no statistical difference across skill (education) levels, suggesting that the markets for skilled and unskilled labour are similarly affected by segmentation, which is not driven by minimum wages.

Commander et al. (2013) used the 2003 and 2004 waves of ULMS and estimate that the share of employment in the informal sector in Ukraine increased from 10–16 % in 1991 up to 17–23 % in 2004, excluding people involved in agricultural production for their own use. They also focus on multiple job holding as a prevalent feature of the informal economy, which is connected with the formal economy. They design an analytical model of an economy with state and private sectors, incorporating formal and informal as well as full- and part-time work, to study the impact of changes in non-monetary compensation on the reallocation of labour. The likelihood of switching into the informal sector will be decreasing in relation to the size of the firm (a proxy for the probability of detection in payroll tax evasion), and increasing in predicted relative wages in the informal sector. The likelihood of switching into the formal/informal sector will be affected positively by the social benefits and negatively by subsidy.

Lehmann (2014) posits that the incidence and determinants of informal employment in transition economies depend on the definition used. Studies that attempt to test for labour market segmentation in transition economies along the formal–informal divide provide inconclusive results. Hence, more work needs to be done before making definitive statements about whether labour markets are integrated or segmented in transition economies. At last, he introduces a new research area linking risk preferences and selection into labour market states, showing that if individuals have a choice, non-risk averse workers have an increased likelihood of chosing informal employment and self-employment.

Shehu and Nilsson (2014) carried out standardised surveys across 20 countries—among which was Ukraine in 2013—taking jobs as the observation units as regards both components of informal employment defined in the 17th International Conference of Labour Statisticians (ICLS): within the informal sector and the formal sector including unprotected jobs. The main findings are that informal and formal wage earners seem to share many wage determinants. In both sectors, educational attainment generates a higher income, except at the primary level where it is only significant for informal workers. Experience at the current job is highly significant for formal workers, but insignificant for informal workers. Average hourly wage of formally and informally youth employees by educational attainment does not show a wage premium for education. However, the distribution of average hourly wage is positively (negatively) associated with educational attainment for unprotected jobs in the formal sector versus jobs in the informal sector.

The Case of Ukraine: Data Sources, Definition, Methodology

Data

Various data sources are available with regards to the labour market in order to investigate informal employment.

On the demand side, the World Bank designed a pilot labour demand survey in 2007 upon 1,127 respondents, in order to identify the occupational profile of jobs destroyed, jobs created and vacancies; and to assess the difficulty employers have with filling vacancies (Rutkowski 2009).

The three sources focus on the supply side:

The LFS is designed alongside the guidelines from the International Labour Organization (ILO) upon a multi-level stratified monthly sample of 18,500 households. As for 2007, there were 141,900 respondents and the response rate among urban and rural households was 80.3 % and 89.2 %, respectively (ETF 2009).

The Youth Transition from Education to Work Survey in 2007 investigated the determinants of (successful or unsuccessful) transition from education to the labour market upon a sample of 2,015 individuals aged 15–34 years old.

The main data source for our study is the Ukrainian Longitudinal Monitoring Survey (ULMS). It consists in three waves of panel data (2003, 2004 and 2007)[1] and provides an in-depth overview of household life conditions and employment of individuals. It is designed as a statistically representative sample of the Ukrainian working-age population stratified by age, gender, rural/urban area and regional structure. The 2007 wave collected questionnaire results from 3,101 households and 6,774 individuals. Although they differ between survey waves by the structure, the main questions in the ULMS questionnaires were saved in order to trace information. Such is the case for primary and secondary employment (as well as multiple job holding), job search efforts, non-employment and participation in labour market programs, education and skills, changes of residence, spatial mobility, wages, in-kind payments, unpaid leave and the rest (Lehmann et al. 2012).

We present preliminary results for the 2007 wave of the ULMS. As far as our knowledge is concerned, no Mincer earnings function was applied to this wave and we provide some added value in connection with this.

Defining Informal Employment for the Ukrainian Labour Market

Informality in the labour market may be defined as "unreported income from the production of legal goods and services, either from monetary or barter transactions, hence all economic activities that would generally be taxable were they reported to the tax authorities" (Schneider and Enste 2000). However, two approaches to define informal employment are the most commonly used: productivity definition and legalistic definition (Khamis 2009).

The *productivity definition* identifies informal employment by the job characteristics: according to this definition under the category of "informal" fall less-skilled, domestic workers and workers in small firms of up to five employees. The *legalistic approach* defines informal employment by non-compliance with the regulations in terms of labour market rules and the social security system. According to the second definition, the informality is characterised by employees and self-employed that are not compliant with the labour market rules, or, in another words, are not registered.

The current state of informal employment in Ukraine is estimated since 1999 according to the methodology approved by the State Statistics Committee of Ukraine. It was developed on the basis of the Resolution on employment in the informal sector, adopted at the 15th ICLS in 1993 (ILO 2013). According to this methodology classification, the enterprises participating in informal sector must simultaneously meet the following criteria: market orientation of economic activity of the enterprise; a limited number of employees (up to five people); not be registered as a business enterprise (unincorporated).

This method is based rather on productivity approach because, according to the national methodology, the informal sector includes all persons who were employed in unregistered enterprises, which belong to the households' sector by their size (number of employees) according to the UN System of National Accounts.

In accordance with the 17th ICLS Resolution (ILO 2002), the number of informal employees was expanded in order to include those people who worked under oral agreement with the employer in the formal sector, without a formal labour agreement (contract), which results in the absence of minimum social guarantees (SSSU 2012). We follow the legalistic definition because this consistent approach is well observable based on the available data.

We use data from the ULMS 2007 in order to investigate individuals according to their employment status: formal employee, informal employee, formal self-employed, informal self-employed and unemployed. The individuals are classified into these five categories based on their survey responses. To be regarded as an employee or self-employed, an individual needs to have worked at least one hour during the reference week. From the response to the question whether the employee/self-employed person is officially registered or not (based on a written contract) we can identify the status: formal employee (FE) and formal self-employed (FSE) or informal employee (IE) and informal self-employed (ISE). An individual that has not worked during the reference week but was looking for a job is classified as unemployed (U).

Methodology

We study the labour market, divided into five categories according to job position or status: formal employees, informal employees, formal self-employed, informal self-employed and unemployed within active labour force (15–70 years old). The entry of workers into each of these segments may vary and we assume that experience and educational attainment plays a part in this entry. Hence, we apply to the Ukrainian labour market the following Mincer model:

$$\ln Income_{ij} = a_j + \sum_r \beta_{rj} x_{rij} + \gamma_j Education_{ij} + \delta_j Experience_{ij} + u_{ij}$$

where w_{ij} denotes the hourly wage of the worker in the state j; x_r is the set of individual characteristics (age, gender, place of residence, working schedule, children, marital status, size of the household, multiple job holding); a, β and δ are unknown coefficients and u_{ij} represents a random disturbance and measurement error.

Results

Personal Background Characteristics

We look first at the Ukrainian labour market distribution in 2007. According to Table 2, formal working population (formal employee and formal self-employed) constitute 86 %, and informal employment

Table 2 Distribution of the labour market, 2007

Occupation	*Number of individuals*	*To employed population*
Employed population	**3,300**	**1.00**
Formal employee (FE)	2,674	0.81
Informal employee (IE)	303	0.09
Formal self-employed (FSE)	160	0.05
Informal self-employed (ISE)	163	0.05
Unemployed	**337**	**0.10**
Total formal employment (FE + FSE)	2,834	0.86
Total informal employment *(IE + ISE)*	**466**	**0.14**

Source: Authors' own calculations based on the ULMS 2007 wave

(informal employee and informal self-employed) is revealed as 14 % of the overall workforce. Unemployed individuals amount to 10 % and are excluded from "employed population".

The economically active population (aged 15–70 years old) in 2007 amounted to 22.3 million, which makes it a 62.6 % activity rate. The economically inactive population was 13.3 million. As regards the distribution of economically active population, the 15–24-years-old age group constituted 13.9 %; the 25–39 age group represented 37.4 %; the 40–59 age group amounted to 43.7 %; and the 60–70 age group was 5.1 % (ETF 2009).

According to the ULMS 2007, the distribution of age groups of the total work force and the informal workforce is respectively as follows: 18.9 and 24.9 % (15–24-years-old age group); 21.9 and 35.6 % (25–39 age group); 37.2 and 36.3 % (40–59 age group); 22 and only 3 % (60–72 age group). The ULMS sample is obviously younger than the LFS sample and the same applies to the informal work force.

We first analyse means and standard deviations of the variables chosen for each of the occupation statuses in order to highlight the Ukrainian labour market divide. Table 3 displays averages and standard deviations for personal background characteristics, by the occupation categories: formal employee (FE), informal employee (IE), formal self-employed (FSE), informal self-employed (ISE) and unemployed (U). See Table 5 in the Appendix for the description of variables.

There are fewer women on average among entrepreneurs, in respect to other workers. They dominate in the category of formal employees, although with a small difference to men. The proportion of unemployed men and women is almost the same. According to the SSSU (2012), men are slightly more engaged in the informal economy than women (22.4 % and 22.2 % respectively). Table 3 is in accordance with this.

Table 3 Personal background characteristics by occupation category: averages and standard deviations (in brackets): 2007

Variable	*Formal employee (FE)*	*Informal employee (IE)*	*Formal self-employed (FSE)*	*Informal self-employed (ISE)*	*Unem-ployed (U)*	*Total*
Gender	0.49 (0.5)	0.56 (0.5)	0.53 (0.5)	0.67 (0.47)	0.51 (0.5)	0.51 (0.5)
Age	41.08 (12.3)	34.17 (12.3)	40.68 (9.24)	39.4 (12.4)	36.17 (12.5)	39.97 (12.41)
Marital status	0.71 (0.45)	0.55 (0.5)	0.81 (0.39)	0.69 (0.46)	0.58 (0.49)	0.69 (0.46)
Size of the household	2.76 (1.11)	2.96 (1.17)	2.68 (1.14)	2.81 (1.28)	2.84 (1.13)	2.78 (1.13)
Children	1.69 (0.68)	1.75 (0.99)	1.65 (0.68)	1.84 (0.96)	1.93 (0.89)	1.72 (0.74)
Educational attainment	2.55 (0.88)	2.26 (0.67)	2.65 (0.91)	2.31 (0.77)	2.27 (0.7)	2.5 (0.86)
Education years	13.45 (2.01)	12.48 (2.01)	13.78 (1.97)	12.65 (2.26)	12.71 (1.83)	13.28 (2.04)
Place of residence	0.56 (0.49)	0.56 (0.5)	0.74 (0.44)	0.39 (0.49)	0.39 (0.49)	0.55 (0.5)
Working schedule	0.96 (0.19)	0.91 (0.28)	0.92 (0.27)	0.72 (0.45)	–	0.94 (0.24)
Experience years	9.03 (9.91)	2.08 (3.27)	5.77 (4.39)	5.58 (6.62)	4.45 (4.44)	8.03 (9.36)
Multiple jobs	0.02 (0.13)	0.01 (0.11)	0.03 (0.17)	0.03 (0.17)	–	0.02 (0.13)
Income	915.90 (586.26)	798.09 (601.34)	1732.55 (2430.92)	988.62 (1068.334)		934.56 (767.21)
Number	2674	303	160	163	337	3637

Source: Authors' own calculations based on the ULMS 2007 wave

The age group with the lowest participation is that of the informal employees (average age of 34.17 years), followed by unemployed (36.17 years). Formal workers and self-employed are the oldest (41.08 and 40.68 years respectively).

Marital status shows that married individuals are present among formal employees and formal self-employed; however, all groups are represented in the majority of "non-single" individuals. The variable "size of the household" differs slightly among the five categories and shows that a labour market participant in Ukraine lives in a household of less than three people on average. The average number of children is less than two and proves quite similar across categories, although slightly higher for informal self-employed.

Educational attainment indicates that workers with the highest level (higher learning) are formal self-employed and formal employees. Interestingly, unemployed are not less educated than informal self-employed and employees (2.27 % in respect to 2.26 % and 2.31 %). The variable "education years" displays the same pattern and accounts for an obvious formal/informal divide.

Regarding the place of residence, informal self-employed and unemployed are present in rural areas, the highest number of urban workers is present in the formal self-employed category (0.74). Working schedule does not show a significant difference between categories, although the less engaged in full-time job are informal entrepreneurs (0.72).

"Experience" is very different considering each category: the highest experience is relevant to formal employees (9.03 years), while the lowest is informal employees (2.08 years). Informal employees and informal self-employed have almost the same average number of years of experience. The variable "multiple jobs" does not show a significant difference across categories.

Income varies across categories, which proves labour income inequality, being the highest for formal self-employed (UAH 1,732.55 where UAH stands for "Ukrainian Hryvnia"), followed by informal self-employed (UAH 988.62) and formal employees (UAH 915.90), and with the lowest for informal employees (UAH 798.09). For the year 2007, minimum salary increased from UAH 420 to UAH 460 (UAH 440 on average) and the living wage rose from UAH 492 to UAH 532 (UAH 516 on average), whereas unemployment benefit increased from UAH 292.6 to UAH 313.7.

Income distribution varies also within the four categories. The most dispersed income is for formal self-employed with a median of UAH 1,000 and standard deviation of UAH 2,340.92, which is twice as high as the income itself. Formal employees experience the lowest income dispersion with a median value of UAH 800 and standard deviation of UAH 586.26. Slightly higher dispersion characterises informal employees with a median value of UAH 700 and standard deviation of UAH 601.34. As for informal self-employed, there is a median of UAH 725 and standard deviation of UAH 1,068.33.

The Mincer Model

We build a Mincer model to study key factors that determine the income of individuals. Table 4 presents the coefficients of Mincer equations using ordinary least squares regressions for the four categories of workers. The model includes variables generally included in a standard human capital accumulation model (years of education, educational attainment dummies, experience, experience squared and a gender dummy). We use the "education" variable both as continuous (years of schooling) and discrete (educational attainment). Results indicate very clearly that returns on education are very low in the informal sector.

Comparing results for the four categories of workers, we see that gender is not significant for informal employees and formal self-employed, age—for formal self-employed and informal self-employed (in the model with education level, but not in the model with education as a continuous variable)—is more significant on the long run. Neither marital status, nor the household size improve the model for all statuses. This is relevant also for the "children" variable in as much as the number of children is similar in all five categories. Place of residence is positive for all categories except for formal self-employed; however, the coefficient is significant only for formal employees. Working schedule is highly significant for all categories except for formal self-employed. The "multiple job holding" variable is significant, positively related for both formal and informal self-employed and negatively for informal workers.

Interestingly, education variables (continuous and discrete) behave differently with the same set of factors. The model with the "education level" variable has slightly higher significance, suggesting that educational achievement is better valued than duration of schooling, and that a diploma has a signalling impact on the demand side. Returns to education are positive and the highest for formal employees, as well positive but not significant for formal self-employed, and negative and not significant for informal workers. Hence, educational attainment generates a higher income only for those who are formally employed. Other factors that we did not capture, such as social capital, may explain the formal/informal divide.

Table 4 Mincer model of income determination: dependent variable–log income, 2007

	FE	*IE*	*FSE*	*ISE*	*FE*	*IE*	*FSE*	*ISE*
	(1)	*(2)*	*(3)*	*(4)*	*(5)*	*(6)*	*(7)*	*(8)*
Variables	*Lincome*	*Lincome*	*Lincome*	*Lincome*	*Lincome*	*Lincome*	*Lincome*	*Lincome*
Gender	0.365***	0.122	0.218	0.596***	0.350***	0.138	0.173	0.575***
	(0.027)	(0.129)	(0.168)	(0.164)	(0.027)	(0.129)	(0.164)	(0.166)
Age	0.024***	0.061*	0.034	0.097*	0.023***	0.064*	0.022	0.079
	(0.008)	(0.034)	(0.072)	(0.050)	(0.008)	(0.034)	(0.066)	(0.049)
Age2	−0.000***	−0.001*	−0.000	−0.001**	−0.000***	−0.001*	−0.000	−0.001**
	(0.000)	(0.000)	(0.001)	(0.001)	(0.000)	(0.000)	(0.001)	(0.001)
Education (years)	0.060***	−0.047	0.020	−0.041				
	(0.007)	(0.032)	(0.046)	(0.030)				
Education (level)					0.148***	−0.052	0.187*	−0.019
					(0.015)	(0.096)	(0.102)	(0.091)
Experience	0.013***	0.202***	0.149**	−0.081***	0.013***	0.211***	0.146**	−0.075***
	(0.004)	(0.066)	(0.065)	(0.028)	(0.004)	(0.066)	(0.063)	(0.028)
Experience2	−0.000	−0.019***	−0.008*	0.003***	−0.000	−0.019***	−0.008*	0.003***
	(0.000)	(0.007)	(0.005)	(0.001)	(0.000)	(0.007)	(0.004)	(0.001)
Residence	0.180***	−0.045	0.176	0.248	0.185***	−0.059	0.110	0.235
	(0.027)	(0.129)	(0.197)	(0.153)	(0.026)	(0.129)	(0.197)	(0.155)
Working schedule	0.527***	0.644***	0.378	0.637***	0.526***	0.659***	0.337	0.647***
	(0.067)	(0.237)	(0.376)	(0.174)	(0.066)	(0.237)	(0.369)	(0.176)
Children				0.064				0.096

				(0.088)				(0.086)
Marital status	0.004		−0.164	0.018	0.001		−0.157	−0.013
	(0.031)		(0.231)	(0.195)	(0.031)		(0.224)	(0.196)
Size of the household	−0.009	−0.019	−0.061	−0.056	−0.010	−0.013	−0.060	−0.065
	(0.012)	(0.055)	(0.071)	(0.067)	(0.012)	(0.055)	(0.069)	(0.068)
Multiple job holding		−0.992*	1.017*	0.817**		−0.978*	0.856	0.856**
		(0.540)	(0.609)	(0.409)		(0.547)	(0.605)	(0.413)
Constant	4.667***	5.186***	5.372***	5.006***	5.130***	4.624***	5.526***	4.901***
	(0.187)	(0.776)	(1.459)	(1.038)	(0.166)	(0.666)	(1.365)	(1.048)
Observations	2,558	286	98	93	2,560	286	99	93
R-squared	0.147	0.120	0.191	0.455	0.153	0.114	0.211	0.443

Source: Authors' own calculations based on the ULMS 2007 wave

Standard errors in parentheses

*** $p<0.01$, ** $p<0.05$, * $p<0.1$

The experience variable is very important for all four categories, although negative for informal entrepreneurs. In the long run, experience has a negative influence on income, but not for informal self-employed.

Concluding Remarks

We used the data on individuals from the Ukrainian Longitudinal Monitoring Survey for the year 2007 in order to study the current state of the labour market and informal employment in Ukraine by distinguishing five employment statuses of individuals: formal employee, informal employee, formal self-employed, informal self-employed and unemployed. We showed that the Ukrainian labour market is quite heterogeneous across the five categories, as regards size of each of these categories, income distribution and personal background characteristics of the individuals.

Informal employment constitutes 14 % of active labour force, whereas over four out of five people are formal workers. Formal labour market participants tend to be older and not single, reside in an urban area, have higher educational attainment, are more experienced and have higher incomes (especially the entrepreneurs). These three last characteristics are consistent with human capital theory. Interestingly, the unemployed are not less educated than informal workers. We also show that the income for formal self-employed is less stable and has the highest dispersion across all labour market segments.

We further designed a Mincer earnings function for the Ukrainian labour market. Empirical evidence documents inequality in earnings between formal and informal workers according to various factors, especially education. Education plays an important role for formal employment; moreover, educational achievement is better valued than duration of schooling and a diploma has a signalling impact on the demand side. Education has a significantly positive impact on the earnings of formal employees. Experience is important and generates higher income for all labour market segments, except for informal self-employed. Another two important factors that determine earnings are the working schedule and multiple job holding that both have a positive impact, albeit only on informal workers for the latter.

ETF (2009) points out that ULMS data are likely to be less reliable than official LFS data because of the smaller size of the sample and the lower response rate. In the first wave of ULMS, the response rate averaged about 66 % for individuals and 87 % for households; with unchanging samples, the rate is falling from one wave to another. Furthermore, the ULMS is not as regular as the LFS. However, the former provides more information than the latter in order to understand the trajectories of individuals.

Note

1. The Fourth wave (2012) of the ULMS has not been available for the public use at the time of publication.

Appendix

Table 5 Description of the variables

Variable	*Description*
Gender	0 = female; 1 = male
Age	Age of the individual in the year 2007
Marital status	0 = Single, widowed, divorced, separated; 1 = Registered/non-registered marriage
Size of the household	Number of members of the household: min – 1, max – 6
Children	Number of children
Education (level)	1 = None or at most primary school; 2 = Medium school; 3 = Secondary school; 4 = Higher education; 5 = Vocational or professional training
Education (years)	Duration of schooling, continuous in years
Place of residence	0 = Rural: village, urban settlement, small town (up to 20,000 inhabitants); 1 = Urban: medium town (20–99,000), city (100–499,000), large city (over 500,000)
Occupation (status)	1 = formal employee (FE); 2 = informal employee (IE); 3 = formal self-employed (FSE); 4 = informal self-employed (ISE); 5 = unemployed (U)
Working schedule	0 = Always part-time, sometimes full-time and sometimes part-time; 1 = Always full-time
Experience (years)	Duration in years: Year of survey – year of the first job – years of non-employment
Multiple jobs	0 = no; 1 = yes
Income	Net monthly salary for employees; net income for self-employed; in UAH
Income	Net monthly salary for employees; net income for self-employed; in UAH

References

Adair, P. (2012). Non-observed economy in the European Union countries (EU-15): A comparative analysis of estimates. In M. Pickhardt & A. Prinz (Eds.), *Tax evasion and the shadow economy. Cheltenham, UK* (pp. 83–121). Edward Elgar Publishing Limited.

Angel-Urdinola, D. F., & Tanabe, K. (2012). *Micro-determinants of informal employment in the Middle East and North Africa region.* Social protection and labor. The World Bank (1201). Available from: http://www-wds.worldbank.org/servlet/WDSContentServer/WDSP/IB/2012/02/01/000333038_20120201032926/Rendered/PDF/665940NWP00PUB0Box365795B0SPDP01201.pdf.

Bochi, A., & Povoroznyk, V. (2014). *Shadow economy in Ukraine: Causes and solutions.* Kyiv. Available from: icps.com.ua.

Clementi, F., & Giammatteo, M. (2014). The labour market and the distribution of earnings: An empirical analysis for Italy. *International Review of Applied Economics, 28*(2), 154–180.

Commander, S., Isachenkova, N., & Rodionova, Y. (2013). Informal employment dynamics in Ukraine: An analytical model of informality in transition economies. *International Labour Review, 152*, 445–467.

European Training Foundation. (2009, January). *ENPI 08-14 Black Sea labour market reviews* (Ukraine country report).

Feige, E. L. (2015). Reflections on the meaning and measurement of unobserved economies: What do we really know about the "shadow economy"? *Journal of Tax Administration, 2* (MPRA paper No. 68466), 1–51. Available from: https://mpra.ub.uni-muenchen.de/68466/.

Feige, E. L., & Urban, I. (2008). *Measuring underground (unobserved, non-observed, unrecorded) economies in transition countries: Can we trust GDP?* (p. 1–34).

Gorodnichenko, Y., & Sabirianova Peter, K. (2005). Returns to schooling in Russia and Ukraine: A semiparametric approach to cross-country comparative analysis. *Journal of Comparative Economics, 33*(2), 324–350.

International Finance Corporation and World Bank Group. (2009). *The costs of tax compliance in Ukraine*, Kyiv. Available from: http://www.ifc.org/wps/wcm/connect/725f0b804b5f7ae59f06bf6eac26e1c2/UTCCS_eng.pdf?MOD=AJPERES&CACHEID=725f0b804b5f7ae59f06bf6eac26e1c2.

International Labour Organization. (2002). *Decent work and the informal economy.* Geneva. Available from: http://www.ilo.org/public/english/standards/relm/ilc/ilc90/pdf/rep-vi.pdf.

International Labour Organization. (2013). *Measuring informality: A statistical manual on the informal sector and informal employment.* Geneva. Available from: http://unstats.un.org/unsd/EconStatKB/Attachment563.aspx.

Khamis, M. (2009). A note on informality in the labor market. *Journal of International Development, 24*(7), 894–908 Available from: http://ftp.iza.org/dp4676.pdf.

Kuddo, A., & Rutkowski, J. (2011). *Policies to reduce informal employment. An international survey. Technical note for the government of Ukraine.* Washington, DC: The World Bank. Available from: http://siteresources.worldbank.org/UKRAINEINUKRAINIANEXTN/Resources/455680-1310372404373/PoliciestoReduceInformalEmploymentEng.pdf.

Lehmann, H. (2014). *Informal employment in transition countries: Informal employment in transition countries: Empirical evidence and research challenges* (IZA discussion paper No. 8687(8687)).

Lehmann, H., Muravyev, A., & Zimmermann, K. F. (2012). *The Ukrainian longitudinal monitoring survey: Towards a better understanding of labor markets The Ukrainian longitudinal monitoring survey: Towards a better understanding of labor markets in transition* (7090), p. 21. Available from: http://ftp.iza.org/dp7090.pdf.

Mincer, J. (1974). *Schooling, experience, and earnings.* National Bureau of Economic Research, p. 167. Available from: http://papers.nber.org/books/minc74-1.

Mincer, J. (1981). *Human capital and economic growth.* National Bureau of Economic Research (803), p. 29. Available from: http://www.nber.org/papers/w0803.pdf.

Ogreba, S. (2012). International experience of statistical assessment of the shadow economy. *Journal of Social Sciences, 1*(2), 95–102.

Ott, K. (2002). The underground economy in Croatia. *Institute of Public Finance* (pp. 1–29). Available from: https://www.google.com.ua/url?sa=t&rct=j&q=&esrc=s&source=web&cd=1&cad=rja&uact=8&ved=0ahUKEwiP54ihkq7QAhXJFSwKHWzDCjUQFggaMAA&url=http%3A%2F%2Fwww.csd.bg%2FfileSrc.php%3Fid%3D10322&usg=AFQjCNFkFU9kc29FB8rKAALIvuQ8zziGCQ&sig2=uUUQ6qFdq4dFzdbqZuXGQ

Pagés, C., & Stampini, M. (2009). No education, no good jobs? Evidence on the relationship between education and labor market segmentation. *Journal of Comparative Economics, 37*(3), 387–401.

Polachek, S.W. (2007). *Earnings over the lifecycle: The mincer earnings function and its applications* (3181), p. 109. Available from: http://ftp.iza.org/dp3181.pdf.

Rutkowski, J. (2009). *Ukraine labour demand study.* Available from: http://siteresources.worldbank.org/UKRAINEEXTN/Resources/WB_Book_Report_labor_demand_EN_prew.indd.pdf.

Schneider, F., & Enste, D. (2000). Shadow economies: Size, causes, and consequences. *Journal of Economic Literature, 38*(1), 77–114.

Schneider, F., Buehn, A., & Montenegro, C. E. (2010, July). New estimates for the shadow economies all over the world. *International Economic Journal, 24.*

Shehu, E., & Nilsson, B. (2014). Informal employment among youth: Evidence from 20 school-to-work transition surveys (SWTS). In *Work4Youth publication series.* Geneva: International Labour Office.

Shumska, S., & Nezhyvenko, O. (2013). Shadow economy in Ukraine: Methodology and evaluation. *Actual Problems of Economics, 10*, 74–83.

State Statistics Service of Ukraine. (2012). *Economic activity of the population of Ukraine* (pp. 1–203).

Tansel, A., & Kan, E. O. (2012). The formal/informal employment earnings gap: Evidence from Turkey. *Munich Personal RePEc Archive*, (38498). p. 45. Available from: http://mpra.ub.uni-muenchen.de/38498/1/MPRA_paper_38498.pdf.

Tkachenko, O., & Mosiychuk, T. (2014). Labour force availability as an economic development factor in post socialist countries. *Economics & Sociology, 7*(2), 64–79. Available from: http://www.economics-sociology.eu/files/10_33_Tkachenko_Mosiychuk.pdf.

United Nations Economic Commission for Europe. (2010). *Non-observed economy in national accounts. Survey of country practices.* New York/Geneva: United Nations. Available from: http://www.unece.org/fileadmin/DAM/stats/publications/NOE2008.pdf.

Approaching Informality: Rear-Mirror Methodology and Ethnographic Inquiry

Marius Wamsiedel

Introduction

Soon after beginning fieldwork at the triage of an emergency department in Romania, I became exposed to nurses' and clerks' expressions of sheer frustration and annoyance with patients attempting to use personal connections in order to secure faster admission and better care. Even though they never rejected other staff members' requests to grant favors of access to various people, most of the nurses and clerks that I had interacted with regarded connection work as an irksome presence at the triage. Oftentimes, they conveyed their sense of frustration by rolling their eyes or staring at me after the end of encounters involving favors of access. Occasionally, they mimicked the speech mannerisms and bodily movements of those would-be patients attempting to bypass the ordinary admission procedures by making reference to some personal connection within the hospital world.

However, never during the long fieldwork hours did informality of access surface spontaneously as a topic for casual discussion. When I

M. Wamsiedel (✉)
The University of Hong Kong, Department of Sociology,
Pokfulam Road, Hong Kong
e-mail: mariusw@connect.hku.hk

A. Polese et al. (eds.), *The Informal Economy in Global Perspective*, International Political Economy Series,
DOI 10.1007/978-3-319-40931-3_6

addressed the issue in formal interviews, my respondents acknowledged the omnipresence of connection work (*cunoștințe*) at the triage, but none of them was willing to go into more detail. Two reactions were common. Some of the nurses and registrars condemned the practice in general terms but were reluctant to discuss any specific occurrence (and some of them even refused to disclose how frequently it happened). Others provided an ambivalent reading of the practice, arguing that it did not necessarily work or did not influence too much the regular flow of activities. All things considered, relying exclusively on triage workers' narratives and taking the statements at face value would have rendered any attempt to make sense of the practice futile.

Informality of access was not the only topic raising methodological concerns. I have encountered similar reactions towards other practices, such as the manipulation of registry entries (Wamsiedel 2016), or towards certain categories of patients whose appearance was considered burdensome to the emergency department. Thus, although ethnicity itself seldom appeared in conversations among members of staff, post-hoc comments regarding the behavior of specific patients belonging to the Roma community were legion. Similarly, non-clinical judgments on the undesirable traits of persons looking for emergency healthcare were expressed in brief comments after handling persons considered to exhibit them. Apart from these verbal side notes to the proceedings, more often than not allusive and sibylline in content, information was suggested in oblique fashion through bodily cues including smiles, stares, sighs and nods of the head. Attempts to systematically delve into these topics through formal interviews met other obstacles, the most salient of which being respondents' propensity to bend towards a normative interpretation of the events. In this process, empirical evidence contradicting the statements was either refuted or trivialized, negative judgments on the clientele were softened or nuanced, and respondents treated the objectionable characteristics of the patients with a leniency rarely displayed in direct encounters.

With the advantage of hindsight, I present in this chapter some practical solutions devised in situ for dealing with the concealment maneuvers employed by the participants to the research. They have to do primarily with positionality, rapport and choice of research methods. By drawing upon reflections from the field, I make the case for extending the "rear-mirror methodology" (Ledeneva 2011) and adapting it to the ethnographic investigation of informality and other social phenomena occurring in an open secrecy context.

The data comes from six months of ethnographic fieldwork conducted in 2013 and 2014 in the emergency wards of two public hospitals in Romania. I carried out the research as part of a doctoral project on the non-clinical evaluation of patients in post-socialist contexts. Fieldwork consisted in daily observation of the interaction between medical personnel and patients at the triage, consultation and surveillance and monitoring rooms; casual talk with nurses, doctors and patients; and formal, semi-directed interviews with nurses in charge of the admission and triage.

Moral Ambiguity and Open Secrecy

Informality is inextricably related to the state (Ledeneva 2008, p. 119; Polese and Morris 2015, p. 3), in the sense that the attribute of 'informality' is given only to those social norms and practices that fall outside or beyond state-sponsored, formal rules. Nevertheless, the relation between formality and informality is rarely a straightforward one. Informal ways of doing things can develop in the absence of state-devised alternatives (Davies and Polese 2015, p. 36) or when such alternatives exist but are unable to meet people's demands and expectations (Kovács 2015). Moreover, informality occupies a wide spectrum of possibilities, ranging from legal to illegal, and from socially acceptable to unacceptable (Hartnett and Dawdy 2013; Polese 2014; Yalçın-Heckmann 2014).

The nature of a practice is, thus, contingent upon the cultural and legal contexts in which it is embedded, and it is by no means exceptional to witness a radical shift in the meaning of a practice once the social fabric of the society changes. For instance, in countries passing from a socialist to a market economy, the status of pilferage and idleness at work has undergone a major transformation. In spite of being illegal and violating the basic tenets of the socialist work ethic, pilferage used to be tolerated by authorities and accepted by society at large (Chelcea 2002, p. 27; Heinzen 2013, p. 934) as long as the appropriation of public resources complied with some basic norms of propriety. Labor withholding was equally common in socialist factories and cooperative farms (O'Neill 2015, pp. 389–390; Sampson 1987, p. 134). Supervisors and managers tended to treat it with forbearance, particularly given that occasional bottlenecks on the production line were inevitable in the command economy. While practices of this sort continued to exist (Morris 2014) after the structural conditions leading to their existence had vanished, the hysteresis of the socialist habitus was accompanied by an abrupt normative shift: pilferage and idleness were resignified as socialist habits incompatible with the ethos of the market economy, and evils to be eradicated in the path to modernization (Chelcea 2015; Morrison 2003). At the same time, people who had gained work experience during socialism began to be stigmatized as carriers of a poor work ethic (Kideckel 2002; Stenning 2005), many of them finding a hard time in maintaining employment in the new economic order (Stillo 2015).

Notwithstanding these fluctuations in meaning, informality has always inhabited a morally ambiguous space due to its inherent social ambivalence. Since "[i]nformal practices …compensate for defects in the formal order while simultaneously undermining it," (Ledeneva 2006, p. 7) and the transition between the stabilizing and the predatory sides of informality is slippery (Stan 2012), extricating oneself from the negative aspects of involvement in informal actions becomes a face-saving necessity for participants. Individuals commonly respond to the moral ambiguity surrounding informality by denying the use of informality as a means to get by in life, and by rhetorically constructing their personal involvement in practices of this sort as disinterested (Ledeneva 1998, pp. 60–67). In a similar vein, the state minimizes its responsibility for creating favorable conditions for the spread of informality by banning it from public discourse (Ledeneva 2008, p. 123), refusing to acknowledge the structural problems that made it possible (Yang 1994, pp. 63–64), and placing the burden of responsibility for its existence on individual flaws alone (Ledeneva 1998, p. 68). The tendency of social actors to distance themselves from informality while allowing it to exist and occasionally engaging in it turns informality into an "open" (Ledeneva 2011) or "public secret" (Taussig 1999), that is to say a widely recognized yet generally unacknowledged social fact.

Open secrecy refers to the discursive tendency of people involved in, assisting to or having knowledge of informal practices to overtly conceal but covertly reveal the nature of proceedings.[1] In other words, informality is usually neither talked about in plain language nor kept entirely hidden: it surfaces in discussions in numerous roundabout ways, including "knowing smiles" (Ledeneva 2011), puns (Hanser 2006, p. 482) and allusive statements (Praspaliauskiene 2016, p. 13). Open secrecy is both a reflection of the moral limbo in which informal transactions are embedded and a prerequisite for maintaining ambivalence. It diverges from other forms of collective concealment in at least a couple of ways, both of them raising important methodological challenges.

First, the open secrecy context concurrently accommodates contrary meanings in ways that make joint action possible. Hence, the secrecy of content is secondary and instrumental to the secrecy of gaze, a cultivated ability to see without noticing, thus integrating the secret into the social texture that secreted it and to which it gives coherence. Selective inattention creates the climate of ambiguity necessary to stage mutual pretense and doubletalk,[2] which are two of the building blocks of open secrecy.

Second, open secrets blur the insider–outsider dichotomy. Groups involved in ordinary types of secrecy operate a strict demarcation between those entitled and those not entitled to get access to the information that makes the object of the cover up (Bok 1989, p. 6; Goffman 1956, p. 88; Simmel 1906, p. 470), and make use of mendacity in order to maintain a strict delineation of boundaries (Bok 1989, p. xv). In secrets of a public kind, concealing the nature of proceedings has nothing to do with the intention to create social divisions and/or gain personal advantages. Instead, it emerges as a concerted accomplishment by all participants to encounters. Because what is not to be discussed is out in the open, amenable to scrutiny, prevarication plays a minor part in the repertoire of concealment maneuvers. On the contrary, the performance of open secrecy occasionally includes cues about its staginess, the effect of which is to enhance the overall ambiguity surrounding interactions.

Rear-Mirror Methodology and Open Secrets

Despite numerous punctual considerations pertaining to challenges encountered throughout the research process and solutions devised to overcome them, open secrets have not so far received a systematic methodological examination. Alena Ledeneva's "rear-mirror methodology" (2011), an outline of the principles that guided her research on informal practices, provides a brief but noteworthy elaboration in this direction. To study open secrets, she recommends that the researcher assume a marginal position, approach the topic indirectly, and frame questions in a way that detaches the respondent from personal involvement in the morally ambiguous practice.

> Speak about generic practice, not personal experience; let the experience trickle down through the narrative; speak about others (neighbors, other firms, friends); speak about the past if the research is about know-how that is no longer in use. ... [T]he most direct way of studying an open secret is to study it indirectly, to find it one should not look for it, to develop mar-

> ginality to see what is on the inside, to go away to see the bigger picture (Ledeneva 2011, p. 729).

Ledeneva's insight into the study of open secrets invites further exploration and clarification. Her recommendations are not operationalized, even though her previous works provide examples of strategies used to cast aside the veils of secrecy and taken-for-grantedness surrounding informal intermediation of access. Also, her framework is devised for interview research, which leaves unaddressed the peculiarities of ethnographic investigation of collective concealment. It is the purpose of this chapter to reflect upon the adaptations necessary in order to extend rear-mirror methodology to the ethnographic exploration of informality as an open secret. I discuss the issues of positionality, rapport and choice of data collection methods by using as a starting point my field experience in post-socialist hospitals.

Positionality

The researcher's position relative to the participants has been acknowledged as a key issue of methodological concern in qualitative studies. Positionality delineates the space of autonomy enjoyed by researchers in the field and constrains their access to data. What and how informants disclose and what they conceal, silence or misrepresent, on the one side, and how the researcher makes sense of the dynamics of the research process and the data therein gathered, on the other side, are inextricably bound up with the places they occupy in the social space. Positionality is difficult to fix precisely, requires ongoing negotiation with participants and is susceptible to change over the course of the fieldwork (Merriam et al. 2001, pp. 411–412; Reeves 2010, p. 323; Sherif 2001). These characteristics make it more suitable for retrospective than for prospective considerations. However, for the particular context of researching open secrets, I argue in favor of the researcher's positioning at the midpoint of the insider–outsider continuum and adoption of the role of naïve newcomer to the field.

The status of insider brings along with it faster and easier entrance to the site, privileged access to information, commonality of experience with the population under scrutiny and deep understanding of the local culture (Labaree 2002, p. 103–105). As public secrecy is commonly referred to by members of the social order through variegated indirect references (Mookherjee 2006, p. 435; Taussig 1999, p. 133; Turner 2005, p. 43), the holder of insider status enjoys exposure to these linguistic intricacies that are valuable resources for the understanding of the phenomenon. Nevertheless, being "one of them" also means that the customary interdiction of openly addressing the secret applies, which reduces the possibilities of questioning participants about the practice, at least in overt ways.

At the other end of the spectrum, as Merriam and her colleagues (2001, p. 411) observed, the outsider has freedom to inquire about topics that are taboo. Nescience and unboundedness to customary constraints allow the researcher to bring to the fore issues whose direct examination is forbidden. However, that does not mean to say that respondents have any obligation to provide insights into arcane knowledge. On the contrary, they tend to give outsiders explanations tailored to their status. In my research, this propensity appeared clearly during tape recorded interviews. Open secrets, to which references had been made constantly throughout the months of observation, were suddenly resignified. Respondents dealt with them by sticking to the normative version of the events, downplaying or completely ignoring evidence that suggested different interpretations.

Partial Insider Status

Given the complementarity of the two statuses, assuming an intermediary position that makes the artful vacillation between insider and outsider positions possible appears as a necessary compromise for the student of open secrecy. As a "partial insider" (Enguix 2014, p. 88; Sherif 2001), one is entitled to receive information that is out of the reach of strangers, particularly information whose way of being delivered (through jokes, puns, sibylline remarks) exempts the speaker from responsibility for the content (Goffman 1956, p. 121, 1967, p. 30). At the same time, the social distance inherent to the partial insider status qualifies the researcher to discuss topics difficult to address among full members of the social order.

In my research, the status of partial insider was relatively easy to achieve and maintain. I was granted formal access to the field by the deputy director of the hospital, who also instructed me to use a medical gown throughout my stay in the emergency ward. While the professional garment did not necessarily confer me recognition as member of the team, wearing it signaled that I was neither a patient nor a visitor. In a social context where the distribution of positions is so neatly delineated, the gown brought me inevitably closer to the members of staff. Apart from the uniform, I shared with triage nurses a number of characteristics whose importance in the research site it did not take me long to figure out, including nationality and milieu of residence. Other characteristics, apparently less salient—gender, level of instruction and experience of living abroad for extended periods of time—set me apart from them. Positioning is contingent not only upon individual characteristics, but also upon socialization to the culture of the population under study (Reeves 2010, p. 323). In this respect, the lack of medical training and socialization to both the occupational culture and hospital culture alienated me to a certain extent from the nurses, but also created an unexpected opportunity for gathering data.

As the journal entry excerpt below shows, it became evident to me after a couple of weeks in the field that I was accepted as a member of the group, but one who was entitled only partially to the benefits and obligations of membership.

> My observation sheets and journal entries are replete with information on the progressive acceptance of my presence in the triage room of the emergency ward. However, it would be hasty or plainly dull to believe that I became "one of them", that is to say a person entitled to fully participate to the life of the ward and from whom nothing is to be kept hidden. A recent field note made me aware of it:
>
> *Lena, an elderly nurse, is upset on a colleague in the emergency ward who allegedly does not work hard enough and is boisterous. She refers to her as Chihuahua, the smallest breed of dog. When asked why she nicknamed her this way, Lena says that her coworker got her teeth and started biting. Triage nurses all laugh, suggesting agreement with the opinions of the elder nurse. However, Lucia asks her not to speak like that, because I am taking notes.*
>
> *Lena: It doesn't matter. [To me:] Write everything. She is a Chihuahua because she's teething and started biting. [Laughter again]*
>
> *Lucia: Come on, don't give away!*
>
> So far, frictions among personnel have been hidden from me. Occasionally, I witnessed some mild negative reactions towards colleagues that were absent—for example, saying about another triage nurse that she was loudmouth or expressing preference for a different shift partner—but sharp expressions of disregard were never disclosed. Breaking the norm of secrecy was encountered with astonishment by other nurses, who jestingly invited the elder nurse to refrain from further comments because I might include them in my notes. The language used to frame the request is particularly relevant. "To give away", which in Romanian is literally "to give away from the house", shows my interme-

> diary status in the hospital: I find myself in the "house" without being part of the household, a provisional member towards whom customary secrecy should apply. (3 April 2013)

Two observations are necessary here. First, I was positioned differently on the insider–outsider continuum by the nurses I interacted with. Lucia and some of her colleagues were very careful in the lines they adopted during my presence in the triage room, and they extended their caution to other members of the staff as well. On some occasions, the advice of censoring the content of the communication was made overtly, as in the journal entry above.[3] Other times, it took more devious forms, such as turning the head towards me when the interlocutor made very informal remarks, so that my presence would become conspicuous. At the same time, Lena and other coworkers felt more comfortable to discuss things freely during my observation hours, and felt no need to justify or rectify their stances afterwards.

Secondly, regardless of the inclination to stick to the etiquette or to assume more informal lines of acting, the attitudes towards me did not differ significantly. All nurses acted friendly, discussed at length the cases that I expressed interest in, and occasionally cracked jokes or relaxed the atmosphere, especially after tense moments. But they also maintained a safe distance in relation to me, and never commented on the decisions of the management or voiced discontentment with the doctors on duty. Therefore, I have reason to believe that my positioning on the insider–outsider spectrum, in spite of the variations, revolved around the ideal-type of partial insider.

An indicator of this status comes from the jocular ascription of fictive identity. During the months of fieldwork I was referred to as "the media", "journalist", "writer" and "secret service [officer]", and my notebook was referred to as "the novel". Sometimes nurses introduced me to other members of the staff by saying that I went there to write a book about hospital life, instead of a doctoral dissertation. The playful mockery accompanying these remarks conveys feelings of familiarity and closeness. The identity ascribed in jest, however, suggests externality and social distance. Thus, the mélange of comic objectification and intentional misrepresentation carries the message of partial acceptance as member of the social order.

Naïve Newcomer Role

Being a marginal insider gives the researcher the opportunity to play the role of the naïve newcomer, which is a privileged one for getting immersed into the habitual ways of doing things. The newcomer enjoys temporarily freedoms that a proper member of the community or a stranger knowledgeable of the community does not have: to push minor boundaries without being challenged for the transgression, to ask questions that are usually avoided either because the answers are tacitly known or because the issue is considered secret, to feign misinterpretation of facts and act accordingly. By making adroit use of maladroit stances, the researcher invites to be socialized by the others in a way that is not threatening for them.

When I entered the field, I left aside the indirect knowledge acquired through reading the academic literature on moral evaluation of patients and hospital ethnography. I also gave no clue to nurses and doctors that I was conversant with the situation of the Roma ethnic minority and that my previous research dealt with Roma access to healthcare services. I deliberately made conversational faux pas, by bluntly asking things that were properly discussed only in convoluted ways and, in order to check that my understanding of the events was correct and to elicit more information, I sometimes pretended to be puzzled by what was going on. This strategy, which made sense only as part of the naïve newcomer role, gave me valuable insight into controversial areas of nursing practice. The data collected as part of my socialization to the triage work included numerous references to the characteristics of the patients and the horizon of expectations associated to those characteristics; the ways in which demeanor in the emergency ward was used to make inferences about the health condition of the patient; and the functioning of informal referrals.

Socialization and Rapport

Useful as it is, the naïve newcomer role cannot be played for too long without incurring the risks of disturbing the regular flow of activities, making the staff irate and projecting an unfavorable image of the self. Sticking to it long after the inception of fieldwork indicates that the researcher's socialization to the culture of the studied population has failed, and this is likely to become a source of strain.

The need to abandon the initial role raises the problem of optimum rapport with the participants in the research. It is generally agreed that achieving a certain complicity with the participants represents a precondition for the success of qualitative research (Enguix 2014, p. 89) and that "participant disclosure ... can be heightened if there is a level of rapport between researcher and participant" (Dickson-Swift et al. 2007, p. 331). Meanwhile, excessive familiarity with participants and conflation of the roles of researcher and friend turns the researcher into a complete insider. When open secrets make the topic of inquiry, the most reasonable option seems to be that of partial intimacy: being intimate enough to construct an environment of trust and camaraderie that would stimulate participant disclosure, but at the same time not intimate to the point where the interdictions peculiar to any social world of addressing specific topics apply.

To achieve this, I engaged in reactive self-disclosure. I talked about myself only when prompted to do so or when the participant increased the level of familiarity and closeness to the point where failing to reciprocate would have created disequilibrium in interpersonal relations. However, I never crossed the boundaries in a way that brought the statuses of researcher and friend dangerously close.

In my case, socialization and rapport building went hand in hand. Unlike Reeves (2010, p. 323), whose familiarization with participants was built upon the intimate knowledge of the site of investigation gained through temporary employment on the premises before the inception of the study, I was a complete stranger when I started fieldwork. The complete strangeness, lack of acquaintanceship with the culture of the emergency ward and disconnection from the major problems affecting the ordinary performance of the tasks by nurses created the conditions for both establishing rapport and socialization. A particularity of the field site contributed to this. The researcher's allegiances are important in contentious spaces (Drake and Harvey 2013, p. 5), and the emergency ward where I conducted fieldwork was prone to disagreement between providers and beneficiaries of healthcare. Therefore, I was tabula rasa in a field of confrontation in which, in order to become an ally, I had to be taught how to read "in a proper way" the proceedings.

Nurses also sensed the situations in which their behavior did not make sense if divorced from the context in which they originated and were eager to provide me with the necessary background information. This context, amalgamating personal experiences, judgments on the clientele, organizational constraints and departmental norms was remarkably stable among triage nurses, which explains the regularities encountered in the non-clinical evaluation of patients. Understanding it would have been a more ungracious enterprise were it not for the willing, unprompted disclosure by nurses.

Data Collection Methods

As compared to other forms of collective concealment, whose existence relies in prohibiting outsiders to get access to particular information, open secrecy has more fluid boundaries between insiders and outsiders and less rigid regulations concerning the preservation of the secret. The master norm of public secrecy is indirectness. What makes the object of concealment cannot be discussed in plain language, but is commonly alluded to through intricate linguistic roundabouts. In open/public secrets, "language becomes manifestly treacherous, both sharpening and disarming the critical faculty through hazy ambiguities" (Taussig 1999, p. 104). Instead of directly articulating the sensitive information, people communicate through "insinuation, fragments, and hints" (Turner 2005, p. 43) and various "idioms of secrecy" (Mookherjee 2006, pp. 437–442). However, through repeated use in a particular context, the semantic ambiguity surrounding open secrets dissipates and participants to the social order can "assume enough shared understanding so that the meanings of deliberately vague utterances can be decoded" (Penglase 2009, p. 57). Therefore, one of biggest challenges for the ethnographer studying open secrets lies in the ability to acquire an emic understanding of the vague references to the secret.

This is complicated by participants' tendency to produce divergent discourses in formal and informal contexts. Thus, when interviewed, participants often tend to stick to normative accounts to the expense of descriptive ones, that is they talk about "how things *ought to be* rather than how they *actually are*" (Scott et al. 2006, p. 33). To get past this difficulty, researchers favored casual talk (Brewer 1993, p. 139) and the analysis of humor, ribaldry, rumor and gossip (Brewer 1993, p. 135; Frohlick 2008, p. 24; Mookherjee 2006, p. 446; Scott et al. 2006, p. 35) over direct questioning through formal interviews.

In my research, I encountered the same neat cleavage between formal and informal contexts. Casual conversations with nurses, particularly on the handling of specific patients, proved useful for understanding the social categorization as a process, because they contained fine-grained distinctions, were made in direct reference to particular cases and allowed the occasional expression of ideas that were not consistent with the standards of occupational practice. Through their immediacy and grounding in specific social situations, casual talk was separated from the participants' elaborate efforts at crafting a favorable presentation of self. Moreover, the accumulation of seemingly trivial things developed into standard patterns of action and thus rendered amenable to investigation a content that would have been obscured in the formal interviews. In day-to-day conversations, information was circulated with the primarily aim to instill in me the tacit knowledge underlying the assessment of situations. Formal interviews, on the other hand, generated accounts oriented towards making the behavior intelligible and acceptable not only to me, but to a potential audience unacquainted with the contingencies of hospital life. They provided a more sophisticated, internally consistent representation of the triage work. As a consequence, nurses preferred generalizations rather than discussing particular cases and situations and dismissed evidence that contradicted the general scheme of interpretation. Besides that, they tended to show in the formal accounts a benevolence towards the clientele, particularly that part of the clientele suspected of mischievous use of the emergency services, that was not granted in face-to-face encounters or in the ensuing conversations inside the triage room. In interviews, nurses talked empathically about the social circumstances of the alleged misusers, allowed phenomenological explanations for the disagreements over priority ranking, created nuanced representations of stigmatized groups, such as Roma, and overall projected a flattering image of the self, as competent, responsible and sensitive individuals.

While casual talk is oriented towards sense-making, formal interviewing leads to account-making. Sense-making aims to render intelligible and morally acceptable things that are controversial or fuzzy, or prone to misinterpretation. It is situational and immediate in character and, even if some coherence is generally sought, this is not necessarily achieved. The fragmentary character of sense-making creates discordance and contradictions. However, the accretion of punctual explanations forms an abundant set of data, the analysis of which permits to distinguish patterns of thought and patterns of action that would be difficult to reconfigure using different methods. Account-making, on the other hand, is an attempt to produce an overall representation of the facts that is consistent, coherent and morally acceptable. Capturing it allows one to grasp the general picture, providing the intellectual context in which decisions take place and some of the contingencies that have shaped that context. However, as a creative effort to give a story that is acceptable to the outside audience, it involves rhetorical maneuvers that silence rather than speak, and blur rather than sharpen the reality. Therefore, instead of privileging one method over the other, I exploited their complementarity and delved deeper into the apparently contradictory evidence the two techniques produced. It was in the very space of contradictions and inconsistencies that I found the most valuable ways to go past what could not be openly articulated, but was merely hinted at.

This approach seems to me particularly suitable to investigations of open secrecy in post-socialist contexts, where the legacy of doubletalk is still present. As in the past, participants in the social dramaturgy of everyday life put in practice a complex game of extended pretense, in which one interactant departs from the formal rules while taking complicated measures to safeguard the appearance of formality, whereas the coactant(s) sustain the elaborate play by acting as if nothing out of ordinary, that is to say, nothing falling out of the normative, took place. This practical entanglement of formality and informality allows participants to switch back and forth between one and the other versions of the reality according to momentary interests. Thus, dismissing the legitimacy of a patient's presentation on the grounds of his ethnicity (that allegedly makes him prone to exaggerate the symptoms in order to cheat the system and get faster access than his condition would entitle him to) in an informal discussion following the triage admission encounter coexists with a resolute statement, made by the same nurse, this time in a formal, tape-recorded interview, that ethnicity does not matter and that all patients are treated in just the same way.

Conclusion

The "rear-mirror" methodological framework represents a useful approach for the study of open secrets. In this paper, I have attempted to disambiguate the recommendations made by Ledeneva (2011) for narrative research and to adapt them to the peculiarities of ethnographic inquiry. The article makes the case for methodological flexibility and indirectness in approaching topics that are not amenable to conventional scrutiny. Researchers of open secrecy are invited to assume the status of partial insider and the role of naïve newcomer; to entertain rapport with but also maintain a certain distance from participants; and to combine casual talk with formal interviews, paying particular attention to the apparent inconsistencies between data generated by the two techniques.

In a larger sense, my contribution makes the call for greater reflexivity in the ethnographic study of informality. In spite of the remarkable vitality of the field, there are still disappointingly few published considerations on the manner in and extent to which the field situation impacts the production of knowledge. Based on my research experience in Romanian emergency departments, I reflect upon the practical solutions devised in order to elicit meaningful information from participants operating in a mutual pretense awareness context (Glaser and Strauss 1965). Such examinations are necessary to set the ground for the standardization of data-gathering strategies and practices, which, in turn, would facilitate the cross-cultural comparison of findings.

The methodological framework is particularly suitable for organizational ethnography, a type of research notoriously underrepresented in the field of informality. The state is ubiquitous in ethnographies of informal practices. It defines the rules of the game, by formalizing some aspects of social life while leaving other things unregulated. It also decides what is legal and what is not, which legal rules are to be enforced and which can be ignored, and how severe are the consequences for transgressing the formal ways of acting. Street-level bureaucrats are the ones in charge of putting such indications into practice, and it is by no means surprising that they feature so prominently in recent studies. However, their presence is generally discrete and equivocal, because more often than not they are introduced into the story by other participants. Occasionally, street-level bureaucrats are the key figures of studies, but even then they are extracted from the social milieu in which they construct, negotiate and alter the meanings attached to informality, and that of the organization. Hopefully, this chapter gives an impetus to organizational ethnographies conducted in state agencies and public services, such as tax offices, police precincts, hospitals, schools, welfare agencies, custom authorities and local authorities.

Even though this chapter originates in a study of informality and aims primarily towards the community of scholars working on post-socialist informal structures and practices, the methodological framework proposed herein is suitable to the scrutiny of any context in which contradictions between competing representations of reality are silenced in order to sustain the conduct of everyday affairs. Topics as eclectic as sexual tourism

(Frohlick 2008), adventure tourism (Fletcher 2010), the memory of wartime rape (Mookherjee 2006), racial and economic inequality (Radcliffe 2008) and drug trafficking (Penglase 2009) constitute public secrets that are amenable to investigation through the amended version of rear-mirror methodology advanced in this paper.

Notes

1. "Open" and "public secrets" are defined in strikingly similar terms. Alena Ledeneva (2011, p. 725) refers to open secrets as "unarticulated knowledge that everybody who is part of a transaction knows about but that no one discusses in a direct way", whereas public secrets are equated by Michael Taussig (1999) with "knowing what not to know" (2, 50), "that which is generally known but cannot be articulated" (5), and "that which is generally known but cannot be spoken" (50). Both authors consider that secrecy inhabits spaces of contradiction and tension, and that linguistic vitality is necessary in order to convey its protean nature (Ledeneva 2011, p. 725; Taussig 1999, p. 50). Ledeneva derives open secrecy from her studies on socialist and post-socialist informal practices, whereas Taussig draws upon a composite body of data, including anthropological studies of ordinary life under dictatorship, ethnographic accounts of initiation rituals in the Land of Fire, media reports on the destruction of national symbols in the USA and Australia, and literary works. In spite of some variations, the two forms of secrecy are consubstantial, and I treat them interchangeably in this chapter.
2. Failure to exert selective inattention is to open secrets what revealing the hidden information is to ordinary ones—a breach of the definition of the situation that leads to the impossibility of sustaining it any longer. Nowhere is this transgression of open secrecy more clear than in authoritarian regimes, whose legitimacy requires keeping the ideological façade intact in spite of all practical inconsistencies. In these regimes, seeing what should not be seen—the neglect of the ideology by the ruling force and all sorts of tolerated departures from formal rules in the conduct of everyday public life—albeit not violating any of the formal rules, is commonly treated as a major infraction. Perpetrators are subject to persecution, imprisonment or confinement to psychiatric wards (Zdravomyslova and Voronkov 2002, pp. 65–66) and to social marginalization and stigmatization (Yang 1994, p. 67).
3. The directness was softened in this case by framing the recommendation as a joke and the use of an idiom.

References

Bok, S. (1989). *Secrets: On the ethics of concealment and revelation*. New York: Vintage.

Brewer, J. D. (1993). Sensitivity as a problem in field research: A study of routine policing in Northern Ireland. In C. M. Renzetti & R. M. Lee (Eds.), *Researching sensitive topics* (pp. 125–145). Newbury Park: Sage Publications.

Chelcea, L. (2002). The culture of shortage during state-socialism: Consumption practices in a Romanian village in the 1980s. *Cultural Studies, 16*(1), 16–43.

Chelcea, L. (2015). Post-socialist acceleration: Fantasy time in a multinational bank. *Time & Society, 24*(3), 348–366.

Davies, T., & Polese, A. (2015). Informality and survival in Ukraine's nuclear landscape: Living with the risks of Chernobyl. *Journal of Eurasian Studies, 6*(1), 34–45.

Dickson-Swift, V., James, E. L., Kippen, S., & Liamputtong, P. (2007). Doing sensitive research: What challenges do qualitative researchers face? *Qualitative Research, 7*(3), 327–353.

Drake, D. H., & Harvey, J. (2013). Performing the role of ethnographer: Processing and managing the emotional dimensions of prison research. *International Journal of Social Research Methodology, 17*(5), 489–501.

Enguix, B. (2014). Negotiating the field: Rethinking ethnographic authority, experience and the frontiers of research. *Qualitative Research, 14*(1), 79–94.

Fletcher, R. (2010). The Emperor's new adventure: Public secrecy and the paradox of adventure tourism. *Journal of Contemporary Ethnography, 39*(1), 6–33.

Frohlick, S. (2008). Negotiating the public secrecy of sex in a transnational tourist town in Caribbean Costa Rica. *Tourist Studies, 8*(1), 19–39.

Glaser, B., & Strauss, A. (1965). *Awareness of dying: A study of social interaction*. Chicago: Aldine.

Goffman, E. (1956). *The presentation of self in everyday life*. Edinburgh: University of Edinburgh Social Science Research Center.

Goffman, E. (1967). On face-work: An analysis of ritual elements in social interaction. In *Interaction ritual: Essays in face-to-face behavior* (pp. 5–46). New York: Anchor Books.

Hanser, A. (2006). Sales floor trajectories: Distinction and service in postsocialist China. *Ethnography, 7*(4), 461–491.

Hartnett, A., & Dawdy, S. L. (2013). The archaeology of illegal and illicit economies. *Annual Review of Anthropology, 42*(1), 37–51.

Heinzen, J. (2013). Thirty kilos of pork: Cultural brokers, corruption, and the 'bribe trail' in the postwar stalinist Soviet Union. *Journal of Social History, 46*(4), 931–952.

Kideckel, D. A. (2002). The unmaking of an East-Central European working class. In C. Hann (Ed.), *Postsocialism: Ideals, ideologies and practices in Eurasia* (pp. 114–132). London/New York: Routledge.

Kovács, B. (2015). Managing access to full-time public daycare and preschool services in Romania: Planfulness, cream-skimming and 'interventions'. *Journal of Eurasian Studies, 6*(1), 6–16.

Labaree, R. V. (2002). The risk of 'going observationalist': Negotiating the hidden dilemmas of being an insider participant observer. *Qualitative Research, 2*(1), 97–122.

Ledeneva, A. (1998). *Russia's economy of favours: Blat, networking and informal exchange*. Cambridge: Cambridge University Press.

Ledeneva, A. (2006). *How Russia really works: The informal practices that shaped post-soviet politics and business.* Ithaca/London: Cornell University Press.

Ledeneva, A. (2008). Blat and Guanxi: Informal practices in Russia and China. *Comparative Studies in Society and History, 50*(1), 118–144.

Ledeneva, A. (2011). Open secrets and knowing smiles. *East European Politics and Societies, 25*(4), 720–736.

Merriam, S. B., et al. (2001). Power and positionality: Negotiating insider/outsider status within and across cultures. *International Journal of Lifelong Education, 20*(5), 405–416.

Mookherjee, N. (2006). 'Remembering to forget': Public secrecy and memory of sexual violence in the Bangladesh war of 1971. *The Journal of the Royal Anthropological Institute, 12*(2), 433–450.

Morris, J. (2014). Moonlighting strangers met on the way: The Nexus of informality and blue-collar sociality in Russia. In J. Morris & A. Polese (Eds.), *The informal post-socialist economy: Embedded practices and livelihoods* (pp. 51–66). London/New York: Routledge.

Morrison, C. (2003). Labour and technological discipline: Chaos and order in a Russian textile company. In N. Dannhaeuser & C. Werner (Eds.), *Anthropological perspectives on economic development and integration* (Research in economic Anthropology) (Vol. 22, pp. 171–197). Oxford: Emerald Group Publishing.

O'Neill, B. (2015). Bored stiff: Sex and superfluity in a time of crisis. *Public Culture, 27*(2), 387–405.

Penglase, B. (2009). States of insecurity: Everyday emergencies, public secrets, and drug trafficker power in a Brazilian Favela. *PoLAR: Political and Legal Anthropology Review, 32*(1), 47–63.

Polese, P. (2014). Drinking with Vova: An individual entrepreneur between illegality and informality. In J. Morris & A. Polese (Eds.), *The informal post-socialist economy: Embedded practices and livelihoods* (pp. 85–101). London/New York: Routledge.

Polese, A., & Morris, J. (2015). My name is Legion. The resilience and endurance of informality beyond, or in spite of, the state. In J. Morris & A. Polese (Eds.), *Informality in post-socialism* (pp. 1–21). London: Palgrave.

Praspaliauskiene, R. (2016). Enveloped lives: Practicing health and care in Lithuania. *Medical Anthropology Quarterly*, 1–28. Accepted author manuscript. doi:10.1111/maq.12291.

Radcliffe, V. S. (2008). Public secrecy in auditing: What government auditors cannot know. *Critical Perspectives on Accounting, 19*(1), 99–126.

Reeves, C. L. (2010). A difficult negotiation: Fieldwork relations with gatekeepers. *Qualitative Research, 10*(3), 315–331.

Sampson, S. L. (1987). The second economy of the Soviet Union and Eastern Europe. *Annals of the American Academy of Political and Social Science, 493*, 120–136.

Scott, S., Miller, F., & Lloyd, K. (2006). Doing fieldwork in development geography: Research culture and research spaces in Vietnam. *Geographical Research, 44*(1), 28–40.

Sherif, B. (2001). The ambiguity of boundaries in the fieldwork experience: Establishing rapport and negotiating insider/outsider status. *Qualitative Inquiry, 7*(4), 436–447.

Simmel, G. (1906). The sociology of secrecy and of secret societies. *American Journal of Sociology, 11*(4), 441–498.

Stan, S. (2012). Neither commodities nor gifts: Post-socialist informal exchanges in the Romanian healthcare system. *Journal of the Royal Anthropological Institute, 18*, 65–82.

Stenning, A. (2005). Where is the post-socialist working class? Working-class lives in the spaces of (post-)socialism. *Sociology, 39*(5), 983–999.

Stillo, J. (2015). We are the losers of socialism!' tuberculosis, the limits of bio-citizenship and the future of care in Romania. *Anthropological Journal of European. Cultures, 24*(1), 132–140.

Taussig, M. T. (1999). *Defacement: Public secrecy and the labor of the negative*. Stanford: Stanford University Press.

Turner, S. (2005). The Tutsi are afraid we will discover their secrets'—on secrecy and sovereign power in Burundi. *Social Identities, 11*(1), 37–54.

Wamsiedel, M. (2016). Accomplishing public secrecy: Non-monetary informal practices and their concealment at the emergency department. *Journal of Contemporary Central and Eastern Europe, 24*(3): 307–320.

Yalçın-Heckmann, L. (2014). Informal economy writ large and small: From Azerbaijani herb traders to Moscow shop owners. In J. Morris & A. Polese (Eds.), *The informal post-socialist economy: Embedded practices and livelihoods* (pp. 165–186). London/New York: Routledge.

Yang, M. M.-H. (1994). *Gifts, favors, and banquets: The art of social relationships in China*. Ithaca/London: Cornell University Press.

Zdravomyslova, E., & Voronkov, V. (2002). The informal public in soviet society: Double morality at work. *Social Research, 69*(1), 49–69.

Explaining the Informal Economy in Post-Communist Societies: A Study of the Asymmetry Between Formal and Informal Institutions in Romania

Colin C. Williams and Ioana A. Horodnic

Introduction

In recent decades, a burgeoning literature has brought out of the shadows the magnitude of the informal economy in post-communist societies and its important role in helping people get by (Abbot and Wallace 2009; Kapelyushnikov et al. 2012; Kukk and Staehr 2014; Polese and Rodgers 2011; Sauka and Putniņš 2011; Williams et al. 2013). With some quarter of national income in the post-communist economies of Central and Eastern Europe not declared to the authorities and an equivalent proportion of employment occurring through the informal economy (Schneider and Williams 2013), tackling the informal economy is not some minor issue. Addressing these practices is important however, not only because of the money being lost by governments which could otherwise pay for social

C.C. Williams
Management School, University of Sheffield, Sheffield, UK

I.A. Horodnic (✉)
Faculty of Economics and Business Administration, Alexandru Ioan Cuza University of Iași, Iași, Romania
e-mail: ursachi_ioana_alexandra@yahoo.com

A. Polese et al. (eds.), *The Informal Economy in Global Perspective*, International Political Economy Series,
DOI 10.1007/978-3-319-40931-3_7

protection. The informal economy also results in poorer quality working conditions and causes unfair competition for legitimate businesses, placing increased pressure on legitimate businesses themselves to start flouting the formal regulations, thus resulting in a vicious levelling down of working conditions in post-communist economies (Andrews et al. 2011; Davidescu 2014; Drechsler and Xenogiani 2008; ILO 2014).

Until now, the prevalence of the informal economy in these post-communist societies has been explained largely in terms of country-level structural conditions such as their economic under-development and lack of modern governance, public sector corruption and high taxes, or the inadequate levels of state intervention and protection of workers (see Williams 2013, 2015a, b, c, d, 2016; Williams and Horodnic 2015, 2016a, b; Williams and Windebank 2015). The problem with this approach that highlights country-level structural causes of the informal economy, however, is that this fails to explain why some citizens in a country participate in the informal economy and others do not. In other words, it fails to take agency into account in its explanations.

The aim here is to advance a new way of theorising the informal economy in post-communist economies that takes agency into account. Drawing inspiration from institutional theory (Baumol and Blinder 2008; Helmke and Levitsky 2004; North 1990; Webb et al. 2009), the informal economy is here theorised as arising when there is a lack of alignment of the codified laws and regulations of a society's formal institutions with the norms and values of its citizens that produce socially shared unwritten rules and understandings (i.e. informal institutions). The proposition is that the greater the non-alignment of formal and informal institutions, the higher the prevalence of the informal economy. If valid, this has consequences for how the informal economy is tackled. A policy approach based on reducing this institutional asymmetry necessitates a very different approach towards the informal economy to that currently employed.

To evaluate this, the first section briefly reviews past explanations of the informal economy and their shortcomings and then proposes a new explanation grounded in institutional theory. This proposes that the less norms, values and beliefs are aligned with the codified laws and regulations of formal institutions, the greater is the propensity to participate in the informal economy. To evaluate this, the second section then introduces the methodology and data used, namely an ordered logistic regression analysis of the association between participation in the informal economy and the degree of institutional asymmetry using data from interviews conducted in Romania in 2013. The third section then presents the findings followed by a discussion of the theoretical and policy implications in the fourth section, before the final section summarises the findings along with acknowledging the limitations of the study and suggesting avenues for future research.

At the outset, however, the informal economy must be defined. For Castells and Portes (1989, p. 15), the informal economy is "a specific form of income generating production … unregulated by the institutions of society in a legal and social environment in which similar activities are regulated". Although defining the informal economy through the lens of both the formal ("legal") and informal ("social") institutions in a society, this definition fails to recognise first, that the informal economy, even if unregulated by formal institutions, is regulated by the rules of informal institutions and second, that such activity can be "legitimate" from the viewpoint of informal institutions even if "illegal" from the viewpoint of formal institutions (Siqueira et al. 2014; Webb et al. 2009). Here, therefore, and reflecting the consensus in the literature, we define the informal economy as socially legitimate activity which is legal in all respects other than it is not declared to the authorities for tax, social security or labour law purposes (European Commission 2007; OECD 2012; Williams 2014a, b). If it is not legal and legitimate in all other respects, it is not part of the informal economy. Whilst the formal economy is legal (from the viewpoint of formal institutions) and legitimate (from the viewpoint of informal institutions), the informal economy is illegal but legitimate, unlike the criminal economy (e.g. forced labour) which is both illegal and illegitimate (Ponsaers et al. 2008).

Explaining the Informal Economy in Post-Communist Economies

It is now widely recognised that the informal economy is a large and persistent feature of many post-communist economies. Schneider (2013), for example, estimates that the informal economy is the equivalent of 31.9 % of GDP in Bulgaria, 29.1 % in Romania, 28.5 % in Lithuania, 28.2 % in Estonia, 26.1 % in Latvia, 24.4 % in Poland, 23.6 % in Slovenia, 22.5 % in Hungary, 16 % in the Czech Republic and 15.5 % in the Slovak Republic. Similarly, Williams (2014a) estimates that the share of employment in the shadow economy in 2013 was 26.2 % in Latvia, 22.7 % in Croatia, 21.6 %

in Estonia, 20.4 % in Lithuania, 19.6 % in Slovenia, 15.7 % in Bulgaria, 14.6 % in Romania, 13.4 % in Slovakia, 12.6 % in Hungary, 11.6 % in the Czech Republic and 11 % in Poland.

To show the consequences for governments and societies of having informal economies of this magnitude, Murphy (2012) examines the total tax revenue lost, and to provide a measure of what is foregone as a result, measures the tax lost as a percentage of total healthcare spending. As Table 1 reveals, based on 2009 figures the average size of the shadow economy in these ten post-communist East-Central European countries was 29.7 % of GDP and, as a result of the informal economy, 23.3 % of the total tax revenue was lost. This represents the equivalent of 127 % of current healthcare spending; in other words, if those operating in the informal economy paid their taxes, spending on healthcare in these countries could more than double.

Amongst the post-communist economies of East-Central Europe, as shown most studies reveal that the informal economy in Romania is one of the largest and most persistent of all these post-communist economies. Unsurprisingly therefore, the last decade or so has witnessed a proliferation of studies on the Romanian informal economy (Adair 2004; Drechsler and Xenogiani 2008; Neef 2002). These have largely sought to evaluate its magnitude using either direct survey methods (Albu and Nicolae 2003; Drechsler and Xenogiani 2008; Parlevliet and Xenogian 2008) or indirect methods using proxy indicators (Dobrescu 2001; Pelinescu 2003; Scutaru et al. 2002) such as the amount of cash in circulation (Tudorel et al. 2010), as well as more sophisticated multiple proxy indicators (Schneider 2013). Both these later studies find that the informal economy is around 30 % of GDP. There have also been studies of its pervasiveness in the health sector (Fărcăşanu 2010; Stepurko et al. 2013; Ungureanu et al. 2013) and agriculture (Thomka 2005), as well as amongst the retired—who turn towards the informal economy as a survival strategy in the absence of adequate social protection (Weber 2014).

To explain the informal economy, and as Williams (2014a) highlights, most studies have adopted one of three competing theoretical explanations. Firstly, "modernisation" theory explains the informal economy in terms of the lack of economic development and modernisation of state bureaucracies (Geertz 1963; ILO 2013; Lewis 1959), secondly, "neo-liberal" theory explains the informal economy as resulting from high taxes and over-burdensome rules and regulations (De Soto 1989, 2001; Nwabuzor 2005) and third and finally, "political economy" theory explains

Table 1 Tax revenue lost as a result of the informal economy in ten post-communist East-Central European societies

Country	*GDP 2009*	*Size of shadow economy 2009*	*Tax burden 2009*	*Tax revenue lost as a result of shadow economy*	*Gov't spending as % of GDP*	*Tax lost as a % of gov't spending*	*Healthcare spending as % of GDP*	*Tax lost as % of healthcare spending*
	Euro'm	%	%	*Euro'm*	%	%	%	%
Bulgaria	36,000	35.3	28.9	3,673	37.3	27.4	7.4	137.9
Czech Rep	145,000	18.4	34.5	9,205	42.9	14.8	7.6	83.5
Estonia	15,000	31.2	35.9	1,680	39.9	28.1	4.3	260.5
Hungary	98,000	24.4	39.5	9,445	49.2	19.6	8.2	117.5
Latvia	18,000	29.2	26.6	1,398	38.5	20.2	8.1	95.9
Lithuania	27,000	32.0	29.3	2,532	37.4	25.1	7.8	120.2
Poland	354,000	27.2	31.8	30,620	43.3	20.0	7.1	121.8
Romania	122,000	32.6	27.0	10,738	37.6	23.4	5.4	163.0
Slovakia	66,000	18.1	28.8	3,440	34.8	15.0	8.5	61.3
Slovenia	36,000	26.2	37.6	3,546	44.3	22.2	9.1	108.3
Total or unweighted average	917,000	29.7	35.6	76,277	–	23.3	–	127.0

Source: Derived from Murphy (2012)

it to result from inadequate state intervention and a lack of safeguards for workers (Castells and Portes 1989; Dau and Cuervo-Cazurra 2014; ILO 2014; Meagher 2010; Slavnic 2010). The problem with all these explanations which focus upon country-level conditions is that they are unable to take agency into account and explain why some individuals participate in the informal economy and others do not.

This is increasingly recognised to be important. Earlier studies assumed that participation in the informal economy was necessity-driven and a result of exclusion from the formal economy (Castells and Portes 1989; Gallin 2001). An array of more recent studies, however, have displayed that for the majority of participants, it is more a matter of choice, rather than lack of choice, to work informally, not least to escape the public sector corruption and burdensome bureaucracy that confronts those seeking to operate formally (Gerxhani 2004; Round et al. 2008; Williams et al. 2013).

In this chapter, therefore, the objective is to advance a new way of explaining the informal economy which takes agency into account. We here argue that an institutionalist analysis provides such a theoretical lens (Baumol and Blinder 2008; Helmke and Levitsky 2004; North 1990). Institutions prescribe the norms regarding the acceptability of activities; they set the "rules of the game" (Baumol and Blinder 2008; Denzau and North 1994; Mathias et al. 2014; North 1990). All societies not have only codified laws and regulations (i.e. formal institutions) that set the legal rules of the game (prescribing "state morality") but also informal institutions which are the norms, values and beliefs of the citizens—the "socially shared rules, usually unwritten, that are created, communicated and enforced outside of officially sanctioned channels" (Helmke and Levitsky 2004, p. 727). These prescribe "civic morality".

The norms, values and beliefs of a society's informal institutions are either "complementary" if they reinforce formal institutions or "substitutive" if the rules they prescribe are incompatible with those of the formal institutions (Helmke and Levitsky 2004; North 1990; Williams and Vorley 2014). When symmetry exists between the formal and informal institutions, therefore, the informal economy will be largely absent since citizens will seek to adhere to the legal rules of the game. The only reason informality will take place is because citizens unintentionally engage in it, such as due to the rules being not simple enough to understand or to complex too fulfil. However, if there is asymmetry between a society's formal institutions and its informal institutions, such as due to a lack of trust in government, the informal economy will be larger. Indeed, as the conclusions to one of the only major contemporary studies of the informal economy in Romania states, "Informality in Romania is above all an expression of the lack of trust in public institutions, the negative perception of the role of the state and the limited understanding of the benefits derived from social security" (Drechsler and Xenogiani 2008, p. 2). To test this new institutional theory of the informal economy, the following proposition can be therefore evaluated:

Institutional asymmetry thesis: the greater the asymmetry between formal and informal institutions, the greater is the propensity to participate in the informal economy.

Data and Methodology

To evaluate the validity of this institutional asymmetry thesis, we here examine a post-communist society shown above to have one of the largest informal economies, namely Romania, and which therefore should display a high level of institutional asymmetry. To explore this, we report data from special Eurobarometer survey no. 402, which involved 1,027 face-to-face interviews conducted in 2013. A multi-stage random (probability) sampling methodology was employed which ensured that on the issues of gender, age, region and locality size, both the Romanian national-level sample as well as each level of the sample, was representative in proportion to its population size. For the univariate analysis, therefore, we employ this sample weighting scheme as recommended in both the wider literature (Sharon and Liu 1994; Solon et al. 2013) and the Eurobarometer methodology, to obtain meaningful descriptive results. For the multivariate analysis, however, a debate exists over whether to use a weighting scheme (Pfeffermann 1993; Sharon and Liu 1994; Solon et al. 2013; Winship and Radbill 1994). Reflecting the dominant viewpoint, the decision was taken not to do so.

The face-to-face interviews first asked participants attitudinal questions regarding their views on the acceptability of various forms of informal work, followed by questions on whether participants had purchased from the informal economy and finally whether they had engaged in the informal economy over the past year. Here, the focus is firstly upon the attitudinal questions on the acceptability of working in the informal economy, which measure the degree of institutional asymmetry, and secondly the questions on whether they had participated in the informal economy.

To measure the level of institutional symmetry, participants were asked to rate the acceptability of six types of informal work on a 10-point Likert scale (where 1 means absolutely unacceptable and 10 means absolutely acceptable). These six types were: an individual is hired by a household for work and s/he does not declare the payment received to the tax or social security authorities even though it should be declared; a firm is hired by a household for work and it does not declare the payment received to the tax or social security authorities; a firm is hired by another firm for work and it does not declare its activities to the tax or social security authorities; a firm hires an individual and all or a part of the wages paid to him/her are not officially declared; someone receives welfare payments without entitlement; and someone evades taxes by not declaring or only partially declaring their income. An aggregate institutional asymmetry index is then created by collating participants' responses to each of the six questions. The Cronbach's Alpha coefficient is 0.86, which shows an excellent internal consistency of the scale (Kline 2000). The index has been represented here in the 10-point Likert scale's original format. The higher the index value, the higher the institutional asymmetry.

The dependent variable is therefore the institutional asymmetry index. As the dependent variable is a 10-point Likert scale index, we here employ an ordered logistic regression analysis. To evaluate whether institutional asymmetry is associated with participation in the informal economy, we include the following variable to measure this:

- *Participation in the informal economy*: a dummy variable with recorded value 1 for persons who answered "yes" to the question, "Have you yourself carried out any undeclared paid activities in the last 12 months?" and with recorded value 0 otherwise.

Drawing upon previous studies of attitudes towards working in the informal economy which have been conducted in various countries, revealing how gender, age, marital status, social class, occupation, income level and area influence the acceptability of participation in the informal economy (Alm and Torgler 2006; Cannari and D'Alessio 2007; Daude and Melguizo 2010; Daude et al. 2013; Kastlunger et al. 2013; Lago-Peñas and Lago-Peñas 2010; Martínez-Vázquez and Torgler 2009; Williams and Martinez-Perez 2014a, b), the independent variables selected are (details in Table A1 in Appendix):

- *Gender*: a dummy variable with value 1 for men and 0 for women.
- *Age*: a numerical variable for the exact age of the respondent.
- *Marital Status*: a categorical variable for the marital status of the respondent with value 1 for married/remarried individuals, value 2 for cohabiters, value 3 for single people, value 4 for those separated or divorced, and value 5 for widowed and other.
- *Social class*: a categorical variable for the respondent perception regarding social class of society to which a person reports that they belong with value 1 for the working class, value 2 for the middle class and value 3 for the upper class, other or no class.
- *Household composition aged 15+*: a categorical variable for the number of people 15+ years old in the respondent's household (including the respondent) with value 1 for one person, value 2 for two persons, value 3 for three persons, and value 4 for four persons or more.
- *Number of children* (up to 14 years old in the household): a categorical variable for number of children with value 1 for individuals with no children, value 2 for the presence of children less than ten years old living in respondent's household, value 3 for the presence of children aged ten to 14 years old living in respondent's household, and value 4 for the presence of children less than ten years old and children aged ten to 14 years old living in respondent's household.
- *Occupation*: a categorical variable for the occupation of the respondent with value 1 for self-employed, value 2 for employed, and value 3 for not working.
- *Difficulties paying bills*: a dummy variable for the respondent having difficulties in paying bills with value 1 for having difficulties and value 0 for not having difficulties in paying bills.
- *Area*: a categorical variable for the area where the respondent lives with value 1 for rural area or village, value 2 for small or medium-sized town, and value 3 for large town.
- *Region*: a categorical variable for the region where the respondent lives with value 1 for Nord-Est, value 2 for Sud-Est, value 3 for Sud-Muntenia, value 4 for Sud-Vest-Oltenia, value 5 for Vest, value 6 for Nord-Vest, value 7 for Centru, and value 8 for Bucuresti-Ilfov.

To analyse the results, firstly a descriptive analysis of the level of institutional asymmetry is provided, secondly, a Wilcoxon rank-sum is used to test whether the level of institutional asymmetry of Romanian individuals participating in the informal economy is greater than that of those not participating; finally, an ordered logistic regression analysis is used to, on the one hand, test the hypothesis that there remains an association between institutional asymmetry and participation in the informal economy when other independent control variables are introduced and held constant, and on the other hand, to identify socio-demographic, socio-economic and spatial variables strongly associated with less adherence to the formal institutions, in order to identify potential population groups where there is high institutional asymmetry.

Findings

The institutional asymmetry index for the Romanian population as a whole regarding the acceptability of participating in the informal economy is 2.29 (where 1 is totally unacceptable and 10 totally acceptable). The formal and informal institutions are therefore not wholly aligned (i.e. the institutional asymmetry index is not 1.00).

Nevertheless, the social acceptability of participation in the informal economy varies according to whether a firm or individual participates. As Fig. 1 displays, the Romanian population deems it more unacceptable for firms than individuals to operate in the informal economy. The mean tax morale score for a firm hiring an informal worker is 2.15, and it is 2.21 for a firm doing informal work for a household, while it is even lower (2.11) for firms doing informal work for another firm (i.e. the lower the score, the more unacceptable the activity). Meanwhile, the Romanian population is more tolerant of individuals participating in the informal economy. The acceptability of a person partially or completely concealing their income is 2.32, and 3.40 for an individual engaging in informal work for a household. The exception is those claiming benefits without entitlement, such as whilst working informally. This is the most unacceptable of all behaviours, scoring 1.83, doubtless because such individuals are here viewed as "taking our money" rather than seeking to "keep their own money". Similar patterns regarding the relative social acceptability of these different types of informal work are replicated across not only the EU15 but also the new member states of the European Union, where the overall institutional asymmetry is lower, at 2.22 and 2.75 respectively.

Is it the case, therefore, that there is a relationship between the level of institutional asymmetry and participation in the informal economy? To evaluate this, the first step is to test whether the level of institutional asymmetry of Romanian individuals participating in the informal economy is

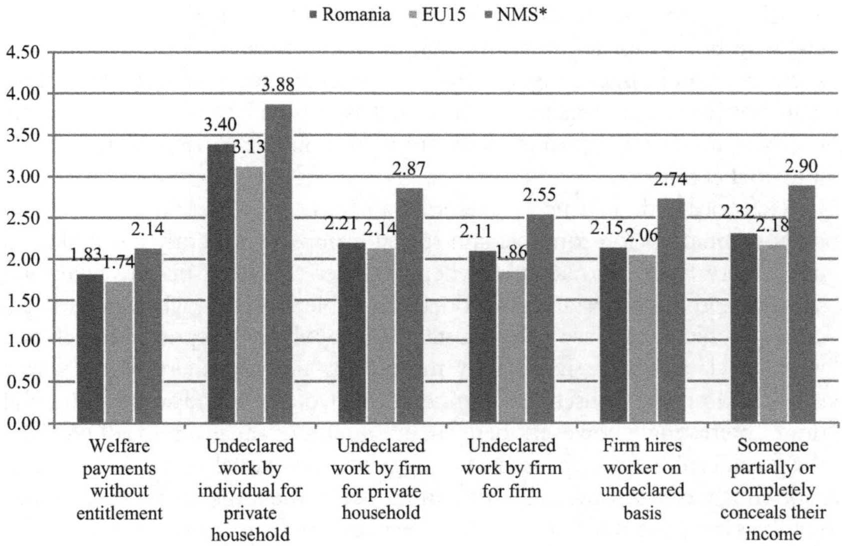

Fig. 1 Acceptability of different work in the informal economy; a comparison of average scores for Romania, EU15 and new member states (*Notes*: NMS (Romania excluded) – Bulgaria, the Czech Republic, Cyprus, Estonia, Hungary, Latvia, Lithuania, Malta, Poland, Slovenia, Slovakia, Croatia. EU15 Austria, Belgium, Denmark, Germany, Greece, Finland, France, Ireland, the Netherlands, Italy, Luxembourg, Portugal, Spain, Sweden, United Kingdom)

greater than of those not participating. Given that the distribution of the acceptability of working informally is non-parametric, a Wilcoxon rank-sum test, also known as the Mann–Whitney two-sample statistic, is used. The finding is a strong statistically significant difference in the median institutional asymmetry index of those participating in the informal economy, which is 4, compared with those not engaging in informal work, whose median score is 2 (see Table A2 in Appendix). Those participating in the informal economy are thus significantly less likely to agree with the formal rules than those not participating in the informal economy. This provides support for the institutional asymmetry thesis.

To determine whether this association remains significant when other characteristics are taken into account and held constant, Table 2 reports the results of an ordered logistic regression analysis. The first row in models 1–3 reveals that adherence to the formal rules remains strongly associated with participation in the informal economy across all models, whether socio-demographic variables alone are analysed, or whether socio-economic and/or spatial characteristics are added and held constant. This positively confirms the institutional asymmetry thesis; the greater the non-alignment with formal institutions, the higher is participation in the informal economy.

This ordered logistic regression analysis also identifies the socio-demographic, socio-economic and spatial groups significantly more likely to not adhere to the formal rules when all other characteristics are taken into account and held constant. As model 1 in Table 2 reveals, when other socio-demographic factors are held constant, those who self-report themselves as working class remain significantly more likely not to adhere to the formal rules, as do those households composed of two adults and with young children. Interestingly however, there are no significant variations in adherence to the formal rules through, for instance, gender or marital status. When socio-economic characteristics are added in model 2, the same socio-demographic variables remain significant. However, neither employment status nor whether one has difficulties paying the bills significantly influence adherence to the formal rules. The unemployed and those witnessing financial difficulties, for example, are not significantly more likely to not adhere to the formal rules than those in employment and those without financial problems. Finally, when model 3 adds the spatial characteristics, the socio-demographic variables that continue to be significant are that the working class and those with several children display less adherence to the formal rules, and the additional finding is that there is no association between whether one lives in an urban or rural area and one's adherence to the formal rules, but there are significant regional variations. People living in the poorest north-eastern region of Romania adhere less to the formal rules than those living in all other regions.

Discussion and Conclusions

This chapter has proposed a new way of conceptualising informal employment as representing a violation of the social contract that exists between the state and its citizens, and explains informal employment as arising when the norms, values and beliefs of citizens (social morality) do not align with the codified laws and regulations of a society's formal institutions (state morality). The proposition is that the wider the gap between state morality and social morality, the greater the likelihood of participation in informal employment.

Table 2 Toleration of shadow economy: ordered logistic model

	Model 1	*Model 2*	*Model 3*
Informal work (not engaged)			
Engaged	1.435** (0.598)	1.416** (0.601)	1.536*** (0.578)
Gender (women)			
Men	−0.0589 (0.134)	−0.108 (0.136)	−0.0626 (0.139)
Age (exact age)	−0.00519 (0.00512)	−0.00544 (0.00549)	−0.00373 (0.00570)
Marital status (re/married)			
Single living with partner	0.195 (0.257)	0.147 (0.268)	0.223 (0.267)
Single	0.372 (0.259)	0.356 (0.269)	0.370 (0.269)
Divorced or separated	0.221 (0.414)	0.177 (0.416)	0.161 (0.439)
Widow and other	0.189 (0.272)	0.108 (0.275)	0.178 (0.291)
Social class (The working class of society)			
The middle class of society	−0.275** (0.137)	−0.237* (0.140)	−0.156 (0.144)
The upper class/Other/None	−0.697** (0.340)	−0.703** (0.329)	−0.731** (0.347)
Household composition aged 15+ (One)			
Two	0.489* (0.281)	0.471* (0.285)	0.473 (0.293)
Three	0.387 (0.309)	0.379 (0.310)	0.410 (0.311)
Four or more	0.362 (0.323)	0.368 (0.325)	0.481 (0.335)
Number of children (no children)			
Children < 10 years	0.397* (0.211)	0.325 (0.213)	0.353 (0.218)
Children 10–14 years	−0.320 (0.210)	−0.321 (0.215)	−0.386* (0.227)
One or more < 10 years and 10–14 years	0.872*** (0.303)	0.849*** (0.299)	0.652** (0.278)
Occupation (self-employed)			
Employed		−0.292 (0.217)	−0.248 (0.234)
Not working		−0.209 (0.219)	−0.220 (0.234)
Difficulties paying bills last year (not having difficulties)			
Having difficulties		0.224 (0.137)	0.173 (0.138)

(*continued*)

Table 2 (continued)

	Model 1	*Model 2*	*Model 3*
Area respondent lives (Rural area or village)			
Small/middle town			−0.0854 (0.166)
Large town			0.00393 (0.196)
Region (Nord Est)			
Sud-Est			−0.226 (0.258)
Sud-Muntenia			−1.268*** (0.255)
Sud-Vest-Oltenia			−1.522*** (0.312)
Vest			−1.157*** (0.256)
Nord-Vest			−0.913*** (0.254)
Centru			−1.159*** (0.257)
Bucuresti-Ilfov			−1.576*** (0.309)
Constant cut1	−0.470 (0.466)	−0.652 (0.513)	−1.480*** (0.570)
Constant cut2	0.675 (0.468)	0.499 (0.514)	−0.262 (0.569)
Constant cut3	1.593*** (0.470)	1.432*** (0.516)	0.749 (0.567)
Constant cut4	2.465*** (0.475)	2.312*** (0.519)	1.688*** (0.568)
Constant cut5	3.286*** (0.492)	3.137*** (0.539)	2.540*** (0.582)
Constant cut6	4.142*** (0.517)	3.964*** (0.549)	3.382*** (0.586)
Constant cut7	4.856*** (0.583)	4.678*** (0.608)	4.106*** (0.634)
Constant cut8	5.558*** (0.693)	5.380*** (0.708)	4.813*** (0.727)
Constant cut9	6.950*** (1.154)	6.772*** (1.169)	6.208*** (1.178)
N	796	789	789
Pseudo R^2	0.0196	0.0219	0.0491
Log likelihood	−1249.2925	−1232.9936	−1198.64
χ^2	52.64	59.59	120.46
p>	0.0000	0.0000	0.0000

Notes: Significant at *** $p<0.01$, ** $p<0.05$, * $p<0.1$ (robust standard errors in parentheses); All coefficients are compared to the benchmark category, shown in brackets

Evaluating the validity of this social contract violation thesis using data on Romania, the above analysis positively confirms this thesis. It reveals that the greater the asymmetry between state morality and social morality, the higher the propensity to participate in the informal economy, and this remains strongly significant when other socio-demographic, socio-economic and spatial variables are introduced and held constant. This Romanian survey thus confirms that the informal economy arises when in society there is a lack of adherence to the formal rules.

This view that the informal economy arises when there is a lack of adherence to the formal rules has direct implications for how this realm is tackled. According to institutional theory, two basic mechanisms exist for tackling institutional asymmetry: disincentives (sticks) to prevent socially legitimate but illegal activities, or incentives (carrots) to encourage desirable legal activities (Mathias et al. 2014; North 1990).

Conventionally, when tackling the informal economy, the Romanian government, akin to other governments, has used disincentives to ensure that the cost of being caught and punished is greater than the pay-off from participating in the informal economy (Allingham and Sandmo 1972; Dekker et al. 2010). First, penalties and sanctions have been raised and/or second, the likelihood of detection has been improved, such as by increasing workplace inspections and by improving data sharing and matching to identify individuals engaged in informal employment (e.g. Hasseldine and Li 1999; Williams 2014a). The problem with this dominant disincentives approach, however, is that introducing tougher sanctions and improving detection reduces voluntary compliance because it undermines respect for the fairness of the system and leads to greater rather than less informal employment (Chang and Lai 2004; Murphy 2005; Murphy and Harris 2007).

Hence, a different policy approach is needed if informal employment is to be tackled. Two possibilities exist. First, incentives to behave legally can be offered, such as direct and indirect tax incentives to either suppliers or consumers of informal employment, in order to encourage them to operate in the formal economy. The problem, nevertheless, is that such incentives are in effect bribes offered to citizens precisely because they would not otherwise comply with the codified laws and regulations (i.e. state morality). The argument here is that the medium- to long-term approach should be to align social morality with state morality, which will in the long term be a far more effective and cost-efficient means of tackling the problem of the informal economy. Here, therefore, a second and rather different policy approach to providing incentives to behave legally is advocated.

To reduce participation in the informal economy, what is required is a policy shift away from the currently dominant approach of detecting and punishing those participating in the informal economy and towards an approach that seeks to reduce the gap between social morality and state morality. On the one hand, this requires policies that change social morality so as to realign it with state morality. Such measures include education and awareness-raising campaigns regarding the importance and benefits of paying taxes, such as by providing information on the public goods and services paid for by taxation. Drechsler and Xenogiani (2008, p. 2): "Long term sustainable change requires a transformation of people's attitudes and beliefs. More innovative policies, such as information campaigns on the benefits of formal work and the risks of informality can gradually change people's opinions." For example, "your taxes are paying for this" signs can be prominently positioned in hospitals, schools, on ambulances and around other public sector construction projects. Until now, the Romanian government has not sought to do this. In April–July 2015, however the National Agency for Fiscal Administration conducted an awareness and education campaign for the taxpayers called "Romania works with your taxes", simultaneously using the newspapers, radio, TV, online and outdoor media in order to address as many people as possible (National Agency for Fiscal Administration 2014). This education and awareness-raising campaign, as Table 2 reveals, could be usefully targeted at those populations whose social morality least adheres to state morality, namely those defining themselves as working class, those with several children and those living in the poorest north-eastern region of Romania. Gender, age, marital status, number of adults in the household, employment status, whether they have financial difficulties and live in an urban or rural area do not significantly influence adherence to the formal rules.

On the other hand, an alignment of social morality and state morality also requires changes in formal institutions. Drawing inspiration from a large body of research at the organisational level where there has been a shift from "hard" to "soft" HRM, and from bureaucratic to post-bureaucratic management (Legge 1995; Thompson and Alvesson 2005; Watson 2003), a similar shift is here advocated at the societal level when tackling participation in informal employment. In other words, a policy shift is advocated away from the conventional low commitment, low trust and adversarial "hard" policy approach, which has sought compliance using tight rules, close supervision and monitoring, prescribed procedures and centralised structures. Rather, and replicating how behaviour change is being elicited at the organisational level, a high trust, high commitment "soft" policy approach could instead be pursued, which nurtures self-regulation through internalised commitment. At the societal level, this requires a shift away from a "cops and robbers" approach, which treats citizens as criminals, and towards a customer service-oriented approach which treats citizens as clients. To move towards this, enhancements in the procedural and redistributive justice and fairness of formal institutions are required so that citizens believe that the authorities are treating them in a respectful, impartial and responsible manner, believe that they pay their fair share and believe that they receive the goods and services they deserve (Molero and Pujol 2012; Murphy 2005).

This chapter has not only provided a new conceptualisation and explanation of the informal economy in Romania but also a new policy approach. Nevertheless, there are limitations to the chapter. The major limitation is that although the above quantitative analysis displays the importance of aligning social morality with state morality, it has not been able to identify the reasons for the social morality of the Romanian population deviating from the codified laws and regulations (i.e. state morality). As Drechsler and Xenogiani (2008, p. 1) assert about Romania, "Workers fail to see the link between social security contributions and benefits, and in any case deplore the low quality of public services. Corruption in Romania's public sector is a further disincentive to joining the formal sector." Studies have also revealed the extent of corruption (Bocean 2010; Marinescu and Jora 2013; Ristei 2010). Future qualitative research is therefore required to identify the reasons, such as whether it is due to a perception that tax rates are too high, a lack of understanding of the taxation system and how taxes are used, a lack of acceptance of what taxes are spent on, or the tax, social security and labour law regulations. This will then enable an identification of what policy approaches are required in order to better align social morality with state morality.

In sum, this chapter has outlined a new explanation for participation in informal employment and policy approaches for tackling the informal sector. Whether this is valid in other European countries and global regions now requires consideration. If this chapter thus inspires such evaluations, it will have achieved one of its objectives. However, if governments also start recognising that informal employment arises when a gap exists between social morality and state morality and begin exploring policy measures to close this gap, rather than persisting with the detection and punishment of those participating in informal employment, then this chapter will have achieved its broader aims too.

Acknowledgement This work was supported by the Alexandru Ioan Cuza University of Iasi through Grants for young researchers, project code no. GI-2015-18.

Appendix

Table A1 Variables used in the analysis: definitions and descriptive statistics

Variables	*Definition*	*Mode or mean*	*Min / Max*
Tax Morality Index (dependent variable)	Constructed index of self-reported tolerance towards tax non-compliance	2.39	1 / 10
Undeclared work	Dummy variable of undeclared paid activities carried out in the last 12 months, apart from regular employment	No undeclared activities (96.19 %)	0 / 1
Gender	Dummy for the gender of the respondent	Female (51.72 %)	0 / 1
Age	Respondent age (exact age)	44 years	15 / 87
Marital status	Respondent marital status in categories	Married/ Remarried (60.79 %)	1 / 5
Social class	Respondent perception regarding social class of society to which it belongs in categories	Middle class of society (51.91 %)	1 / 3
Household composition aged 15+	People 15+ years in respondent's household (including the respondent) in categories	Two people (51.15 %)	1 / 4
Number of children	Presence of children (up to 14 years old) in the household in categories	No children (72.92 %)	1 / 4
Occupation	Respondent occupation in categories	Not working (52.04 %)	1 / 3
Difficulties paying bills	Dummy for the respondent difficulties in paying bills	Not having difficulties (56.53 %)	0 / 1
Area respondent lives	Size of the area where the respondent lives in categories	Rural area/ village (43.57 %)	1 / 3
Region	Region where the respondent lives in categories	Nord-Est (16.74 %)	1 / 8

Source: Eurobarometer 79.2 (2013): Undeclared Work in the European Union

Table A2 Two-sample Wilcoxon rank-sum (Mann-Whitney) test

		Obs.	*Rank sum*	*Expected*
People not engaged in undeclared work		790	319544.5	323900
People engaged in undeclared work		29	16245.5	11890
Combined		819	335790	335790
Unadjusted variance	1565516.67			
Adjustment for ties	-115791.06			
Adjusted variance	1449725.61			

Ho: Tax morality of people not engaged in undeclared work = Tax morality of people engaged in undeclared work
z = −3.617
Prob> |z| = 0.0003

References

Abbot, P., & Wallace, C. (2009). Patterns of participation in the formal and informal economies in the Commonwealth of Independent States. *International Journal of Sociology, 39*(2), 12–38.

Adair, P. (Ed.). (2004). *Informal economies and social transformation in Romania* (Vol. 5). Münster: LIT Verlag.

Albu, L.-L., & Nicolae, M. (2003). *Use of household survey data to estimate the size of the informal economy in Romania* (MPRA paper no. 14286). Available from: http://mpra.ub.uni-muenchen.de/14286. Accessed 6 Dec 2014.

Allingham, M., & Sandmo, A. (1972). Income tax evasion: A theoretical analysis. *Journal of Public Economics, 1*(2), 323–338.

Alm, J., & Torgler, B. (2006). Culture differences and tax morale in the United States and in Europe. *Journal of Economic Psychology, 27*(2), 224–246.

Andrews, D., Caldera Sanchez, A., & Johansson, A. (2011). *Towards a better understanding of the informal economy* (OECD Economics Department Working Paper No. 873). Paris: OECD.

Baumol, W. J., & Blinder, A. (2008). *Macroeconomics: Principles and policy.* Cincinnati: South-Western Publishing.

Bocean, G. C. (2010). The shadow economy and corruption in Romania. *Ovidius University Annals, Economic Sciences Series, 10*(1), 543–546.

Cannari, L., & D'Alessio, G. (2007). *Le Opiniomi degli Italiani sull'Evasione Fiscale* (Temi di Discussione). Rome: Bank of Italy.

Castells, M., & Portes, A. (1989). World underneath: The origins, dynamics and effects of the informal economy. In A. Portes et al. (Eds.), *The informal economy: Studies in advanced and less developing countries* (pp. 1–19). Baltimore: John Hopkins University Press.

Chang, J. J., & Lai, C. C. (2004). Collaborative tax evasion and social norms: Why deterrence does not work. *Oxford Economic Papers, 56*(2), 344–368.

Dau, L. A., & Cuervo-Cazurra, A. (2014). To formalize or not to formalize: Entrepreneurship and pro-market institutions. *Journal of Business Venturing, 29*(5), 668–686.

Daude, C., & Melguizo, A. (2010). *Taxation and more representation? On fiscal policy, social mobility and democracy in Latin America* (OECD Development Centre Working Paper 294). Paris: OECD.

Daude, C., Gutiérrez, H., & Melguizo, A. (2013). What drives tax morale? a focus on emerging economies. *Review of Public Economics, 207*, 9–40.

Davidescu, A. (2014). Evaluating the relationship between official economy and shadow economy in Romania: A structural vector autoregressive approach. *Journal of Social and Economic Statistics, 3*(2), 57–65.

De Soto, H. (1989). *The other path: The economic answer to terrorism*. London: Harper and Row.

De Soto, H. (2001). *The mystery of capital: Why capitalism triumphs in the West and fails everywhere else*. London: Black Swan.

Dekker, H., Oranje, E., Renooy, P., Rosing, F., & Williams, C. C. (2010). *Joining up the fight against undeclared work in the European Union*. Brussels: DG Employment, Social Affairs and Equal Opportunities.

Denzau, A. T., & North, D. (1994). Shared mental models: Ideologies and institutions. *Kyklos, 47*, 3–30.

Dobrescu, E. (2001). Some estimations concerning the informal economy in Romania. *Journal for Economic Forecasting, 1*, 7–15.

Drechsler, D., & Xenogiani, T. (2008). *The two faces of informal employment in Romania* (No. 70). OECD Publishing.

European Commission. (2007). *Stepping up the fight against undeclared work*. Brussels: European Commission.

Fărcășanu, D. (2010). Population perception on corruption, informal payments and introduction of co-payments in the public health system in Romania. *Management in Health, 14*(1), 8–13.

Gallin, D. (2001). Propositions on trade unions and informal employment in time of globalisation. *Antipode, 19*(4), 531–549.

Geertz, C. (1963). *Old societies and new states: The quest for modernity in Asia and Africa*. Glencoe: Free Press.

Gerxhani, K. (2004). The informal sector in developed and less developed countries: A literature survey. *Public Choice, 120*(3–4), 267–300.

Hasseldine, J., & Li, Z. (1999). More tax evasion research required in new millennium. *Crime, Law and Social Change, 31*(1), 91–104.

Helmke, G., & Levitsky, S. (2004). Informal institutions and comparative politics: A research agenda. *Perspectives on Politics, 2*, 725–740.

ILO. (2013) *Women and men in the informal economy: Statistical picture*. Available from: http://laborsta.ilo.org/informal_economy_E.html. Accessed 18 Nov 2014.

ILO. (2014). *Transitioning from the informal to the formal economy*. Report V (1), International Labour Conference, 103rd Session. Geneva: ILO.

Kapelyushnikov, R., Kuznetsov, A., & Kuznetisova, O. (2012). The role of the informal sector, flexible working time and pay in the Russian labour market mode. *Post-Communist Economies, 24*(2), 177–190.

Kastlunger, B., Lozza, E., Kirchler, E., & Schabmann, R. (2013). Powerful authorities and trusting citizens: The slippery slope framework and tax compliance in Italy. *Journal of Economic Psychology, 34*(1), 36–45.

Kline, P. (2000). *The handbook of psychological testing* (2nd ed.). London: Routledge.

Kukk, M., & Staehr, K. (2014). Income underreporting by households with business income: Evidence from Estonia. *Post-Communist Economies, 26*(2), 257–267.

Lago-Peñas, I., & Lago-Peñas, S. (2010). The determinants of tax morale in comparative perspective: Evidence from European countries. *European Journal of Political Economy, 26*, 441–453.

Legge, K. (1995). *Human resource management: Rhetorics and realities*. Basingstoke: Macmillan.

Lewis, A. (1959). *The theory of economic growth*. London: Allen and Unwin.

Marinescu, C., & Jora, O.-D. (2013). Assessment on the "institutional economics" of corruption. Business and development in Romania, between formal and informal practices. *The Amfiteatru Economic Journal, 15*(Special 7), 603–616.

Martínez-Vázquez, J., & Torgler, B. (2009). The evolution of tax morale in modern Spain. *Journal of Economic Issues, 43*, 1–28.

Mathias, B. D., Lux, S., Crook, T. R., Autry, C., & Zaretzki, R. (2014). Competing against the unknown: The impact of enabling and constraining institutions on the informal economy. *Journal of Business Ethics, 127*(2), 251–264.

Meagher, K. (2010). *Identity economics: Social networks and the informal economy in Nigeria*. New York: James Currey.

Molero, J. C., & Pujol, F. (2012). Walking inside the potential tax evader's mind: Tax morale does matter. *Journal of Business Ethics, 105*, 151–162.

Murphy, K. (2005). Regulating more effectively: The relationship between procedural justice, legitimacy and tax non-compliance. *Journal of Law and Society, 32*, 562–589.

Murphy, R. (2012). *Closing the European tax gap: A report for Group of the Progressive Alliance of Socialists and Democrats in the European Parliament*. Downham Market. Tax Research LLP.

Murphy, K., & Harris, N. (2007). Shaming, shame and recidivism: A test of re-integrative shaming theory in the white-collar crime context. *British Journal of Criminology, 47*, 900–917.

National Agency for Fiscal Administration. (2014). *Press release*. Available from: https://static.anaf.ro/static/3/Anaf/SCAN%20488_20.04.2015.pdf. Accessed 20 Dec 2014.

Neef, R. (2002). Aspects of the informal economy in a transforming country: The case of Romania. *International Journal of Urban and Regional Research, 26*(2), 299–222.

North, D. C. (1990). *Institutions, institutional change and economic performance*. Cambridge: Cambridge University Press.

Nwabuzor, A. (2005). Corruption and development: New initiatives in economic openness and strengthened rule of law. *Journal of Business Ethics, 59*, 121–138.

OECD. (2012). *Reducing opportunities for tax non-compliance in the underground economy*. Paris: OECD.

Parlevliet, J., & Xenogian, T. (2008). *Report on informal employment in Romania*. Paris: OECD.

Pelinescu, E. (2003). Causes and size of informal economy in Romania. *Journal for Economic Forecasting, 1*, 86–97.

Pfeffermann, D. (1993). The role of sampling weights when modelling survey data. *International Statistical Review, 61*(2), 317–337.

Polese, A., & Rodgers, P. (2011). Surviving post-socialism: The role of informal economic practices. *International Journal of Sociology and Social Policy, 31*(11/12), 612–618.

Ponsaers, P., Shapland, J., & Williams, C. C. (2008). Does the informal economy link to organised crime? *International Journal of Social Economics, 35*(9), 644–650.

Ristei, M. (2010). *Competing formal and informal institutions in a democratizing setting: An institutional analysis of corruption in Romania*. Kalamazoo, Michigan: Western Michigan University.

Round, J., Williams, C. C., & Rodgers, P. (2008). Corruption in the post-Soviet workplace: The experiences of recent graduates in contemporary Ukraine. *Work, Employment & Society, 22*(1), 149–166.

Sauka, A., & Putniņš, T. (2011). *Shadow economy index for the baltic countries 2009 and 2010*. Riga: Stockholm School of Economics in Riga.

Schneider, F. (2013). *Size and development of the shadow economy of 31 European and 5 other OECD countries from 2003 to 2013: A further decline*. Available from: http://www.econ.jku.at/members/Schneider/files/publications/2013/ShadEcEurope31_Jan2013.pdf. Accessed 6 Nov 2014.

Schneider, F., & Williams, C. C. (2013). *The shadow economy*. London: Institute of Economic Affairs.

Scutaru, C., Pauna, C., & Pauna, B. (2002). A micro-econometric approach for assessing the determinants of the informal economy in Romania. *Journal for Economic Forecasting, 3*, 29–51.

Sharon, L., & Liu, J. (1994). A comparison of weighted and unweighted analyses in the National Crime Victimization Survey. *Journal of Quantitative Criminology, 10*(4), 343–360.

Siqueira, A. C. O., Webb, J., & Bruton, G. D. (2014). Informal entrepreneurship and industry conditions. *Entrepreneurship Theory and Practice, 40*(1), 177–200.

Slavnic, Z. (2010). Political economy of informalisation. *European Societies, 12*, 3–23.

Solon, G., Haider, S.J., & Wooldridge, J. (2013). *What are we weighting for?* (Working Paper No. 18859). Cambridge: National Bureau of Economic Research.

Stepurko, T., Pavlova, M., Gryga, I., & Froot, W. (2013). Informal payments for health care services: Corruption or gratitude? A study on public attitudes, perceptions and opinions in six Central and Eastern European countries. *Communist and Post-communist Studies, 46*, 419–431.

Thomka, A. (2005). The informal economy and viability of small family farms in Romania. *Eastern European Countryside, 11*, 89–109.

Thompson, P., & Alvesson, M. (2005). Bureaucracy at work: Misunderstandings and mixed blessings. In P. du Gay (Ed.), *The values of bureaucracy* (pp. 121–140). Oxford: Oxford University Press.

Tudorel, A., Ştefănescu, D., & Oancea, B. (2010). Quantitative Methods for Evaluating the Informal Economy. Case Study at the Level of Romania. *Theoretical and Applied Economics, 7*(7), 15.

Ungureanu, M. I., Litan, C. M., Rus, I. A., & Chereches, R. M. (2013). A brief insight into the study of informal health care pay-ments in Romania. *Transylvanian Review of Administrative Sciences, 39*, 212–219.

Watson, T. J. (2003). *Sociology, work and industry*. London: Routledge.

Webb, J. W., Tihanyi, L., Ireland, R. D., & Sirmon, D. G. (2009). You say illegal, I say legitimate: Entrepreneurship in the informal economy. *Academy of Management Review, 34*(3), 492–410.

Weber, G. A. (2014). After a Lifetime of Labor: Informal Work among the Retired in Romania. *Anthropology Now, 6*(1), 15–24.

Williams, C. C. (2013). Evaluating cross-national variations in the extent and nature of informal employment in the European Union. *Industrial Relations Journal, 44*(5/6), 479–494.

Williams, C. C. (2014a). *Confronting the Shadow Economy: Evaluating tax compliance and behaviour policies*. Cheltenham: Edward Elgar.

Williams, C. C. (2014b). Out of the shadows: A classification of economies by the size and character of their informal sector. *Work, Employment and Society, 28*, 735–753.

Williams, C. C. (2015a). Explaining cross-national variations in the scale of informal employment: An exploratory analysis of 41 less developed economies. *International Journal of Manpower, 36*(2), 118–135.
Williams, C. C. (2015b). Explaining the informal economy: An exploratory evaluation of competing perspectives. *Relations Industrielles. Industrial Relations, 70*(4), 741–765.
Williams, C. C. (2015c). Explaining cross-national variations in the informalisation of employment: Some lessons from Central and Eastern Europe. *European Societies, 17*(4), 492–512.
Williams, C. C. (2015d). Out of the margins: Classifying economies by the prevalence and character of employment in the informal economy. *International Labour Review, 154*(3), 331–352.
Williams, C. C. (2016). Tackling employment in the informal economy: A critical evaluation of the neo-liberal policy approach. *Economic and Industrial Democracy: An International Journal.* http://dx.doi.org/10.1177/0143831X14557961.
Williams, C. C., & Horodnic, I. A. (2015). Evaluating the prevalence of the undeclared economy in Central and Eastern Europe: An institutional asymmetry perspective. *European Journal of Industrial Relations, 21*(4), 389–406.
Williams, C. C., & Horodnic, I. A. (2016a). Evaluating the illegal employer practice of under-reporting employees' salaries. *British Journal of Industrial Relations.* doi:10.1111/bjir.12179.
Williams, C. C., & Horodnic, I. A. (2016b). Cross-country variations in the participation of small businesses in the informal economy: An institutional asymmetry perspective. *Journal of Small Business and Enterprise Development, 23*(1), 3–24.
Williams, C. C., & Martinez-Perez, A. (2014a). Explaining cross-national variations in tax morality in the European Union: An exploratory analysis. *Studies in Transition States and Societies, 6*, 5–17.
Williams, C. C., & Martinez-Perez, A. (2014b). Why do consumers purchase goods and services in the informal economy? *Journal of Business Research, 67*(5), 802–806.
Williams, N., & Vorley, T. (2014). Institutional asymmetry: How formal and informal institutions affect entrepreneurship in Bulgaria. *International Small Business Journal, 33*(8), 840–861.
Williams, C. C., & Windebank, J. (2015). Evaluating competing theories of informal employment: Some lessons from a 2013 European survey. *International Journal of Business and Globalisation, 15*(1), 45–62.
Williams, C. C., Round, J., & Rodgers, P. (2013). *The role of informal economies in the post-Soviet world: The end of transition?* London: Routledge.
Winship, C., & Radbill, L. (1994). Sampling weights and regression analysis. *Sociological Methods and Research, 23*(2), 230–257.

Post-Socialist Informality Rural Style: Impressions from Bulgaria

Diana Traikova

Introduction

Transition affected both rural and urban areas, but in a different way. After the regime change in Bulgaria, the regional disparities in post-socialist areas increased. It is not uncommon that every area offers a different set of resource endowments and opportunities for economic activities, but the transition diminished the attractiveness of rural areas significantly. In Bulgaria, after joining the European Union, once again the rules changed significantly, with the most important repercussions for rural areas coming from the Common Agricultural Policy. The transition has been a bumpy ride. Today, a quarter of a century after the fall of the communist regime, the majority of one whole generation is looking at the ruins of its life-long efforts and tries to make sense of the situation. The most pressing problem for rural areas is the lack of employment opportunities. If it is difficult to obtain a waged job, people can attempt to migrate or stay and try to work on their own account. If things go well, they might even create some jobs. Depending on their understanding of the new rules, their life stage, experience, resource endowments and ambitions, rural people

---

D. Traikova (✉)
Leibniz Institute of Agricultural Development in Transition Economies, Halle (Saale), Germany

A. Polese et al. (eds.), *The Informal Economy in Global Perspective*, International Political Economy Series,
DOI 10.1007/978-3-319-40931-3_8

draft their 'road maps' for how to move on with their lives and careers. It is well known that in transitional societies the written rules do not correspond to the lived practices of average people (Williams and Horodnic 2015a, b, c, d). Disappointed and feeling let down by the government, individuals seek to avoid the state and transfer many of their activities into the informal realm (Morris and Polese 2014; Williams and Franic 2015, 2016; Williams et al. 2014, 2015). This chapter contributes to the literature on context-specific research in informal rural entrepreneurship (for reviews, see Williams 2016; Williams and Nadin 2010). This is illustrated with practices for dealing with the post-socialist challenges in rural areas of Bulgaria.

The chapter proceeds with a short outline of some peculiarities of Bulgarian rural areas and rural entrepreneurship in particular. Then data and the method are introduced. The heart of the chapter encompasses descriptions of practices of rural entrepreneurs in their effort to take control of their economic faith. Examples for interwoven influences of perceived institutions, locational characteristics and individual preferences illustrate the complexity of the rural informality phenomenon and call for more nuanced quantitative approaches for the future.

Rurality and Post-Socialism

Rural and urban disparities are not a new issue. Similar to other former communist countries, in Bulgaria, rural outmigration existed long before 1990. At times, it has been also fueled by the ideology of overcoming rural backwardness and adopting the new "modernity" which was associated with the big cities. In order to restrict the outflow from rural areas, the Bulgarian Communist Party introduced quotas for urban living permits and located industrial complexes in the rural areas. This was done not because of a locational competitive advantage, but with the main goal of ensuring employment for the rural population. After 1990, this artificially created structure broke down. Dramatic institutional shifts occurred, affecting both the subjective and objective realities of rural dwellers in Bulgaria. The essence of the transition is privatization. State-owned assets were given back to the heirs of the owners, who had "volunteered" them in the dawn of the communist state. In Bulgaria, the privatization process happened in a hurry and without transparent procedures. A bitter aftertaste of injustice and power abuse by the strong of the day tainted the rural spirit and gave an uneven start to a small privileged group. Only after that was a pure market economy philosophy adopted, where all individuals are supposed to compete following free market rules. Then, rural transition took its course. First, non-agricultural production almost came to a stand-still, with its systems being dismantled and sold in pieces. As a consequence, decades of education and working experience tailored to local rural needs (targeting the nearby factories) become obsolete within a few years with the downsizing and closure of the big state-owned enterprises. The winds of change also swept away the proud symbols of socialist agriculture—the cooperatives and the huge agro-industrial complexes. This interrupted the vertical integration links, previously centrally coordinated by the communist government. Without the food-processing factories and with the disappearance of the traditional export markets, millions of rural people were confronted with unemployment, and challenged to start all over from scratch. After the massive lay-offs, many sought refuge in the small plots they received from the dismantled agricultural cooperatives. Struggling with budget deficits and tough requirements for fiscal discipline, the post-socialist governments could not offer decent pensions and unemployment benefits to those in need. Especially in the times of hyperinflation in 1996–1997, Bulgarian people learned to rely on themselves and on real tangible assets instead of on the state. Initially seen as a temporary phenomenon, the widespread existence of subsistence farms is still persisting and crystalized as a typical characteristic of Bulgarian rural areas (Davidova et al. 2012). By definition, they are based on informal (not officially registered) activities, with occasional sales of surplus produce on the road or to wholesale markets. As a whole, this phenomenon is considered a problem, not only because of the low efficiency of such small-scale production and the non-payment of taxes, but because it does not really provide a stable livelihood. Still, in the face of a weak social support system, it remains one of the core coping strategies for rural households. It is also deeply rooted in Bulgarian culture.

Another peculiarity of rural Bulgaria is the high fragmentation of its agricultural land (Kostov and Lingard 2002). Different to, for example, Eastern Germany, where state property is privatized but kept in existing production structures, the land in Bulgaria is restituted in real boundaries. Sometimes one farmer has ten small plots, which are a few kilometers away from each other. This has implications for the applicability of machine cultivation, for the long-term investment in agricultural improvements and also for the incentives to register formally as a farmer. It took a long time before a functioning land market was put in place in Bulgaria. Legal claims and conflicts are common and slow down the progress of structural adjustment even today.

What appears as efficient on the macro-level (increasing average farm-size plots enabling economies of scale) may be linked to individual perception of unjust outcomes from legal disputes in the courts, which are known to be notoriously corrupt. The uneasy feeling of being betrayed and abandoned by the state is growing in the hearts of many disappointed rural Bulgarians. Becoming a part of the big European family gave a push for many institutional improvements, but few rural people benefit from them. With every year the average plot size is increasing, but even so, in recent years, it has become evident how unprepared the country was for the adoption of the Common Agricultural Policy (CAP) of the European Union. In its direct payments part, it offers funds as income compensation to the farmers, but their distribution is based on farm size (derived from land size). In Bulgaria, there is a minimum requirement of 0.5 ha in order to fulfill the eligibility criteria for participation in the single area payment scheme. According to the official data (Bulgarian Ministry of Agriculture and Food 2014), only 30 % of farmers have officially registered as agricultural producers, leaving the remaining 70 % without access to this aid. Despite the financial incentive, for some reason these farmers have stayed informal.

At the same time, empty rural schools, deteriorating infrastructure, pensions perceived as insultingly low, a corrupt healthcare system and distrust towards courts, police and almost any manifestation of the state, motivate the trend towards individualism, skepticism towards any collective endeavors and the importance of the family.

Still, life goes on and rural people are also doing business. Some rural entrepreneurs are well-off and plan to grow, while others are struggling to make ends meet and fear whether or not their venture will be there in a few months' time. Economic activities follow universal principles regardless of their location, but there are some peculiarities of rural entrepreneurship which need to be considered when analyzing informality in rural businesses. This chapter will highlight them.

Methodology and Data

The ideas presented here are inspired by the review of the literature on entrepreneurship, rural development, non-farm diversification and cognitive decision-making (Ajzen 1991; Ellis 2000; Ellis et al. 1999; Grilo et al. 2007; van der Zwan et al. 2010). Further, concrete insights from field work in Bulgaria provide examples of how rural people manage the challenges of rurality when doing business. Data from more than 100 in-depth interviews on the topics of structural adjustment and rural livelihood strategies were used to derive statements. The regions of Varna, Burgas, Pazardjik and Plovdiv were visited on several occasions between 2004 and 2015. They were chosen in six research projects as representing different levels of economic development, climate and soil conditions, as well as farming practices in Bulgaria. About 20 villages were visited and hundreds of hours of interviews were conducted, transcribed and analyzed. The main focus was not put on informal business practices, but this aspect arose throughout the stories rural people shared.

Informality in Rural Areas

Rural business decisions should not be understood solely as means of maximizing income generation, but as strategic acts as a part of an overall livelihood strategy, balancing the interests of all household members while considering also their bargaining and decision-making power.

The concept of pluriactivity may help to understand the importance put on a specific business activity, why it is conducted informally or why it is just partially formalized. Researchers aiming to entangle the drivers of rural informal business practices should try to understand the purpose of the rural venture as seen by the household as the unit of analysis. This is especially important because of the prevalence of small family businesses in rural areas. Family businesses try to satisfy the needs of all family members involved. Before delving into the details of the particular underreporting or non-reporting of taxable income, one should look at the bigger picture. Is the rural venture a primary income generator or just a complementary income source? Is it planned just as a temporary solution for overbridging one winter or is it something more permanent? Would the own business activity be abandoned at the first serious dependent employment offer? Are we dealing here with a tentative attempt to make ends meet or are there ambitious growth plans, which policymakers eagerly showcase in their programs? All these have implications for the motivation to formalize the particular activity or not.

As a whole, informal practice can render different sets of business opportunities feasible and attractive, compared to when the law is strictly applied and tax and insurance are paid. Coupled with rurality (meaning mainly dominance of agriculture and dependence of seasonal variations, higher transaction costs for reaching remote markets, low population density, most people from the village knowing each other, and limited off-farm employment opportunities), a favorable environment is at hand for informal business activities. The next sections reveal the impressions the author gained during extensive rounds of data collection in rural Bulgarian villages.

Informality and Rural Start-Ups

Usually rural entrepreneurs start with the resources they have at hand, trying to keep the initial investment costs as low as possible. For this they harness the resources the household already controls (family savings and own physical assets), but also make heavy use of their personal networks. Especially in rural areas, the role of social capital should be underlined, since it is often accumulated over decades of interactions and is intertwined with the traditions and the enclosure of the rural place.

In order to understand the alternatives of informal rural businesses, scholars should watch for several crucial aspects in the rural context. Is there something left from the former state-owned enterprises which offers employment? Are there any job opportunities which match the qualifications of the household members? If yes, is the payment acceptable for covering the household needs and aligning with the preferences of the household members?

A typical problem of transition is that most of the people in the village show similar qualification profiles. This is no surprise because they visited regional schools which prepared them for the needs of the local large-scale industry during communist times. Back then, one big state-owned enterprise gave employment to thousands. With such an abundance of similarly qualified labor, but only limited purchasing power, entrepreneurship was a way to introduce some diversity in the post-socialist rural economy. This sounds better than it feels in reality. With rural people not having any significant savings as start-up capital and without appropriate managerial training, they mostly orient themselves towards activities targeting local customers, which do not require high qualifications and significant starting capital. One typical example is grocery shops. Severe competition and minimal profits are the logical consequence. In particular, less entrepreneurial individuals are pushed to accept low-paid jobs, which are short-term or even one-offs. They are a last resort solution but offer at least some income. Sometimes there are jobs in the next town, but they are out of reach for many rural people because of the high transport costs. Due to increasing depopulation in some Bulgarian rural areas, many bus routes are not maintained anymore or have had to reduce service frequency. As a result, one can get out of the village only by car, or only every other day. This poses difficulties for taking up a normal job outside some remote villages and, accordingly, rural people try to be as self-sufficient as possible. From this background, any local employment opportunity, even if it is not officially registered and secured by a written contract, becomes attractive.

In Western societies, the social system offers a safety net of social transfer payments, but in Bulgaria social protection is not sufficient to cover even the basic needs of pensioners, the handicapped and families with small children. Given that the largest share of the costs of Bulgarian households goes on food, rural households engage in farming to offset this effect. The long tradition of subsistence farming is complemented by the necessity to save cash for other services and goods, which the household cannot produce alone.

In some villages, the soil is fertile and the land is flat (no hills is good news for machine cultivation), allowing specialization in agriculture and going beyond the subsistence orientation. Again, because many people in the village apply the same strategy, the profit margins of those selling surplus remain slim and the incentives to formalize imply a high threshold of quantities produced. For example, elderly pensioners sell their surplus production along the village road, hoping that cars passing by will stop and buy. They do this only in the season and depending on the availability of surplus. This is seen as normal and acceptable and most customers do not expect to get invoices from such transactions.

The matter is different with bigger producers, who aim to make use of the support programs foreseen by the CAP and the complementing national measures for producer support and rural development. Such entrepreneurs react quickly to the incentives of the respective policies and create businesses tailored to the funding criteria. Those who believe that they will be able to fulfill the requirements, plan their business entry with the clear intention strictly to follow the law. After several corruption scandals in the last ten years, the impression prevails that law enforcement in this area has dramatically increased: controls are tightened and land use is monitored via satellites, the paperwork is extensive and there are also examples of how subsidy violators have had to return the support they received plus interest. Those who are aware of their inability to fulfill the requirements stay on the margin and plan to operate informally for the long run, as long as their health, production surplus and market access allow it. For example, as mentioned above, one requirement for receiving farm subsidies is to have at least 0.5 ha of cultivated land. Another is to have stables corresponding to animal welfare standards, which should also be located outside the village. Usually this compliance requires significant investments, which most rural people cannot accomplish on their own. After a wave of private insolvencies following the introduction of accessible credits prior to 1997, rural people seem to be reluctant to take the path of approaching the bank and would rather rely on personal savings and informal credit. Another issue is the culturally rooted attachment to the land, which the banks would ultimately take as collateral. Bulgarians have a saying, “one can acquire land only through war and through marriage”, which seems to be shared by the majority of the visited households. Another reason for the unwillingness to sell land is the single area payments scheme under CAP, which distributes support based on the land used and not based on the type of farm production. This limits the recognized business opportunities rural people can enact (e.g. farmers opt for grains and not horticulture) and job creation potential is often simply not there from the very gestation of the new businesses.

Many of the rural people who dream about having their own business do so because they are tired of job hopping and the lack of control of their work situation. After observing how others employ workers without contracts or pay them just the minimum wage, they believe they can achieve some income while working for their own account. A frustrated woman in her.

fourties, owner of a small coffee shop shared:

“I have been working without a contract for so long. I was always promised that at some point I will get a decent insurance, but whenever I checked, this was never the case. So if they can do it and get away with it, why should I stick to them? I can try a business on my own and at least insure me on the minimal wage.”

The desire to be one’s own boss was reported repeatedly as one of the most important motives for becoming self-employed. The craving for predictability and the freedom from having to obey what someone else tells you marry with a trend towards individualization in rural areas after the fall of the communist regime. In their poverty, people encapsulate themselves within the family and in the first place try to improve the situation of their own household. Community spirit is no longer the highest priority. It is rather unusual to observe businesses which are planned to be founded collectively, and this limits the start-up capital of the new ventures and increases the probability that such businesses will be informal or semi-formal.

Informality and Growth of Rural Businesses

The most typical challenge for rural employment is its dependence on agriculture and the linked seasonality of production. Most rural households are involved in some kind of farming. This has implications for the time budget of the household members. One day has just 24 hours and the different business activities compete for each working hour. Usually, whenever livestock is involved, the person responsible is blocked from giving a hand in alternative income generating activities. Livestock is known to have an income stabilizing role, but farmers have been complaining for years about the falling prices of their milk and meat production and more and more of them turn to crops. In order to achieve growth, a company (regardless of whether it is formal or informal) needs investment—in contacts, know-how acquisition, transport to new markets and expansion of storage facilities or employing additional workers. In rural areas the timing of such investments is linked to the pulse of agricultural production, especially in the lack of formal credits or the unwillingness to use banks. Farmers can invest money only after they sell their products and get paid. This may slow down the exploitation of promising business opportunities. Another implication is that only gradual growth can be achieved, so growth per se can be given up as a business strategy.

According to most interviewed respondents, the main important advantage of informality is its flexibility. This is especially the case for seasonal activities like harvesting or planting, where manual work is required for a limited time span. Despite the possibility for short-term contracts, farmers still prefer to do this informally. One producer explained:

> I am the biggest producer of cucumbers here. I need many workers for the harvest in a short time. At first I tried to use the labor office. But this is not very convenient for me – I had to go to the town and wait for several hours. Then when my turn came I was told that there are no sufficient workers for my campaign, some other farmers had already reserved them for their harvest. So for me it does not pay to invest this time and in the end to still have to search for workers on my own. Since then I go the old way – I spread the word in the village pub and whoever is interested, is coming. Then if this is not enough, I go to the Roma street and announce that I am searching for workers. I send one truck to collect them. They arrive, jump in the field and start picking. When the noon heat sets in, they sleep under the big trees for few hours and continue in the afternoon until we are finished. Then at the end of the day I pay them 20 leva (10 Euro) and everybody is happy. No paperwork, no hassle. Next time when the harvest approaches they come and ask on their own if I can take them again.

Besides farming, another typical activity for the informally employed in post-socialist rural areas is guarding. It is usually performed by pensioners, who need to top up their income. They do not demand formal contracts, since they already have pensions. Employers prefer them to younger individuals who insist on insurance payments. The need for guarding comes through the land fragmentation after the privatization and the difficulties for locals to swap fields (many land ownership issues are still not solved or are blocked in court). Farmers make efforts to unite the land they cultivate, but this is not so easy. So low-cost (informal or semi-formal) guarding is needed to make production in remote fields worthwhile. Without guarding, it is to be expected that 50–100 % of the harvest will be stolen. Farmers mostly blame the Roma for this—they are pushed by poverty and lack of employment opportunities (Roma get jobs with greater difficulty than ethnic Bulgarians), especially after the end of the construction boom in 2009, which gave employment to many Roma people. Facing ever-shrinking profit margins, farmers opt for the cheaper informal employees, in order to extensively expand their production. Without this practice, they would have to abandon the more remote fields.

Informal or semi-formal entrepreneurs need to maintain a low profile in order to remain unnoticed by the tax authorities. This pushes them to carefully pick their business partners from a limited pool of well-trusted individuals. Trust takes time to build and reputation is a costly thing to lose. In the context of weak law enforcement and distrust towards most unknown business partners, reputation is priceless. Lacking the chance to advertise their activities in the newspapers, such entrepreneurs rely more on word-of-mouth marketing and only slowly expand beyond the boundaries of their villages. Here is one vivid example from a farming family, which is in the process of establishing their almond orchard:

> We are registered as farm producers and receive subsidies for our plots with wheat and coriander. But we decided to diversify with almonds. This is a long-term investment and the quality of the young almond trees is crucial for our future profitability. We searched for local suppliers, but we could not find any who had the necessary number of trees, good references and could give us an invoice. So we decided to follow the recommendations of other almond farmers we trust and bought the young trees from a producer 200 km away, who sold them unofficially. He did not give us an invoice and the amount of this investment (about 10,000 Euros) was significant for our household budget. Of course, without an invoice we cannot claim

> it as a cost and get tax relief. Still, in our eyes this is worth it, if the trees develop well and we get good quality almonds in the next decade to come. We have to wait five years and see if this is the case or not. We do not want to cause trouble to this guy, without him for us it would be much more risky and costly.

Rural informal entrepreneurs usually focus on activities which do not require extensive training. But with the time, skills and a good reputation can make the difference. When the moment comes to hire an additional employee in order to handle the increased volume of orders, the problem with the mismatching education of the rural population arises. Rural informal firms are doomed to invest in training without being able to tap any support funds for at least partially compensating this cost. Semi-informality (paying just the minimum wages formally and the rest in an envelope) solves the issue to some extent, but attracts control attention. So, after undergoing the test-bed phase and proving a particular business idea viable, the incentives for formalization increase also in rural areas. The author traced the development of a rural window frame producer, who could not find a suitable employee in the course of six years. He complained that once he trains people, theyleave the village in search of better employment with these skills in the city. After doing this for a while, he said he is no longer going to take on employees unless he knows them very well and is sure they will stay in the village for the years to come. He was uncertain if he would be willing to cover the training on his own again or will search for some funding. He was not aware of relevant support programs, but believed that formalization might help him to continue in more sustainable way—now he had accumulated a sufficient number of reliable and well-paying customers.

Another reason for the widespread informality in rural villages is that rural people mostly know each other. This is known to hinder tax inspectors from surprising entrepreneurs. Knowing the local policemen or warning the others once the first instance of inspection hits is a natural thing for rural people. Despite the individualism when trying to make ends meet, they appear to share a general distrust towards the state and its institutions and demonstrate solidarity when it comes to avoiding inspections. Given that many operate informally, they have no interest in having inspectors at their neighbor's house. The act of reporting a business to the tax authorities was seen in the same category as setting someone's house on fire. This illustrates the importance of fairness perception when it comes to justifying informal business operations. Maybe when some critical mass of formally operating businesses is reached, the prevailing morale will flip and it will become justified to chase informal competitors in rural areas too.

Regardless of the mentioned solidarity when it comes to avoiding tax controls, small farm producers distrust others and are not really eager to cooperate in other ways. Depending on the experience with the local cooperatives during communist times, this is more or less pronounced. Not surprisingly, lack of coordinated action and pooling of resources hinders growth and limits the bargaining power of small producers. Official cooperation facilitates access to new markets, but requires formal registration and licensing. Farmers who are uncertain about the future of their production also do not feel inclined to enter into associations.

An interesting example is the effort to restore the deteriorated irrigation system in one village. After the regime change the pipes were stolen, the route of the water was blocked or the channels were not maintained. Despite the fact that irrigation is crucial for farm development and cash generation in the village, farmers did not manage to solve the problem for about 20 years. Again, land fragmentation, unclear property rights and heavy administrative procedures blocked this collective effort. Still, it is a matter of finding a single motivated and enduring individual, to overcome all of this for quite big areas. The author met such an individual, who made it his life's task to restore an efficient irrigation system and bring water to three villages. He spent years visiting each farming household and helping with solving property problems until he got the right to register a voluntary cooperative, which was eligible for funding from the European Union for restoring the irrigation network. The presence of such individuals and the clear advantages of the business idea (a horticulture region is better-off when irrigation is efficient and predictable, especially in drought times when prices, for example, for watermelons are high) helped many farmers to stabilize their yields and increase their motivation for official registration. This also facilitates better supply chain integration (e.g. supermarkets prefer to buy bigger quantities from single organizations instead of handling hundreds of small suppliers to reach the desired quantity). Another favorable factor for this is the changing preferences of Bulgarian consumers for buying national fruit and vegetables. In the long run, the pressure to cooperate will become stronger and those who dare to go this way might have better chances of survival.

In the short run, informality can offer also a way out from a crisis. Such a crisis can happen when weak law enforcement in rural areas is combined with difficult access to markets. The story of one shepherd from a mountain village illustrates this.

> My former processor was buying sheep milk from the shepherds in several villages. For some reason this dairy company experienced liquidity problems and offered to pay the producers not with money, but with cheese. This caused frustration among shepherds, because we were not experienced in selling cheese. Those who decided to wait until the solvency problem is solved remained without any payment – the processor went broke. Those who took the cheese had to find a way to sell it. I could rely on a friend to help me out with potential customers, who were ready to buy without invoice and trust the quality. Without this, I would have gone broke too. Even if we decide to bring the case to the court, it will take years until a decision is made and it will cost a lot because of the lawyers. The legal way of selling cheese with official registration, cooling tanks, quality certificates and so on appeared as too long and clumsy for such a short-term solution. And I did not plan to turn from a shepherd to cheese trader for the future. Still, this freed up the money I needed and I could continue with the animals. The others from the village went broke and had to slaughter their animals, because they did not have money for the fodder. It was quite bitter…

Quite often, rural businesses are founded with the clear intention to keep them small. Besides the limitations of capital endowment, the preference for being free and less dependent on the rules is also reported as a strong driver. Lifestyle entrepreneurs (making occasional sales through hobby activities) do not pursue growth and would most likely not react to a policy seeking formalization efforts.

Concluding Remarks

The chapter has provided a snapshot picture of some rationales for being involved in informal or semi-formal practices in post-socialist rural areas. The phenomenon can be better understood if a holistic livelihood approach is taken, which accounts for the specific rural properties. Special attention deserves to be given to farming and its profitability, the make-up of local formal and informal institutions and the preferences of decision-making individuals. Further research could extend and validate the understanding of rural informality in the post-socialist context and clarify if rural-specific policy measures are appropriate to tackle it.

References

Ajzen, I. (1991). The theory of planned behavior. *Organizational Behavior and Human Decision Processes, 50*, 179–211.

Bulgarian Ministry of Agriclutre and Food. (2014). *Agricultural report 2014*. Sofia, Bulgarian Ministry of Agriclutre and Food. Available from: http://www.mzh.government.bg/mzh/Documents/AgrarenDoklad.aspx.

Davidova, S., Fredriksson, L., Gorton, M., Mishev, P., & Petrovici, D. (2012). Subsistence farming, incomes and agricultural livelihoods in the new member states of the European Union. *Environment and Planning C, Government and Policy, 30*(2), 209–227.

Ellis, F. (2000). The determinants of rural livelihood diversification in developing countries. *Journal of Agricultural Economics, 51*(2), 289–302.

Ellis, N. E., Heal, O. W., Dent, J. B., & Firbank, L. G. (1999). Pluriactivity, farm household socio-economics and the botanical characteristics of grass fields in the Grampian region of Scotland. *Agriculture, Ecosystems & Environment, 76*(2–3), 121–134. doi:10.1016/S0167-8809(99)00081-X.

Grilo, I., Van der Zwan, P., & Thurik, A. R. (2007). Modeling latent and actual entrepreneurship SCALES. Zoetermeer.

Kostov, P., & Lingard, J. (2002). Subsistence farming in transitional economies: lessons from Bulgaria. *Journal of Rural Studies, 18*(1), 83–94.

Morris, J., & Polese, A. (2014). *The informal post-socialist economy. Embedded practices and livelihoods*. New York: Routledge.

van der Zwan, P., Thurik, R., & Grilo, I. (2010). The entrepreneurial ladder and its determinants. *Applied Economics, 42*, 2183–2191.

Williams, C. C. (2016). Tackling enterprise in the informal economy: An introductory overview. *International Journal of Entrepreneurship and Small Business, 28*(2/3), 139–153.

Williams, C. C., & Franic, J. (2015). Tackling the propensity towards undeclared work: Some policy lessons from Croatia. *The South East European Journal of Economics and Business, 10*(1), 18–31.

Williams, C. C., & Franic, J. (2016). Explaining participation in the informal economy in post-socialist societies: A study of the asymmetry between formal and informal institutions in Croatia. *Journal of Contemporary Central and Eastern Europe, 24*(1), 51–65.

Williams, C. C., & Horodnic, I. A. (2015a). Evaluating the prevalence of the undeclared economy in Central and Eastern Europe: An institutional asymmetry perspective. *European Journal of Industrial Relations, 21*(4), 389–406.

Williams, C. C., & Horodnic, I. A. (2015b). Tackling the informal economy in South East Europe: An institutional approach. *Journal of South East European and Black Sea Studies, 15*(4), 519–539.

Williams, C. C., & Horodnic, I. A. (2015c). Explaining and tackling the shadow economy in Estonia, Latvia and Lithuania: A tax morale approach. *Journal of Baltic Economics, 15*(2), 81–98.

Williams, C. C., & Horodnic, I. A. (2015d). Marginalisation and participation in the informal economy in Central and Eastern European nations. *Post-Communist Economies, 27*(2), 153–169.

Williams, C. C., & Nadin, S. (2010). Entrepreneurship and the informal economy: an overview. *Journal of Developmental Entrepreneurship, 15*(4), 361–378.

Williams, C. C., Franic, J., & Dzhekova, R. (2014). Explaining and tackling the undeclared economy in Bulgaria: An institutional asymmetry perspective. *The South-East European Journal of Economics and Business, 9*(2), 33–45.

Williams, C. C., Horodnic, I. A., & Windebank, J. (2015). Explaining participation in the informal economy: An institutional incongruence perspective. *International Sociology, 30*(3), 294–313.

Exploring the Practice of Making Informal Payments in the Health Sector: Some Lessons from Greece

Adrian V. Horodnic, Colin C. Williams, Abel Polese, Adriana Zait, and Liviu Oprea

Background

Despite a wide array of measures often being adopted to tackle informal payments in the healthcare sector, this practice continues to be a widespread phenomenon. Although some individual and isolated cases of informal payments exist in countries such as Austria and Germany in Western Europe (European Commission 2013), they are more common

A.V. Horodnic (✉) • L. Oprea
Grigore T. Popa University of Medicine and Pharmacy, Faculty of Medicine, Iași, Romania
e-mail: adrian-vasile-horodnic@umfiasi.ro

C.C. Williams
University of Sheffield, Management School, Sheffield, UK

A. Polese
Dublin City University, School of Law and Government, Dublin, Ireland

University of Sheffield, Management School, Sheffield, United Kingdom

Tallinn University of Technology, Tallinn School of Law, Tallinn, Estonia

A. Zait
Alexandru Ioan Cuza University of Iași, Faculty of Economics and Business Administration, Iași, Romania

A. Polese et al. (eds.), *The Informal Economy in Global Perspective*, International Political Economy Series,
DOI 10.1007/978-3-319-40931-3_9

in low- and middle-income countries in the former USSR and Eastern and Central Europe (Cohen 2012). Therefore, various countries are seeking to deal with informal payments for healthcare—such as Albania (Burak and Vian 2007), Bulgaria (Atanasova et al. 2013; Atanasova et al. 2012; Stepurko et al. 2013; Belli 2002), Hungary (Gaal and McKee 2005; Gaal and McKee 2004; Gaal et al. 2006a, 2006b; Szende and Culyer 2006), Lithuania (Stepurko et al. 2015; Stepurko et al. 2013), Moldova (Mokhtari and Ashtari 2012), Poland (McMenamin and Timonen 2002; Shahriari et al. 2001; Stepurko et al. 2015), Romania (Belli 2002; Manea 2015; Stan 2012; Stepurko et al. 2013; World Bank 2001), Ukraine (Polese 2014; Stepurko et al. 2015; Stepurko et al. 2013; Williams and Onoshchenko 2015) or Russia (Aarva et al. 2009; Fotaki 2009; Gordeev et al. 2014).

Not only are informal patient payments more common in low- and middle-income countries in the former USSR and Eastern and Central Europe but also in some high-income Southern European countries such as Italy (European Commission 2013) and Greece (Atanasova et al. 2013; European Commission 2013; Liaropoulos et al. 2008). Therefore, as reflected in the work of Cohen (2012), due to the link with the issue of corruption, research has so far paid more attention to informal patient payments in low- and middle-income countries rather than in higher-income nations.

Usually defined as "payments to individual and institutional providers, in kind or in cash, that are made outside official payment channels" (Lewis 2000), the literature offers various perspectives on the informal payments issue. Even though "gratitude payments" or "grey payments" can be seen, in some countries, as legal or vague activities (Cohen 2012), usually labeled "black payments", informal patient payments are considered a form of corruption (Cohen 2012; Gordeev et al. 2014).

Considered a payment given illegally for better treatment, "black payments" to health workers or healthcare institutions can include different actions, such as direct payments to the doctor or nurse in order to avoid waiting lists, giving money or gifts to the doctor before or after the care was given, or making donations to research funds at the hospital in order to receive better treatment (Cohen 2012). Indeed, a variety of explanations have been given for informal payments. From connections between informal payments and cultural aspects (Gaal and McKee 2004; Lewis 2000) or economic behaviour (Gaal and McKee 2004) to structural explanations, all provide different perspectives to the complex phenomenon of informal payments in healthcare. Yet, structural explanations are perhaps the most common in the literature. Given certain conditions and constraints, it is asserted that the propensity to give informal patient payments will increase. Not only are socio-demographic characteristics therefore investigated (Belli 2002; Cockcroft et al. 2008; Liaropoulos et al. 2008; Szende and Culyer 2006), but so too the type of medical insurance, methods of paying for healthcare services (Cohen 2012), failure of government to provide adequate funding and failure to regulate (Ensor 2004), patients' dissatisfaction, lack of information about the healthcare services which patients deserve or structural conditions of basic corruption in the public service (Belli et al. 2004 in Cohen 2012).

Previous studies rarely reveal a relationship between socio-economic status and informal payments. Moreover, it is argued that these payments are found in all socio-economic groups in various countries (European Commission 2013). However, some studies find a positive association between the prevalence of informal patient payments and income or educational level, and a negative association with age (Cockcroft et al. 2008; Liaropoulos et al. 2008). An association with gender is revealed in the work of Stepurko et al. (2015), the likelihood of making informal payments being higher for females in Bulgaria, Hungary and Lithuania. Similarly, fewer family members or a higher household income in Hungary, Lithuania and Romania increase the propensity to make informal payments (Stepurko et al. 2015). Corruption, as another structural factor, is found to be related to informal payments. For instance, along with market and government failure, corruption is considered by Lewis (2000) another reason for the incidence of informal payments. Similarly, in Bolivia, informal patient payments are related to the perception that corruption exists in the healthcare system (Gray-Molina et al. 1999).

Focusing on informal patient payments in Greece, Liaropoulos et al. (2008) find that 36 % of those receiving treatment in public hospitals report at least one informal payment to a doctor, of whom 42 % state it was given because of the fear of receiving sub-standard care (if they did not pay) and 20 % because the doctor demanded such a payment. Kaitelidou et al. (2013) similarly find that 74 % using public obstetrics services had made informal payments, whilst Souliotis et al. (2016) reports under-the-table payments for 32.4 % of public hospital admissions.

Grounded in structural explanations, this chapter aims to explore the practice of making informal patient payments in Greece by analysing (1) the association between the likelihood of making informal patient payments and the acceptability of corruption, (2) informal patient payments variations according to socio-economic status and (3) doing so across Greek regions. The chapter commences with an introduction to the methodology used in the analysis, continues by reporting the results and concludes with the policy implications of the findings.

Methodology

To analyse whether the likelihood of making informal patient payments in Greece is associated with a high acceptability of corruption, and to explore socio-spatial variations across patients making extra informal payments or valuable gifts to medical practitioners or making hospital donations additional to the official fees, data is reported from Special Eurobarometer No. 397 ("Corruption") (European Commission 2014). Conducted as part of wave 79.1 of Eurobarometer Series and employing the same sampling methodology as other Eurobarometer studies, the survey was carried out in the national language with adults aged 15 years and older. Overall, during February and March 2013, 27,786 interviews were conducted, of which 1,001 took place in Greece. At the country level, 621 out of 1,001 respondents had visited a public healthcare practitioner or institution in the last 12 months prior to survey.

According to Eurobarometer methodology, a multi-stage random (probability) sampling procedure was used to ensure that the sample was representative in proportion to its population size on the issues of gender, age, locality and region. The whole territory was covered according to Greek regions and urban–rural distribution of the population. We here used weights to ensure that the sample was proportionate to the universe of the population.

In the analysis below, the dependent variable is whether Greek patients offered informal payments for healthcare services. To discover this, the respondents were firstly asked if they had "been to a public healthcare practitioner such as a GP (general practitioner) or a public healthcare institution such as a public hospital in the past 12 months". Secondly, they were asked whether they had offered informal payments for healthcare services. Therefore, we here use a dummy dependent variable with recorded value 1 for patients who answered "yes" to the question "Apart from official fees did you have to give an extra payment or a valuable gift to a nurse or a doctor, or make a donation to the hospital?" and with recorded value 0 otherwise.

To explore the practice of informal payments, three categories of variables were selected: corruption related variables, socio-demographic variables and spatial variables. For analysing the association between the likelihood of making informal patient payments and corruption, along with the general perception on the extent of corruption in public institutions in Greece, the acceptability of corruption was used. The acceptability of corruption is a categorical variable, evaluating patients' acceptability to give money, to give a gift and to perform a favour in order to get something from the public administration or public services (with value 1 for "acceptable", value 2 for "tolerated" and value 3 for "unacceptable").

For evaluating informal patient payment variations according to socio-economic status, we here used gender (male, female), age (15–24 years old, 25–34, 35–44, 45–54, 55–64, 65+), marital status (unmarried, (re) married/single with a partner, divorced or separated, widowed), level in society (lowest level in society, middle level in society, highest level in society), occupation (self-employed, employed, not working), and difficulties in paying bills (most of the time, from time to time, almost never/never). Spatial variations are evaluated using the type of community (rural area or village, small or medium-sized town, large town) and Greek regions (Voreia Ellada [Northern Greece], Kentriki Ellada [Central Greece], Attiki [Attica], Kriti [Crete]) (see Table 4 in Appendix for details).

To analyse the results, a descriptive analysis is firstly used and, secondly, a logistic regression analysis is employed to evaluate the association between the likelihood of making informal patient payments and the acceptability of corruption, and to explore socio-spatial variations across patients making informal payments.

Results

Of the 5,058 interviews conducted in 2013 in Southern Europe, 74 % were with respondents who reported that they have visited a public healthcare practitioner or a public healthcare institution during the past 12 months, of whom one in 33 (3 %) offered extra informal payments or valuable gifts to medical practitioners or made hospital donations additional to the official fees. Table 1 reveals that even if the proportion of people experiencing public healthcare services is lower in Greece (60 %) compared with the Southern European average (74 %), the percentage of patients who have made an informal payment is higher (11, compared with 3 %). Therefore, with a large deviation from the South European average, it seems to be that Greece is a particular case.

Moreover, the proportion using public healthcare services and making additional informal payments is not evenly distributed across Greek regions. For instance, those living in Attiki (Attica) or Voreia Ellada (Northern Greece) received public healthcare services in a higher number of instances (65 % and 62 % respectively) than those living in Kriti (Crete) (43 %). However, the proportion of patients making informal payments is larger in Crete, Central Greece and Attica (23 %, 15 % and 13 % respectively) and much smaller in Northern Greece (4 %).

Table 1 Informal patient payments and acceptability of corruption in Greece, by region

Southern Europe	*n = 5,058*				*n = 3,601*
Greece	*n = 1,001*				*n = 621*
Region/ Country	*Public healthcare – experience*	*Informal payments*	*Acceptability of corruption*		
			Acceptable	*Tolerated*	*Unacceptable*
	(%)	*(%)*	*(%)*	*(%)*	*(%)*
Southern Europe	74	3	2	28	70
Greece	60	11	4	47	49
Voreia Ellada (Northern Greece)	62	4	2	41	57
Kentriki Ellada (Central Greece)	54	15	13	48	39
Attiki (Attica)	65	13	2	50	48
Kriti (Crete)	43	23	3	61	36

Source: Authors' own calculations based on Special Eurobarometer No. 397 ("Corruption")

Of those making informal payments, and as Table 1 shows, 70 % consider it unacceptable to give money, a gift or to perform a favour in order to get something from the public administration or public services in Southern Europe, but only 49 % think so in Greece. There are also marked regional variations, with 36 % of patients in Crete considering corruption unacceptable, 39 % in Central Greece, 48 % in Attica and 57 % in Northern Greece. Not surprisingly, the highest percentage of patients considering corruption as unacceptable (57 % in Northern Greece) corresponds to the lowest prevalence of informal payments (4 %).

Examining the groups more likely to make informal payments for healthcare services apart from the official fees, Table 2 shows that there is little gender variation, with 10 % of men and 11 % of women making informal payments. However, not all patient groups are equally likely to make such payments. For instance, informal payments are more prevalent amongst patients aged 35–44 or 45–54 years than patients aged 55–64 years (15 % and 13 % of patients aged 35–44 or 45–54 years respectively gave informal payments but only 5 % of those aged 55–64 years did so). So too are divorced or separated patients more likely to make informal payments, as are those employed or those having difficulties in paying bills most of the time (16 %, 13 % and 12 % respectively). Turning to the spatial variations, Table 2 displays that patients living in rural areas or villages are more likely to give

Table 2 Informal patient payments and acceptability of corruption in Greece, by socio-economic and spatial characteristics

			n = 621	
Socio-economic/ Spatial characteristics	*Informal payments*	*Acceptability of corruption*		
		Acceptable	*Tolerated*	*Unacceptable*
	(%)	*(%)*	*(%)*	*(%)*
Gender				
Male	10	4	45	51
Female	11	4	49	47
Age				
15–24 years	10	3	33	64
25–34 years	9	5	39	56
35–44 years	15	3	45	52
45–54 years	13	5	50	45
55–64 years	5	4	47	49
65+ years	11	4	56	40
Marital status				
Unmarried	9	3	37	60
Re)Married/Single with a partner	10	5	48	47
Divorced or separated	16	3	57	40
Widowed	12	4	56	40
Level in society				
Lowest level in society	10	7	47	46
Middle level in society	11	2	51	47
Highest level in society	11	5	38	57
Occupation				
Self-employed	9	5	41	54
Employed	13	6	43	51
Not working	10	4	49	47
Difficulties paying bills last year				
Most of the time	12	3	46	51
From time to time	10	5	46	49
Almost never/Never	7	7	51	42
Type of community				
Rural area or village	13	2	54	44
Small or medium-sized town	6	9	40	51
Large town	11	4	45	51

Source: Authors' own calculations based on Special Eurobarometer No. 397 ("Corruption")

additional informal payments than patients living in smaller or larger urban areas (13 % compared with 6 and 11 %).

Data on the acceptability of corruption presented in Table 2 reveals that younger age groups view it as more unacceptable to give money, a gift or to perform a favour in order to get something from the public services

(64 % in the case of patients between 15 and 24 years old). It is similarly the case for unmarried patients or for those placing themselves in the highest level ofsociety (60 and 57 % respectively). Hence, these descriptive statistics tentatively display that socio-spatial variations exist in the prevalence of informal patient payments in Greece and a relationship exists between the prevalence of such payments and the acceptability of corruption.

To determine whether the association between informal patient payments and the acceptability of corruption is significant when other characteristics are taken into account and held constant and also to evaluate if socio-economic and spatial variations are significant when using multivariate analysis, Table 3 reports the results of a logistic regression. The additive models in Table 3 analyse corruption-related variables, socio-demographic variables and spatial variables. The first stage model examines the association between informal payments and corruption (Model 1) and the second and third stage models add socio-economic and spatial variables to examine their association with the informal payments for healthcare services (Model 2 and Model 3).

Model 1 in Table 3 reveals that patients who consider it unacceptable to give money, a gift or to perform a favour in order to get something from the public administration or public services are significantly less likely to make additional informal payments for healthcare services. A strong association thus exists between the likelihood of making informal patient payments and the acceptability of corruption. Not only are patients who consider corruption unacceptable significantly less likely to make informal payments but so too are those who consider that the problem of corruption is not a very widespread phenomenon.

When Model 2 and Model 3 add the socio-economic and spatial variables to the corruption-related variables, there are no major changes to the influence of the corruption-related variables on the propensity to make informal payments. However, according to Model 2, no significant associations were identified in respect to the respondent`s gender, age, marital status, level in society, occupation or difficulties in paying bills. This therefore shows that informal patient payments are observed in all investigated groups, irrespective of their socio-economic status.

Model 3 in Table 3, meanwhile, reveals that patients living in small/ medium-sized towns or large towns are significantly less likely to make extra informal payments or valuable gifts to medical practitioners or to make hospital donations additional to the official fees. Moreover, when considering the Greek regions, the finding is that compared with patients living in Northern Greece, patients living in Attica and Crete are significantly more likely to make informal payments. As such, informal patient payments vary according to region and type of community.

Table 3 Logistic regressions of the propensity to make additional informal payments for public healthcare services in Greece

Variables	*Model 1*			*Model 2*			*Model 3*		
	β	$se(\beta)$	$Exp(\beta)$	β	$se(\beta)$	$Exp(\beta)$	β	$se(\beta)$	$Exp(\beta)$
Corruption (Acceptable)									
Tolerated	−0.175	0.545	0.839	−0.261	0.586	0.770	−0.709	0.657	0.492
Unacceptable	−1.532***	0.589	0.216	−1.760***	0.639	0.172	−2.056***	0.722	0.128
Corruption extent Very widespread)									
Fairly widespread, Fairly/ Very rare	−0.849**	0.345	0.428	−0.760**	0.359	0.467	−1.095***	0.421	0.334
Gender (Male)									
Female				−0.119	0.298	0.888	−0.075	0.306	0.928
Age (15–24 years old)									
25–34				−0.526	0.829	0.591	−0.217	0.785	0.805
35–44				−0.026	0.893	0.974	0.024	0.881	10.024
45–54				−0.304	0.928	0.738	−0.341	0.909	0.711
55–64				−1.342	0.985	0.261	−1.060	0.932	0.346
65+				−0.591	0.975	0.554	−0.526	0.927	0.591
Marital status (Unmarried)									
(Re)Married/Single with a partner				0.248	0.627	10.282	0.281	0.597	10.325
Divorced or separated				0.945	0.787	20.572	0.587	0.852	10.799
Widowed				0.625	0.822	10.868	0.487	0.814	10.628
Level in society (Lowest level in society)									
Middle level in society				0.187	0.361	10.206	0.288	0.395	10.334
Highest level in society				0.444	0.439	10.559	0.619	0.467	10.857
Occupation (Self-employed)									
Employed				0.235	0.476	10.265	0.187	0.508	10.206
Not working				0.293	0.462	10.340	0.298	0.485	10.347
Difficulties paying bills last year (Most of the time)									

(*continued*)

Table 3 (continued)

Variables	*Model 1*			*Model 2*			*Model 3*		
	β	*se(β)*	*Exp(β)*	*β*	*se(β)*	*Exp(β)*	*β*	*se(β)*	*Exp(β)*
From time to time				−0.241	0.326	0.786	−0.199	0.336	0.820
Almost never\ Never				−0.785	0.497	0.456	−0.650	0.504	0.522
Type of community (Rural area or village)									
Small or medium-sized town							−1.386**	0.60	0.250
Large town							−1.371**	0.60	0.254
Region (Voreia Ellada [Northern Greece])									
Kentriki Ellada (Central Greece)							0.841*	0.465	20.320
Attiki (Attica)							1.790***	0.632	50.990
Kriti (Crete)							3.190***	0.799	24.30
Constant	−1.256**	0.512	0.285	−1.181	1.08	0.307	−1.188	10.097	0.305
N			27,396			27,392			27,392
Subpop. N			611			607			607
Prob > F			0.0001			0.0007			0.0000

Source: Authors' own calculations based on Special Eurobarometer No. 397 ("Corruption")

Notes: Significant at *** p < 0.01, ** p < 0.05, * p < 0.1

All coefficients are compared to the benchmark category, shown in brackets

Sample size is lower due to missing data

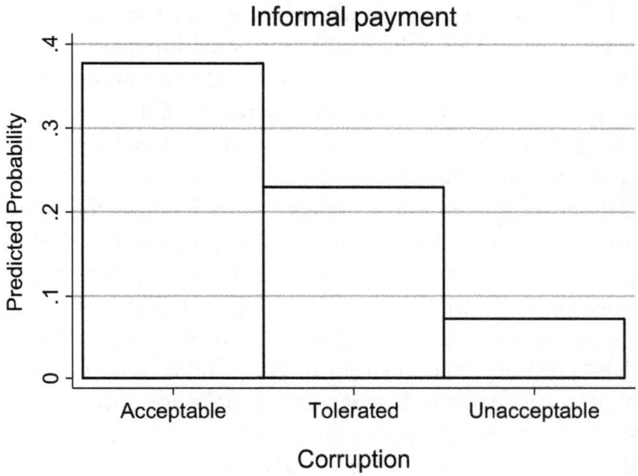

Fig. 1 Predicted probability of informal payments for a "representative patient" in Greece: by acceptability of corruption (*Source*: Authors' own calculations based on Special Eurobarometer No. 397 ("Corruption"))

To better understand the association between informal patient payments and the acceptability of corruption, Fig. 1 shows the predicted probability of informal payments for a "representative patient" in Greece, according to them possessing different views on the acceptability of corruption. The "representative patient" is derived by taking the modal values of the other independent variables. Hence, the "representative patient" in Greece is a female who considers that corruption is very widespread, aged over 65 years, (re)married or single living with a partner, places herself in the middle class of society, not working, faces difficulties most of the time in paying bills and lives in a large town in Attica. As Fig. 1 displays, the representative Greek patient who is more accepting of corrupt behaviour is far more likely to make informal payments. For this representative patient, as the level of corruption acceptability increases, the predicted probability of making informal payments increases as well.

Conclusions

Grounded in a structural explanation of informal payments in the healthcare sector, this chapter has examined the association between making such extra payments or valuable gifts (apart from official fees) and the acceptability of corruption, along with how making informal payments varies socio-spatially.

Based on 1,001 interviews conducted in Greece, the finding is that 621 respondents had visited a public healthcare practitioner or institution in the last 12 months prior to survey and that 11 % had made an informal payment. In a South European regional context, therefore, although the number of people visiting public healthcare services is lower in Greece compared with Southern Europe (60 % compared with 74 %), the instances of informal payments are much higher (11 % compared with 3 %). This underlines that Greece represents a particular case in Europe, given this high prevalence of informal patient payments. Indeed, this chapter reveals a strong association between corruption awareness, corruption acceptability and informal payments. Patients who consider that the problem of corruption is widespread in Greece and consider that corruption is acceptable, are more likely to give extra payments or valuable gifts when they experience public care health services. As such, the structural explanation of informal patient payments seems to be valid when the case of Greece is analysed.

One important outcome of this research, however, is that no significant association is identified between socio-economic characteristics and the likelihood of making informal payments. This might be explained by the neutral or even positive attitude which persists towards patients making informal payments, and which makes it difficult to find efficient ways for tackling the phenomenon. This homogenous spread of informal patient payments for healthcare public services across all analysed groups is yet to be explored. Is it a consequence of the patients' gratitude toward received health services, implying the "brighter" side of informal payments? Or is it an expression of prudence and fear, derived from the unethical behaviour of the medical personnel involved? The current dataset cannot answer. In-depth qualitative research is required in order to answer such a question.

What is to be done, then, about tackling the informal payments that patients make in Greece? There are at least two main approaches. Either deterrents or incentives can be used in order to reduce the instances of informal payments made by patients when using public healthcare services. Thus, as a first approach, tougher penalties for those caught making informal payments might be implemented or measures might be taken to increase the risks of detection, for example sending government officials undercover into public healthcare services to identify those who demand such payments from patients. This might significantly reduce the incidence of public healthcare professionals demanding informal payments. Another approach is to recognise what is perhaps one of the major reasons for healthcare professionals demanding these additional payments, and to provide higher salaries (i.e. an incentive) to the medical staff so that they do not need additional financial support for assuring their living. An alternative approach is that rather than use deterrents or incentives, indirect controls could be employed, as is being advocated when tackling the undeclared economy more widely (Williams 2014, 2016; Williams and Franic 2016; Williams et al. 2016). In the case of healthcare services, this might well involve using awareness raising campaigns among healthcare professionals and the wider population regarding the negative impacts of making and receiving informal payments for healthcare services (Williams and Onoshchenko 2015) or may well involve reforming the culture of healthcare services in a manner whereby procedural justice and fairness is promoted (Williams and Horodnic 2015a, b, c). These indirect controls can be used as complementary measures to the traditional "sticks" and "carrots" approach of using deterrents and incentives. For example, it might be the case that a government will first use awareness raising campaigns, followed by incentives for the medical staff and only after doing this use punishments for those who continue to claim such payments from their patients. However, what is certain is that a laissez-faire approach is not an option. Given that this form of corruption is a widespread phenomenon, action from the public authorities is needed to tackle it.

Appendix

Table 4 Variables used in analysis

Variables	*Description*	*Mode*
Informal payment (dependent)	Dummy variable for extra payment, valuable gift to a nurse or a doctor or a donation to the hospital (apart from official fees) for public healthcare services.	No (89 %)
Corruption	Patient acceptability of corruption in categories.	Unacceptable (49 %)
Corruption extent	Dummy for the perceived corruption extent.	Very widespread (70 %)
Gender	Dummy variable for the gender of the respondent.	Female (54 %)
Age	Respondent age in intervals.	65+ years (28%)
Marital status	Patient marital status in categories.	(Re)Married/Single with a partner (61 %)
Level in society	Patient perception regarding the level in society to which it belongs in categories.	Middle level in society (45 %)
Occupation	Patient occupation in categories.	Not working (64 %)
Difficulties paying bills last year	Patient difficulties in paying bills in categories.	Most of the time (46 %)
Type of community	Type of community where the patient lives in categories.	Large town (56 %)
Region	Region where the patient lives in categories.	Attiki (Attica) (40 %)

Source: Authors' own calculations based on Special Eurobarometer No. 397 ("Corruption")

References

Aarva, P., Ilchenko, I., Gorobets, P., & Rogacheva, A. (2009). Formal and informal payments in health care facilities in two Russian cities, Tyumen and Lipetsk. *Health Policy and Planing, 24*, 395–405.

Atanasova, E., Pavlova, M., Moutafova, E., Rechel, B., & Groot, W. (2012). Out-of-pocket payments for health care services in Bulgaria: Financial burden and barrier to access. *European Journal of Public Health, 23*(6), 916–922.

Atanasova, E., Pavlova, M., Moutafova, E., Rechel, B., & Groot, W. (2013). Informal payments for health services: The experience of Bulgaria after 10 years of formal co-payments. *European Journal of Public Health, 24*(5), 733–739.

Belli, P. (2002). *Formal and informal household spending on health: A multicountry study in Central and Eastern Europe.* Boston, MA, Harvard School of Public Health International Health Systems Group, Central and Eastern European Health Network. Available from: https://www.hsph.harvard.edu/ihsg/publications/pdf/lac/MerckReportFINAL.pdf.

Belli, P., Shahriari, H., & Gotzadze, G. (2004). Out of pocket and informal payments in the health sector: evidence from Georgia. *Health Policy, 70*, 109–123.

Burak, L., & Vian, T. (2007). Examining and predicting under-the-table payments for health care in Albania: An application of the theory of planned behavior. *Journal of Applied Social Psychology, 37*(5), 1060–1076.

Cockcroft, A., Andersson, N., Paredes-Solis, S., Caldwell, D., Mitchell, S., Milne, D., Merhi, S., Roche, M., Konceviciute, E., & Ledogar, R.J. (2008). An inter-country comparison of unofficial payments: Results of a health sector social audit in the Baltic States. *BMC Health Services Research, 8*(15), doi:10.1186/1472-6963-8-15.

Cohen, N. (2012). Informal payments for health care – the phenomenon and its context. *Health Economics, Policy and Law, 7*, 285–308.

Ensor, T. (2004). Informal payments for health care in transition economies. *Social Science and Medicine, 58*, 237–246.

European Commission. (2013). *Study on Corruption in the Healthcare Sector.* Luxembourg: Publications Office of the European Union.

European Commission. (2014). *Eurobarometer 79.1 (2013).* TNS Opinion, Brussels [producer]. GESIS Data Archive, Cologne. ZA5687 Data file Version 1.0.0, DOI:10.4232/1.11855.

Fotaki, M. (2009). Informal payments: A side effect of transition or a mechanism for sustaining the illusion of 'free' health care? The experience of four regions in the Russian Federation. *Journal of Social Policy, 38*(4), 649–670.

Gaal, P., & McKee, P. (2004). Informal payment for health care and the theory of 'INXIT. *The International Journal of Health Planning and Management, 19*, 163–178.

Gaal, P., & McKee, M. (2005). Fee-for-service or donation? Hungarian perspectives on informal payment for health care. *Social Science and Medicine, 60*, 1445–1457.

Gaal, P., Belli, P., McKee, M., & Szocska, M. (2006a). Informal payments for health care: Definitions, distinctions and dilemmas. *Journal of Health Politics, Policy and Law, 31*, 251–293.

Gaal, P., Evetovits, T., & McKee, M. (2006b). Informal payment for health care: Evidence from Hungary. *Health Policy, 77*, 86–102.

Gordeev, V. G., Pavlova, M., & Groot, W. (2014). Informal payments for health care services in Russia: Old issue in new realities. *Health Economics, Policy and Law, 9*(1), 25–48.

Gray-Molina, G., de Rada, E.P., & Yañez, E. (1999). *Transparency and accountability in Bolivia: Does voice matter?* Working paper #R-381. Inter-American Development Bank. Available from: http://www.iadb.org/res/publications/pubfiles/pubr-381.pdf.

Kaitedlidou, D. C., Tsirona, C. C., Galanis, P. A., Siskou, O., Mladovsky, P., Kouli, E. G., et al. (2013). Informal payments for maternity health services in public hospitals in Greece. *Health Policy, 109*(1), 23–40.

Lewis, M. (2000). *Who is paying for health care in Eastern Europe and Central Asia?* Washington D.C.: World Bank, Europe and Central Asia Region.

Liaropoulos, L., Siskou, O., Kaitelidou, D., Theodorou, M., & Katostaras, T. (2008). Informal payments in public hospitals in Greece. *Health Policy, 87*, 72–81.

Manea, T. (2015). Medical bribery and the ethics of trust: The Romanian case. *Journal of Medicine and Philosophy, 40*, 26–43.

McMenamin, I., & Timonen, V. (2002). Poland's health reform: Politics, markets and informal payments. *Journal of Social Policy, 31*(1), 103–118.

Mokhtari, M., & Ashtari, M. (2012). Reducing informal payments in the health care system: Evidence from a large patient satisfaction survey. *Journal of Asian Economics, 23*, 189–200.

Polese, A. (2014). Informal payments in Ukrainian hospitals: On the boundary between informal payments, gifts, and bribes. *Anthropological Forum: A Journal of Social Anthropology and Comparative Sociology, 24*(4), 381–395.

Shahriari, H., Belli, P., & Lewis, M. (2001). *Institutional issues in informal health payments in Poland*. Available from: https://openknowledge.worldbank.org/handle/10986/13679.

Souliotis, K., Golna, C., Tountas, Y., Siskou, O., Kaitelidou, D., & Liaropoulos, L. (2016). Informal payments in the Greek health sector amid the financial crisis: Old habits die last.... *European Journal of Health Economics, 17*(2), 159–170.

Stan, S. (2012). Neither commodities nor gifts: Post-socialist informal exchanges in the Romanian healthcare system. *Journal of the Royal Anthropological Institute, 18*(1), 65–82.

Stepurko, T., Pavlova, M., Gryga, I., & Groot, W. (2013). Informal payments for health care services – Corruption or gratitude? A study on public attitudes, perceptions and opinions in six Central and Eastern European countries. *Communist and Post-Communist Studies, 46*(4), 419–431.

Stepurko, T., Pavlova, M., Gryga, Y., Murauskiene, L., & Groot, W. (2015). Informal payments for health care services: The case of Lithuania, Poland and Ukraine. *Journal of Eurasian Studies, 6*(1), 46–58.

Szende, A., & Culyer, A. J. (2006). The inequity of informal payments for health care: The case of Hungary. *Health Policy, 75*(3), 262–271.

Williams, C. C. (2014). *Confronting the shadow economy: Evaluating tax compliance and behaviour policies*. Cheltenham: Edward Elgar.

Williams, C. C. (2016). Tackling enterprise in the informal economy: An introductory overview. *International Journal of Entrepreneurship and Small Business, 28*(2/3), 139–153.

Williams, C. C., & Franic, J. (2016). Beyond a deterrence approach towards the undeclared economy: Some lessons from Bulgaria. *Journal of Balkan and Near Eastern Studies, 18*(1), 90–106.

Williams, C. C., & Horodnic, I. A. (2015a). Tackling the informal economy in South East Europe: An institutional approach. *Journal of South East European and Black Sea Studies, 15*(4), 519–539.

Williams, C. C., & Horodnic, I. A. (2015b). Explaining and tackling the shadow economy in Estonia, Latvia and Lithuania: A tax morale approach. *Journal of Baltic Economics, 15*(2), 81–98.

Williams, C. C., & Horodnic, I. A. (2015c). Explaining and tackling envelope wages in the Baltic Sea region. *Baltic Journal of Management, 10*(3), 295–312.

Williams, C. C., & Onoshchenko, O. (2015). An evaluation of the persistence of blat in post-Soviet societies: A case Study of Ukraine's health services sector. *Studies of Transition States and Societies, 7*(2), 46–63.

Williams, C. C., Horodnic, I. A., & Burkinshaw, L. (2016). Evaluating competing public policy approaches towards the informal economy: Some lessons from the United Kingdom. *International Journal of Public Sector Management, 29*(4), 365–380.

World Bank. (2001). *Diagnostic surveys of corruption in Romania*. World Bank. Available from: http://www1.worldbank.org/publicsector/anticorrupt/romenglish.pdf.

Violent Pressure on Business and the Size of the Informal Economy: Evidence from Russian Regions

Michael Rochlitz

This chapter was originally written as a paper for the IAPP Summer School "Multiple Moralities and Shadow Economies in Post-Socialism" held in Zagreb, Croatia 29 August 29–1 September 2015. I want to thank Galina Belokurova for permission to use her data on violence against businessmen.

Introduction

Why do firms decide to conduct their activities in the informal economy? What are the effects on the formal economy of a sizeable shadow economy? And what can be done to bring businesses back from the informal to the formal sector?

Since the early 2000s, the question of what determines the size of the shadow economy has been increasingly studied. An extensive number of empirical studies has looked at the tax and regulatory burden (Antunes and Cavalcanti 2007; Aruoba 2010; Botero et al. 2004; Busato et al. 2011; Cebula 1997; Dabla-Norris et al. 2008; Elgin 2010; Giles and Tedds 2002; Johnson et al. 1998; Sabirianova-Peter 2009), institutional quality (Choi

M. Rochlitz (✉)
Higher School of Economics, Moscow, Russia
e-mail: michael.rochlitz@gmail.com

A. Polese et al. (eds.), *The Informal Economy in Global Perspective*, International Political Economy Series,
DOI 10.1007/978-3-319-40931-3_10

and Thum 2005; Dreher et al. 2009; Echazu and Bose 2008; Torgler and Schneider 2009; Williams and Horodnic 2015a, b, c), inequality (Chong and Gradstein 2007; Rosser et al. 2000) and the political system, for example federal versus centralized state structures (Teobaldelli 2011; Teobaldelli and Schneider 2012) as potential determinants for the size of the informal economy. The role played by business associations (Nugent and Sukiassyan 2009), entry costs (Auriol and Warlters 2005), foreign debt (Buch et al. 2000), trust (D'Hernoncourt and Méon 2012), competition in general terms (Karlinger 2009) as well as competition from the informal sector (Estrin and Mickiewicz 2010) and even average national IQ (Salahodjaev 2015) have also been studied empirically.

In this chapter, we will look at the role played by physical violence and violent pressure on firms and businesses, either by criminal groups or by predatory state officials. Will businesses that are under the pressure of corporate raiders, predatory state agencies or other forms of violence flee to the informal economy to escape violent pressure, in order to hide and "stay under the radar"? Or does a high level of violence and predatory pressure on the contrary lead to firms seeking protection in the formal economy, even if this means being subject to higher regulatory burdens and higher taxes? Finally, does the level of violence per se have an effect on the size and dynamics of the shadow economy, or are other determinants more important?

We will study this question by looking on the Russian economy under Putin. While Russia was characterized by a high level of business-related violence during the 1990s (see for example Volkov 2002), violent pressure on business has remained a defining feature of the Russian economy throughout the 2000s to the present day (Belokurova 2014; Gans-Morse 2012b; Kazun 2015; Rochlitz 2014; Rochlitz et al. 2016; Yakovlev et al. 2014). At the same time, according to most measures, the size of the informal sector in Russia has markedly increased during the last 15 years (Baranov et al. 2015; Gimpelson and Kapeliushnikov 2014; Lehman et al. 2011; Lehman and Zaiceva 2015).

Looking at the interaction between both phenomena in Russia might thus offer interesting insights into the relationship between violence and informality. In addition, another advantage of studying the Russian context is that Russia's large number of regions makes it possible to investigate regional heterogeneity in the size of the informal sector and the intensity of violent pressure on business while keeping other factors such as language, culture or national laws and regulations constant, thus avoiding the pitfalls cross-country studies are often suffering from.

Using various measures of informal employment, shadow economy size and business-related violence in Russian regions, this chapter finds that there indeed seems to be a strong link between informality, violence and violent pressure on business. However, the direction of the link is less clear, and depends on the measures of informality and violence used. This chapter finds that higher levels of physical violence such as the numbers of murders, violent robberies and the number of businesspeople that are victims of violent attacks are correlated with a larger part of the workforce being employed outside the corporate sector. At the same time, though, higher levels of physical violence are also correlated with officially registered firms facing less competition from the informal economy. On the other hand, competition from the informal economy increases the less secure are property rights, measured for example by the number and intensity of corporate raiding attacks in a given region.

These findings are consistent with a theory à la Shleifer and Vishny (1993) where contexts with *decentralized* corruption and predation are also economically less dynamic. While characterized by higher levels of physical violence, regions where the state is less able to secure the monopoly of violence might also be characterized by lower levels of centralized state predation, thus driving a lower number of dynamic firms into the informal economy. Conversely, in regions where corruption and predation are centralized in the hands of various state agencies, the risk of officially declaring your business might actually be higher for dynamic firms, thus resulting in a larger part of such firms seeking shelter in the informal sector.

The chapter is organized as follows. The next section will describe the development of the shadow economy and its interaction with business-related violence in Russia from the late 1980s until today. The third section discusses the data and methodology, the fourth section presents results, followed by the conclusion in the fifth section.

Insecure Property Rights, Business-Related Violence and the Informal Economy in Russia

The shadow economy has a long history in Russia (see Barsukova and Radaev 2012, for an overview). During the Soviet Union, the use of official position to steal state-owned resources which then could be resold on the black market was a widespread phenomenon (Grossman 1989). This so-called second economy was tolerated to a certain extent, as it helped to alleviate the widespread consumer shortages and bureaucratic bottlenecks from which the official Soviet economy was suffering (Sampson 1987).

After 1991, the Russian economy went through a stage characterized by a severe shortage of liquidity, which manifested itself through the widespread prevalence of barter exchange and payment arrears (Gaddy and Ickes 2002). Once money was flowing back into the system in the second part of the 1990s, this "virtual economy" was then gradually replaced by a large informal economy with widespread tax evasion (Barsukova and Radaev 2012), as the weakened Russian state remained unable to effectively enforce the payment of taxes. While tax evasion was often relatively risk-free for firms and businesses (Yakovlev 2000), tax collection by the state was further complicated by the sharing of tax bases between different levels of government, leading to perverse incentives for tax collecting agencies. For example, regional governors had strong incentives to collude with local enterprise directors to keep part of their profits off the book, as officially collected taxes had to be shared with the federal budget (Treisman 1999).

At the same time, resulting from the weakness of Russia's underfunded security agencies, criminal groups all across the country had started to run extortion schemes, by offering businesses protection from other criminals and themselves for a share of the profits. The state security agencies that had lost the monopoly of violence in the country were not only helpless against these numerous criminal groups, but often actively competed themselves on the market for protection money in order to complement their meagre salaries (Volkov 2000, 2002). As a result, during this period, businesses often had no choice but to stay in the informal economy if they wanted to survive, as protection money had to be paid anyway, while effective tax rates were often prohibitively high if actually paid (Johnson et al. 2000).

The situation changed in many respects during the early 2000s. The 2001 tax reform lowered tax rates and simplified the tax system, making it less costly for businesses to conduct their activities in the formal economy. At the same time, Russia's economic recovery and rising oil prices led to a significant increase in funding for the state security agencies, which subsequently were able to regain the monopoly of violence on the territory of the Russian state. All this lead to a significant decrease of the informal economy during the early 2000s, as dealing with non-state violence became increasingly costly and risky for businesses (Barsukova and Radaev 2012, p. 9). Joining the formal economy instead had become a real option, with state institutions such as for example arbitration courts gradually becoming a viable alternative to the use of criminal groups and "violent entrepreneurs" as a way to enforce contracts and solve disputes between business entities (Gans-Morse 2012a).

However, it did not take long for the state security agencies to start using their newly gained power for illicit gain. While a series of liberal market reforms during the early 2000s together with rising oil prices had laid the foundations for Russia's economic recovery, the state-led attack against Mikhail Khodorkovsky's Yukos oil company in 2003 started an adverse dynamic of state-led predation from which the Russian economy has been suffering ever since (Sakwa 2014).

After being pushed out of the market for protection as a result of the re-consolidation of the Russian state, many former criminal groups started to legalize their structures and transformed into private security agencies. Using their experience and connections from the 1990s, they offered protection and started to consult firms that were involved in corporate conflicts. Companies that were interested in taking over a rival firm approached these newly founded agencies, and soon the former violent entrepreneurs were carrying out corporate raids for a number of corporations and business groups that wanted to extend and consolidate their economic holdings (Bloom et al. 2003). According to Aldabergenova (2010), in 2004 no less than 100 such agencies were offering their services in Moscow alone, while Privalov and Volkov (2007) speak of "several dozen professional groups" throughout Russia.

One particular feature of these private security consultancies were the close links they maintained with state security agencies. When Russia was no longer able to finance the Soviet Union's massive security apparatus in the early 1990s, many state security officials were relieved of their position or were being paid only symbolic salaries. As a consequence they started offering their skills and services to criminal groups and violent entrepreneurs (Volkov 2002), while nonetheless keeping close contact with colleagues who continued to work for the state (Volkov 2000). After the turn of the century and the re-consolidation of Russia's state security services, these former policemen then used their connections to facilitate the work and corporate raids of the security agencies for whom they were now working.

As a result, the increasing number of corporate raiding attacks characteristic for Russia's economy from the early 2000s onwards were more and more carried out with the active support and participation of law enforcement agencies, tax officials or the judiciary (Gans-Morse 2012b; Rochlitz 2014). It seems that over the years state agencies even became the main initiators of such attacks, resulting in a couple of high-profile cases, such as the attack against the investment fund Hermitage Capital Management in

2007. From an environment where powerful economic players were able to directly control and influence the state to advance their interests in the first decade of economic transition (Hoffman 2002), Russia's economy during the 2000s was thus increasingly characterized by business capture through various state agencies (Frye 2002; Yakovlev 2006; Yakovlev 2011). Apart from direct expropriation through raiding activities, corrupt state actors and especially Russia's security services have also been feeding on businesses through extracting bribes and protection payments. Some observers of the Russian economy such as the lawyer Yuri Gervis even claim that certain state agencies have a strong interest in businesses staying in the informal sector because this makes it easier to extract bribes.[1]

A related feature of Russia's business environment is relatively high levels of physical violence against entrepreneurs (Belokurova 2014). While corporate raiding attacks have become less violent in nature during the 2000s, with a shift from the use of physical violence towards the use of forged documents and various semi-legal schemes, Belokurova (2014, p. 37) documents how general levels of business-related violence remained high from 1991 to 2010. Belokurova finds spikes in business-related violence around regional legislative elections where businessmen-candidates compete for office, with attacks often being initiated by competitors. That a seat at a regional legislative assembly can be highly profitable for a regional business has been shown by Szakonyi (2015), who finds that firms connected to businessmen who narrowly won a seat at a regional legislature as compared to those who narrowly lost can net on average an extra $100,000 in profits because of their political connection. Once in parliament, businessmen can also block access to, for example, public procurement contracts for their competitors. It thus is conceivable that certain businessmen might use violence in order to prevent a competitor from winning public office.

The question we ask in this chapter is how business-related violence and state predation can affect the propensity of businesses to conduct their activities either in the formal or in the informal economy. One possibility might be that businesses hide in the informal sector to escape the attention of predatory state agencies. As one entrepreneur put it in an interview with the author, a successful mid-level businessperson in Russia has to try to "stay under the radar" of those state or criminal elements who might potentially become interested in her or his businesses. If this hypothesis holds, we might expect a larger informal economy in regions characterized by high levels of state predation and corporate raiding.

One the other hand, being part of the formal economy might offer businesses better protection against predation and violence. Following the argument made by Yuri Gervis, having a legally registered business would make it more difficult for corrupt state officials to extract bribes or construct a pretext for a raiding attack (although shifting from the informal to the formal economy might cause problems with those officials that had been feeding on the business in the informal economy). Being part of the official economy might also make it easier to apply for protection from the police in case of violent attacks by competing businesses. In this case, we would expect a smaller shadow economy in regions with high levels of predation and violence.

Data and Methodology

One key problem when studying the informal economy is the question of how to measure informality. The Russian federal statistical service, Rosstat, provides a measure of informal employment as a percentage of overall employment in Russian regions (www.gks.ru). While this measure has the advantage of being available for all Russian regions for the years 2001, 2004 and then continuously from 2006 onwards, the disadvantage is that Rosstat uses the productivity-based definition of informality (Gimpelson and Kapeliushnikov 2014, p. 9). The problem with this measure is that it links informality to characteristics of enterprises and not to the fact of being officially registered and paying taxes. In other words, while all those working for "legal entities" (corporations or the government) are considered to work in the formal sector, the self-employed as well as those working for unincorporated microbusinesses or private individuals are counted as informally employed, irrespective of being registered with tax authorities and social protection agencies or not. The Rosstat indicator therefore is more a measure of the quality and precariousness of a job position, rather than a measure of informality per se. While it is probably a decent proxy for the amount of small businesses on the border between the formal and the informal economy in a given region, it is less well-suited to account for the number of firms of all sizes that make a conscious decision to stay in the informal economy.

A better measure for this second group of firms are two questions added to the most recent Business Environment and Enterprise Performance Survey (BEEPS) that was conducted in 37 Russian regions by the European Bank of Reconstruction and Development and the World Bank in 2011, and that was published in 2012 (from now on BEEPS 2012, http://ebrd-beeps.com/). The BEEPS (2012) survey consists of a detailed survey of 71 to 122 firms per region, where firms were asked, among other things, if "this establishment competes against unregistered or informal firms" (question E.11), and "to what extent are practices of competitors in the informal sector an obstacle to the current operations of this establishment" (question E.30). While these measures arguably account better for the actual size of the shadow economy in a given region, they are for now unfortunately only available for the year 2012 and for 37 out of Russia's 85 regions (although these 37 regions do include most economically important regions in Russia).

This chapter uses both the Rosstat and the BEEPS (2012) measures as proxies for the size of the informal economy. Because the Rosstat measure is available for seven continuous years between 2006 and 2012, we also use percentage changes from year to year as an additional dependent variable, to look both at the absolute size of informality and at dynamics over time.

Using the responses to question E.11 from the BEEPS (2012) survey, we construct a variable measuring the overall percentage of firms that experienced competition from the informal sector in a given region, which gives us our third dependent variable. Finally, for the question on informal practices as an obstacle to the current operations of a firm, respondents were able to rank their answers on a five-point scale from "no obstacle" (0) to "very severe obstacle" (4). For each region, we sum the answer ranks given by firms in a region and then divide the result by the number of firms that took part in the survey, to obtain an indicator of the intensity to which informal competition is an obstacle to firms, which provides us with our fourth dependent variable.

To measure the extent of property rights insecurity, predation and business-related violence, we use a range of indicators both from newspaper sources and official Russian statistics. Through a systematic analysis of Russian national and regional newspaper archives, Rochlitz (2014) built a database of 312 cases of corporate raiding that took place between 1999 and 2010 in Russia. The particularity of corporate raids in Russia is that they are often implemented with the help of illegal methods, and that the objective and result are in many cases not a simple transfer of property, but asset-strapping and theft that then result in the ultimate destruction of the target company. To distinguish raiding attacks from other forms of corporate takeover, a case was only added to the database if two independent sources confirmed that illegal methods (e.g. blackmail, bribery, forged documents or the use of physical force through armed groups or bribed police officers) were used in an attempted or successful attack on a given firm (Rochlitz 2014, p. 93).

We take the number of raiding attacks in a region per year divided by the overall number of firms in the region as an explanatory variable ("raiding attacks"). To supplement this measure, we also use the overall number of applications per region between 2011 and 2013 to the organization Business against Corruption (BaC), weighted by the number of firms in the region. BaC is an entity that helps entrepreneurs to organize a defense against corporate raiding attacks and cases of state predation, and although its potential remains limited due to the opposition and entrenched nature of Russia's law enforcement agencies, it is the most important such organization to date with 471 applications being filed between February 2011 and March 2013 (Yakovlev et al. 2014).

Our main proxy for business-related violence is an indicator constructed by Galina Belokurova (2014). Using online archive databases of Russian news agencies, Belokurova collected a database of over 6,000 incidents of business-related violence, which she defines as "attacks resulting in physical violence against entrepreneurs, including deliberate destruction of their property and exposure to explicit threat of physical harm" (Belokurova 2014, p. 4). Her paper focuses particularly on physical violence, as opposed to commissioned legal attacks that may also result in the weakening of a business organization. In our chapter, we use the number of victims of business-related violence per year and region divided by the population of a given region as an independent variable. We then also use various indicators of violence and violent crime that are published yearly by Rosstat, such as the number of murders, robberies and violent robberies as additional explanatory variables, also in per capita terms.

Finally, we use data on gross regional product (GRP), gross regional product growth, the percentage of people living under the poverty line and the percentage of unemployment, as well as the percentage of people living in cities and the percentage of the population classified as ethnically "Russian", as controls. All this data has also been obtained from Rosstat.

In order to investigate the effect violent pressure on business has on the size and dynamics of the shadow economy, we first use an OLS panel data model with region and time fixed effects, standard errors clustered on regions and data from 2001, 2004 and 2006–2010, depending on the availability of data for the Rosstat measure of informal employment (Eq. 1),

$$Y_{it} = \beta_0 + \beta_1 V_{it} + \beta_2 P_{it} + \beta_3 X_{it} + \beta_4 r_i + \beta_5 y_t + \epsilon \tag{1}$$

where Y_{it} is either the percentage share of informal employment or the yearly change in this share (from Rosstat), and V_{it} is either the number of victims from violent attacks against businessmen (from Belokurova 2014), or the number of murders, robberies or violent robberies, respectively, per year and region. P_{it} is the number of raiding attacks per capita, year and region, X_{it} is a vector of controls, r_i are region and y_t are year-fixed effects to control for region and time-specific characteristics, and ϵ is the error term.

We then also use an OLS model for the year 2012 with data for 37 regions, with the BEEPS measures on competition from the informal economy as dependent variable (Eq. 2),

$$Y_{it} = \beta_0 + \beta_1 V_{it} + \beta_2 P_{it} + \beta_3 X_{it} + \epsilon \tag{2}$$

where Y_{it} is either the percentage of firms that have experienced competition from the informal sector in a given region, or the indicator measuring the intensity of such competition (BEEPS 2012). V_{it} is either the per capita mean of the overall number of violent attacks against businessmen in a given region between 1998 and 2010 (from Belokurova 2014), or the number of murders, robberies or violent robberies, respectively, per year and region. P_{it} is the per capita mean of the overall number of raiding attacks per region between 1999 and 2010, X_{it} is a vector of controls, and ϵ is the error term.

Results

Table 1 presents our first set of results, using the Rosstat measure of informal employment (i.e. employment outside the corporate sector) as an independent variable. In specifications 1–4, we look on the effect of business-related and other forms of violence on the dynamics of informal employment in Russian regions, while specifications 5 and 6 look on how these measures affect informal employment as a percentage share of overall employment.

It seems that a strong link between various forms of violence and non-corporate employment does indeed exist. Interestingly, while various proxies for violence are positively and significantly correlated with the growth of self-employment and unincorporated microbusinesses (as opposed to incorporated businesses), other non-violence related crime indicators such as the amount of non-violent robberies do not seem to have an effect.

Here it is important to note that the forms of small businesses at the border between legality and illegality captured by the Rosstat measure of informality are not necessarily the small and medium businesses often hailed as the most innovative and dynamic elements in a market economy, but rather precarious forms of low-quality employment. The results we find thus make intuitive sense. In regions with high levels of violence, the percentage of workers engaged in various semi-legal and low-quality activities is also higher.

For now, our specification does not allow us to make any claims on causality. In other words, while it makes sense that higher shares of various low-quality activities are correlated with higher levels of violence, we cannot say for certain that higher levels of violence are causing an increase in informal employment, although violence seems to have a positive effect on the growth rate of informal employment for the years 2006–2010. Using the Rosstat measure, we also cannot draw conclusions on the propensity of larger firms to stay in the shadow economy. Indeed, property rights insecurity as proxied by the amount of raiding attacks does not seem to have an effect on informal employment in our various specifications.

In order to see what affects the decisions of larger economic entities to conduct their activities in the informal economy or not, it might thus make more sense to use the informality measure derived from the BEEPS (2012) survey instead (Table 2). Here we see that the intensity of corporate raiding activity in a given region now has indeed a positive and significant effect on the size of the informal sector. In regions where competition from the informal sector was more intense (specifications 1–4, Table 2) and where more firms experienced competition from the informal sector (specifications 5 and 6, Table 2), the average number of raiding attacks was also significantly higher. In addition, the number of applications to the self-defense organization BaC also has a positive correlation, although here the effect is not statistically significant.

Interestingly, in contrast to the results described in Table 1, the degree of physical violence now seems to have a consistently *negative* effect on the amount of competition from the informal sector across various measures and specifications.

One possible interpretation for these findings is that firms do indeed hide in the informal sector from predatory pressure by state officials and criminal groups. This result would be in accord with anecdotal and interview evidence described elsewhere (Rochlitz 2014). Up to a certain size and extent of corporate activity, staying in the shadow economy could

Table 1 Informal Employment (Rosstat), Violence and Violent Pressure on Business (OLS)

	Informal Employment (% change from last year)				*Informal Employment (% share of overall employment)*	
	1)	*2)*	*3)*	*4)*	*5)*	*6)*
Violent attacks on businessmen[1]	**428.91***** **(126.5)**				**315.13***** **(83.73)**	
Murder cases[1]		**314.28*** **(185.29)**				116.82 (71.26)
Robberies[1] (article 161)			5.884 (9.584)			
Violent robbery[1] (article 162)				**135.48*** **(79.114)**		
Raiding attacks[2]	28.628 (97.803)	111.63 (107.93)	52.754 (106.23)	24.87 (112.53)	57.3 (65.44)	55.44 (81.441)
GRP	0.0098 (0.032)	0.0053 (0.029)	−0.004 (0.033)	−0.008 (0.319)	−0.004 (0.022)	−0.001 (0.021)
GRP growth	0.051 (0.066)	0.058 (0.07)	0.072 (0.07)	0.08 (0.065)	−0.046 (0.039)	−0.024 (0.04)
Population below poverty line (in %)	−0.0009 (0.0019)	0.0006 (0.0018)	0.0004 (0.0019)	0.0008 (0.0019)	**−0.002***** **(0.0006)**	**−0.001***** **(0.0005)**
Unemployment	0.001 (0.0032)	0.0019 (0.0025)	0.0016 (0.0026)	0.0026 (0.0026)	−0.0003 (0.001)	0.0001 (0.001)
% of population living in cities	−0.0065 (0.116)	−0.0069 (0.0112)	−0.0067 (0.0116)	−0.007 (0.011)	**−0.006**** **(0.002)**	**−0.006**** **(0.002)**

Population	0.108	0.096	0.107	0.16	0.0046	−0.0001
	(0.078)	(0.063)	(0.082)	(0.079)	(0.0212)	(0.002)
% Russians	−0.932	0.137	0.092	0.121	−0.107	0.06
	(1.287)	(0.188)	(0.196)	(0.196)	(0.2)	(0.2)
Time & Region FE	yes	yes	yes	yes	yes	yes
Observations	306	322	322	322	537	566
R-squared	0.2879	0.3037	0.2783	0.2902	0.8512	0.856

Ordinary Least Squares; standard errors clustered on regions; *** 1 % significance level, ** 5 % significance level, * 10 % significance level; 1) per capita in a given region; 2) divided by the number of firms in a given region.

thus help firms to evade the attention of predatory state agencies that might only become aware of the firm's activities once the firm has to apply for and comply with the manifold regulations and controls that come with being registered officially in Russia's economy.

On the other hand, in regions with high levels of physical violence, the trade-off between hiding from the authorities and benefiting from at least a certain degree of protection from the police might play in favour of keeping your business officially registered. This might explain the consistent negative correlation between physical violence and informality we find in Table 2.

A similar but somewhat more sinister interpretation is that in regions where state agencies have successfully managed to establish control over the local economy, levels of violence are lower as the monopoly of violence is in the hands of the state (and not in the hands of various competing criminal groups that periodically would fight over influence, thus creating spikes in violence). Because regional state agencies control the economy, predation and corruption are centralized (as described in Shleifer and Vishny 1993). The problem is that if all firms would be registered in the formal economy, they have to pay taxes which are less easy to steal and probably have to be transferred to the federal centre. On the other hand, firms in the informal economy can pay regional state agencies directly for protection instead of having to pay taxes to the state, and those state agencies can then more easily keep the money for themselves. As put by Yuri Gervis (Moscow News 2010):

> For the businessman, it really makes no difference whom he pays – whether it's the cops in a grey scheme or the government in a white scheme. But people who make money off this don't like it one bit – they don't want the businessman to pay to the government.[2]

In sum, the empirical evidence described in Tables 1 and 2 is consistent with a story where some regions are characterized by competing criminal groups, higher levels of physical violence, decentralized predation, less sophisticated economic activity and a higher percentage of low-quality and precarious employment. Such regions would most probably also be less economically dynamic, with the firms in the official economy not experiencing significant levels of competition from the informal economy.

On the other hand, in regions where state agencies have the monopoly of violence and have thus managed to limit the level of physical violence, predation might have a more centralized nature with various raiding and

Table 2 Competition from the Informal Sector (BEEPS 2012), Violence and Violent Pressure on Business (OLS)

	Competition from Informal Sector as obstacle to current operations (BEEPS 2012, question E.30)				*Competition from the Informal Sector (BEEPS 2012, quest. E.11)*	
	1)	*2)*	*3)*	*4)*	*5)*	*6)*
Violent attacks on businessmen[1, 3]	**−52.689*****			**−46.729****	**−21.261*****	**−19.917****
	(18.19)			**(21.731)**	**(6.943)**	**(7.126)**
Murder cases[1]		**−2.932***				
		(1.656)				
Violent robbery[1] (article 162)			**−1.682***			
			(0.975)			
Raiding attacks[2,4]	**18.443****	**18.188***	**19.493***		**6.553****	
	(8.653)	**(9.549)**	**(10.127)**		**(2.91)**	
BaC applications[2, 5]				0.655		0.254
				(0.9504)		(0.349)
GRP	0.139	**0.3008****	**0.22***	0.152	0.049	0.542
	(0.116)	**(0.117)**	**(0.115)**	(0.126)	(0.046)	(0.053)
GRP growth	−2.355	−1.44	−0.97	−1.231	−0.119	0.297
	(2.099)	(2.316)	(2.59)	(2.27)	(0.559)	(0.589)
Population below poverty line (in %)	0.009	0.005	0.003	0.002	0.009	0.0067
	(0.018)	(0.019)	(0.015)	(0.0197)	(0.006)	(0.007)
Unemployment	−0.009	0.031	0.024	0.0095	0.0017	0.0085
	(0.033)	(0.034)	(0.039)	(0.036)	(0.0117)	(0.0121)
% of population living in cities	−0.001	−0.003	0.0002	0.003	0.0004	0.002
	(0.007)	(0.007)	(0.008)	(0.007)	(0.0017)	(0.0016)
Population	−0.0003	−0.008	−0.003	−0.0005	−0.0003	−0.0004
	(0.0056)	(0.005)	(0.005)	(0.0053)	(0.002)	(0.0022)

(*continued*)

Table 2 (continued)

	Competition from Informal Sector as obstacle to current operations (BEEPS 2012, question E.30)				*Competition from the Informal Sector (BEEPS 2012, quest. E.11)*	
	1)	*2)*	*3)*	*4)*	*5)*	*6)*
% Russians	0.008	−0.075	0.09	−0.049	0.025	0.0026
	(0.354)	(0.349)	(0.331)	(0.39)	(0.089)	(0.091)
Observations	37	37	37	37	37	37
R-squared	0.2775	0.2326	0.2337	0.2371	0.2657	0.2269

Ordinary Least Squares; standard errors clustered on regions; *** 1 % significance level, ** 5 % significance level, * 10 % significance level; 1) per thousand people in a given region; 2) per thousand firms in a given region; 3) mean of the overall number of violent attacks against businessmen in a given region between 1998 and 2010, source Belokurova (2014); 4) mean of the overall number of raiding attacks per region between 1999 and 2010, source Rochlitz (2014); 5) overall number of applications between 2011 and 2013.

predatory activities by state agencies being more intense. These regions are richer and are also characterized by a higher degree of competition from the informal sector (as seen by the positive and significant link between GRP and informal competition in some specifications of Table 2).

While one possible explanation for the higher share of informality in these regions might be that successful firms prefer to stay unregistered to hide from predatory state agencies, an alternative explanation is that state agencies actually encourage or force firms to stay informal, as this makes it easier to extract various informal payments and enforce transfers of property.

Conclusion

What determines the decision of firms to stay in the informal economy is a question that has been studied from many different angles. This chapter explores the significant heterogeneity in business-related violence and informal sector size that can be found across Russia's regions to study the relationship between violence and informality.

As compared to cross-country studies, such an approach has the advantage that country-specific effects such as language, culture or national laws and regulations can be held constant. Apart from having a large number of heterogeneous regions, Russia is also well-suited to study this question as levels of business-related violence have remained high throughout the 2000s, while the size of the informal economy has after a decline at the beginning of the decade again continuously increased, despite high levels of economic growth during the first two presidencies of Vladimir Putin.

Using different measures of informality and business-related violence, the chaper finds that that regions where firms experience a higher degree of competition from the informal sector are also characterized by higher levels of corporate raiding attacks, while exhibiting lower levels of direct physical violence. These findings are consistent with a story where firms evade or are forced to stay in the informal economy in regions with centralized predation, but prefer to stay in the formal economy in regions with decentralized predation.

Notes

1. Yuri Gervis (lawyer of Evroset founder Evgenyi Chichvarkin) in an interview with the author; see also Arutunyan, A. (2010) "Customs, Contraband and Chichvarkin", *The Moscow News*, 11 September 2010, v.4484, no. 61, p. 11, http://themoscownews.com/business/20101108/188185233.html.

2. http://themoscownews.com/business/20101108/188185233.html (accessed on 14 August 2015).

References

Aldabergenova, B. (2010). Reyderstvo – sestra korruptsii ili chleb bednykh chinovnikov? (Raiding – sister of corruption or daily bread of poor state officials?). *Yevraziskiy Yuridicheskiy Zhurnal, 1*(20), 116–120.

Antunes, A., & Cavalcanti, T. (2007). Start up costs, limited enforcement, and the hidden economy. *European Economic Review, 51*(1), 203–224.

Aruoba, B. (2010). *Informal Sector, Government Policy and Institutions* (Working Paper).

Auriol, E., & Warlters, M. (2005). Taxation base in developing countries. *Journal of Public Economics, 89*, 625–646.

Baranov, A., Malkov, E., Polishchuk, L., Rochlitz, M., & Syunaev, G. (2015). How (Not) to mesure Russian regional institutions. *Voprosy Ekonomiki, 87*(2), 69–103.

Barsukova, S., & Radaev, V. (2012). Informal economy in Russia: A brief overview. *Economic Sociology, 13*(2), 4–12.

Belokurova, G. (2014). *When does business turn violent? Elections and business-related violence in Russia, 1995–2010* (Working paper).

Bloom D., Ratnikov K., Osipov K., & Areshev S. (2003). Corporate Takeovers, Russian Style: How to Defend Against Them. New York: Coudert Brothers LLP.

Botero, J., Djankov, S., La Porta, R., Lopez-de-Silanes, F., & Shleifer, A. (2004). The Regulation of Labor. *Quarterly Journal of Economics, 119*(4), 1339–1382.

Buch, C., Heinrich, R., Lusinyan, L., & Schrooten, M. (2000). *Russia's Debt Crisis and the Unofficial Economy* (Kiel Working paper No. 978). Kiel: Institute of World Economics.

Busato, F., Chiarini, B., & Marchetti, E. (2011). Indeterminacy, underground activities and tax evasion. *Economic Modelling, 28*(3), 831–844.

Cebula, R. (1997). An empirical analysis of the impact of government tax and auditing policies on the size of the underground economy: The case of the United States, 1973–94. *American Journal of Economics and Sociology, 56*(2), 73–186.

Choi, J., & Thum, M. (2005). Corruption and the shadow economy. *International Economic Review, 46*(3), 817–836.

Chong, A., & Gradstein, M. (2007). Inequality and informality. *Journal of Public Economics, 91*, 159–179.

Dabla-Norris E., & Inchauste G. (2008). Informality and Regulations: What Drives the Growth of Firms? *IMF Staff Papers*, 55(1): 50–82.

D'Hernoncourt, J., & Meon, P. (2012). The not so dark side of trust: Does trust increase the size of the shadow economy? *Journal of Economic Behavior & Organization, 81*(1), 97–121.

Dreher, A., Kotsogiannis, C., & McCorriston, S. (2009). How do institutions affect corruption and the shadow economy? *International Tax and Public Finance, 16*(6), 773–796.

Echazu, L., & Bose, P. (2008). Corruption, centralization, and the shadow economy. *Southern Economic Journal, 75*(2), 524–537.

Elgin, C. (2010). *Political turnover, taxes and the shadow economy* (Working paper). Bogazici University.

Estrin, S., & Mickiewicz, T. (2010). Shadow economy and entrepreneurial entry. *Review of Development Economics, 16*(4), 559–578.

Frye, T. (2002). Capture or exchange? Business lobbying in Russia. *Europe-Asia Studies, 54*(7), 1017–1036.Gaddy C., & Ickes B. (2002). *Russia's Virtual Economy.* Washington, D.C.: Brookings Institution Press.

Gaddy C., & Ickes B. (2002). *Russia's Virtual Economy* Washington, D.C.: Brookings Institution Press.

Gans-Morse, J. (2012a). *The end of a violent era: The role of force in Russian business conflicts* (Working paper). Northwestern University.

Gans-Morse, J. (2012b). Threats to property rights in Russia: From private coercion to state aggression. *Post-Soviet Affairs, 28*(3), 263–295.

Giles, D., & Tedds, L. (2002). *Taxes and the Canadian underground economy* (Canadian Tax Papers 106). Toronto: Canadian Tax Foundation.

Gimpelson, V., & Kapeliushnikov, R. (2014). *Between light and shadow: Informality in the Russian labour market* (IZA discussion papers No. 8279).

Grossman, G. (1989). Informal personal incomes and outlays of the Soviet urban population. In A. Portes et al. (Eds.), *The informal economy: Studies in advanced and less developed countries* (pp. 150–170). Baltimore and London: The Johns Hopkins University Press.

Hoffman, D. (2002). *The Oligarchs: Wealth and power in the New Russia.* New York: Public Affairs.

Johnson, S., Kaufman, D., & Zoido-Lobaton, P. (1998). Regulatory discretion and the unofficial economy. *American Economic Review Papers and Proceedings, 88*, 387–392.

Johnson, S., Kaufman, D., McMillan, J., & Woodruff, C. (2000). What do firms hide? Bribes and unofficial activity after communism. *Journal of Public Economics, 76*, 495–520.

Karlinger, L. (2009). The underground economy in the late 1990s: Evading taxes, or evading competition? *World Development, 37*(10), 1600–1611.

Kazun, A. (2015). Violent corporate raiding in Russia: Preconditions and protective factors. *Demokratizatsiya, 23*(4), 459–484.

Lehman, H., & Zaiceva, A. (2015). Redefining informality and measuring its determinants: Evidence from the Russian labour market. *Journal of International Development*. doi:10.1002/jid.3062.

Lehman, H., Razzolini, T., & Zaiceva, A. (2011). *Job separations and informality in the Russian labour market* (IZA discussion paper No. 6230). Bonn: Institute for the Study of Labor.

Nugent, J., & Sukiassyan, G. (2009). Alternative strategies for firms in oppressive and corrupt states: Informality or formality via business associations? *Contemporary Economic Policy, 27*(4), 423–439.

Privalov, A., & Volkov, A. (2007). Rashushdeniye o reyderstve po metode Barona Kyuve (Thinking about raiding by following the method of Baron Cuvier). *Ekspert*, May 14, 18(559). Available from: http://expert.ru/expert/2007/18/sobstvennost/.

Rochlitz, M. (2014). Corporate raiding and the role of the state in Russia. *Post-Soviet Affairs, 30*(2–3), 89–114.

Rochlitz, M., Kazun A., & Yakovlev A. (2016). Unter Räubern - Russland: Investitionsrisiko Unternehmensplünderungen. *Osteuropa*(66(5), 95–110.

Rosser, J., Rosser, M., & Ahmed, E. (2000). Income inequality and the informal economy in transition economies. *Journal of Comparative Economics, 28*(1), 156–171.

Sabirianova-Peter, K. (2009). *Income tax flattening: Does it help to reduce the shadow economy?* (IZA discussion papers No. 4223).

Sakwa, R. (2014). *Putin and the oligarch: The Khodorkovsky-Yukos affair*. London: I.B. Tauris.

Salahodjaev, R. (2015). Intelligence and shadow economy: A cross-country empirical assessment. *Intelligence, 49*, 129–133.

Sampson, S. (1987). The second economy of the Soviet Union and Eastern Europe. *Annals of the American Academy of Political and Social Science, 493*, 120–136.

Shleifer, A., & Vishny, R. (1993). Corruption. *The Quarterly Journal of Economics, 108*(3), 599–617.

Szakonyi, D. (2015). *Renting higher office: Firm-;level returns from connections to elected politicians* (Working paper). Columbia University.

Teobaldelli, D. (2011). Federalism and the shadow economy. *Public Choice, 146*(3–4), 269–289.

Teobaldelli, D., & Schneider, F. (2012). *Beyond the veil of ignorance: The influence of direct democracy on the shadow economy* (Working Paper).

Torgler, B., & Schneider, F. (2009). The impact of tax morale and institutional quality on the shadow economy. *Journal of Economic Psychology, 30*(2), 228–245.

Treisman, D. (1999). Russia's tax crisis: Explaining falling revenues in a transitional economy. *Economics and Politics, 11*(2), 145–169.

Volkov, V. (2000). Between economy and the state: Private security and rule enforcement in Russia. *Politics & Society, 28*(4), 483–501.

Volkov, V. (2002). *Violent entrepreneurs: The use of force in the making of Russian capitalism*. Ithaca: Cornell University Press.

Williams, C. C., & Horodnic, I. A. (2015a). Evaluating the prevalence of the undeclared economy in Central and Eastern Europe: An institutional asymmetry perspective. *European Journal of Industrial Relations, 21*(4), 389–406.

Williams, C. C., & Horodnic, I. A. (2015b). Tackling the informal economy in South East Europe: An institutional approach. *Journal of South East European and Black Sea Studies, 15*(4), 519–539.

Williams, C. C., & Horodnic, I. A. (2015c). Explaining and tackling the shadow economy in Estonia, Latvia and Lithuania: A tax morale approach. *Journal of Baltic Economics, 15*(2), 81–98.

Yakovlev, A. (2000). Pochemu v Rossii Vozmozhen Bezriskovy Ukhod ot Nalogov? (Why Is Low-Risk Tax Evasion Possible in Russia?). *Voprosy Ekonomiki, 11*, 142–146.

Yakovlev, A. (2006). The evolution of business-state interaction in Russia: From state capture to business capture. *Europe-Asia Studies, 53*(1), 1033–1056.

Yakovlev A. (2011). State-Business Relations in Russia in the 2000s: From the Capture Model to a Variety of Exchange Models? Bofit Discussion Paper No. 10/2011.

Yakovlev, A., Sobolev, A., & Kazun, A. (2014). Means of production versus means of coercion: Can Russian business limit the violence of a predatory state? *Post-Soviet Affairs, 30*(2-3), 171–194.

Labor Informality in Mexico: An Indicator Analysis

Rogelio Varela Llamas, Ramón A. Castillo Ponce, and Juan Manuel Ocegueda Hernández

Introduction

The recent performance of Mexico on some economic indicators has been a cause for concern for policymakers, the business and consumer sectors, and international organizations including the Organization for Economic Co-operation and Development (OECD) and the International Labour Organization (ILO). Weak growth of gross domestic product, and a rise in unemployment, has led to the worsening of poverty and an increase in social marginalization. Individuals joining the labor force and not finding a job represent a challenge for economic policy. Likewise, informal labor, which is tied to small and micro establishments with low productivity and

R.V. Llamas (✉) • J.M.O. Hernández
Department of Economics and International Relations, Universidad Autónoma de Baja California (UABC), Tijuana, Mexico
e-mail: rvarela@uabc.edu.mx, jmocegueda@uabc.edu.mx

R.A.C. Ponce
Department of Economics and International Relations, Universidad Autónoma de Baja California (UABC), Tijuana, Mexico

Department of Economics and Statistics, California State University, Los Angeles, CA, USA
e-mail: racastillo2000@yahoo.com

A. Polese et al. (eds.), *The Informal Economy in Global Perspective*, International Political Economy Series,
DOI 10.1007/978-3-319-40931-3_11

limited capacity for innovation and entrepreneurship, also constitutes a fundamental challenge that needs to be addressed. In this context, and in light of recent developments, analyzing the phenomenon of informality in the labor market is of fundamental importance.

The objective of this chapter is to identify some of the factors that explain the probability of belonging to the informal labor market. To that end, data from Mexico's National Survey of Occupation and Employment (ENOE) is examined. The survey provides unit-level data that allows for the study of individual households in the Mexican economy. The chapter is divided into four sections. The main theoretical approaches that shed light on the phenomenon of informality, as well as the empirical evidence, are described in the first section, "Review of the Literature on Informality". In the second section, "Indicators of Economic Performance and Informality", a discussion on indicators of labor market performance is conducted. An empirical exercise considering a logistic regression is developed in the next section, "Logistic Regression Analysis: Discussion of Results", followed by a conclusion.

Review of the Literature on Informality

Theoretical Approaches: An Explanation

The literature examining the phenomenon of informality in the labor market considers various theoretical approaches. The discussion we present here is not intended to be an exhaustive survey of them, but rather a broad description of the most commonly referred to approaches: *exclusion* and *exit* (Perry et al. 2007; Williams and Round 2010; Williams and Youssef 2014; Williams et al. 2011). In general, exclusion leads to a type of informality that is basically involuntary, derived from a segmentation of the labor market, while under the exit viewpoint informality is seen as voluntary and associated with net benefits. In particular, the exclusion approach suggests the existence of a dual economy where dynamic competitiveness in the labor market does not prevail and there are barriers for the workforce to navigate between the formal and informal sectors (Harris and Todaro 1970). The existence of modern and stagnant sectors is considered, where the latter is at a productive and technological disadvantage. The modern sector is where formal jobs are generated. It faces structural problems that limit its capacity to generate the jobs that the workforce demands. Ros (2010), for instance, states that informality is the result of the inability of the formal sector to absorb the workforce. This situation is closely related to a process of slow economic growth. On the other hand, the exit approach posits that a worker's decision to join a sector is both voluntary and optimal. Perry et al. (2007) stress this point and illustrate the labor market as highly competitive.

Meanwhile, De Soto (1989) suggests that the phenomenon of informality is not explained by the existence of institutional rigidities, barriers to entry or mobility between sectors, as highlighted by the exclusion approach. In his opinion it arises from difficulties with the regulatory framework some governments implement to take action against certain social groups. The author argues that workers conduct a cost–benefit analysis and decide to participate in the informal sector voluntarily and rationally. For Maloney (2004), an individual's decision to join a given sector is influenced by the existence of incentives. The fact that a worker becomes part of the informal sector does not necessarily mean that said worker is at a relative disadvantage.

The processes of exclusion and exit that pushes workers towards labor informality vary from country to country, between regions and productive sectors. The literature states that being an informal worker does not make one part of a social segment where there is a higher rate of poverty and lower standards of living. On average, formal workers earn higher salaries, but there may be exceptions where an informal worker earns an even higher wage. Beyond the wage gap between workers and sectors, it is also important to emphasize that the growth of informal activities is related to incentives that encourage it. Levy (2008) claims that social security provides such an incentive. He makes the point using the Mexican social security program. He notes that the informal population does not choose to venture into formality because of the low cost of social insurance relative to acquiring non-government provided forms of social security, but rather because they receive a net benefit from being informal.

From an exclusion perspective, society should strive to implement proactive policies that affect economic growth in the medium and long term to strengthen the capacity to generate formal employment and labor productivity. The exit viewpoint proposes the elimination of factors that encourage the decision to join the informal sector. It promotes the creation of a competitive and productive modern sector so there can be improvements in workers' wages and social security.

Another important aspect about informality highlighted in De Soto (1989) refers to the complexity of the rules that can inhibit the transition of small businesses towards the formal labor market. Significant taxation, accompanied by excessive regulations, can lead firms to remain in the informal sector, thereby harming their growth dynamic and productive efficiency. It should be noted that beyond the arguments formulated under the exclusion and exit approaches, in the case of the Latin American and Caribbean economies the phenomenon of informality is multidimensional. That is, not only does slow growth and institutional inefficiency influence the development of the informal sector, but other factors such as work experience, level of education, gender, marital status and whether workers live in an urban or rural area affect the worker's decision to become informal.

Saracho et al. (2015), for instance, point out that informality is closely related to corruption, which is linked to low productivity and lack of competitiveness in the economy. They suggest that, in addition to formalizing companies, employment should also be formalized. Typically, informality increases in periods of crisis and decreases during expansions. However, in some countries the informal sector has surged even though the economy was growing. This suggests that there are other factors, apart from economic cycles, that influence workers entering the informal sector.

In sum, explaining informality in the labor market is not a trivial task and requires going beyond the traditional approaches. This point is highlighted in Samaniego (2008), who views informality as heterogeneous and complex in its nature and causes. He recommends reconciling both approaches, rather than stressing the predominance of one approach or another. According to the author, the economic policies they propose could be complementary, not exclusionary.

Empirical Literature: Some Findings

Empirical exercises evaluating the phenomenon of informality have considered different explanatory variables, historical contexts and databases. In the case of the Mexican economy, Alcaraz et al. (2008) find that formal workers earn more, on average, than their informal counterparts. It is thought that in the short term informal workers may profit. In the long run, however, they experience a wage penalty. As such, the existence of rigidities in the labor market increases informality. In this discussion, it is also noted that the level of education of a worker should be included as an explanatory variable. In less developed countries the levels tend to be inferior relative to developed economies. This results in a negative effect on labor productivity and integration into the formal sector (Brandt 2011). Moreover, Levy (2008) reasserts that social insurance can be a distorting element in the labor market. In this sense, Zonszein (2012) acknowledges that informality is the result of the absence of an industrial policy that promotes productive investment capable of generating employment. Rivera (2011) proposes several variables that may explain informality. For example, the author notes that women, because of their activities at home such as child care, are more likely to participate in the informal sector. For Freije (2002), age is also a relevant variable. Young workers with little work experience are more likely to enter informality.

Maloney (1999) finds evidence that workers move between the formal and informal sectors, which supposes unrestricted mobility and the existence of non-segmented markets. Mobility across sectors would be produced by certain incentives that trigger informality and not because the worker is predisposed to belong to it. Ruiz and Ordaz (2011) identify the Mexican economy as one that has not generated sufficient formal employment, where temporary jobs have increased in relation to permanent jobs. Recently, Robles (2015) determined that informality is a product of both exit and exclusion factors. The author notes that a married individual is more likely to participate in the informal sector if he is excluded from formal activities. It is argued, as well, that as the age of an individual increases, he is less likely to transit from formality to informality, because of the social insurance that the formal sector provides. Education, regarded as an exclusion variable, may also contribute to informality: having a greater level of education reduces the probability of being part of informality as educated workers reap the benefits of high human capital.

Various studies have identified labor informality in Mexico as high and persistent. It declines during periods of economic recovery and rises in times of crisis (OIT 2014). According to Bayón From the first quarter of (2006), job creation in Mexico in recent years has been associated with traditional sectors, primary and secondary, where microenterprises play a major role. He notes that domestic work and unqualified self-employment constituted almost half of the urban population in 2002. Hence, a large number of people lived without social protection in the country. Another relevant study for the case of Mexico is Esquivel and Ordaz (2008), who empirically evaluate the hypothesis that social programs have increased labor informality. Their results indicate that there is no impact. The authors find that the informality rate remained stable over the period of study and also that there was no wage premium for informal work. Finally, in Loayza and Sugawara (2009) informality is modeled not as the result of a single cause, but a consequence of a set of factors that have to do with the shortcomings of public services and the existence of a burdensome regulatory regime.

Indicators of Economic Performance and Informality

To understand the phenomenon of labor informality in Mexico, it is necessary to recognize the performance of aggregate economic activity and the evolution of formal unemployment, as both variables are closely related to informality. The annual change in real gross domestic product (GDP) has been relatively unstable, especially during the period from the first quarter of 2005 to the third quarter of 2015. From 2006 to 2008 GDP decreased, accelerating its decline in 2009 when the growth rate was −8 %. Without doubt, this behavior is linked to the international crisis initiated in the USA during 2008–2009. In early 2010 a recovery in economic activity was observed, reaching a positive change in the second quarter of 2010 of about 6 %. However, thereafter the level of activity has fallen. Until the third quarter of 2015, growth was slightly above 2 % (see Fig. 1). This situation has meant a loss in the economy's capacity to generate formal employment and the ability to meet social demands in terms of employment. The trajectory exhibited by GDP variation is most likely the

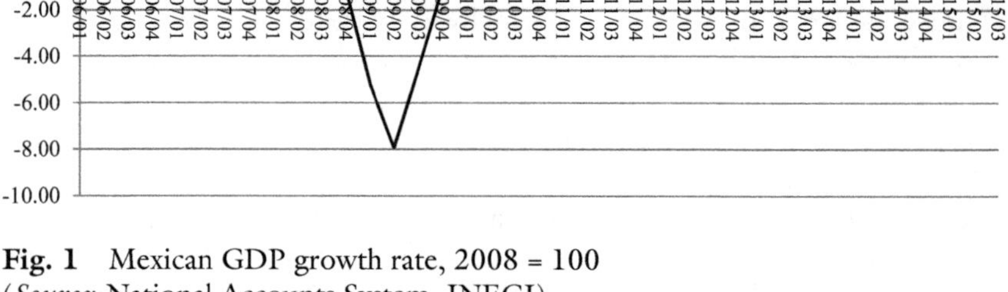

Fig. 1 Mexican GDP growth rate, 2008 = 100
(*Source*: National Accounts System, INEGI)

result of structural failures, including low productivity and competitiveness, exacerbated by transitory events. Another factor that may be contributing to this performance is inadequate physical and human capital formation, which has limited the productive potential of the economy. It is equally important to note that the labor force has shown significant growth, representing additional pressure on the labor market.

In terms of the unemployment rate, it fluctuated around 3 % from 2005 to 2008. However, between the third and fourth quarters of 2009 it slightly exceeded 6 %. It practically doubled from one year to another, suggesting that the decline in economic activity significantly affected the labor market. From the first quarter of 2010 to the third quarter of 2015, the rate exhibited a downward trajectory, revealing a slight recovery in formal employment. It should be noted that, although the trend is downward, the unemployment rate has not descended to the levels exhibited prior to 2008, between 3 % and 4 %. The current expectation is that, as the economy recovers and grows at 3 % or higher, the level of employment will also rise.

When analyzing employment by gender, some peculiarities in the data are found. In the period before the crisis, the unemployment rate of men was inferior to that of women. That is, women had a more difficult task in finding jobs than men. Beginning in 2009, both rates spiked and remained at a level of about 5 % on average until 2014. In the third trimester of 2015, however, the unemployment rate of women slightly exceeded that of men again. Also, the gap in unemployment by gender was more pronounced before the crisis (see Fig. 2).

Another strategic indicator of the labor market reported by National Institute of Statistics and Geography (INEGI from its name in Spanish) is participation rate in the informal sector. This measure is reported at the national and state levels. The variable ORIS_1 represents the proportion of the employed population working in an informal non-agricultural economic unit (establishment), with respect to the total working population. ORIS_2 is the proportion of the employed population working in a non-agricultural and informal economic unit relative to total non-agricultural employment. Both correspond to a definition of informality strictly linked to an informal establishment, defined as one that conducts business activities based on household resources and that is not constituted as formal business. Its income and equipment are not independent and/or distinguishable from those of the household. The graphical illustration of the evolution of these two indicators shows that ORIS_2 is higher than ORIS_1, that is

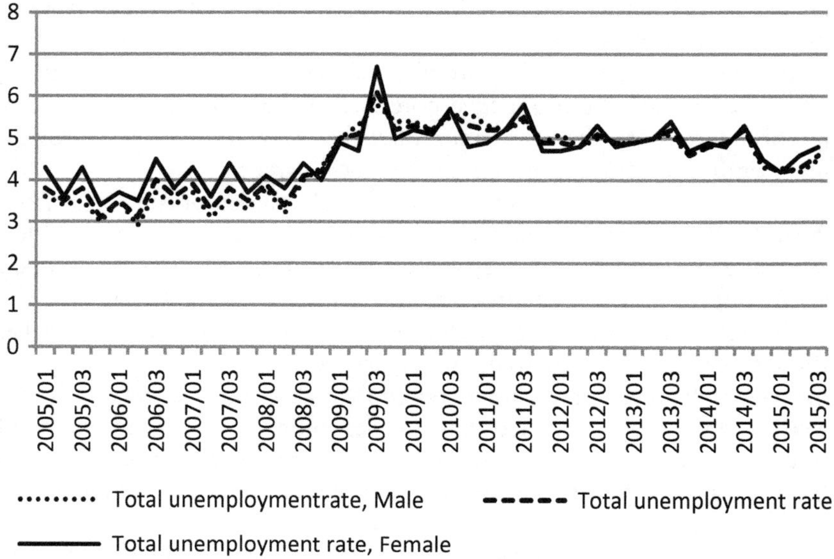

Fig. 2 Unemployment rate of the Mexican economy (*Source*: National Survey of Occupation and Employment, ENOE-INEGI)

to say, the ratio of those employed in the non-agricultural informal sector with respect to the total non-agricultural employed population is higher. We notice that ORIS_2 is located within a range of 31.2 % and 33.7 %, while the ORIS_1 fluctuates between 26.8 % and 29.1 %. In both cases it is interesting to note that they have remained virtually unchanged over time; no significant highs or lows are observed (see Fig. 3).

The rate of labor informality (RLI) is also reported by INEGI. Its computation considers the number of people working in unregistered economic units or in the informal sector, and also those occupied in the paid domestic sector with no social security, self-employed in subsistence agriculture, non-paid workers and subordinate paid employees that lack social security. RLI is a broad indicator that covers the phenomenon of informality from the establishment to the different modalities of informal employment. Specifically, RLI_1 measures the proportion of the working population previously described with respect to the total working population. On the other hand, RLI_2 measures the proportion of the non-agricultural occupied population in the informal sector but

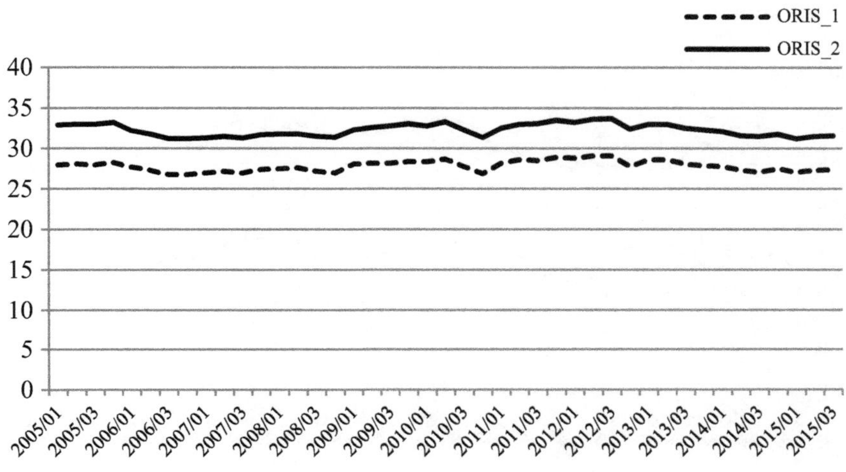

Fig. 3 Participation rate in the informal sector (ORIS)
(*Source*: National Survey of Occupation and Employment, ENOE-INEGI)

with respect to the total non-agricultural working population (INEGI 2014). From the first quarter of 2005 RLI_1 tended to decline, reaching a minimum level of 57.7 % in the third quarter of 2007. Thereafter it exhibited an upward trend with a peak in the fourth quarter of 2009 at 60 %. Starting in 2010 a decline in informality could be observed, it fell to 57.6 % in the first quarter of 2015 and 57.8 % in the third quarter of the same year (see Fig. 4).

From the graphical evidence above, it is clear that when the unemployment rate decreases labor informality does not fall sharply. According to the OIT (2014), the reduction of formal unemployment has coexisted with a high and persistent informal employment. Notice that in the sample period the highest rate of informality was 60 %, which was reached in the fourth quarter of 2009. For the third quarter of 2015 the same remained at 58.8 %, not a very significant decline. Given the nature of the phenomenon under study, the question that comes to mind is *what policies have been implemented to reduce informality in Mexico?*

Samaniego (2008) outlines policies that can be bundled into three phases, the first comprises the period known as "stabilizing development" (1955–1975). During this period informality is considered a temporary phenomenon that would decline as the economy develops. The second phase has its origins in the middle of the 1970s, where informality increases

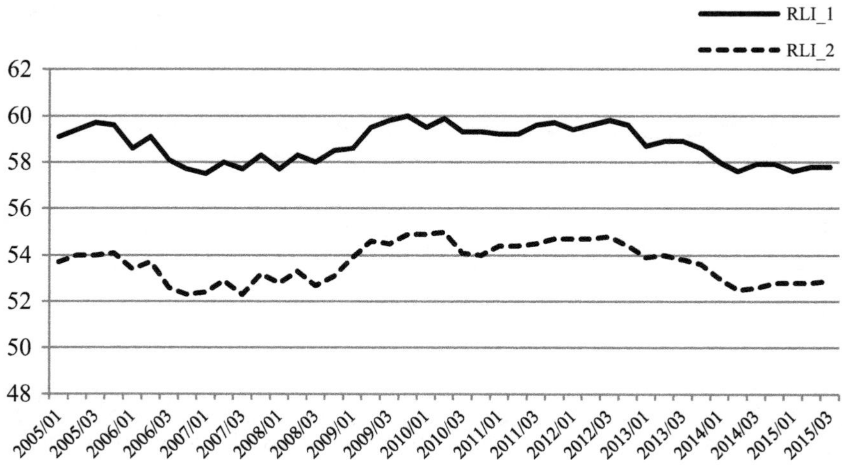

Fig. 4 Informality rates (RLI)
(*Source*: National Survey of Occupation and Employment, ENOE-INEGI)

and is associated, according to the author, with a loss of dynamism in the modern sector of the economy. It is then that policymakers start to appreciate the size and importance of the phenomenon. At the start of the 1980s, employment policies directed at the formal sector are implemented. They included programs to promote employment, placement services, and retraining of the workforce that was displaced by the debt crisis. The third phase is implemented sometime during the 1980s and 1990s, when scattered and poorly focused actions are the norm. For example, soft loans and tax advice are offered at the national and regional levels. Success stories are widely publicized to promote political agendas but are not part of an articulated nationwide plan to address informality.

Currently, the ILO recommends not ignoring the phenomenon of informality or just viewing it as a residual event that will be solved with higher growth and the promotion of formal employment. It argues that an appropriate strategy should not only address the need for formal employment, but also the need to align incentives to encourage the transition from one sector to another. It warns of the need to boost exports for companies linked to international trade in order to generate more jobs and supply chains within domestic markets. The ILO itself suggest, as part of corporate development, implementing measures to facilitate the creation of formal enterprises and promote compliance with tax authorities. Also, financial institutions should not tighten the flow of credit. Instead, development banks must have a higher capacity to allocate loans so that micro, small and medium firms have greater liquidity.

Given the persistence of high rates of informality, the Mexican government in conjunction with the Ministry of Labor and Social Security unveiled in July 2013 the Programa para la Formalización del Empleo (Program to Formalize Employment). The document recognizes that, in the short term, informality is a viable alternative to the problem of unemployment. However, it also warns that informality has negative implications for a firm's productivity and competitiveness. It limits worker's access to social security, and also results in low wages and poor working conditions. It is considered a subsistence activity with no access to credit, technology or training. From a fiscal point of view, it weakens public spending and the pension system; socially, it heightens inequality for workers. One of the objectives of the program is to create a robust formal market that may improve workers' quality of life, increase productivity and competitiveness, improve access to healthcare and provide pensions.

Public policies were defined in order to achieve this and other objectives. With respect to education, for example, the proposal calls for strengthening the human capital of the workforce to boost their productivity and improve welfare. This action is framed within the context of the recent educational reform approved in Mexico, which essentially seeks to improve the quality of basic education in accordance with international standards. In regards to the labor market, the enactment of new legislation is expected to streamline the hiring process, promote productivity and encourage higher wages. The goal is to create a more competitive and flexible formal labor market. This would facilitate the incorporation of women and young workers into the formal sector. As part of the labor reform, the National Productivity Committee was created. This committee is responsible for developing policies and strategies to combat informality. For instance, it is well known that labor informality is mainly concentrated in small establishments, which normally face liquidity constraints because of barriers to access financial markets. One of the possible strategies that the committee would consider is to facilitate access to financial markets for small and medium-size firms. Sustained funding may result in more capital and improve firms' innovative capacity and ability to grow. Overall, the new strategy to reduce the levels of informal labor is framed in a series of actions linked to recent economic reforms.

At the international level, the discussion centers on the content and realism of policies directed to address the phenomenon of informality. While some commentators argue that for the most part the proposals are prudent, others recognize their theoretical value but point to a disconnect with their empirical implementation. To be fair, the content of the Program to Formalize Labor incorporates actions that are at the core of some of the proposals of international organizations such as the ILO and the Organization for Economic Cooperation and Development. For example, making an effort to improve productivity in the formal sector in order to boost wages has long been championed by these institutions. If acquiring skills and knowledge increases workers' productivity and produces higher wages, then individuals would have an incentive to improve their human capital and opt to participate in the formal sector of the economy.

Overall, the expectation is that recently adopted labor, educational and financial reforms will have a positive effect on the economy in the medium and long term. While expectations are high, one should recognize that the impact will depend on the efficiency of their implementation. It should also be noted that the Mexican economy is currently facing an adverse economic climate, which is related to the fall in international oil prices, the gradual depreciation of the peso against the dollar and forecasts of low growth for 2016. All of these factors can undermine the decline of informality in the short term.

Logistic Regression Analysis: Discussion of Results

The phenomenon of informality can be analyzed from different angles. For example, research has evaluated its consequences, evaluated the effectiveness of public policies aimed at lowering it and identified its determinants. In recent years there has been a special emphasis in the latter line of analysis. In this chapter we pursue this avenue and conduct an empirical investigation of the profile of informal workers. The methodology considers the estimation of a multivariate logit model. Our exercise builds on the study of Rivera (2011), which in turn follows Portes and Haller (2004). The authors characterize informal workers according to regional and cultural differences, and also structural economic elements. More importantly, they note that there are socio-economic factors that explain the probability of joining the informal sector. To develop the econometric exercise, microdata from the National Survey of Occupation and Employment is used. The sample considers the first quarter of 2015. We selected variables that describe specific characteristics of heads of household that were between the ages of 15 and 65. The estimated model fits the following econometric specification.

$$p(y_i = 1) = \frac{1}{1 + \ell^{-(\beta_0 + \beta_1 E_i + \beta_2 IM_i + \beta_3 S_i + \beta_4 B_i + \beta_5 L1_i \, \beta_6 L2_i + \beta_7 L3_i)}} \quad (1)$$

The dependent variable takes the value of 1 if the worker chooses informal labor and 0 if he chooses formal labor. The logistic function takes into account the number of school years (E_i) and monthly income (IM_i); both variables are numeric. Also, a dummy variable is introduced for gender (S_i). It takes the value of 1 for man and 0 for woman. A categorical variable that controls for the size of the communities where heads of households live is also introduced: L_1_i (communities with more than 100,000 people), L_2_i (communities with 15,000 to 99,999 people), L_3_i (communities with 2,500 to 14,999 people) and L_4_i (communities with less than 2,500 people). Finally, we build a variable B_i, which takes the value 1 if the person searches for a job or 0 otherwise.

Prior to discussing the results, it is worth mentioning some specifics about the data. The original sample size was 404,432 observations, which became 15,535 after making adjustments. We considered only heads of households with ages ranging from 15 to 65 years, consistent with the

Table 1 Summary statistics

	E_i	IM_i
Median	90.94	5235
Mean	9	4300
Mode	9	0
Standard deviation	40.5	6299
Range	22	154,800
Minimum	0	0
Maximum	22	154,800

Dummy variables
$p(y_i=1)$, S_i, B_i, L_1_i, L_2_i y L_3_i

age range for people included in the labor force. Monthly income and education are scale variables; all other variables are dummies. Table 1 reports summary statistics for E_i and IM_i. In the case of education, the average is about ten years with a maximum of 22. Average income is about US$ 300 (at a peso–US dollar exchange rate of 17 pesos per dollar) with a maximum of about US$ 9,000.

The results of the estimation are presented in Table 2. All of the variables are statistically significant at a 95 % confidence interval and the statistical adjustments are, given the nature of the database, reasonably acceptable. In regards to E_i, an inverse relation is observed. The exponential coefficient of E_i indicates that the advantages of being an informal worker decline as the worker acquires one additional year of education. Hence, more education decreases the probability of participating in the informal sector. Monthly income, while significant, shows a very small coefficient. The coefficient of S_i has a negative sign, indicating that a male is less likely to become part of the informal sector relative to a female. The coefficient of B_i suggests that there is a positive relationship between seeking an

Table 2 Estimation results

Variable	$\hat{\beta}$	*Significance*	$\exp\left(\hat{\beta}\right)$
E_i	−1.57	0.00	0.855
IM_i	0.00	0.00	1.000
S_i	−0.27	0.00	0.762
B_i	0.97	0.00	2.641
L_1_i	−1.05	0.00	0.350
L_2_i	−0.69	0.00	0.503
L_3_i	−0.36	0.00	0.707

Goodness of fit statistics
Nagelkerke's R^2: 0.27
−2 log likelihood: 18,073.6
N: 15535
Hosmer-Lemeshow: $\text{chi}^2 = 66.84$, sig(0.000)
The results include the constant
Forward stepwise method (conditional). An increase of goodness of fit is observed in each step

Source: Authors' own estimations with SPSS software

additional job and the probability of finding one in the informal sector as a result of the search. This means that a worker may end up being part of labor informality to the extent that the worker is a seeker of an additional job. One possible explanation for this result is that workers searching for an additional job may not feel satisfied with their current employer or that their present job is perceived to be of low quality.[1] Regarding the communities variables, L_1_i, L_2_i and L_3_i, which refer to urban areas, we notice that the partial coefficients indicate a negative relationship. This suggests that, on average, a worker is less likely to be in the informal sector if he resides in an urban center.[2] This is perhaps given by the fact that in urban areas there is a great diversity of jobs and production diversity. It must be noted that the ratio of advantages, or [$\exp\left(\hat{\beta}\right)$], is less than one in all three of the cases mentioned.

Conclusions

Reducing informality in the Mexican labor market poses a challenge for policymakers. While it may represent an alternative to formal unemployment when economic growth is sluggish, it also negatively impacts productivity, wages and competitiveness. Given the persistence of the phenomenon and its magnitude, it is imperative to identify and understand the factors that influence the decision of a worker to opt for informal employment. In this sense, the empirical exercise conducted here reveals the importance of improving education levels of the labor force. Ideally, the education reform recently enacted in Mexico will produce positive outcomes and help reverse the informality figures in the medium term. Also, our results call for intensifying the efforts to motivate women to enter or remain in the formal market. It is clear that the generation of formal employment must be accompanied by greater labor market flexibility in order to integrate women more rapidly and efficiently. Moreover, it is important to highlight that the process of needing to find a new job to supplement an existing one may be an indication of the persistence of low quality jobs in the economy. Accordingly, the generation of quality jobs as measured by wages and working conditions should be a key objective for public policies in the medium and long term. Without doubt, the only way to strengthen the transition from an informal labor market to a formal one will be the creation of attractive job opportunities.

Notes

1. For an accurate observation of the extent to which the advantages of being an informal worker increase or decrease, when a there is a continuous or discrete change in the variables see the *odd-ratio* (last column of Table 2).
2. According to the National Institute of Statistics and Geography, a rural population has a population of 2,500 or less.

References

Alcaraz, C., Chiquiar, D., & Ramos-Francia, M. (2008). Diferencias salariales intersectoriales y el cambio en la composición desempleo urbano de la economía mexicana en 2001–2004. *Working paper, Banco de México, 6*, 1–41.

Bayón, C. M. (2006). Precariedad social en México y Argentina. *CEPAL Magazine*, April (88), 133–152.

Brand, N. (2011). *Informality in Mexico* (Economics Department Working Paper 896). Paris: OCDE.

De Soto, H. (1989). *The other path: The invisible revolution in the third world*. New York: *Harper Collins*.

Esquivel, G., & Ordaz, D. J. (2008). Es correcto vincular la política social a la informalidad en México? Una prueba simple de las premisas de esta hipótesis. *CEPAL*, Diciembre (104), 1–32.

Freije, S. (2002). El empleo informal en América Latina y el Caribe: causas, consecuencias y recomendaciones de política. *Banco Interaméricano de Desarrollo*, 1–49. http://publications.iadb.org/handle/11319/3772

Harris, R. J., & Todaro, M. P. (1970). Migration, unemployment and development: A two sector analysis. *The American Economic Review, 60*(1), 126–142.

Instituto Nacional de Estadística y Geografía. (2014). *La informalidad laboral, marco conceptual y metodológico*. Encuesta Nacional de Ocupación y Empleo. ENOE.

Levy, S. (2008). *Good intentions, bad outcomes, social policy, informality and economic growth in Mexico*. Washington, DC: Brookings Institution Press.

Loayza, N., & Suguwara, N. (2009). El sector informal en México: Hechos y explicaciones fundamentales. *El Trimestre Económico, LXXVI*(304), 887–920.

Maloney, W. F. (1999). Does informality imply segmentation in urban labor markets? Evidence from sectoral transitions in Mexico. *The World Bank Economic Review, 13*(2), 275–302.

Maloney, W. F. (2004). Informality revisited. *World Development, 32*(7), 1159–1178.

Organización Internacional del Trabajo. (2014). *El empleo informal en México: situación actual, políticas y desafíos* (pp. 1–10). Oficina Regional para América Latina y el Caribe.

Perry, E. G., Maloney, F. W., Arias, S. O., Fajnzylber, P., Mason, D. A., & Saavedra, J. (2007). *Informalidad: escape y exclusion*. Washington, DC: World Bank.

Portes, A., & Haller, W. (2004). La economía Informal. *CEPAL, División de Desarrollo Social*, serie (100), 1–49.

Rivera Huerta, R. (2011) Estrategias para la informalidad. In: U. F. Novelo (Ed.), *La UAM ante la sucesión presidencial* (pp. 477–513). Universidad Autónoma Metropolitana.

Robles, O. D. (2015). Escape y Exclusión: algunos determinantes de la informalidad en México. *Análisis Económico, XXX*(73), 139–161.

Ros, J. (2010). Employment, Structural Adjustment and Sustainable Growth in Mexico. *The Journal of Develoment Studies, 36*(4), 95–116.

Ruíz, N. P., & Ordaz, D. J. L. (2011). Evolución reciente del empleo y el desempleo en México. *Economíaunam, 8*(23), 91–105.

Samaniego, N. (2008). El crecimiento explosivo de la informalidad. *Economía UNAM, 5*(13), 30–41.

Saracho, A. (2015). *Informalidad, corrupción y competitividad. En IMCO, la corrupción en México, transamos y no avanzamos.* México DF: Primera edición.

Williams, C. C., & Round, J. (2010). Explaining participation in undeclared work: A result of exit or exclusion. *European Societies, 12*(3), 391–418.

Williams, C. C., & Youssef, Y. A. (2014). Is informal sector entrepreneurship necessity- or opportunity-driven? Some lessons from urban Brazil. *Business and Management Research, 3*(1), 41–53.

Williams, C. C., Rodgers, P., & Round, J. (2011). Explaining the normality of informal employment in Ukraine: A product of exit or exclusion? *The American Journal of Economics and Sociology, 70*(3), 729–755.

Zonszein, S. (2012). Seguro popular, incentivo a la informalidad? Centro de Estudios de las Finanzas Públicas. *Finanzas Públicas, 4*(8), 125–180.

The Interplay Between Formal and Informal Firms and Its Implications on Jobs in Francophone Africa: Case Studies of Senegal and Benin

Ahmadou Aly Mbaye, Nancy Claire Benjamin, and Fatou Gueye

We are grateful to participants of a workshop organized by Development Policy Research Unit, at the University of Cape Town, in November 2015, for useful comments on an earlier draft of this chapter. The results presented here are drawn from a bigger project on the informal sector in francophone Africa, sponsored by IDRC-Canada and the World Bank. In particular, insights from Pirella Paci and Flaubert Mbiekop in the design of the project are acknowledged. The usual disclaimer does apply.

Introduction

The informal sector is overwhelming in West African economies, with a share of GDP ranging between 50 % and 70 % and its share of employment peaking at up to more than 95 % (Mbaye and Benjamin 2015; Golub and Hayat 2015). While a growing body of literature covers many aspects of the informal labor force and household enterprises, very little is known

A.A. Mbaye (✉) • F. Gueye
University Cheikh Anta Diop, Dakar, Senegal
e-mail: mbayealy93@yahoo.fr

N.C. Benjamin
World Bank, Washington, DC, US

A. Polese et al. (eds.), *The Informal Economy in Global Perspective*, International Political Economy Series,
DOI 10.1007/978-3-319-40931-3_12

about the bigger actors of the large informal sector spectrum, or the deep interrelations between the various segments of this sector and the formal one. When they do exist, such studies use either the World Bank Investment Climate Assessment (ICA) surveys (Gonzalez and Lamanna 2007), or 123 survey databases (Bohme and Thiele 2014). Using data on Latin America, the former find that formal firms which are exposed to competition from informal ones tend to have lower levels of productivity than the others (see also Williams et al. 2016b). They also find the magnitude of this impact to vary a lot depending on several factors, such as firms' intrinsic characteristics as well as their business environment. In contrast, Ali and Najman (2015), using World Bank Enterprise surveys for 33 sub-Saharan African countries, find greater informal competition shows a positive relation with the labor productivity of formal firms. Bohme and Thiele identify two types of interaction between formal and informal firms: forward linkages and backward linkages, with backward linkages being more frequent. They also examine the intensity of such linkages and conclude that level of formality as well as size of capital stock are the main factors influencing them. Our view is that neither of the datasets used can allow for a comprehensive explanation of this complex interplay in Africa. ICA surveys deal mostly with formal firms. And informal firms as well as their relationship to formal ones are only marginally covered both in their samples and in the survey instruments. Regarding 123 surveys, these mostly cover small family enterprises, with very few bigger firms included in their samples. In this report we combine quantitative and qualitative approaches to yield a better understanding of the types of interaction being developed by informal and formal firms in francophone Africa. Results of semi-structured and focus group discussions led in Benin and Senegal have been extensively used. Data used in the quantitative part of the report are based on surveys completed in West and Central Africa about the informal sector in general (Benjamin and Mbaye 2012; Mbaye et al. 2015), as well as on a more recent survey focusing more on the type of interrelations in terms of competition, trade and subcontracting. Our data cover a larger spectrum of the informal sector, encompassing various degrees of formality/informality (see Williams and Shahid 2016), based on a given set of criteria.

The main objective of this study is to improve understanding of the relationship between formal and informal businesses and how it could improve firm performances and employment. The remainder of the chapter is organized as follows: the next section lays out our methodology and data sources; the following section is entitled "A Qualitative Assessment of the Interplay Between Formal and Informal Actors in Africa", looking at these in terms of trade, outsourcing and competition, using some sectors as case studies. The next section, "The Interactions Between the Formal and Informal in Africa", examines the same interrelations using our survey data, and in the following section "The Determinants of the Interrelations Between Formal and Informal Firms: An Econometric Analysis", we use a simple econometric setting to analyze the determinants of such interactions, while there comes a "Conclusion" to round things off.

Methodology

Benjamin and Mbaye (2012) define the informal sector as a continuum, by considering the following criteria: size, registration, honest accounting, the lack of payment of tax or the type of tax paid, mobility of workplace and the access to bank credit. By combining this set of criteria, they identify several levels of informal firms according to the number of criteria they meet. In this study, we use the same method as Benjamin and Mbaye and target the group of all formal and informal firms of West and Central African countries considered in our sample: Benin, Burkina Faso, Senegal, Guinea Bissau, Cameroon and Gabon. The unit of analysis is the firm. To specifically address the issue of the interactions between formal and informal firms, a more targeted survey was implemented in Benin and Senegal in 2015, focusing specifically on this aspect of the study. In addition to the data from our surveys, our study also uses secondary statistics and qualitative data collected from semi-structured interviews and focus groups. These concurrent sources of data allowed us to conduct an in-depth analysis of various facets of the informal sector—mainly its impact on business climate and growth as well as employment and living conditions. The same approach is used to study the interrelations between formal and informal firms.

Quantitative Data

Considering our goal to include in our sample the different segments of the informal sector spectrum, we opted for a stratified sampling strategy, obtained by combining the different levels of informality (small informal, large informal, formal) and the different sectors of activity (commerce, other services, industry). The base for the polling is the total population of firms corresponding to different tax regimes. According to the tax regime to which the company belongs, we distinguish:

a) the subset of firms subject to regular taxation,
b) the subset of firms subject to the presumptive lump sum tax plan,
c) the subset of all other firms that are either unknown to tax records or are not subject to any of the above regimes.

From these subsets, we have drawn a stratified sample of firms in the industry, trade and services sectors (see Mbaye et al. 2015 for more details). This approach has been used in different periods of time to gather information on formal and informal firms in West and Central Africa. A narrower sample of firms with similar characteristics was drawn in each of the cities of Dakar and Cotonou, and administered a version of the questionnaire centered on the patterns and magnitudes of interactions between small informal and larger formal firms.

Qualitative Data

The results of the qualitative analysis are essentially gathered from semi-structured interviews and focus groups that were set up to collect the opinions of the different actors on the topic under investigation. These interviews are more focused than the surveys, and concern the administrative agents in charge of the informal sector (tax services, Ministry of Commerce, small and medium-sized businesses, industry and craft, the national agencies in charge of the development of the small and medium-sized businesses, national services of statistic etc.). We also questioned the chambers of commerce and industry, the employers' associations for the formal and informal sectors, the main clients, suppliers of the informal sector and donors involved in the sector. The objective of these interviews is mostly to collect the opinions of the actors that know the sector well and are therefore able to deliver a pertinent opinion. The interviews also served as a base which certain information from surveys may be checked against.

Another dimension of the qualitative analysis is that it facilitated the review of all relevant documentation on the informal sector: the legal texts, the writing of sociologists and anthropologists on the networks of informality in Africa, as well as their international implications.

A Qualitative Assessment of the Interplay Between Formal and Informal Actors in Africa

The relationships between formal and informal sectors are quite complex. The two sectors are sometimes highly complementary and interact to produce goods or services, and sometimes they can engage in very strong competition. Several cases of competition are observed. The drug distribution industry is a case in point. In Francophone Africa, drug distribution channels are similar from one country to another. Very few drugs are manufactured locally; most are imported and the government and professional organizations, such as the federation of pharmacists, play an important role. In almost all countries, we note a very well-structured distribution channel paralleled by a more informal one. The latter relies mainly to fraudulent imports of drugs, most of which are usually counterfeit, and on extraction of good quality drugs from public hospitals and other formal organizations, through theft and bribery. The market is rather segmented with the bulk of the population, mostly from low income households, being supplied by informal "drugstores" which are much cheaper but also much riskier. Distribution of adulterated petroleum products in Africa is another case of competition between formal and informal sectors. This is widely observed in Benin and to a lesser extent in Cameroon. In both cases, petroleum products mainly come from illegal imports from Nigeria. This product is designated by *Zoua Zoua* in Cameroon and *Kpayo* in Benin. Formal gas stations are very scarce in most of Benin and in Douala (Cameroon). The bulk of car owners use adulterated gas which is much cheaper than regular gas, but poses big challenges to safety and the environment. Competition between used cars importers and traders on one hand and formal car dealers on the other is another important feature of francophone African economies, and in particular Benin. Benin is a special case, given its position vis-à-vis Nigeria. Imports of used vehicles, which are estimated at over 10 % of GDP, are intended to cover the needs of Benin's domestic market, as well as Nigeria's, and to a lesser extent Chad, Niger, Mali and Burkina. In the capital of Benin, huge open air parks have been built for the trade of used vehicles. These parks, completely controlled by informal actors, have a very light administrative structure. According to some estimates, total car imports to Benin amounted to 150,000 units in 2014. Out of which only 1,500 units (around 1 %) were imported by formal dealers (Mbaye and Gueye 2015). Public transport by motorcycle taxis is a reality in many African cities. Douala (Cameroon) and Cotonou (Benin) are good examples. The number of motorcycle taxis is close to 65,000 in Benin. The development of this mode of transport has been possible thanks to the dual effect of rapid population growth and low incomes. The prices are very low and the drivers show a boundless availability to transport passengers, whatever the road conditions or the time at which they are asked to make the trip. Competition from this type of transport also reduces formal services of transport to a very low level. Many instances of competition between formal and informal actors are observed in Africa, with informal actors usually offering poor quality goods or services that target low to medium income households.

The interplay between formal and informal firms is not always contentious though. Several cases of trading and outsourcing relations are also noted. Outsourcing is increasingly promoted in African countries, many of which have set up national subcontracting fairs. These fairs, which are intended to facilitate the outsourcing of certain services by large companies to smaller ones, are directly managed by the private sector, in partnership with the government and the support of UNIDO (United Nations Industrial Development Organization). These fairs are intended primarily for industrial partnerships and national-level fairs have been connected to the regional level. The main objective is to facilitate exchanges between enterprises of different sizes, by sharing information and putting them in touch. They also seek to help small actors develop such attitudes as punctuality and reliability, to make them inspire trust and creditworthiness to their bigger counterparts. Unfortunately, except in rare cases, outsourcing fairs do not work very well. Indeed, they are faced with funding problems that threaten even the retention of their staff, which they often end up losing. The IT sector is an area where the potential for outsourcing is huge. Indeed, in the business of wiring for Internet and developing and managing certain applications, there is room for major operators who wish to remain in business and subcontract to smaller ones. In the sub-region, most telephone companies are multinational corporations that coexist with a number of local actors, mainly SMEs. In general, the latter are involved in the development of software applications, sales of computer hardware, computer wiring, computer network management and so forth. These SMEs often complain that large operators do not give them enough work. Instead, they prefer to bring on site technicians from the parent company. Most SME managers we interviewed expressed their frustration about not having access to these markets. According to them, there is also a serious corruption problem with bribery in both the public and the private sector regarding big outsourcing contracts. Indeed, except in very rare cases, outsourcing from large formal to small rather informal firms is not a usual practice in Africa. The main reason for this is the lack of expertise, inadequate training and limited capital that prevent small informal businesses meeting even basic requirements from larger firms.

While subcontracting to informal firms is marginal in Africa, trading relations are widespread and span a very diverse set of activities. Distribution of manufactured products made by the formal sector by informal actors is an important area of cooperative interaction between the two categories. For most of these products, the companies that manufacture them go through wholesalers or retailers, most of whom are informal. The standard distribution channel consists of selling the products to wholesalers that in turn parcel out to a network of informal retailers. In the service sector, sales of prepaid phone credits and management of cyber cafés are cases of positive interactions between the major telecommunications companies and actors in the informal sector, and such interactions occur in almost all African capitals. There is a small thriving business of prepaid phone cards, phone-transferable credits from one mobile phone to another and internet services. These sales are made in retail, and are used for even modest amounts of money. Real estate brokerage is another area in which the formal and informal sectors interact. This activity consists of connecting the supply and demand of buildings or land used for residential or office space, and to facilitate land and real estate transactions, in return for a commission, which is generally very negotiable. We distinguish the formal brokerages, which consist of the well-known agencies, from informal trading which is done by individuals who bring together customers and suppliers of goods and services in the field of land and real estate, against payment of commission. In Africa, the bulk of distribution is controlled by the informal sector. Locally produced goods as well as imported ones actually often use the same distribution channels, which are widely informal.

The Interactions Between the Formal and Informal in Africa

In this section, we focus on the interrelations between the formal and informal sectors, based on our survey data. These interactions are assessed in terms of competition and in terms of trade relations and subcontracting. The data used in this section are from surveys performed on 600 firms in Benin and Senegal in 2007 and 2009. They are further complemented by data from a more targeted survey on 300 units, implemented in the same countries in 2015, focusing specifically on relationships between formal and informal firms.

Trade and outsourcing are palpable realities in the relations between large (formal) and small (informal) firms. Table 1 shows that 52.5 % of firms in Dakar and a third of companies in Cotonou work with intermediaries. Moreover, 64 % of such firms in Dakar and 90 % in Cotonou consider that their use of intermediaries is following a growing trend over time.

Table 2 is even more explicit in this regard. It shows that 77.5 % of enterprises in Dakar and 65 % in Cotonou trade with households or informal family businesses for the most part.

Furthermore, the pattern of subcontracting is rather counterfactual, with mainly bigger firms delivering services to small ones, rather than the opposite. This is observed in Cotonou, where a significant proportion of large companies (12.5 %) carry out services for the profit of small ones. In Table 3, we see the sectors most affected by the interplay between formal and informal firms. Not surprisingly, trade leads with almost 32 % of reported cases of interactions. As shown in previous sections, the actors in commerce (wholesalers as well as retailers) are mostly retailers of manufactured goods. Even in services, intense trading activities link the formal to informal sectors.

Table 1 Share of firms working with intermediaries (%)

City		*Dakar*	*Cotonou*
Firms using different size counterparts as clients		52.50 %	33.33 %
Share of firms selling to	Big enterprises	1.67 %	12.50 %
	Small enterprises	36.67 %	21.67 %
Appreciation of the trend of interaction over time	Increasing	64.52 %	90.00 %
	Decreasing	6.45 %	2.50 %
	Stable	16.13 %	7.50 %

Source: Author's own calculations

Table 2 Share of firms trading with the government, households and household enterprises

	Sales to the government	*Trading with households or household enterprises*
Dakar	10.17 %	77.50 %
Cotonou	31.67 %	65.00 %

Source: Author's own calculations

Table 3 Sectors affected by subcontracting

	Dakar	*Cotonou*
Insurance	3.33 %	2.50 %
Building and public work	16'67 %	27.50 %
Commerce	31.67 %	42.50 %
IT	1.67 %	
Customs clearance	1.67 %	
Kitchen utensils	3.33 %	
Carpentry		12.50 %
Other	41.67 %	15.00 %
Total	100.00 %	100.00 %

Source: Author's own calculations

Table 4 Firms trading output to smaller enterprises, by informal criteria or correlates

	Fixity of workplace	*Payment of Tax*	*Registration*	*Access to bank loan*	*Honest accounts*	*More than five employees*	*Social Security coverage*
Dakar	53.68 %	56.52 %	59.46 %	65.00 %	55.56 %	73.81 %	80.95 %
Cotonou	77.50 %	33.01 %	43.75 %	37.50 %	35.71 %	54.55 %	53.85 %

Source: Author's own calculations

It is often not about outsourcing, strictly speaking, but distribution that is done in several ways. Building and public work are an important sector where subcontracting is observed (16.7 %). Here, the major companies who are the only ones with the financial strength and expertise needed to win bids, subcontract to piece workers who are mostly informal.

Table 4 shows the profile of informal enterprises that engage in business interaction with formal ones, using different criteria and correlates for informality. Small informal actors are often used as intermediaries by large firms, both from the formal and the informal sectors: 53.68 % and 77.5 % in Dakar and Cotonou respectively. In general, whatever the criterion or correlate retained for informality, our respondents tend to play the role of intermediary. Thus, this activity concerns 55.56 % and 35.71 % of companies not using honest accounting, both in Dakar and Cotonou respectively. They represent, in both cities: 80.95 % and 53.85 % for actors failing to provide their employees with any kind of social protection, 73.81 % and 54.55 % for small businesses (with fewer than five employees), 65 % and 35.5 % for companies excluded from bank credit; 59.46 % and 43.75 % for unregistered businesses; and finally 56.52 % and 33.01 % for companies not paying tax or taxed at package.

Table 5 Appreciation of level of punctuality and professionalism of small firms in their relation to bigger counterparts, by criteria or correlates of informality

		Fixity of workplace	*Payment of Tax*	*Registration*	*Access to bank loan*	*Honest accounts*	*More than five employees*	*Social Security coverage*
Dakar	Satisfactory	93.88 %	95.65 %	93.02 %	91.67 %	94.87 %	93.55 %	94.12 %
	Not satisfactory	4.08 %	0.00 %	6.98 %	0.00 %	2.56 %	6.45 %	5.88 %
	No response	2.04 %	4.35 %	0.00 %	8.33 %	2.56 %	0.00 %	0.00 %
Cotonou	Satisfactory	80.65 %	82.35 %	85.71 %	100.00 %	84.00 %	88.89 %	85.71 %
	Not satisfactory	9.68 %	14.71 %	9.52 %	0.00 %	14.29 %	11.11 %	7.14 %
	No response	9.68 %	2.94 %	4.76 %	0.00 %	4.00 %		7.14 %

Source: Author's own calculations

Table 5 presents the perception of the quality of trade relations and subcontracting between formal and informal actors. It turns out that the level of satisfaction of subcontracting[1] firms is quite high, both in Dakar and in Cotonou. These results remain robust to different criteria used to categorize small informal businesses. A proportion between 80 % and 100 %, according to the criterion, expressed great satisfaction with the timeliness and level of professionalism of the outsourcing (Table 5).

In Table 6, relations with outsourced companies are highlighted and it appears that almost 35 % of companies in Dakar and 67.5 % in Cotonou are outsourcing to relatives or friends. This personalization of industrial relations, rather surprising at first glance, is quite understandable to anyone who grasps the level of risk associated with the informal sector. That is what explains why economic relations involving the informal sector often go through networks of religious, family, social or other contacts (Hansen-Lewis and Golub 2012). In Benin, the cases of outsourcing through these networks represent 87.5 % of the total.

The informality of transactions between companies is also evident in Tables 7 and 8, where 97.5 % of such transactions involve a loan to the subcontracted company, often informal and lacking working capital. The way in which these loans are made is also noteworthy: in 89 % of cases in Dakar and in 100 % of cases in Benin, these transactions are made in cash.

Finally, Table 9 compares different performance indicators between commercial companies that trade with informal firms and those not trading with informal firms. When considering productivity levels (Table 9), no clear pattern emerges. While in West Africa, formal firms trading with informal firms have a higher level of productivity, in Central Africa by contrast, it is the firms that do not trade with informal

Table 6 Relationship to the subcontracted firms

Relationship	*Dakar*	*Cotonou*
Friend	34.69 %	67.50 %
Relative	2.04 %	12.50 %
Same kinship network	4.08 %	2.50 %
Same religious network	2.04 %	5.00 %
Professional	57.14 %	12.50 %
Total	100 %	100 %

Source: Author's own calculations

Table 7 Loans granted to subcontracted firms

		Dakar	*Cotonou*
Existence of loans		41.94 %	97.50 %
Type of loan	In cash	88.89 %	100 %
	In kind	11.11 %	
Modalities of repayment	Weekly	3.28 %	
	Daily	14.75 %	
	Monthly	80.33 %	
	Other	1.64 %	100 %
Appreciation of level of repayment	Good	40.74 %	100 %
	Excellent	14.81 %	
	Fair	29.63 %	
	Other	14.81 %	

Source: Author's own calculations

firms that have a higher level of productivity. When considering the size of firms across all countries, those who trade with informal firms tend to be of a smaller size than the others (Table 9). By contrast, when compared with those commercial companies not trading with informal firms (Table 9), among the firms that have expressed confidence in the future of their business, there is no particular difference noted. The same observation can be made for firms that have expressed a desire to change activities (Table 9).

We have also examined the competition between formal and informal firms in different sectors and their implications for different formal sector performance indicators. Competition from small informal firms seems not to affect the productivity of large firms (formal and informal). Table 9 shows in fact that among the companies that have a level of productivity above the median (which is the case for most large companies), no significant productivity gap is observed based on whether there is competition from small informal firms or not. Similarly, it appears in Table 10 that exporting firms are less subject to competition from small informal firms than other firms. A proportion ranging from 88.5 % in Libreville to 96.6 % in Dakar of non-exporting companies are subject to competition from small informal firms.

Likewise, large corporate firms, which are members of a professional association are less subject to competition from small informal than others (Table 11).

Table 8 Levels of loan recovery from smaller firms, by criteria or correlates of informality

		Fixity of workplace	*Taxation*	*Registration*	*Access to bank loan*	*Honest accounts*	*More than five employees*	*Social Security*
DAKAR	Excellent	15.38 %	16.00 %	17.65 %	0.00 %	16.67 %	36.36 %	42.86 %
	Good	42.31 %	44.00 %	35.29 %	20.00 %	44.44 %	27.27 %	42.86 %
	Fair	26.92 %	24.00 %	35.29 %	80.00 %	22.22 %	36.36 %	14.29 %
	No response	15.38 %	16.00 %	11.76 %	0.00 %	16.67 %	0.00 %	0.00 %
Cotonou	Excellent	100.00 %	100.00 %	100.00 %	100.00 %	100.00 %	100.00 %	100.00 %
	Good	0.00 %	0.00 %	0.00 %	0.00 %	0.00 %	0.00 %	0.00 %
	Fair	0.00 %	0.00 %	0.00 %	0.00 %	0.00 %	0.00 %	0.00 %
	No response	0.00 %	0.00 %	0.00 %	0.00 %	0.00 %	0.00 %	0.00 %

Source: Author's own calculations

Table 9 Distribution of larger firms trading and not trading with small informal firms, based on various characteristics (%)

Cities	*Description*	*Share of firms with productivity higher than median*	*Share of firms with size larger than average*	*Share of firms whose managers expressed confidence in the future*	*Share of firms whose managers have recently changed area of activity*
Dakar	Large formal and informal firms trading with small informal	91.7	33.3	83.3	16.7
	Large formal and informal firms not trading with small informal	75	42	80.4	31.3
Cotonou	Large formal and informal firms trading with small informal	85.7	33.3	100	12.5
	Large formal and informal firms not trading with small informal	72.5	38.6	95	19.4
Ouaga	Large formal and informal firms trading with small informal	100	25	75	0
	Large formal and informal firms not trading with small informal	86.2	32.4	89.6	10.9
Douala	Large formal and informal firms trading with small informal	50	6.3	81.3	18.8
	Large formal and informal firms not trading with small informal	68.2	33.6	94.5	10.9
Yaoundé	Large formal and informal firms trading with small informal	46.7	20	86.7	0
	Large formal and informal firms not trading with small informal	73.2	44.6	92.9	12.5
Libreville	Large formal and informal firms trading with small informal	50	50	100	0
	Large formal and informal firms not trading with small informal	81.5	67.7	96.9	9.2

Source: Author's own calculations

Table 10 Share of exporting firms exposed to small informal competition (%)

	Exporting	*Big firms exposed to small informal competition*	*Big firms not exposed to small informal competition*
Dakar	Yes	3.4	15.5
	No	96.6	84.5
Cotonou	Yes	7.7	19
	No	92.3	81
Ouaga	Yes	4	8.6
	No	96	91.4
Douala	Yes	14	13.5
	No	86	86.5
Yaoundé	Yes	4.5	16.3
	No	95.5	83.7
Libreville	Yes	11.5	10
	No	88.5	90

Source: Author's own calculations

Table 11 Share of firms with professional membership which are exposed to competition from small informal (%)

	Existence of a professional membership	*Bigger firms exposed to small informal competition*	*Bigger firms not exposed to small informal competition*
Dakar	Yes	30.5	36.2
	No	69.5	63.8
Cotonou	Yes	9.7	37.5
	No	90.3	62.5
Ouaga	Yes	15.4	19.4
	No	84.6	80.6
Douala	Yes	25.6	40.5
	No	74.4	59.5
Yaoundé	Yes	9.1	23.3
	No	90.9	76.7
Libreville	Yes	11.5	20
	No	88.5	80

Source: Author's calculations

The Determinants of the Interrelations Between Formal and Informal Firms: An Econometric Analysis

Beyond the descriptive statistics presented in the previous section, we performed econometric regressions to understand the determinants of the relationship between small informal firms on one hand, and larger formal and informal enterprises on the other. The simple model that we considered is:

$$y = c + \alpha X + \beta y + \varepsilon$$

y is a dummy variable taking the value 1 when the company answers yes to the question of whether it is a partner to (merchant or contractor with) informal firms and 0 otherwise. That is the case for Model 1. Alternatively, in Model 2, it takes the value 1 when the firm competes with informal firms and 0 otherwise. C is a constant.

X is a vector of control variables: size, access to bank credit, the age of the firm, share of exports in turnover, wage, a dummy variable set for the building and public work sector, a variable capturing trading with large firms, and another one capturing supplying large firms.

Υ is productivity.

All results are presented in Table 12.

Model 1 shows that productivity is negatively correlated with the dependent variable: formal companies maintaining partnerships with informal ones (in the form of trade or outsourcing), have significantly lower levels of productivity. This variable is significant at 1 %. The size is another significant variable to 1 %, indicating that larger firms are less likely to enter into partnership with the small informal than others. Age is only significant at 5 %, with a negative sign indicating that older firms are less likely to be partners than other small informal. The coefficients of the industry's fixed effects were obtained by taking the "trade" sector as a reference. The literature indicates it is at the level of the industry and services that we are most likely to find cases of formal–informal partnerships. What is surprising is that the coefficient of the construction sector is not significant even though the industry is known as home to multiple cases of subcontracting between the small informal and large companies. This can be explained by the low number of degrees of freedom associated with the underrepresentation of such enterprises in our sample.

Table 12 An econometric analysis of the deter-inants of partnership (trading or subcontracting) and competition between formal and informal

	(1)	*(2)*
Variables		
LogProdvte	−0.243***	−0.0531
	(0.0910)	(0.0601)
Logsize	−0.338***	−0.297***
	(0.128)	(0.0804)
Logwage	−0.108*	−0.0401
	(0.0632)	(0.0508)
LogAge	−0.389**	−0.0753
	(0.182)	(0.126)
Customer: large enterprises		−0.490**
		(0.227)
Supplier: large enterprises		0.0166
		(0.216)
Exporting	−0.715	−0.454
	(0.760)	(0.380)
Access to bank loan	−0.277	−0.330
	(0.378)	(0.234)
Sector. *(Ref. Trade)*		
Building and public work	0.0169	−0.637
	(0.797)	(0.448)
Other Industries	1.082***	0.279
	(0.416)	(0.264)
Services	1.175***	0.228
	(0.406)	(0.273)
Constant	3.889**	1.969*
	(1.630)	(1.085)
Observations	472	440

Source: Author's own calculations

Standard errors in parentheses

***$p < 0.01$, **$p < 0.05$, *$p < 0.1$

When looking at Model 2, we have the most correlated variables to the dependent variable that measures the likelihood of being exposed to competition from small informal businesses. The productivity factor is not significant here. This largely confirms Table 5, which does not show any difference in productivity between rivaled and non-rivaled companies. The size of the firm has a significant coefficient at 1 %, indicating that large companies are less exposed to competition from small informal ones. Of course, firms that have large companies as clients seem less exposed to competition than others.

Conclusion

In francophone Africa, as in most developing countries, the informal sector plays an important role in the economy. In Africa, as elsewhere, the informal sector is very heterogeneous and strongly connected with the remainder of the economy. The relationship between the formal and the informal sectors are either competitive or complementary. In some sectors such as distribution of drugs, gasoline or used cars, we observe a strong competition which favors the informal sector, due to its lower prices, even though it is to the detriment of quality. In other sectors like commerce, transport, buildings and public work, we alternatively notice stronger complementarities between formal and informal. Subcontracting is indeed noted between both sectors, but with a very limited scope. Only activities like building and public works and customs clearance are concerned. In the IT sector, outsourcing is scarcer, and usually involves small and medium-sized enterprises originating from developed countries rather than from Africa. Because technical and managerial capacities are weaker in Africa, SMEs, overwhelmingly informal, are not trusted by multinationals, especially in the area of telecommunications and IT. Informal firms are mainly concentrated in industries like commerce or public transport, which are very simple and not at all intensive in technology or human capital and are not deemed reliable enough to be subcontracted by bigger firms for activities that require expertise and technical capabilities.

When we now turn to the impact of competition on formal firms' performance, we do not detect any significant effect on productivity. Moreover, bigger firms are less exposed to competition from informal businesses than smaller ones. Likewise, exporting firms and those which are members of a professional association are less exposed.

A simple econometric model has been tested with our data, to complete the descriptive statistical analysis we have undertaken. The results show formal firms trading with informal firms have a significantly lower level of productivity than those that do not. Apart from productivity, firm size and age are also correlated with the probability of trading or subcontracting with informal firms. Nevertheless, being exposed to competition from informal firms does not seem to negatively affect firms' productivity. Like the descriptive statistics, our econometric results confirm that exporting firms and bigger ones seem less exposed to competition from the informal sector.

Note

1. Throughout the section outsourcing is considered in general terms, including trading.

References

Ali, N., & Najman, B. (2015). *Informal competition and labour productivity: A possible explanation for new growth patterns in Sub-Saharan Africa* (Working Paper, University of Paris East).

Benjamin, N., & Mbaye, A. A. (2012). *The informal sector in francophone Africa: Firm size, productivity and institutions.* Washington, DC: World Bank.

Bohme, M., & Thiele, R. (2014). Informal-formal linkage and informal enterprise performance in Urban West Africa. *The European Journal of Development Research, 26*(4), 473–489.

Gonzales, A. S., & Lamanna, F. (2007). *Who fears competition from informal firms? Evidence from Latin America* (World Bank Policy Research Working Paper, 4316).

Mbaye, A. A., & Gueye, F. (2015). *The interplay between formal and informal firms in francophone Africa.* Unpblished report to the World Bank.

Mbaye, A. A, Ekomié, J. J., Saha, J. C., Kobou, G., Charmes, J., Benjamin, N., Golub, S., Haughton, D., Cissé, R., Diop, I. T., Gueye, F., Diop, A. N., Doucouré, F. B., & Diallo, N. A. (2015). *Secteur informel, environnement des affaires et croissance économique: une analyse comparative de l'Afrique de l'Ouest et du Centre.* CRDI.

Williams, C. C., & Shahid, M. (2016). Informal entrepreneurship and institutional theory: explaining the varying degrees of (in)formalisation of entrepreneurs in Pakistan. *Entrepreneurship and Regional Development, 28*(1–2), 1–25.

Williams, C. C., Shahid, M., & Martinez, A. (2016b). Determinants of the level of informality of informal micro-enterprises: Some evidence from the city of Lahore, Pakistan. *World Development, 84*, 312–325.

Governing Informal Payments by Market in the Chinese Healthcare System

Jingqing Yang

Introduction

Informal payments refer to cash or in-kind contributions that patients give to doctors beyond formal payments in the course of seeking medical services in predominantly public health institutions. The practice is endemic in many developing countries, and is particularly widespread in former and current socialist countries in Asia and Central and Eastern Europe (Lewis 2010) where informal economies have existed for decades (Morris and Polese 2015). Given their nature of secrecy and informality, they are considered illegal or at least illegitimate, and thus have become a major concern of health authorities in these countries. China is one of those countries undergoing market transition, although it remains a socialist state, at least in name. While its market reform has been largely successful and commendable in other sectors, its market-based health reform has been predominantly a failure acknowledged even by the authorities (Ge and Gong 2007). A main adverse outcome of the health reform is the prevalence of informal economies, of which informal payment is a major component. The Chinese government has made long-term and persistent efforts to

J. Yang (✉)
School of International Studies, University of Technology Sydney,
Broadway, NSW, Australia

A. Polese et al. (eds.), *The Informal Economy in Global Perspective*, International Political Economy Series,
DOI 10.1007/978-3-319-40931-3_13

contain the practice. Apart from resorting to a hierarchical regulatory structure, it has made even greater efforts to establish a market model to lift the efficiency of healthcare and the morale of health professionals, and has introduced some particular market-based mechanisms to curb informal economies. But the result is apparently not satisfactory.

This chapter aims to evaluate the governance of informal payments through market mechanisms in the Chinese healthcare system, analyzing why the market is unlikely to be a feasible solution to the problem.

Informal payments, which are called red packets (*hongbao*) in Chinese, emerged in the late 1980s, and have since become increasingly widespread. Today, the practice of giving red packets to doctors has become a deep-rooted social norm for hospitalized patients. An investigation conducted between 2008 and 2009 in ten cities surveyed 4,000 patients who had been hospitalized in recent years. The results showed that 54.4 % of them gave red packets to doctors (Kong et al. 2011). Almost everyone who received operations gave red packets to their surgeons. Only 4.7 % of patients gave their red packets as a token of gratitude. Over 95 % of them were motivated for reasons other than gratitude. The study thus concluded that giving red packets had become a "latent norm" and "a rule of the profession", although 73.5 % of patients believed it was not right for doctors to take red packets from them. Other studies also confirm that informal payment has been so ubiquitous that it has become a social norm (Bork et al. 2011; Eggleston and Yip 2004; Hong 2012; Huang 2004; Lu et al. 2010; Zhou and Zhang 2004).

Given the prevalence of informal payments and other forms of misconduct in the healthcare system, there is little wonder the government has been under constant criticism for not doing enough, in spite of the fact that it has always taken a firm stance against misconduct and has made tremendous governance efforts to contain this in the healthcare system since the early 1990s. Generally speaking, two models of governance have been employed. One is usually termed as "government" in which the power and control is hierarchically exercised from the top down (Kjær 2004). The other is the market, in which the governance of informal payments is exercised through market-based mechanisms. Accordingly, criticisms have concentrated on two aspects: hierarchical regulation and marketization.

In terms of hierarchical governance, scholars almost unanimously call for the government to step up its efforts to strengthen regulatory and supervisory devices and institutions to control informal economies in hospitals. But, as I have pointed out elsewhere (Yang 2015), the criticism is largely misplaced. There is ample evidence that the party-state has put in tremendous efforts, mobilized considerable resources from both the Chinese Communist Party (CCP) and the government and established complicated and omnipresent hierarchical governing structures to regulate and redress medical misconduct. The problems which have led to the poor performance and outcomes of the party-state's regulation lie less in its regulatory efforts than in the flaws in the institutional design of the hierarchical governance.

Throughout the reform era, however, the Chinese government and health authority, aligning health reform with the market-oriented economic reform that has dominated the transition inaugurated in the late 1970s, have favored market more than hierarchy as a governance solution to informal economies in the healthcare system. As Wang Shaoguang notes, the Chinese government has a superstitious belief in the almighty power of economic growth and the market, embracing them as the elixir for social and political problems (Wang 2003). But scholars are divided on whether the market is a culprit or a solution for informal payments. One opinion blames marketization for some endemic problems that haunt the Chinese healthcare system today. Blumenthal and Hsiao (2015), critics of healthcare marketization in China, note that since 1984, the Chinese healthcare system has undergone three major stages of reform. During the stage between 1984 and 2003, the healthcare system experienced drastic free market reforms featuring the retreat of the state from financing public health insurance and facilities, decentralization and privatization, leading to widespread public outcries and discontent. From 2003, the government introduced some modest insurance schemes to cover rural populations and urban employees in the private sector and unemployed residents, but these schemes were not successful as the party-state was reluctant to make significant financial commitment to healthcare. In the latest, ongoing round of reform starting from 2008, the government, realizing the drawbacks of a healthcare system based on market principles, attempted to abandon market-oriented incentives and commit to "providing affordable basic healthcare for all Chinese people by 2020" (Blumenthal and Hsiao 2015, p. 1283). But hospitals resisted the reform efforts, forcing the government to continue to rely on market mechanisms.

Informal payments are believed to have emerged in the context of market-based health reforms. Since for-profit activities are encouraged and incentivized, medical professionals naturally take advantage of their dominating market position in their relationship with patients and maximize their personal gains. As salaries for medical professionals are controlled by the state and are set at a low level, a black market has emerged in which doctors receive informal extra payments from patients to compensate their low incomes (Bork et al. 2011; Cao 2010; Chen 2006a; Xu 2006; Zhou and Zhang 2004). As a result, the scholars of this view advocate that the state must be brought back to dominate the organization and delivery of healthcare—only thus can problems and corruption in the system be solved (Ge and Gong 2007; Li 2005; Xu 2006). However, these scholars usually overlook the fact that the state has always been heavily involved, especially in the hierarchy that governs illegitimate economic behaviors of practitioners in public hospitals, but corruption and misconduct are nonetheless endemic. The theory is also weak in explaining why informal payments have to be transacted in a "black" market if the healthcare system has been marketized.

The above view has been vehemently challenged by scholars who argue that blaming the failure of health reform on "marketization" is unwarranted, as no genuine market has ever been established in the healthcare system; or the so-called "market" has been so underdeveloped or heavily intervened in by the state that it can hardly be considered as a market (Fan 2010; Gu et al. 2006; Wong 2010; Wu 2007; Chen 2006b; Zhou 2008). In spite of the fact that public hospitals receive barely any funding from the government and rely predominantly on patients' out-of-pocket payments to survive, they operate in a "market" that is largely closed to private competitors and their market monopoly is heavily protected by the state. Scholars of this view believe that this closed and underdeveloped "market", coupled with excessive regulation in some areas, such as salaries of public doctors and prices for basic services, and insufficient regulation and supervision in other areas, such as pharmaceutical products and highly decentralized hospital management, is the origin of the problems and corruptions that haunt the healthcare system. In other words, they do not believe that genuine marketization would have allowed these problems. It is the state, they argue, that is the culprit. As a result, they claim that a genuine, well-governed healthcare market is the solution to healthcare problems, including informal payments. Some scholars explicitly propose competition (Fan 2010; Peng 2004; Wang and Kuai 2008) and differential pricing (Kong 2004; Lu 2011; Wang 1998; Wang and Kuai 2008; Chen 2006b) as the appropriate market mechanisms to weed out informal payments and other misconduct in public hospitals.

Scholars of this view have demonstrated a better understanding of what the market is, to what extent the Chinese healthcare system has been marketized, and what negative roles the government has played in what they believe is a process of pseudo-marketization. But the solutions they propose may not be the right answer to the problems. Market-based competition and differential pricing have long been implemented in the public healthcare system to boost efficiency and morale, and to fight informal payments. The outcomes of these methods, however, are far from satisfactory. Advocates for market solutions are yet to answer why market elements have failed to produce the intended results.

It is true that the health "market" in China is excessively regulated and closed to private providers of medical services, and is thus highly underdeveloped. Meanwhile, it is also evident that healthcare is highly commercialized as the government has made great and consistent efforts since the mid-1980s to establish market elements in the public healthcare system to boost efficiency, quality and ethics, and, more importantly, to unburden its financial commitment to both the population and public facilities. It is also evident that market mechanisms have been adopted as a major approach to redress informal and unhealthy behaviors and economies in the healthcare system, but these devices are far from successful.

Limited by space, this chapter will not probe what has given rise to informal payments and why the hierarchy has failed to rein in the practice, but will focus on why governance by the market is unlikely to be the solution. In the following text, I will evaluate two leading market mechanisms that have been employed to control informal payments. One is competition, the other differential pricing.

Competition and "Patients Choose Doctors"

The year 2000 is crucial to market-oriented health reform thanks to the promulgation of several important policies. In February the State Council approved a guideline to deepen the reform to the urban healthcare and pharmaceutical systems (State Council Economic Restructuring Office et al. 2000), promising further opening up in both sectors and the establishment of an urban healthcare system that was more compatible with the socialist market economy. A major move in the reform is that public hospitals were encouraged to implement internal competition mechanisms (Ministry of Health and State Bureau of Traditional Medicine Administration 2000). A scheme, called "patients choose doctors" (*bingren xuan yisheng*) which was designed in light of competition principles, was implemented to reshape doctor–patient relationships. Through the promotion of fair competition in every department and in every post within a hospital, medical employees' attitudes and the quality and efficiency of services were expected to improve significantly. It was demanded in the policy that all employees within a public hospital participate in competition, and that their incomes would be determined by their performance in competition against each other. Those who came last in the competition would be disqualified from their medical posts.

What doctors competed for was the patronage of or selection by patients. In general, patients cannot choose their doctors. If they are covered by public insurance, they are not even allowed to choose their hospitals. The reason that the "patients choose doctors" scheme was promoted as a ground-breaking policy lies in the fact that it empowered patients, granting them the right and privilege to choose whatever doctors and nurses they liked, without additional charges. Medical employees, with their incomes linked to the number of patients they served, were pressured to improve their service quality and attitude. Otherwise they would not only face declining incomes, but also the threat of losing their practicing qualification or even unemployment (Zhao 2000, 2001a).

The health authority was not unaware that patients' choice was limited by information asymmetry. To overcome the barrier to information, hospitals were instructed to make easily available and accessible every single doctor's qualification, professional title, specialty, photo and any other relevant information to facilitate patients making their choice. Medical service guides were also appointed to help patients choose appropriate departments and doctors (Ministry of Health and State Bureau of Traditional Medicine Administration 2000). The ministry apparently believed that this would be sufficient for patients to exercise their power of choice.

The decree did not explicitly state that the scheme was intended to target informal payments, but an anti-corruption purpose was doubtlessly embedded in it. As doctors had to curry favor from patients to survive, they would not dare to take, still less solicit, red packets. Based on this assumption, the government has also attached more importance to competition than to hierarchy as an efficient and enduring solution to red packets. In 2004, the Ministry of Health launched a country-wide campaign against improper conduct. One of the major targets was informal payments. Although the ministry specified disciplinary punishment for eight examples of organizational and individual misconduct (taking red packets being one of the individual instances), it emphasized more constructive approaches toward the general ethos of the healthcare system, and undertook to strengthen professional ethics through education and supervision. But, more importantly, it promised further and deeper reform to the system by encouraging fair and orderly competition and advancing the "patients choose doctors" scheme (Ministry of Health 2004). The comments of Ma Wen, one of the leading figures in China's disciplinary hierarchy,[1] were more telling about the government's preference for competition. When looking back at the development of the work of controlling unhealthy tendencies, she noted that since 1997 the government had employed both constructive and rectifying approaches to strike at both the roots and the effects of unhealthy tendencies. "Patients choose doctors" was highly commended as one of the constructive methods striking at the roots of misconduct in the healthcare system (Ma 2008). As a result, there is little wonder that the scheme was considered as the right direction for health reform (Guo 2007).

In spite of the vehement promotion by the government, however, public hospitals were not enthusiastic about the scheme. In 2000, the scheme was pushed through the entire public healthcare system. The health bureau of every province formed local "patients choose doctors" policies in light of the guidance of the ministerial decree, and the majority of public hospitals had implemented or were about to implement the scheme (Zhao 2001b). But in 2007, when a vice minister of health reasserted that the scheme remained the direction of health reform (Guo 2007), many public hospitals had quietly abandoned it. For example, in Nanjing, the scheme was vigorously promoted and implemented in all public hospitals in 2001, but in 2007 only two major hospitals claimed they were still running it, and in a limited form, so limited that even patients were not aware of its existence (Zhou and Chen 2007).

The reason the "patients choose doctors" scheme has been abandoned by hospitals lies in market failures, especially imperfect information and limited competition (Stiglitz 2000, pp. 308–310). What marks medicine as a profession rests on its command of a body of esoteric and scientific knowledge and on "its exclusive mandate to apply this knowledge to the care and treatment of the sick" (Daniel 1990, p. 1). Patients "must rely on the doctor's judgment as to what medicine is required or whether an operation or other procedure is advisable. Because they lack medical expertise, patients cannot effectively assess and evaluate their doctors' advice" (Stiglitz 2000, p. 309). But the "patients choose doctors" scheme is based on the assumption that the former possess sufficient medical knowledge about their illness and are provided adequate information about the doctors they are to consult. When they come to a hospital, they are supposed to already know the nature of their health problems. Then by reading doctors' biographical data publicized somewhere in the hospital, patients should be able to find the right doctors to consult. If they are still not sure which doctors to go to, service guides will provide sufficient information to assist selection. It must be noted that the Chinese healthcare system does not have GPs. Doctors in hospitals are all specialists in a sense. The service guides are usually staffed by nurses who are not qualified to provide medical advice. They only direct patients to the doctors that they think appropriate.

Chinese patients, however, are not smarter or more learned in medicine than those of other countries. In most cases, they do not know what the causes of their illnesses are. That is why they go to doctors to seek help. But, as many critics have pointed out, under the "patients choose doctors" scheme, patients are supposed to first know what their problems are through self-diagnosis, and then go to hospitals with the knowledge of which doctors are able to help. In reality, patients can hardly make sound self-diagnosis due to lack of expertise. Even if their self-diagnosis is accurate to some extent and they go to the right specialties to seek treatment, choosing the right doctors is another hurdle that can hardly be overcome by reading doctors' information or seeking advice from service guides. In short, patients have knowledge of neither their illness nor their doctors (Liu 2000; Yuan et al. 2003; Zhang 2000). Then how do they choose?

It has been widely reported that, due to information asymmetry, many patients make their choice irrationally. Firstly, they choose by the looks of doctors, selecting the good-looking ones or those who look learned or friendly (Li 2001; You 2000; Yuan et al. 2003; Zhu 2002). Secondly, patients may check each doctor's office first, and then choose the one whose office is crowded or has the longest queue (Liu 2000; Shi 2001). Thirdly, and far more frequently, patients choose senior doctors. This is the uttermost concern of both hospital management and doctors.

Public doctors have four professional ranks—doctor (*yishi*), responsible doctor (*zhuzhi yishi*), associate chief doctor (*fu zhuren yishi*), and chief doctor (*zhuren yishi*). Doctors holding the last two ranks are considered senior doctors, and constituted only 12.3 % of the entire medical profession in 2001 (*China Health Year Book* Editorial Board 2002). As patients usually do not have the information of the competence of each doctor, and are not equipped with the knowledge to distinguish the subtleties of doctors' specialisms within the same department, what they trust is what they understand, namely, professional ranks. They naturally believe that senior doctors are more experienced and competent than middle-rank and junior doctors. For the same amount or slightly higher consultation fees, patients flock to senior doctors (Shi 2001; You 2000; Yuan et al. 2003; Zhu 2002).

Hospital managements are deeply concerned about the imperfect competition and its negative effects on the profession that the scheme entails. Firstly, it is unfair to middle-rank and junior doctors as much fewer patients choose them (Gao and Yang 2003; You 2000; Yuan et al. 2003). The lack of patronage is not because they are incompetent or the quality of their services is not up to standard, but solely because they are in the early or middle stages of their careers and patients usually do not trust young doctors as much. Doctors of lower ranks thus have fewer opportunities to build up their medical experience and skills and prepare for higher-rank positions. In addition, as doctors' salaries are determined by the number of patients they serve, fewer patients means less income. Lacking in opportunities to practice and decline in income may compel young doctors to quit their medical jobs and seek career opportunities and higher incomes in other sectors.

Secondly, as patients are granted the power to choose for no additional charge, they tend to choose senior specialists for even minor illnesses such as common cold (Yuan et al. 2003; Zhang and Xu 2007; Zheng 2007; Zhu 2002). This creates tremendous pressure and unmanageable workloads for senior doctors who are always in high demand. To ensure all patients who choose them are served in a timely order, they have to work longer and shorten the time spent on each patient, which inevitably leads to work fatigue and decline of service quality (You 2000; Zhang and Xu 2007; Zhou and Chen 2007). For the hospital management, senior doctors, especially reputed and eminent doctors, doing work that a junior or middle rank doctor can competently accomplish, is a complete waste of human resources (Zheng 2007).

More importantly, the "patients choose doctors" scheme failed to contain informal payments. On the contrary, it fueled the "latent norm". Information asymmetry and imperfect competition doubtlessly push up the demand for the services of senior doctors. Empowered patients found that they are actually in a seller's market and are not that powerful. Due to the spiraling demand, the services of senior and particularly eminent doctors become increasingly scarce. As patients are not charged additional fees for choosing senior specialists, they found that they still have to pay informally to the latter to compete with other patients for scarce preferential services in order to ensure attention and quality. Only now informal payments are concentrated in the hands of senior doctors, leaving doctors of lower ranks losing both formal and informal incomes. This becomes a source of tension between senior doctors and their junior colleagues.

Given the drawbacks of the scheme, there is little wonder that hospitals are not enthusiastic about implementing it and many have phased it out in spite of the insistence of the ministry. This does not necessary indicate that public hospitals resist the market and are unwilling to give patients power of choice. On the contrary, they are keen to empower patients, but they do not want to give the power of choice for free. Fully aware of their monopolistic position in the healthcare "market" and the scarcity of senior and eminent doctors, public hospitals want patients to pay for their choosing power and therefore prefer another market mechanism—differential pricing.

Differential Pricing and "Operation by Nomination"

Differential pricing has a name in the Chinese healthcare system—special medical services (*texu yiliao fuwu*). It was an initiative of the health authority. In 1992, the Ministry of Health promulgated a decree which gave public hospitals the permission to offer special medical services providing that basic medical services were adequately supplied (Ministry of Health 1992). The purpose was to provide choice medical services to meet the increasing demands of well-off patients, and to break the egalitarian income distribution system that employees of the public healthcare sector had been subject to for a long time. Guided by market spirit and the law of value, the decree promised to decentralize the pricing power in special medical services, allowing the prices of such services to float or to be determined by the industry or hospitals themselves.

The ministerial policy was endorsed and reinforced in 1997 by a central government decree which launched an overall reform to the healthcare system in an attempt to make it more adaptive to the socialist market economy (Central Committee of the Chinese Communist Party and State Council 1997). Differential pricing was adopted as a key mechanism to motivate health organizations and personnel. The central government promised relaxation of the regulation of pricing on medical services for special voluntary needs, and clarified this promise in a decree jointly issued by the Ministry of Health and the National Planning Commission (2000).

The decree demanded the market competition mechanism was put to full use. The central government was no longer involved in setting prices for medical services, the responsibility of which was devolved to local municipal governments. Municipal price bureaus were demanded to follow market competition principles, set guidance prices in light of the categories of hospitals and ranks of doctors, and to relax the regulation of pricing of special medical services. Special medical services were embraced by the government as a major policy initiative to bring healthcare in line with the market reform that was making significant progress in other sectors.

Hospitals have been more enthusiastic about special medical services and embraced them eagerly since 1992 as a major source of revenue to compensate for the ever decreasing government funding. Special medical services is the general term for several services, including "operation by nomination" (*dianming shoushu*), "expert outpatient consultation" (*zhuanjia menzhen*), "special wards" (*texu bingfang*) and "special care" (*texu huli*). Expert outpatient consultation allows eminent specialists to charge significantly higher fees for advising outpatients. Special wards refer to expensive, "luxurious" wards that are usually lavishly furnished and better equipped, and contain fewer beds than ordinary wards. Special care is comprehensive full-time care provided by nurses so that relatives of patients do not have to stay in hospitals to provide care.

What is relevant to the current research is the scheme of "operation by nomination" which is explicitly designed to curb informal payments in the healthcare system. The scheme was first adopted by some public hospitals in Beijing and Shanghai in the 1980s (Shu and Wen 1993). With the ministerial endorsement on special medical services in 1992, it became a widespread "standard" service of public hospitals, especially major hospitals. The scheme, which allows patients to choose senior surgeons they prefer by making extra payments for their preferential and prompt services, was designed with an explicit intention to formalize informal payments (Meng and Liu 2004; Shu and Wen 1993; Yuan 1995). As patients were always under the pressure to give red packets to their surgeons, why not formalize them so that both patients and surgeons did not feel guilty of giving and taking (Ni 1993; Shu and Wen 1993; Ye and Liu 1993)? More importantly, the scheme would encourage competition among doctors, especially senior doctors, as only those with excellent skills and good attitudes and manners would be selected by patients. To attract patients, surgeons were compelled to improve their skills and provide quality services to increase their incomes.

Throughout the 1990s, however, the provision of the "operation by nomination" service was chaotic. Even right after the scheme was endorsed by the Ministry of Health, a vice minister of health complained that some hospitals turned basic medical services into special services or forced patients to choose their own surgeons. The scheme also caused confusion and conflicts in the collegial relationship among doctors and hampered the orderly operation of hospitals (Yin 1993).

With the devolution of pricing power to local municipal government, Beijing Price Bureau and Health Department took the lead in 2001 to control the chaos and to regulate special medical services. They decreed the abolition of three special services, namely, after-hour operations, one-on-one care and accompanied delivery, while retaining three special services, including A-class wards, operation by nomination and children's health centers. Surgical operations for which patients were allowed to choose their own surgeons were strictly limited to difficult, complicated and serious cases, and their "special" status must be approved by the experts at each hospital. Only senior surgeons were qualified to provide the service. The maximum annual number of "operations by nomination" must not exceed 30 % of the total number of surgical operations of a hospital. The extra fees for the service that hospitals were allowed to charge were limited to 50 % of the normal fees, with a ceiling of 800 yuan per operation (Beijing Price Bureau and Beijing Municipal Health Department 2001).

The outcome of the regulation, however, was not satisfactory. The Beijing Municipal Government had to ban the scheme from public hospitals entirely in 2006 (Beijing Municipal Commission of Development and Reform and Beijing Municipal Health Department 2006). The reasons that the authorities gave were that the scheme generated more concerns than benefits. Firstly, the scheme disrupted normal surgical arrangements which had been decided by categories and degrees of complexity. As in the case of the "patients choose doctors" scheme, information asymmetry induced patients to choose senior surgeons to do all types of operations, irrespective of degree of complexity. Although it was stipulated that only difficult and complicated operations were qualified for the special surgical service, in reality, the hospital management was inclined to yield to the demands of empowered patients. As a result, senior surgeons always had full schedules of operations, and thus had little time for ward visits, professional development and supervision of junior doctors. In the meantime, junior and middle-rank surgeons lost the opportunities to perform surgery that they were qualified to do. Their careers and incomes suffered as a result. Secondly, the health authority was concerned that the scheme had increased the economic burden on patients. Thirdly, the scheme attracted patients from all over China to seek medical services in Beijing where they could find more medical experts than anywhere else and choose their own surgeons despite additional fees. The surging number of patients created huge pressure on Beijing's healthcare system and prolonged the waiting lists of senior surgeons (Li 2006).

What the government was reluctant to admit was that the "operation by nomination" scheme, which had been intended to turn under-the-table deals above-board via market mechanisms, failed to contain informal payments. Even if patients paid formal nomination fees to the hospital, they still had to pay extra informally to surgeons (Li 2006; Liu 1994; Wang 2006a; Yan 2006; Yuan 1995). The persistence of the practice under the scheme was contributable to patients' distrust of the bureaucratic medical system. Formal nomination fees were paid to the hospital, which in turn paid part of the fees to surgeons formally. Patients viewed this process as an official arrangement and thus it did not serve the purpose of motivating doctors privately. Patients intended red packets to personalize their relationship with surgeons as they believed that only personalized relationships could obligate public doctors. The distrust drove savvy patients to continue to offer red packets even if they had paid additional fees formally for the special service. Moreover, the nomination rates were capped, and only a small share went to surgeons. Surgeons did not feel particularly incentivized, and their incomes did not increase significantly (Li 2006; Wang 2006b). It was reported that on hearing surgeons only took 30–50 % of nomination fees, some patients felt unsettled and voluntarily offered red packets in private to compensate for the surgeons' loss. Consequently, despite the scheme to formalize red packets, informal payments had never disappeared (Yang and Ding 2006; Yuan 1995; Zhang 2006).

A significant change in healthcare ideology also contributed to its falling into disfavor with the government. Unlike "patients choose doctors" which demanded doctors serve patients better and equally, differential pricing, with its emphasis on profit, encouraged hospitals to discriminate against patients and provide unequal services accordingly. This market rationale is incongruent with the CCP's ideological commitment to "serving the people" (Yang 2009). Since 2005 when the failure of health reform was openly admitted and blamed on marketization, the government gradually shifted the kernel of its healthcare ideology from market-based efficiency to social justice and equality. The new health reform plan announced in 2009 distinguished itself from previous reforms with its emphasis on the non-profit nature of public medicine and health, and on its mission to promote equity and fairness (Central Committee of the Chinese Communist Party and State Council 2009). This may explain why the "patients choose doctors" scheme is continuously promoted while the "operation by nomination" scheme was abandoned.

Although the government banned the "operation by nomination" scheme, it did not abolish all special services based on the differential pricing principle. Special services have always been a major source of revenues to compensate for insufficient government funding. As the government is unable to increase investment significantly to cover the operational loss of public hospitals, it has to allow them to continue to provide special services for the sake of generating revenues and balancing the accounts. In the 2009 reform plan and the latest 2015 reform plan, public hospitals are allowed to keep no more than 10 % of wards for special services (Central Committee of the Chinese Communist Party and State Council 2009; General Office of the State Council 2015), which has been interpreted as the government's reluctant concession to hospitals' demands for profit and their preference for differential pricing (Cao 2015; Chen and Du 2010; Du 2010).

"Operation by nomination" as an independent category of special service is no longer offered in hospital, but it has been combined into other types of special services, especially the "special wards" service, and has survived until today. "Special wards" is a euphemism for "luxurious wards" or "VIP wards". They are usually spacious and decorated like five-star hotel rooms. More importantly, special wards are staffed by senior and eminent specialists and the most competent nurses of a hospital, and equipped with the most sophisticated medical technology. Of course, the prices of such wards are remarkably higher than ordinary wards. For example, in 2014, a major public hospital in Guangzhou set up a "five-star delivery service" which offered special wards for about 3000 yuan per day (in comparison, ordinary delivery wards cost about 100 yuan). Would-be mothers hospitalized into special wards could not only enjoy luxurious accommodation and hotel style services, but also pick any obstetricians and nurses as they liked (Yuan 2014). "Special wards" services in public hospitals have been widely and vehemently criticized for encroaching on public resources, making senior doctors less available to ordinary patients and exacerbating health inequality (Bai 2015; He and Jin 2015); but in the foreseeable future, public hospitals are unlikely to give up special services.

Conclusion

Competition and differential pricing are policy initiatives that demonstrate the government's determination to follow market principles to combat informal payments in the healthcare system, but they suffered different fates. The health authority apparently favors competition and the "patients choose doctors" scheme as it ideally combines market mechanisms and the CCP's ideological commitment to equity. But the scheme is not attractive to hospitals. What hospitals are enthusiastic about is differential pricing and "special services" which are more efficient in generating profits. As differential pricing worsens health inequality, however, it has been increasingly disfavored by the CCP, which has been reasserting its devotion to the socialist principle of social justice and equality in healthcare in recent years.

More importantly, the schemes, which were intended to govern informal economic activities by market mechanisms, failed to contain red packets. Both schemes grant choosing power to patients, who are supposed to exercise it rationally in selecting doctors and thus encourage competition and improvement of service quality. But market failures hinder their choice. Due to information asymmetry and imperfect competition, patients usually surrender their choosing power to senior and eminent doctors. Their "irrational" choice only reinforces the professional power and market position of the latter. In other words, these market mechanisms unintentionally push up the demand for senior and eminent doctors, especially eminent surgeons, and exacerbate the scarcity of their services. To compete for their services, patients still have to offer red packets. Senior and eminent doctors thus benefit both formally and informally from market mechanisms to the detriment of the interests of both their patients and colleagues of middle and junior ranks. As a result, market mechanisms do not solve or even abate the problem of informal payments, but just concentrate them in the hands of elite doctors.

It is evident that the market-oriented reform has not established a genuine market for medical services, and therefore it is unfair to blame the prevalence of red packets and other profit-driven misconduct on marketization. Meanwhile, it is still too early to assume that a genuine market would solve the problems of unhealthy tendencies. Health policymakers in China have overwhelmingly focused on reform to health insurances and public health organizations. Little attention has been paid to the governance of doctors as a profession. Perhaps it is time for the Chinese government to shift its policy focus. At the end of the day, it is doctors who serve patients, and it is doctors who take red packets.

Note

1. Ma Wen was the Vice Secretary of the Central Committee of Disciplinary Inspection, Minister of Supervision, and Director of the State Council Office of Rectifying Unhealthy Tendencies, all of which were the top disciplinary organs of the party-state.

References

Bai, J. (2015, June 20). Quxiao texu yiliao fuwu fuhe gonggong liyi (Abolishing special medical services is consistent with public interests). *Renmin ribao (People's Daily)*, p. 19.

Beijing Municipal Commission of Development and Reform and Beijing Municipal Health Department. (2006). *Guanyu jinyibu guifan he quxiao bufen yiliao fuwu xiangmu shoufei de tongzhi (Circular about further strengthening the regulation and cancellation of the rates for some medical service categories)* [online]. Available from: http://www.bjpc.gov.cn/tztg/200602/t111328.htm. Accessed 1 Dec 2015.

Beijing Price Bureau and Beijing Municipal Health Department. (2001). *Guanyu guifan feiyingli yiliao jigou texu yiliao fuwu xiangmu he shoufei biaozhun de tongzhi (Circular on the standardization of the categories and rates of specially needed medical services in non-profit medical organizations)* [online]. Available from: http://law.lawtime.cn/d434230439324.html. Accessed 1 Dec 2015.

Blumenthal, D., & Hsiao, W. C. (2015). Lessons from the East—China's rapidly evolving health care system. *New England Journal of Medicine, 372*(14), 1281–1285.

Bork, T., Gransow, B., Kraas, F., & Yuan, Y. (2011). Marketization and informalization of health care services in mega-urban China. In A. Kramer, M. H. Khan, & F. Kraas (Eds.), *Health in megacities and urban areas*. Heidelberge: Springer.

Cao, X. (2010). Submerged discontent and institutions: Doctors' pay in Chinese hospitals. In *28th International Labour Process Conference*. Rutgers University.

Cao, J. (2015, May 22). Gong yi gaige zhishi yi pian hualili de wenzhang? (Reform of public hospitals is just bravado?). *Yi yao jijing bao (Pharmaceutical and Medical Economy)*, p. 2.

Central Committee of the Chinese Communist Party and State Council. (1997). Guanyu weisheng gaige yu fazhan de jueding (Resolution on health reform and development). *Zhongguo gonggong weisheng guanli (Chinese Journal of Public Health Management), 13*(2), 65–70.

Central Committee of the Chinese Communist Party and State Council. (2009). Guanyu shenhua yiyao weisheng tizhi gaige de yijian (Circular on deepening the reform to the pharmaceutical and health systems). In Z. Hu (Ed.), *Shenhua yiyao weisheng tizhi gaige wenda (Q and A of deepening the reform to the pharmaceutical and health systems)* (pp. 1–25). Beijing: People's Publishing House.

Chen, X. (2006a). Fansi 'hongbao' xianxiang de cunzai jichu ji duice (Reflection on the foundation of 'red packet' phenomenon and policies dealing with it). *Zhongguo yixue lunlixue (Chinese Medical Ethics), 19*(1), 55–57.

Chen, X.-y. (2006b). Clinical bioethics in China: The challenge of entering a market economy. *Journal of Medicine and Philosophy: A Forum for Bioethics and Philosophy of Medicine, 31*(1), 7–12.

Chen, R., & Du, J. (2010, May 21). Gongli yiyuan weihe rezhong texu yiliao fuwu (Why public hospitals are enthusiastic about special medical services?). *Zhongguo shuiwu bao (China Taxation)*, p. 8.

China Health Year Book Editorial Board. (2002). *China health year book 2002.* Beijing: People's Health Publishing House.

Daniel, A. (1990). *Medicine and the state: Professional autonomy and public accountability.* Sydney: Allen and Unwin.

Du, J. (2010, May 12). Lai qian tai rongyi, gongli yiyuan bian xiang da gao texu yiliao fuwu (Public hospitals expand disguised special medical services for easy money). *Haixia cai jing daobao (Straits Financial and Economic Guide)*, p. 5.

Eggleston, K., & Yip, W. (2004). Hospital competition under regulated prices: application to urban health sector reforms in China. *International Journal of Health Care Finance and Economics, 4*, 343–368.

Fan, R. (2010). *Reconstructionist confucianism: Rethinking morality after the West.* Heidelberg: Springer Netherlands.

Gao, H., & Yang, M. (2003). Qianlun zonghexing yiyuan shishi "bingren xuan yisheng" de li yu bi (The advantages and disadvantages of implementing "patients choose doctors" in general hospitals). *Zhongguo weisheng shiye guanli (Chinese Health Service Management), 8*, 470–471.

Ge, Y., & Gong, S. (2007). *Zhongguo yigai: wenti, genyuan, chulu (Chinese health care reform: problems, reasons and solutions).* Beijing: China Development Press.

General Office of the State Council. (2015). *Guanyu chengshi gongli yiyuan zonghe gaige shidian de zhidao yijian (Guiding advice on comprehensive trial reform to urban public hospitals)* [online]. Available from: http://www.gov.cn/zhengce/content/2015-05/17/content_9776.htm. Accessed 22 Aug 2015.

Gu, X., Gao, M., & Yao, Y. (2006). *Zhenduan yu chufang: zhi mian Zhongguo yiliao tizhi gaige (China's health care reforms: A pathological analysis).* Beijing: Social Science Academic Press (China).

Guo, Y. (2007, April 16). Weisheng bu Fu Buzhang Wang Longde: bingren xuan yisheng shi yiliao fuwu gaige de fangxiang (Vice Minister of Health Wang Longde: Patients choose doctors is the direction of medical service reform). *Zhongguo qingnian bao (China Youth)*, p. 7.

He, D., & Jin, C. (2015, August 17). Gongli yiyuan texu fuwu hequ hecong (Speical services in public hospitals: what course to follow). *Jiankang bao (Health News)*, p. 6.

Hong, M. (2012). Yi huan guanxi zhong hongbao xianxiang de yixue lunlixue zai tantao (Revisit medical ethics in the phenomenon of red packets in doctor-patient relationship). *Zhongguo yixue lunlixue (Chinese Medical Ethics), 25*(2), 207–208.

Huang, Y. (2004). Yiyuan "hongbao" xianxiang yu yiliao tizhi zhuanxing ("Red packets" in hospitals and the transition of the health care system). *Shehui (Society), 10*, 28–30.

Kjær, A. M. (2004). *Governance*. Malden: Polity Press.

Kong, G. (2004). Dujue 'hongbao', shi gaishan yihuan guanxi de guanjian zhiyi (Eliminating 'red packet' is one of the keys to improve doctor-patient relationship). *Zhongguo xiandai linchuang yixue (Chinese Journal of Clinical Medicine), 3*(8), 92–93.

Kong, X., Du, Z., Zhao, M., Yang, Y., & Qin, Y. (2011). Hongbao yu yi huan chengxin (Red packets and honesty in doctor-patient relationship). *Yixue yu zhexue (Medicine and Philosophy), 32*(5), 34–37&48.

Lewis, M. (2010). *Informal payments and the financing of health care in developing and transition countries*. Ann Arbor: International Policy Center, Gerald R. Ford School of Public Policy, University of Michigan [Working report]. Available from: http://ipc.umich.edu/working-papers/pdfs/ipc-98-lewis-informal-payments-financing-healt-care-developing-transition.pdf. Accessed 23 Aug 2011.

Li, B. (2001). Bingren xuan yisheng de shishi yu tantao (Implementation and discussion of patients choose doctors). *Yixue yu zhexue (Medicine and Philosophy), 22*(3), 8–10.

Li, L. (2005). Zhongguo ying caiqu zhengfu zhudao xing de yiliao tizhi (China should adopt government-centred health care system). *Zhongguo yu shijie guancha (China and World Affairs), 1*, 156–162.

Li, C. (2006, April 20). Beijing weihe jiaoting 'diandao fei', huanzhe fachou (Why did Beijing call an end to "scalpel nomination fees"). *Renmin ribao (People's Daily)*, p. 15.

Liu, D. (1994). Dui dianming shoushu wenti de shangque (A thought on operation by nomination). *Zhonghua yiyuan guanli zazhi (Chinese Journal of Hospital Management), 10*(9), 532–533.

Liu, W. (2000, October 11). Chongqing: Bingren xuan yisheng caozuo nan yinyou duo (Chongqing: The difficulties and concerns of patients choose doctors). *Zhongguo xiaofeizhe bao (Chinese Consumers)*, p. A02.

Lu, Z. (2011). Qianxi 'kanbing song hongbao' ji zhili duice (A study of 'giving red packet for medical treatment' and policies dealing with it). *Zhongguo yiyao zhinan (Guide of Chinese Medicine), 9*(24), 360–362.

Lu, Z., Wang, X., & Zhang, J. (Eds.). (2010). *Yi huan guanxi xianzhuang, yuanyin ji duice yanjiu—quanguo shi chengshi yi huan guanxi diancha yanjiu baogao (A study of the current state, reasons and solutions of doctor-patient relationship—A research report on the investigation of doctor-patient relationship in ten cities across the country)*. Beijing: Chinese Bookstore.

Ma, W. (2008, December 23). Jiwang kailai yong yu chuangxin anzhao Kexue Fazhan Guan yaoqiu shenru kaizhan jiufeng gongzuo—jinian dang de jilu jiancha jiguan huifu chongjian 30 zhounian (Advance and deepen the work of rectifying unhealthy tendencies innovatively in accordance with the requirements of the Scientific Outlook—On the 30th anniversary of the reinstatement and reconstruction of the Party's discipline inspection organs). *Renmin ribao (People's Daily)*, p. 10.

Meng, Z., & Liu, Y. (2004). *Shoushu dianming fei shi hongbao de hefahua? Huanzhe dao di gai bu gai gei? (Surgical nomination fees are legalized red packets? Should patients give or not?)* [online]. Available from: http://news.xinhuanet.com/newscenter/2004-12/19/content_2353580.htm. Accessed 19 Dec 2010.

Ministry of Health. (1992). Guanyu shenhua weisheng gaige de jidian yijian (Several suggestions on deepening health reform). In Chinese Health Year Book Editorial Board (Ed.), *Chinese health year book 1993.* Beijing: People's Health Publishing House.

Ministry of Health. (2004). *Guanyu jiaqiang weisheng hangye zuofeng jianshe de yijian (Advice on strengthening the construction of good practice in health professions)* [online]. Available from: http://www.moh.gov.cn/publicfiles/business/htmlfiles/mohbgt/pw10405/200804/26860.htm. Accessed 17 Sept 2010.

Ministry of Health and National Planning Commission. (2000). *Guanyu yiliao fuwu jiage guanli de yijian (Suggestions on the reform to the regulation of medical services pricing)* [online]. Available from: http://www.moh.gov.cn/mohghcws/s3577/200804/16456.shtml. Accessed 22 Feb 2016.

Ministry of Health and State Bureau of Traditional Medicine Administration. (2000). *Guanyu shixing bingren xuanze yisheng cujin yiliao jigou neibu gaige de yijian (Advice on promoting 'patient chooses' doctor in order to advance internal reform of medical institutions)* [online]. Available from: http://www.law-lib.com/law/law_view.asp?id=15429. Accessed 17 Nov 2014.

Morris, J., & Polese, A. (Eds.). (2015). *Informal economies in post-socialist spaces: Practices, institutions and networks.* New York: Palgrave Macmillan.

Ni, B. (1993). "Hongbao", ni gai tangtang zhengzheng zou qian men ("Red packets", you should enter from the front door unshamedly). *Jiaoyu yu zhiye (Education and Vocation), 9*, 35.

Peng, Y. (2004). "Yiliao hongbao" xianxiang de sikao yu zhili jianyi (Consideration and suggestions on governing "medical red packets"). *Jiangsu weisheng shiye guanli (Jiangsu Healthcare Administration), 15*(6), 110–112.

Shi, R. (2001, February 6). Ze yi—zhe ganjue hai bucuo (Choose my doctor—I feel good). *Chuncheng wanbao (Spring City Evening News)*, p. 4.

Shu, Z., & Wen, Z. (1993). "Dianming shoushu" gai bu gai? ("Operation by nomination" right or wrong?). *Zhongguo yixue lunlixue (Chinese Medical Ethics), 3*, 51–53.

State Council Economic Restructuring Office, State Economic Planning Commission, State Economic and Trade Commission, Ministry of Finance, Ministry of Labour and Welfare, Ministry of Health, State Bureau of Pharmaceutical Supervision and State Administration of Traditional Chinese Medicine. (2000). *Guanyu cheng zheng yiyao weisheng tizhi gaige de zhidao yijian (Guidelines on the reforms to municipal and township pharmaceutical and health systems)* [online]. Available from: http://www.cnm21.com/yyfg/yyfg_027.htm. Accessed 9 Mar 2016.

Stiglitz, J. E. (2000) *Economics of the public sector* (3rd ed.). New York: W.W. Norton.

Wang, Y. (1998). Dangqian yiyuan hongbao xianxiang de chengyin yu duice (The reasons and countermeasures against the current red packet phenomenon in the hospital). *Jinzhou yixueyuan xuebao (Journal of Jinzhou Medical College), 19*(4), 69–70.

Wang, S. (2003). Zhongguo gonggong weisheng de weiji yu zhuanji (The crisis and hope of Chinese public health). *Bijiao (Comparison)*, p. 7.

Wang, S. (2006a, March 16). Beijing Shi ge yiyuan quxiao shoushu dianming fei: haoshi neng fou ban hao? (Beijing hospitals abolish surgical nomination fees: can a good thing be well done?). *Renmin ribao (People's Daily)*, p. 5.

Wang, S. (2006b). *Shoushu dianming fei' bei jiaoting: dui huanzhe shi fu shi huo? ('Surgeon nomination fee' is put on halt: good or bad news to the patient?)* [online]. Available from: http://news.xinhuanet.com/focus/2006-03/01/content_4241894.htm. Accessed 9 Mar 2016.

Wang, J., & Kuai, S. (2008). Dui yiliao hongbao de sikao (Thoughts on medical red packets). *Weisheng jingji yanjiu (Health Economics Research), 9*, 12–13.

Wong, B. (2010). Wo guo zhun shichang moshi de kuibai yu zhengfu zeren queshi (The failure of quasi-market model and the absence of government accountability in our country). *Dongbei daxue xuebao (Shehui kexue ban) (Journal of Northeastern University (Social Science)), 12*(2), 135–140.

Wu, M. (2007). Wo guo yiliao weisheng lingyu de shichanghua chengdu fenxi (Analysis of the degree of marketization of medicine and healthcare in our country). *Zhongguo weisheng jingji (Chinese Health Economics), 26*(8), 5–8.

Xu, P. (2006). Hongbao' xianxiang de zhidu jingji xue fenxi (An institutional economic analysis of the 'red packet' phenomenon). *Zhongguo weisheng ziyuan (China Health Resources), 9*(4), 147–149.

Yan, Y. (2006, April 12). Shoushu dianming fei: xiang zuo zou haishi xiang you zou (Surgical nomination fee: turning left or right). *Zhongguo gaige bao (China Reform)*, p. 3.

Yang, J. (2009). Serve the people: Understanding ideology and professional ethics of medicine in China. *Health Care Analysis, 18*(3), 294–309.

Yang, J. (2015). Governing informal payments in healthcare: Lessons from China. In J. Morris & A. Polese (Eds.), *Informal economies in post-socialist spaces* (pp. 245–269). New York: Palgrave Macmillan.

Yang, C., & Ding, H. (2006, February 23). Fa gai wei jiao ting "dianming shoushu" fei (Commission of Development and Reform called an end to "operation by nomination" fees). *Huaxia shibao (China Times)*, p. 6.

Ye, R., & Liu, X. (1993, April 6). "Hong bao" yu "shoushu dao" ("Red packets" and "scalpels"). *Chuncheng wanbao (Spring City Evening News)*, p. 2.

Yin, D. (1993). Zai quanguo yizheng gongzuo huiyi shang de baogao (Speech at the National Conference of Medical Administration). *Zhongguo yiyuan guanli (Chinese Hospital Management), 13*(10), 5–12.

You, X. (2000, December 25). Xiri bingren weizhe yisheng zhuan, rujin yisheng weizhe bingren zhuan (Before patients rotated around doctors, now doctors rotate around patients). *Yunnan ribao (Yunnan Daily)*, p. B2.

Yuan, L. (1995). Shui lai "yiliao" teshu yiliao? (Who come to "treat" special medicine?). *Weisheng jingji yanjiu (Health Economics Research), 8*, 29.

Yuan, G. (2014, May 6). Rang "tianjia chanfang" yuanli gongli yiyuan (Keep "exorbitantly priced delivery room" away from public hospitals). *Sichuan ribao (Sichuan Daily)*, p. 6.

Yuan, C., Gong, G., Sun, M., & Han, Y. (2003). Bingren he yisheng dui "bingren xuan yisheng"de yixiang (Patients' and doctors' preference toward "patients choose doctors"). *Zhongguo weisheng shiye guanli (Chinese Health Service Management), 1*, 16–18.

Zhang, Y. (2000, November 4). Bingren xuan yisheng bu yao zouru wuqu (The myth of patients choose doctors). *Jiancha ribao (Supervision Daily)*, p. 3.

Zhang, L. (2006, March 20). Quxiao dianming shoushu fei—Yisheng ruhe pingshuo (Abolishing fees for operation by nomination—doctors' opinions). *Jiankang bao (Health News)*, p. 3.

Zhang, Z., & Xu, B. (2007, April 29). Bingren xuan yisheng: Quanzhou liu nian shijian diaocha (Patients choose doctors: investigation after six years in practice in Quanzhou). *Quanzhou wanbao (Quanzhou Evening News)* [online]. Available from: http://www.qzwb.com/gb/content/2007-04/29/content_2447863.htm. Accessed 1 Jan 2008.

Zhao, Y. (2000, September 23). "Xuan" chulai de bianhua ("Chosen" changes). *Renmin ribao (People's Daily)*, p. 2.

Zhao, Y. (2001a, January 15). Bingren xuan yisheng (Patients choose doctors). *Renmin ribao (People's Daily)*, p. 2.

Zhao, Y. (2001b, January 15). Bingren xuan yisheng zhidu quanmian tuikai ("Patients choose doctors" is implemented country-wide). *Renmin ribao (People's Daily)*, p. 2.

Zheng, Y. (2007, May 1). "Bingren xuan yisheng" kongpa xing bu tong ("Patients choose doctors" may not work). *Shengming shi bao (Life Times)*, p. 5.

Zhou, Q. (2008). *Bing you suo yi dang wen shui? (Who should be consulted about illness?)*. Beijing: Beijing University Press.

Zhou, L., & Chen, Y. (2007, April 17). Nanjing: bingren xuan yisheng zhengce leisheng da yudian xiao (Nanjing: the 'patients chooses doctors' policy is much said but little done). *Jinling wanbao (Jinling Evening Post)* [online]. Available from: http://www.js.xinhua.org/xin_wen_zhong_xin/2007-04/17/content_9808586.htm. Accessed 9 Mar 2016.

Zhou, H., & Zhang, J. (2004). Analysis of the "red packet" phenomenon in China's medical health industry. *China and World Economy, 12*(3), 26–37.

Zhu, H. (2002). Bingren xuan yisheng li bi fenxi ji duice sikao (Analysis of the advantages and disadvantages of patients choose doctors and solutions). *Zhongguo yiyuan tongji (Chinese Journal of Hospital Statistics), 9*(3), 148–149.

Social Mechanisms of the Counterpublic Sphere: A Case of a Coffee Farmers' Cooperative in LAO PDR

Arihiro Minoo

Introduction

The aim of this chapter is to examine the features of the counterpublic sphere by describing the method of constructing connections in two dimensions, namely within the farmers' society and outside of the farmers' society, through the case of a coffee cooperative's representatives in the farming area of Lao PDR (hereafter, Laos).[1] According to the transition from self-sufficient farming to cash crop farming, the monetary-based economy penetrates the farming areas of Laos. At the same time, such farming areas are usually incorporated in the strong bureaucratic organisations constructed by the Lao government. With such current tendencies among the farming areas, how do the small-scale farmers confront the governmental and market powers exercised from beyond the farmers' environments or *lebenswelt* (Habermas 1990)?

Habermas (1989) argues that the transformation of contemporary society is the process wherein the logic of systems—such as the state, the market and the organisation—which is constituted of strategic and instrumental rationalities have colonised the logic of the lifeworld,

A. Minoo (✉)
Faculty of Sociology, Toyo University,
5-28-20, Hakusan, Bunkyō, 112-8606 Tokyo, Japan

A. Polese et al. (eds.), *The Informal Economy in Global Perspective*, International Political Economy Series,
DOI 10.1007/978-3-319-40931-3_14

which consists of communicative actions among people.[2] According to Habermas, the lifeworld is composed of two different realms: the intimate sphere formed by family and kin and the public sphere which is formed by citizens between the systems and the intimate sphere. The public sphere functions to adjust the tensions between private interests or issues, and the interests required by the systems through open-space deliberation. Such spaces are generally utilised through various intermediary groups called "associations", such as churches, cultural circles, academic societies, guilds, political parties and labour unions, all of which consist of citizens who participate on a voluntary basis.[3]

Indeed, it is not appropriate to apply this Habermatian sketch of contemporary society to a Southeast Asian farming society, whose social contexts differ greatly from that of European society (see Hann 1996, pp. 1–26). However, it seems valid to use the Habermatian model of the public sphere in order to grasp comprehensively the power balance among three independent but interrelated domains: the nation-state, the market and the farming society. Yet, Nancy Fraser's criticism of the Habermatian public sphere has important implications for arguments regarding the publicness of the Southeast Asian farming society.

Fraser (1990) criticises the Habermatian public sphere as a bourgeois and dogmatic concept. According to Fraser, the public sphere is capable of being formed only through the exclusion of those who cannot participate in it. Therefore, she proposes an alternative and subaltern concept of the public sphere as a "counterpublic sphere", the space of a political movement composed of those who seek the approval of cultural identity and the distribution of resources (Fraser 1990). Indeed, the farmers' cooperative as the focus of this chapter can be regarded as one of these counterpublic spheres because it functions as a political arena to seek approval for the distribution of economic profits acquired from selling coffee. Therefore, this chapter analyses the mechanism and conditions under which the counterpublic sphere appears in the farming society of Laos.

In order to achieve this aim, this chapter describes connections among the people in coffee producing area. This is because the counterpublic sphere is conceived as something which emerges in the process of the extension of connections among people (Fraser 1990). Therefore, we should find the counterpublic sphere through pursuing the formations of people's connections in the given social context. In this sense, it is important that we regard the cooperative's representatives as key persons to construct connections between governmental and market actors and the farmers. The representatives are the only actors who can negotiate the different interests concerning coffee trading among the government, market actors and farmers. Thus, this chapter illustrates two dimensions of connections by situating the representatives as a pivot. The first dimension is the connection inside the farmers' society, that is, between the farmers' cooperative representatives and the ordinary members of the society, and the second dimension is the connection outside the farmers' society, or that which is between the representatives and the governmental and market actors.[4]

This study is based on the results of my anthropological fieldwork in a coffee producing area of southern Laos in 2008–2009. During this time, I conducted participant observation in the activities of the coffee farmers' cooperative, as well as interviews with key persons from both the government and the private sector on coffee industry, and 150 coffee farmers concerning household income and expenditures. After two years of research, I continued to make short visits a few times a year for follow-up research.

The Historical Background of Coffee Farmers on the Bolaven Plateau

From Shifting Cultivation to Coffee Planting

The Bolaven Plateau extends over four prefectures of southern Laos—Champasak, Sekhong, Attaphu and Salavan—and the area is approximately 4,800 square kilometres (Delang et al. 2013, p. 152). At the centre of this plateau is Paksong District which is situated at 1,200 metres above sea level. The climate conditions on the Bolaven Plateau, which is cooler and receives more rain than in lowland Laos, are considered to be suitable for coffee production (Winston and Op de Leal 2005, p. 9).

On the Bolaven Plateau, the Laven (or, self-professed, Jru) are the ethnic minority group classified in the Mon-Khmer language family, and these people have been settled there for a long period. Whilst they have until recently practiced hunting, gathering and shifting upland rice cultivation for a self-sufficient economy, they have introduced various cash crops such as coffee and tea. These cash crops gradually spread among the people of this area due to the impact of French colonisation (Ducourtieux 1994).

In the 1960s, Lao people, the majority ethnic group, immigrated to the Bolaven Plateau to engage in shifting cultivation and coffee planting. Today, it is not rare to observe villages which consist of Lao and Laven living together. Although one can see cultural and political differences between the Laven-majority villages and the Lao-majority villages, "coffee farmers" in this chapter refers to both the Laven and Lao as there is no significant difference between them in terms of basic agricultural practices, such as cultivation methods and land use.

After Laos converted to a socialist state in 1975, the government began to collectivise the farmers and the farmland. In the case of the Bolaven Plateau, cooperatives for production and commerce (*sahakhon*) as well as the state-managed farms (*nikhom*) were established to specialise in planting coffee and raising cattle. However, almost all the cooperative and state-owned farms in this area fell into dysfunction and disappeared several years after their establishment.

Since Laos introduced a market-driven economy in 1986, international agencies such as the Agence française de développement (AFD), World Bank and the Food and Agriculture Organization of the United Nations (FAO) offered funds and technical assistance to the coffee industry in Laos, as special attention was given to coffee as a means of earning foreign currency (cf. Sallée and Tulet 2010). On the other hand, when several private coffee trade companies were established on the Bolaven Plateau in the 1990s, they purchased coffee from the farmers and then exported the processed green coffee to foreign countries such as Japan, France and Belgium.

The Horizontal Connection Among the Hueaan *as a Household Unit*

Coffee farmers on the Bolaven Plateau make decisions concerning their livelihood, and in this area each unit is constituted by a nuclear family referred to as a *hueaan* (a household or dwelling). Generally, when a couple is married, the groom moves into the *hueaan* of the bride's parents and then engages in farming with the parents on their plots. Several months after the first child is born, the couple then builds a new dwelling near the parents' home, and the father imparts his land to the couple. Even if the couple moves into the new house, the bride's parents occasionally assist by providing them with cash and rice until they can earn sufficient money to make a living. In this way, coffee farmers on the Bolaven Plateau gradually establish their own household.

Tomoko Nakata (2004, p. 24), who conducted research on the Nge society near the coffee planting area on the Bolaven Plateau, conceptualised it as "the egalitarian society in which the social stratum is undifferentiated". The Laven and Lao societies also do not form hierarchical connections among the *hueaan*. The villages in this area are not grouped according to kinship, and there is no strong solidarity among the relatives. In regards to decision-making concerning planting location, plant variety and the buyer, hardly anyone interferes with the members of other *hueaan*.

The Vertical Connection Between Farmers and Middlemen

In the case of the arabica species, which ripens at the end of October, middlemen come to each farmer's house to purchase picked coffee cherries by pickup truck.[5] Then, the farmers directly receive rewards at the time of purchase. The purchase price gradually rises from the end of October, and the peak price comes at the middle of November, when the best quality cherries can be picked.

While the middlemen role in Laos has originally been undertaken by the Chinese and Vietnamese, the number of Laven and Lao middlemen has grown since the 2000s, followed by an increase in the amount of coffee production. Although in many cases people begin engaging in brokerage by utilising their own money for funds, some people obtain a loan with no interest or collateral through D company, the large private coffee export company in Laos, through building a relationship of trust with the D company officer.

Meanwhile, successful middlemen frequently tend to become the informal money lender in farming areas because they hold sufficient capital. In general, because farmers rarely request a loan from formal financial institutions such as the bank, they offer a loan to middlemen through contacting them by mobile phone during the rainy season in August, when their source of income is extremely limited. Middlemen generally offer a 20–30 % reduced price on coffee cherries through an advanced contract compared to the price of the last picking season, while farmers calculate and decide on the amount of coffee cherries they will sell during the picking season at the price offered by the middlemen. This kind of transaction is called "green coffee" (*kaafee khiao*) because it is conducted during the rainy season when the colour of the coffee berry is still green. Once trapped in this transaction, farmers inevitably gain only a low income because they sell the product at a lower price than that during the picking season. Conversely, middlemen can increase the margin because they purchase the coffee at a low price from the farmers and sell it at the normal market price during the picking season.

Because of this connection between farmers and middlemen, even if the trading conditions for the farmers are deplorable, middlemen are required to be a part of this process as a presence to confer cash to farmers flexibly. Therefore, middlemen hold a high economic position in playing a role in the patronage of the farmers. In other words, it can be said that middlemen are connected vertically to farmers, while farmers are connected horizontally to each other through the *hueaan* in regards to financial transactions.

However, it is not necessary for farmers to pledge allegiance to middlemen in order to preserve this connection. As a middleman complained:

> I do not want to lend money to untrustworthy farmers though many farmers call me every day in August. That is why I set the very low price so that farmers avoid borrowing money from me. Notwithstanding, they call me many times. Therefore, I select and contract with only a few farmers whom I can trust. (Interview with a middleman in August 2010)

Why does the middleman trust only a few farmers? In this area, it is often heard that farmers argue with middlemen, stating that no coffee remains since it has already been sold to other buyers, even if the middleman was certainly planning to contract with the farmer. For this reason, he stated that he could not trust farmers very easily. Furthermore, middlemen do not in fact have the power or authority to forcibly implement the contract. Therefore, in order to implement the "green coffee" sale, middlemen must take into account the risk of the contractual default. This implies that it is also a fact that the informal lending of middlemen hardly deserves the non-equivalent contract between the strong and the weak. In this way, although it is certain that the vertical connection between middlemen and farmers represents a relationship between the one who confers the patronage and the one who receives it, both parties at times conduct constant bargaining in the transaction.

In other words, there exists a patron–client relationship which deserves a vertical informal connection rather than one that is bureaucratic and formal, such as village administrations in the coffee transaction, while people on the Bolaven Plateau are living under an egalitarian society whose people are independent in terms of the decision-making of the *hueaan*. Hanks (1962) examined the patron–client relationship in Thailand, which has a social structure and culture similar to that of lowland Laos, and insisted that the relationship between the patron and the client is spontaneous so that it can be cut off either by the patron or the client. Such a condition is quite similar to the connection between middlemen and farmers in Laos. Therefore, the connection is not very strong—to the degree that both possibly create an exclusive relationship between the patronage and the service. Alternatively, it can be said that both establish a strategic and mutually beneficial connection as one utilises the other's services whenever necessary, or one of the two parties can terminate the relationship when desired.

On the basis of the horizontal and vertical connections, the next section will consider the following question: how do the farmers make a connection with the new buyers of the cooperative, who conduct transactions in a different manner from middlemen?

The Cooperative as a New Coffee Buyer

The Public Sphere Space in the Rural Area

In order to discuss the subaltern counterpublic sphere of coffee farmers, I must outline the general situation concerning public speech and political mobilisation in Laos. In the one-party-ruled socialist state of the Lao People's Revolutionary Party (LPRP), speech that criticises the government is strictly prohibited. Therefore, the people's discontent toward the government is hidden in the private sphere.

In Laos, party members of the LPRP always exist in each village and are generally selected as executives of the village organisation such as the village chief and vice village chiefs. Under the influence of the party, even for the smallest unit of administrative organisation, the discontents of everyday life and the troubles between the villagers are negotiated and solved through village meetings that resemble a sort of deliberation, or the praxis of ***diskurs*** in Habermatian terms. Therefore, it can be said that the space of the village is one of the public spheres where conflicts and disputes between the people are exposed publicly.

However, the various discontents related to the coffee trade such as pricing, which is the major concern of coffee farmers, cannot be dealt with in the village meetings. Therefore, farmers' frustrations regarding these types of discontent will only accumulate. Furthermore, raising issues with the middlemen is a daily occurrence. In short, farmers incessantly complain of lying and cheating by middlemen.

These discontents came to be more clearly observed through investigating the case of a coffee farmers' cooperative, the Jhai Coffee Farmer's Cooperative (JCFC), which was established in 2005 by an American NGO, the Jhai Foundation. After the NGO left the region, it has been supported since 2010 by a Japanese fair trade importer, Alter Trade Japan, Inc. (ATJ). The cooperative functions in a different mode from the village organisation as it takes on publicness as a new political arena which deals with the issue of cash allocation over the rewards obtained through coffee sales. This chapter focuses on the public sphere, which is presented in the cooperative with a subaltern nature.

The Revival of the Cooperative

Approximately 20 years after the abolition of state-led cooperatives in the 1980s, an American freelance trading consultant who was employed by the Jhai Foundation organised production groups (PGs) in eleven villages and created a cooperative to bundle them together in order to obtain fair trade certification.[6] Then a newly founded cooperative, the JCFC, started purchasing coffee from its members by contracting with a French fair trade importer in 2005.

Although the JCFC continued to trade with French importers since its establishment, the trading relationship came to an end due to the bankruptcy of the JCFC in May 2010. The JCFC was lost in the competition of coffee purchasing, which was challenged by a government-led cooperative. However, a Japanese importer, ATJ, which had purchased a small amount of the JCFC's coffee for trial in 2009, offered assistance to the JCFC because the JCFC executives (who are also farmers) hoped to continue managing the cooperative. They told an ATJ officer that before bankruptcy farmers could not make any decisions on their own under the oppression of the middlemen and the former general manager.[7] So now they would like to make the organisation one run by the farmers, for the farmers. ATJ approved of these thoughts posed by the farmers' representatives,[8] and agreed upon long-term trading and financial supports in order that they would be able to manage their own organisation individually.

The Profiles of New JCFC Representatives

The renewed JCFC has three farmers' representatives (a president and two vice presidents), and a farmer who previously traded with ATJ for ten years joined in the executive board as a consultant. When the JCFC held the general meeting which aimed to celebrate its renewal in August 2010, nine chiefs of the former PGs participated in the event. Almost all these PGs decided to sell the arabica typica variety of bean to the JCFC while they sell the catimor variety to the government-led cooperative as well as the middlemen.

The president, Mr U, who was born in 1963, and the vice president and financial officer, Mr N, who was born in 1964, have been selling their coffee to Jhai Café, the predecessor of the JCFC, since 2000.[9] They have played important roles in the PG of PO village because they have become familiar with the deputy village chiefs of PO village. When the JCFC board member election was held in 2007, Mr U was elected as the farmers' representative and Mr N was elected as vice representative. On the other hand, Mr K, who was born in 1949 and serves as both vice president and accountant, was discovered by Mr U and Mr N while serving as chief of KP village's PG to be the only person who could write in the accounting book accurately.

Now, we will corroborate the salient features of the cooperative: the method of purchasing, the qualification of members, the buyers, the variety of coffee to be sold and the change in the number of cooperative members. In contrast to the transaction with middlemen, the JCFC has written rules which are shared among the members in order to make coffee transactions organisationally standard. Each PG asks the members how many kilograms of coffee they have sold to the JCFC during the rainy season prior to the coming season. After gathering the information of the quantity, the PG chiefs report it and the JCFC board members adjust the quota of each PG in order to meet the amount ordered by ATJ during the general JCFC meeting held in August. Meanwhile, the JCFC board members,[10] including the representatives and every PG chief, negotiate the purchasing price in the coming season at this meeting with an ATJ staff. After this procedure, ATJ remits 50–70 % of the agreed price to the JCFC account a few months prior to the picking season.

When the picking season arrives, JCFC members generally process coffee cherries picked by each member's family to the parchment——dried but unhulled coffee beans—— through pulping, fermenting, washing and drying them all on their own. Then, they preserve the parchment in the house until the time arrives to send all the parchment to the JCFC's warehouse by the chief's pickup track in January. After the export volume is confirmed and every document is aligned (which is normally in February), ATJ remits the latter amount of the money to the JCFC.

The PG chief allows anyone to become a member of the PG. Therefore, every PG has titular members who do not sell coffee to the JCFC every year, but are only registered in the roster. Actually, there are approximately 650 registered families, but only around 200 families sold to the JCFC in 2011.

Given that the members are not strictly bound to the JCFC and their membership is not exclusive, every member also sells their coffee to other buyers outside of the JCFC. Interestingly, they sell them separately to various buyers such as middlemen and other cooperatives according to their convenience. This is because it is crucial for farmers to sell coffee to middlemen who come to the farmers' houses every day, purchase any quality of coffee and render the reward directly to the purchase site, despite the fact that their purchase price is relatively lower than the cooperative.

In addition, because ATJ only purchases the arabica typica variety in Laos, those who can join the JCFC are only the farmers who plant this variety, which is traded at a high price due to the scarcity of this variety in the area. On the other hand, in 2011 the JCFC also signed a contract with D company to receive rice bags and organic fertiliser in the rainy season in order to reduce their difficulties(see V-2). For this reason, members of the JCFC are able to sell some amount of catimor to D company through the JCFC. Owing to this contract, the operational scale of the JCFC has expanded rapidly, and today the JCFC has come to include around 2,000 families in 55 villages.

The General Meeting as the Political Arena

At the first general meeting of the re-established JCFC in August 2010, as mentioned earlier, the PG chiefs negotiated the guaranteed price for the coming season and confirmed the estimated quantity of coffee. Then they furnished a contract with the JCFC representatives. Here, I will explain how the meeting came to be a political arena through ethnographic description, as follows.

When the meeting started, prompted by Mr K as the moderator, Mr U firstly declared in front of the board members that the JCFC had been re-established as the cooperative for the farmers, by the farmers. Then, Mr K introduced the ATJ officer to allow her to greet the participants, and then the officer proposed to purchase one container of the typica variety of bean. Responding to this proposal, Mr K read aloud a record of the estimated amount collected from every PG in advance, and prompted the chiefs to confirm whether there was any error in this record. Then, the topic of the meeting was moved to the ATJ officer's proposal of the purchase price and the explanation of the benchmark for the pricing. After the officer finished the explanation, a few chiefs raised their hands and expressed their opinions one by one. One of them insisted that "this price is too low. It is hard to pick up Typica and it takes a long time to process it." Responding to this complaint, another chief agreed on this and proposed that the ATJ officer raise the price. Although this debate failed to remove differences on the pricing between chiefs and ATJ, Mr K urged the chiefs to understand ATJ's conditions in the context of the competitive Japanese market. Finally, after he remarked that "those who do not want, do not need to sell. This is not mandatory," he proposed to agree upon the initial price which ATJ offered. All the board members clapped their hands at the approval of his proposal.

Although this controversy was only a part of the general meeting which extended to more than two hours, what can be seen in this controversy is that this meeting acted as the place to negotiate the demands between buyer and seller. Importantly, the JCFC representatives such as Mr K played a role of coordinator through the intermediation. In fact, ATJ and JCFC representatives held a pre-meeting with respect to the purchase price and the export quantity the day before the board meeting was held. However, the board meeting was expected to be a significant opportunity to make decisions on a variety of considerations. In this sense, such a procedure plays an important role in forming a public sphere based on negotiation. In spite of this official and open negotiation, the trade connections between the PG members and the representatives gradually deviated over the first three years.

Connections Within the Farming Society

Changes in the Number of the Members Who Sell Their Coffee to the Cooperative

Since the fresh start of the JCFC in August 2010, the JCFC exported green coffee beans to ATJ three times, until 2013. Table 1 shows the number of member families from 2010 to 2012. According to the table, the number decreased in all the villages except for NY village, and four villages have only one family who sold coffee to the JCFC in 2012. However, it is remarkable that the quantity that the JCFC purchased from these members increased or was unchanged during these three years: 17 tons in 2010, 31 tons in 2011 and 31 tons in 2012. Therefore, at a glance it would seem that a small number of families has increased their amount of production significantly and sold coffee to a small number of families in turn.

However, according to my survey, this is not the case. The actual circumstance is that some members who sold coffee to the JCFC in 2012 purchased coffee cherries from the PG members or non-members, and then processed them by themselves before they sold it to the JCFC. While each member only processed coffee which was picked in his or her plot in 2010, the core members of the PG in some villages have gradually begun to purchase coffee from the farmers in a manner that is precisely that of acting middlemen. ATJ requested the JCFC representatives to clarify membership in order to grasp the facts, including who sells coffee to the JCFC and the exact amounts. Contrary to this, the JCFC has not recorded from whom these core members purchased coffee cherries.

Importantly, these changes in the way of purchasing should not be regarded as a violation of the rules by members. Rather, it should be considered as the manifestation of the JCFC representatives' policy, which states that only a limited few members process the coffee cherries which were purchased from other farmers rather than allowing each member to process the coffee cherries which were picked individually. This is enforced to satisfy the determined amount and quality according to the agreement with ATJ.

Table 1 The change in number of families selling to the JCFC (from 2010 to 2012)

	Village name	*2010 (family)*	*2011 (family)*	*2012 (family)*
1	PO	9	9	1
2	ST	5	3	1
3	NY	–	12	26
4	PD	11	15	8
5	SP	14	16	14
6	NL	44	28	4
7	KP	16	–	1
8	KT	43	–	0
9	PM	18	–	1
10	PD	11	–	0
	Total	181	83	56

Source: Original data collected and compiled by the author

A Case of KP Village: From the Agreement Among the Members to the Personal Networks

KP village is composed of 160 families where Mr K, the accounting officer of the JCFC, resides. The PG of KP village has 53 families, but only 16 families sold coffee to the JCFC in 2010. Because M. K is one of the representatives of the JCFC and is regarded as a person who is familiar with the JCFC's policy, he has a powerful influence on the members' decision of selling although he does not have any position at the local level of the PG. This influence has become a crucial factor in changing the connections among the members as shown in the following case.

ATJ has an agreement with the JCFC regarding the processing steps of coffee cultivation: the harvested coffee cherries must be processed by the members who picked them, and the PG chiefs bring the determined quality of coffee, which was collected from the members in the PG, to the warehouse. In 2010, while all the members brought the green beans to the warehouse according to this agreement, there was a variation in the quality because some members could process them carefully while others could not. Therefore, Mr K has decided to manage the quality of the coffee distributed by all the members of KP's PG since 2011 because the JCFC representatives introduced a set of de-pulping machines, which process coffee cherries to parchment, in Mr K's new KP village plot by receiving the financial support of ATJ.

In 2011, when the JCFC decided to purchase the parchment (which is a previous processing stage of the green beans, rather than the actual green beans) from each PG, Mr K started to purchase coffee cherries from the farmers who grow typica trees inside and outside KP village in order to process them to parchment stage himself. Why did Mr K go through with this kind of action? In August 2011 when I visited some PGs of the JCFC with ATJ staff and Mr K, I asked a PG chief of NY village about the amount of coffee sold to the JCFC the previous year.

NY village is a place where several members of the PG are relatives of Mr K. He told me they sold 1.4 tons of this parchment to the JCFC. Because this amount differs from the amount in the data recorded by the JCFC representatives, I continued to ask whether it was 0.5 tons or not, as it was according to this record. He answered that a member sold 2 tons of coffee cherries to Mr K. Mr. K, who accompanied me, acknowledged the chief's answer without any awareness of the violation of the rules.

In this way, apparently Mr K does not deny purchasing coffee cherries from the other villages beyond his own, and recognises that it is a matter of course. He mentioned his manner of conduct in other locations as it is better for him that he processes coffee himself through the purchasing of coffee cherries. This is because there are quality variations due to the timing of the collection from each member.

ATJ demands JCFC representatives manage the quality of coffee more carefully in exporting, and as Mr K really understands this policy he has requested more discreet quality management by the members. In the case of receiving poor quality parchment, the quality control staff of the JCFC require the members to bring them back to their village and dry the parchment again until it has reached the regulated moisture level on the occasion of examination at the JCFC warehouse in PO village. However, in 2010, a member living in KP village sold his poor quality parchment to a middleman who lives near the warehouse immediately after the parchment was rejected. The individual thought that returning to the village and processing once more would be bothersome. In such a case, the JCFC must re-collect the money which was paid in advance, and then a problem wherein the JCFC cannot meet the amount of coffee specified by ATJ occurs. Therefore, referring to this problem, Mr K explained that he collected the cherries himself both inside and outside the village in order to meet the agreed amount.

As a result, in 2012 Mr K informally collected the cherries from a total of 47 families through his personal network: 30 tons of cherries were collected from 30 families inside KP village, and 10 tons of cherries were collected from 17 families in three other villages which are located near KP village. Because, in terms of the traceability of coffee, ATJ does not formally admit that members ever purchase cherries from elsewhere, the official record showed that only one family sold to the JCFC in KP village (see Table 1).

This purchasing through personal networks leads to a mere superficial shell of decision-making through negotiation among the members, so that it generates dissatisfaction among some of them. In January 2013, while drinking at a local bar in the central area of Paksong with my friend Mr P to celebrate reuniting for the first time in four months, a man who is in fact a PG member in KP village came to meet us. He began complaining that only the relatives of Mr K can sell the amount of coffee they desire. Like him, non-relatives of Mr K are allocated a small amount because Mr K prioritises his relatives when he divides the quota amongst members.

This incidental experience illustrates that a general dissatisfaction has begun to spread: the relatives and the non-relatives are treated differently despite their equal PG membership. Indeed, for the sake of Mr K, there is no evidence as to whether he discriminates against non-relatives intentionally. However, it is certain that a distrust towards Mr K has been generated among the members. On the other hand, Mr K might recognise the dissatisfaction among the members, so that he has struggled in the management of the JCFC. In January 2013, referring to some dissatisfaction among the members, he told me that even if the representatives make an effort to meet all the demands from the members, they would still not bring high quality coffee to the JCFC.

This suggests that Mr K is caught in a dilemma between two contrary prioritisations: the quality and the members' opinions. If the JCFC produced high quality coffee more efficiently, it would be better to purchase coffee from the person who the representatives know well and who works according to the regulations. However, if they purchased from members impartially by prioritising members' opinions, it would occasionally receive defected and low quality coffee because the inexperienced members would thus be included in processing the coffee. Therefore, these cases from KP village demonstrate the process wherein some members are gradually excluded from the process and from decision-making. These are the members who cannot be trusted by the representatives because of their inability to satisfy the JCFC's specified quality and to maintain within the regulations, even though the cooperative's aim is officially to purchase on the basis of the members' consensus.

The Connections Beyond the Farming Society

Negotiation with the Governmental Organisation

The JCFC acquired permission concerning coffee trading from the governor of Paksong district in August 2010. By acquiring permission from the government, the JCFC becomes an organisation which is able to exercise power to achieve their aim in the village under the law of Laos. Therefore, it was very significant for the JCFC to acquire government permission in order to manage the organisation more sustainably.

However, in reality, because the authorisation by the local government to the JCFC is weaker than that of the central government, the basis of the JCFC's trading activities was unstable at that time. In the trading season of

2010, although the JCFC ultimately exported 17.6 tons of green beans to ATJ, it could not meet the previously agreed amount of 19.6 tons. During a meeting between the JCFC and ATJ held in 2011, they reflected on the results of trading in 2010. When I asked why they could not provide the adequate amount of coffee, Mr U explained this inadequacy through lack of authority, as follows: "We do not have *amnaat*, so that we could not prevent the members from selling to other buyers."

Amnaat is a crucial word in considering the exercise of power in the Lao–Thai linguistic world. It is generally translated as "power", but more precisely means the formal authority which is used when the Lao government carries out orders toward the people on the basis of the various regulations such as laws and decrees. In this manner, although the local government of Paksong authorised the JCFC's trading activities, it is not so sufficient that the representatives do not require more effective *amnaat* in the governance of their organisation.

Considering their positions and purposes, it is inevitable that the JCFC representatives seek a direct connection with the central government. In 2011, through the introduction by Mr S who is the consultant of the JCFC, there was talk about the JCFC becoming a member of the Lao Coffee Association (LCA). The LCA is an organisation established in 1995 by the major private coffee trading companies of Laos in order to bridge between the private sector and the governmental sector. Importantly, they are authorised by the central government. When I asked the president of LCA, Mr T, as to why the JCFC should become the member, he told me that the LCA did not have a farmers' group. In the background of this reason, there was a power struggle over the leadership in the coffee industry of Laos with the AGPC, which is the government-led, large-scale cooperative participating with 53 farmers' PGs.

Meanwhile, the president of the JCFC, Mr U, expressed that "if [the] JCFC participates in [the] LCA, we will be able to make the connection with the central government. In that case, it is possible to acquire [a] grant. Indeed, a German aid foundation has already offered [a] renovation project for coffee plots through [the] LCA."

The JCFC's participation in the LCA shows the matched mutual interest between the two parties: the LCA saw the prospect of having a more powerful influence on the Lao coffee industry by connecting with the existing farmers' group of the JCFC under the struggle over the leadership with the AGPC, while the JCFC had the intention of having a more powerful influence on the members by connecting with the agency of the central government. In other words, this suggests that the JCFC can continue to manage the organisation by integrating the members only under the umbrella of *amnaat* brought about by the central government's authority.

On the other hand, if farmers try to order other farmers around, under the circumstance of having no *amnaat*, these farmers are indirectly blamed for excising an unauthorised power through the adoption of such concepts as *itthiphon* by the targeted farmers. While *amnaat* refers to the formal authority, *itthiphon* refers to informal influence.[11] For example, in August 2012 when I conducted a survey on the household economy in KP village, a man told me, "I do not want to sell to [the] JCFC because [Mr K] has *itthiphon*", in response to the question of he did not sell to the JCFC. This man may have been aware that there were people whose coffee was rejected by Mr K at the warehouse for reasons of low quality during the previous season (see the section "A Case of KP Village: From the Agreement Among the Members to the Personal Networks" above).

Generally, in case an action is regarded as *itthiphon*, the farmers attempt to avoid indirect blame as much as possible, because a blamed person will likely become isolated in the village. However, if a person was blamed as he or she was exercising *itthiphon*, the person would be quiet until the backbiting dies down, or conversely they would try to justify their influence by converting the informal influence into a more formal one as performed by the JCFC representatives. That is why it was inevitable that the JCFC hoped to receive the authoritative endorsement by the central government in order to manage its activity sustainably.

What is important to point out in regards to this chapter's argument is the JCFC's self-definition: the JCFC is not the kind of trader that expands personal profit like middlemen in this area, but is rather a farmers' organisation which aims toward negotiation with the buyers to get the best for all members. The president of the JCFC, Mr U, told me in August 2013 that "we do not receive a monthly salary at all. [Meanwhile,] farmers always beg me [for] money. But we cannot make a good relationship with such farmers. We have to endure working for the farmers." This statement suggests that the representatives are appealing to the mentality of self-sacrifice which places the priority on public interest by excluding self-interest.

However, in fact, ATJ pays the management fees to the JCFC of 1,000 kip per kilogram, and requires the JCFC to decide upon the method of utilising it in a consensus among the board members. Even though the total fee is not enough to cover their entire needs, at least the representatives can afford to pay their gasoline and meal costs for the meeting. Because some PG chiefs and members are aware of this treatment, they might think that the mindset of self-sacrifice by the representatives sounds expedient. However, even when the representatives create a connection with the LCA, the LCA recognises the JCFC as an organisation created to pursue a public interest for the farmers, because the LCA does not know of this unstable connection between the representatives and the members inside the organisation.

To conclude, while the JCFC representatives produced the image of public organisation for the farmers as a manipulation tactic to acquire support from the LCA, they gained *amnaat* which created the effect needed to govern the organisation by connecting with the LCA. Therefore, as a consequence they came to have the authority to acquire the obedience of the members.

Negotiation with the Large Export Company

JCFC representatives point out farmers' difficulties while keeping a certain distance in the realm of the market as well as the government. For example, in 2011 the JCFC held a meeting with D company (see section "The Horizontal Connection Among the Hueaan as a Household Unit" above) and was introduced by the consultant of the JCFC, Mr S. According to Mr S, the story of the JCFC's meeting with D company is as follows.

The president of D company called Mr S to consult on business with a Japanese company to which D company has started to export since a few years ago. Because Mr S has been exporting to the Japanese company ATJ since 2004, the president of D company considered that Mr S was a suitable person from whom to gain advice on trading with the Japanese, who are known to demand high quality products. At that time, Mr S brought the JCFC representatives to the meeting and proposed that the president collect coffee through the JCFC because the JCFC had already been successful in exporting to the Japanese market through ATJ since 2010. In regards to making a contract with the JCFC, Mr S requested the president of D company to accept the same conditions as with ATJ (50 % of the payment) in advance. Consequently, D company agreed on these conditions, and the JCFC started to sell 2,000 tons of coffee cherries to D company (interview with Mr S in August 2011).

This explanation of Mr S tells us two points: the JCFC started to create a connection with D company by accepting the consultation of D company, and the JCFC attempted to negotiate with D company while suggesting mutual benefits. This negotiation is worth mentioning in terms of D company's acceptance of the advance payment, which is really necessary for the farmers, by utilising the successful experience of export to a Japanese company. This is because the farmers have reluctantly accepted the price-setting of middlemen who have been superior to farmers in the economic condition in existence until the present day. Apropos trading with the buyers, there are a few cases wherein both sellers and buyers will reach a consensus when taking into account each other's interest in the deliberations, such as in the case of the JCFC and D company. Considering these circumstances between them, the consensus of D company marked a milestone for the farmers.

In regards to the JCFC, it is certain that the pivotal reason for the success in negotiations with D company depended on the successful experience with ATJ. However, special attention must be paid to the fact that the negotiations have succeeded not by utilising the ability of an individual person such as a middleman or an ordinary farmer, but by using a form of the cooperative which is established as the representative body for the farmers. On the other hand, it is also beneficial for D company to purchase a constant quality of coffee through the cooperative as it can grasp the number of members and trace the flow of the product and money, which is very different from purchasing different qualities of coffee from middlemen.

Conclusion

This chapter examined the mechanisms and conditions of the counterpublic sphere through the case of the representatives' activities in a farmers' cooperative in Laos. Contrary to public spheres such as the village, which have been established through top-down planning by nation-states, the public sphere which this case suggests is constructed through the appeals on the issues concerning farmers' distribution of economic resources to actors such as nation-states and markets, without conflicting with the state-led public sphere. This type of public sphere is considered to be one of the counterpublic spheres which Fraser (1990) pointed out. In this counterpublic sphere, it is found that the features of the connections possessed by the cooperative exist in two different but interrelated dimensions: the transformation of connections inside the cooperative, and the construction of connections outside the cooperative.

The former connection demonstrates that it was difficult to form a relationship of trust between the representatives and the members because the members expressed discontent with the representatives, while the representatives select a trustworthy member for purchasing good quality coffee. What can be pointed out through the case in this chapter is that the "distrust towards otherness"——one of the invisible attitudes——may be regarded as a barrier to participating in the public sphere. Various narratives concerning distrust toward otherness have been formed between the middlemen and the farmers as well as between the representatives and the members of the JCFC. Therefore, the middlemen and the representatives are regarded as having a similar tendency by ordinary farmers. While the middlemen sometimes lend money with high interest before picking season, the representatives also pay money in advance prior to the picking season. In any case, the farmers who received money sometimes attempt to escape by not selling his or her coffee to them as promised. In such an untrustworthy relationship, the representatives prefer to construct a connection with a small number of trustworthy members, as do the middlemen in contracting a loan with the farmers. Consequently, therefore, the trade connections have gradually converged on only a certain group of trustworthy people.

The latter connection illustrated that the representatives justified the informal influence *itthiphon* by gaining the formal authority *amnaat* through constructing connections with the central government and a large exporting company, while simultaneously meeting the needs of each organisation by appealing that they are the "public organisation for the farmers". The decisive factor upon which the JCFC was able to build connections with these actors is the representatives' appeal of the JCFC's publicness, specifically their voluntary contribution to the members and their consideration of the farmers' difficulties. This case study suggests that the representatives' tactics are the conversion of the member families' private issues—the difficulties of insufficient funds during the rainy season—into formal issues which the government agency and the company are expected to tackle with the farmers. The private issues regarding almost all of the farmers' difficulties during the rainy season were turned into the public issues, and then grew to be known by the government agency and the export company through the activities of the cooperative.

Both creating and destroying connections are related according to the local composition of power, such as through *amnaat* and *itthiphon*, and the form of trustworthiness. What is found in this chapter is not a simple consequence wherein those mirroring the public interest maintain a connection while the people without it are excluded. Rather, whether the people have "public" interest or not, the representatives in such a case select the connections which they require in order to maintain the organisation.

Notes

1. This chapter is a revised version of the original which was published in *Japanese Cultural Anthropology*.
2. In the preface of the second version in *Strukturwandel der Öffentlichkeit*, Habermas (1990), reflecting on the collapses of the state socialist system of Eastern Europe and the Soviet Union, rejected his own previous perspective that the economy and nation-state were regarded as a practical domain to be integrated systematically. He then presented a new perspective which proposed that the economic system, which functions through the power (*gewalt*) operated by monetary exchange, has a different mechanism from that of the nation-state, which functions through the power operated by the administrative authority. According to his perspective, the public sphere is given the role of sealing the orders that systems operate democratically (Habermas 1990).
3. These examples are taken from the preface of the second edition of the Japanese translation of *Strukturwandel der Offentlichkeit* (1990).
4. Market actors refer to export companies or multinational cooperation in this context because they are assumed to be market-based actors who pursue market mechanisms such as profit maximisation. On the other hand, farmers are not regarded as market actors because they are socially embedded actors who are easily affected by social relationships in decision-making processes even though they are also sell the products.
5. The coffee cherry generally refers to the ripe red berry of the coffee plant.
6. Jhai Café, the predecessor of the JCFC, was established in 2000. This organisation had purchased coffee cherries mainly from PO village and the surrounding area through a contracted middleman at a relatively higher price than the ordinary middlemen.
7. This general manager, who graduated from the university in Laos, was the key person who lived in the city near the coffee farming area. Unlike the JCFC farmers, he could speak English and had access the Internet, so he alone could contact the foreign importers and draft trade contracts. However, the ambiguous accounting figures which he presented to the farmers were met with distrust, and Mr U and Mr K grew to be suspicious of potential corruption on the general manager's part.
8. The representatives consist of the president, Mr U, and two vice presidents, Mr K and Mr N.

9. All village and persons' names are pseudonyms.
10. The board members consist of three representatives and the PG chiefs.
11. Yoshifumi Tamada (1991) refers to *amnaat* and *itthiphon* in Thai. The relationship of both words is quite similar to that of Lao.

References

Delang, C. O., Toro, M., & Charlet-Phommachanh, M. (2013). Coffee, mines, and dams: Conflicts over land in the Bolaven Plateau, southern Lao PDR. *The Geographical Journal, 179*(2), 150–164.

Ducourtieux, O. (1994). *L'Agriculture du Plateau des Bolavens (Évolution du Système Agraire de la Région de Paksong–Sud-Laos)*. Rome: Institut National Agronomique Paris-Grigon.

Fraser, N. (1990). Rethinking the public sphere: A contribution to the critique of actually existing democracy. *Social Text, 25/26*, 56–80.

Habermas, J. (1989). *The structural transformation of the public sphere: An inquiry into a category of Bourgeois Society* (Trans. T. Burger & F. Lawrence). Cambridge, MA: MIT Press.

Habermas, J. (1990). *Strukturwandel der Öffentlichkeit: Untersuchungen zu einer Kategorie der Bürgerlichen Gesellschaft (Mit einem Vorwort zur Neuauflage 1990)*. Frankfurt a.M.: Suhrkamp Verlag.

Hanks, L. M. (1962). Merit and power in the Thai social order. *American Anthropologist, 64*(6), 1247–1261.

Hann, C. (1996). Introduction: Political society and civil anthropology. In C. Hann & E. Dunn (Eds.), *Civil society: Challenging western models* (pp. 1–26). London: Routledge.

Nakata, T. (2004). *The ethnography of village society in southern Laos: "Solidarity" and struggle under the co-living of ethnic groups (in Japanese)*. Tokyo: Akashi Syoten.

Sallée, B., & Tulet, J. (2010). Développement de la Caféiculture Paysanne et Concessions de Terres sur le Plateau des Bolovens (Sud Laos): Synergie ou Antagonisme? *Les Cahiers d'Outre-Mer, 249*, 93–120.

Tamada, Y. (1991). Itthiphon and Amnat: An informal aspect of Thai politics. *Southeast Asian Studies, 28*(4), 445–465.

Winston, E., & Op de Leal, J. (2005). *Arabica coffee manual for Lao-PDR*. Bangkok: FAO Regional Office for Asia and the Pacific.

Formalisation of Entrepreneurship in the Informal Economy in Sub-Saharan Africa and the Role of Formal Institutions: An Analysis of Ghana's Experience

Kwame Adom

Introduction

Informal entrepreneurship is a major lifeline for many dwellers in both rural and urban economies, especially in developing countries, but also in transition economies and the developed world (Adom 2014; Adom and Williams 2012; Sauka et al. 2016; Williams 2014, 2015; Williams and Gurtoo 2017; Williams and Horodnic 2015, 2016; Williams and Shahid 2016; Williams and Youssef 2015; Williams et al. 2016). As Williams (2007) explains, the tendency throughout much of the twentieth century about the informal economy was to perceive it as a remnant from a previous economic era and as something which was disappearing from view as time passed on. During the past few decades, however, the informal economy has attracted attention as it found its place in the development discourse of many academics, governments, policymakers and so on. Although the informal economy is not a new concept, it has acquired a restored currency in a world characterised by an increasing divide between the rich and

K. Adom (✉)
Department of Marketing and Entrepreneurship University of Ghana Business School, Legon - Accra, Ghana
e-mail: kadom@ug.edu.gh

A. Polese et al. (eds.), *The Informal Economy in Global Perspective*, International Political Economy Series,
DOI 10.1007/978-3-319-40931-3_15

the poor. In Ghana, however, it must be argued that in spite of the widespread recognition of its magnitude and even growth entrepreneurship in the informal economy has not received the attention it deserves in the employment policies of the government until now.

There has been no clear policy direction from the formal institutions in terms of their role in formalising informal entrepreneurship. However, the commonly held assumption is that formalisation of economic life is the only route to progress, modernity and advancement and thus formalising entrepreneurship in the informal economy is the route to economic development.

Not only has informal entrepreneurship thus become more and more widespread across various economic landscapes, but also the call for formalisation has become more prominent. Informal entrepreneurship for many represents the site of hopelessness and a road to economic underdevelopment or doom—what I call the "journey of no hope". Since the discovery of the informal sector concept in the twentieth century, it has been widening and has even attracted more attention since the turn of the millennium. Until now, entrepreneurship in the informal economy has been dominated by the view that it is the marginalised and economically vulnerable population who make a living in this arena. Hence, little attention has been given to it. Regardless of the various depictions of informal entrepreneurship as backward, underground, underdeveloped, associated with the black market and so on, formal institutions have failed to prevent or eradicate informal entrepreneurship. For some time now, formalising informal entrepreneurship and ensuring that more decent jobs are available has been part of the development discourse heralded by the International Labour Organization (ILO). In 2015, the ILO overwhelmingly voted for the formalisation of the informal economy enshrined in Recommendation 204 (ILO 2015)

The key question is what is/are the role(s) of formal institutions in ensuring that informal entrepreneurs play by the rulebook (Williams 2007)? Formal institutions are steeped in formal rules (laws and regulations). This chapter therefore seeks to evaluate critically the role of formal institutions in formalising entrepreneurship in the informal economy in Ghana.

From the outset it is appropriate to define informal work to place the debate in perspective. Examining solely paid informal work, Williams and Windebank (1998 p. 1) define informal employment as the "paid production and sale of goods and services that are unregistered by, or hidden from, the state for tax, social security, and/or labour-law purposes but which are legal in all other respects" (see, Portes 1994; Small Business Council 2004). The application of this definition in sub-Saharan African region where informal entrepreneurship involves street vendors (street-preneurs), hawkers, local restaurants (chop bars) and so on may be challenging. One of the main issues confronting the formalisation of informal entrepreneurship is to do with what constitutes informal work and which aspect of that work needs to be formalised.

To address this, therefore, a working definition is adopted so that it becomes clear what is included and excluded. In this paper, and following the ILO definition and subsequent expanded conceptual framework for defining informal work and also examining other definitions, we define the informal economy as:

> "all economic activities by workers and economic units that are in law or practice – not covered or insufficiently covered by formal arrangements" (ILO 2002a, p. 4).

This definition caters for the grey areas between formalisation and informalisation. The implication is that formal institutions will be in a position to assess which aspect of informal entrepreneurship needs to be formalised.

Formal Institutions and Informal Entrepreneurship

Formal institutions in this chapter refers to any institution charged with the responsibility to ensure that the bureaucratic culture is maintained. What makes something formal is its conformity with such an idea or rule (Hart 2006, p. 29). The primary focus is on laws and regulations. Informal activities may break the law through an infringement of health and safety regulations, tax evasion, smuggling, the use of child labour or selling without a license (Hart 2006).

Some believe that lack of or inadequate regulations are responsible for the existence of the informal economy. The outcome is that informality is equated to illegality, with the presumption that workers and enterprises in this arena are unregistered, do not pay taxes, disregard labour laws, are guilty of non-payment of social security and so on. Although this presumption may not be entirely true, strictly, tax evasion is illegal and if informal workers evade tax then their activity does become illegal.

The debate may fall short in certain jurisdictions in that in Ghana in particular most informal players do pay tax, which is determined by the tax authorities as to which evaders could be prosecuted. The illegality of informal work may well to true in advanced economies where formal businesses conduct part or all of their business cash-in-hand or off-the-books (Williams 2009a, 2009b) and thus authorities find it difficult to trace the transactions and assess tax. It is for this reason that Williams and Windebank (1998 p. 1) define informal work as quoted above, and which was also adopted by the Small Business Council in 2004. Their definition is explicit about what is informal work and its legality. The only factor that makes it illegal is the non-payment of tax and social security—the goods and services produced are in fact legal and thus drug trafficking and prostitution are excluded, especially in the UK. The situation in Ghana is different as informality is the norm rather than the exception. Payment of taxes is not the issue because there is a tax payment arrangement present. The real challenge is how to assess workers' income tax in a more progressive manner so that the marginalised and/or low-income populations do not pay more. Again, how could one assess the tax of hawkers, shoeshine boys, domestic servants, streetpreneurs and the like? Although it may seem difficult, in Ghana those operating from a permanent location/premises such as kiosks, containers, stores and in some cases stalls pay a flat-rate tax called tax stamp. This is a sticker made by the Ghana Revenue Authority (GRA) and sold to informal workers to be displayed at their places of business.

Again, the non-payment of tax, especially by informal workers, may not have a universal application, particularly in sub-Saharan Africa. In developed economies the reality is that some formal businesses also do operate partially or wholly in the informal economy (Williams 2007; Williams 2009a, 2009b) and such activities have no paper trail for the tax authorities to trace to assess appropriate tax for those firms.

Formal institutions continue to play a key role in strengthening the informal economy. The reason is not far-fetched. In Ghana, there is an emerging small financial economy; what I call "mobilemoniconomy", which is mainly a system for money transfer through the mobile telephone network. The source of the activity is formal but the intermediaries are informal. The intermediaries are nearly unemployed people who are trying to make a living. They register with the mobile phone companies operating the mobile money transfer and ordinary citizens who want to remit or pay bills or people use these self-employed mobile money operators at vantage locations across cities, town and villages. This business has attracted a lot of people and some mainstream commercial banks are now in the mobile money transfer business. Those in the middle and at the end of this continuum exhibit various degrees of (in)formalisation (Williams and Shahid 2016). This is just one example of such a distribution arrangement within the wide economy. Formal institutions have helped foster informal entrepreneurship for years (Adom and Williams 2012). The formal structure itself promotes informality. Artificial barriers created within formal institutions are a catalyst for ever growing informal entrepreneurship. It is believed that some members of these institutions have become rich and as result protect this source of "free income". Formal, bureaucratic tendencies are a mere ploy to frustrate entrepreneurs into operating informally. However, the term "informal" does not suggest that there are no rules or norms controlling the activities of workers or enterprises (ILO 2002b). Those who take on informal activities have their own "political economy"—their own informal or group rules, arrangements, institutions and structures for mutual help and trust, offering services such as credit provision, training, technological transfer and skills, market and trading access, enforcing obligation and the like (ILO 2002b). Evidence from the literature largely suggests that the informal economy is an unorganised sector and unregistered for tax purposes. However, this may not hold to some extent in Ghana. Informal work may be unorganised activity or unregistered in general but some informal work is organised, registered and tax is paid. Indeed, in Ghana, the Ghana Private Roads Transport Union (GPRTU) is a well-organised informal association with membership of the Trade Union Congress (TUC). According to Croucher (2007), the GPRTU is Ghana's fifth largest union within the TUC fold. They pay what the tax authorities call vehicle income tax (VIT), but the difference here may well be that they pay a fixed form of tax regardless the size of their income. The tax is levied on the vehicle and not on the income that the vehicle generates. Again, the players (vehicle owner, owner-driver, driver and his mate(s)) do not pay any form of tax on their earnings. This form of tax is highly regressive since there is no level playing field for all the drivers in every community across the country. For example, a big vehicle plying rural roads may not make more money but will pay higher VIT than a smaller van/bus (*trotro* as they are called locally) operating in the city of Accra which makes more money regardless of the size but pays less VIT. It is not only the members of the GPRTU but also other organised or unorganised commercial vehicle operators pay the same tax. Ordinary market operators as well as artisans also pay tax stamp. Not only does the GPRTU have membership of the TUC but also it has a huge influence on the government's transport policies, especially road transport. For example, they play a strategic role in fixing transport fares for commercial transport operators across the country.

For many years it has determined transport fares for all commercial drivers across the country with few exceptions. This raises serious question regarding what constitutes informal work and what does not.

Although these workers define themselves as operating in the informal economy, under many definitions they would not be so classified. It is a very complex situation because it is not the drivers and their mates who are paying tax from their income—the tax is on the vehicle. The GPRTU is made up of vehicle owners, owner-drivers and other drivers and their mates. They protect the interest of these members, especially non-owner drivers and their mates, particularly when their employers (vehicle owners) are in breach of their employment terms which are most often in the form of verbal agreement. By many definitions, in consequence, these workers would be defined as formally employed. This shows the importance of being clear on what is being discussed when analysing the informal economy. It is also important to be more explicit here in terms of formality. Apart from the flat-rate tax paid by these informal entrepreneurs, they cannot be termed as formal employees in any other aspects. It is again important to note that it is the wish of the government to formalise the informal economy, which is also consistent with long-term ILO policy.

Formalisation and Its Discontents Among Informal Entrepreneurs

Deregulation of certain sectors of the economy such as the financial and telecommunications in the late 1980s and early 1990s have largely been responsible for the ever growing informal economy. Through mergers and acquisitions employees often are at the mercy of new owners and the outcome is normally downsizing, rendering some unemployed. Trade liberalisation and globalisation have also played key parts in grooming the informal economy. The idea of formalising the informal economy is not new but has attracted current attention in development discourse. In 2015 the ILO moved a little further with the formalisation agenda under the auspices of Recommendation 204 (ILO 2015). Formalisation is, however, seen as crucial for the achievement of sustainable development goals especially goals 1, 5, 8 and so on (ILO 2015). Below are said goals:

Goal 1. End poverty in all its forms everywhere
Goal 5. Achieve gender equality and empower all women and girls
Goal 8. Promote sustained, inclusive and sustainable economic growth, full and productive employment and decent work for all (Hawkes and Popkin 2015; United Nations 2015)

Recommendation 204 epitomises a significant global response, which offers guidance to workers, employers and governments on addressing the subject of the expanding informal economy through transitioning from informality to formality (Adu-Amankwah 2015). Not only does ILO promote formalisation in Africa's informal economy but also in South Asia where it is believed that over 80 % of the labour force is in the informal economy (ILO 2016). Informal entrepreneurs intentionally participate in this sector (de Soto 1989), thus making any formalisation policy unattractive to many of them. When business processes are formalised, these entrepreneurs who willingly evaded tax and social security payments, refusing to play by the rule book (Williams 2009a) and perhaps engaging in illegal processes of producing goods and services, may be discontent with any form of formalisation. In the UK, for many years, formalisation has been pushed down the throat of informal entrepreneurs by adopting deterrent measures (Small Business Council 2004; Williams 2007). However, across the majority of the third world formalisation still lacks clear understanding in terms of policy direction. Even now, there are no clear formalisation policies in most sub-Saharan African countries, with no exception to Ghana. Although evidence suggests that formalisation will bring some benefits to informal entrepreneurs, the entrepreneurs themselves have not welcomed the idea. Part of the reason may be due to the fact that the outcome of any formalisation policy is difficult to ascertain. This puts some doubts, fear and panic into the minds of the entrepreneurs.

Even the ILO believes there are some "good" aspects of informal working life that should remain as the pendulum swings towards formalisation.

According to ILO (2009 p. iii)

> From a policy perspective, transition to formality calls for the development of a comprehensive and integrated strategy cutting across a range of policy areas that eliminates the negative aspects of informality while preserving the significant job-creation and income-generation potential of the informal economy,

> and at the same time promotes the protection and incorporation of informal economy workers and economic units into the mainstream economy.

The key policy direction is the question of how to transform the necessity for informal workers from the survivalist stage to a decent work arena. The first question to be addressed is whether formalisation has occurred already in Ghana? The response to this is clear; formalisation has never happened in Ghana before or after independence. The attempt to formalise has rather resulted in increased informalisation. This is evidenced by the fact that in Ghana the informal economy has been the mainstream economy for years, even before the colonial days, and is now employing about 90 % of the total working population (Adom and Williams 2012; Debrah 2007; Palmer 2007). Evidence across the country also reveals that the informal economy is more resilient, extensive and an integral part of the modern capitalist economy.

Policymakers have mixed views concerning the formalisation of the informal economy. For some, the suggestion is that it would be difficult if not impossible for anybody to attempt to formalise the informal economy considering its current size and its potential for further growth and so on. Any effort or policy to eradicate it may well be a counterproductive, as it may not produce any positive result. It is, however, a permanent phenomenon; it is here with us and will continue to be more resilient in the future. What is important is to recognise and accept that it is part and parcel of the socio-economic fabric of Ghanaian society. Formalisation of the informal economy in Ghana is a dream that may never be realised. The way forward is cooperation and not confrontation between the two seemingly separate economies.

To start with, there is a lack of adequate data on informal workers. The size of the informal economy is always estimated. For example, currently it is estimated that over 80 % of Ghanaians work in the informal economy (Government of Ghana 2015). The evidence from this study also confirms this estimation. On the contrary, there are no proper records to substantiate this claim though this is a global problem. There is therefore the need to build a reliable database if the formalisation objective is to be realised. So far, local government, through the licensing system, has been able to register some informal workers but it is near the ground considering the number of informal operators who are still not registered. One step that may help building a database is to encourage the formation of associations of people who conduct similar or the same business. There are some organised associations in the informal economy but the majority do not belong to any association. This is the time when the TUC is most needed to organise informal workers. According to Asamoah (2015), the TUC has been mobilising and organising informal workers and recently formed the Union of Informal Workers Association (UNIWA) comprising members from existing associate members of the informal economy. When people come under one roof in the name of associations, they are registered and thus the government could collect this data from the individual associations to build a general database without necessarily contacting individual informal workers. The implication for policy is that policymakers would then have access to this data that may bring about evidenced-based policy formulation on the informal economy, since formalisation is inevitable.

The current growth of the informal economy should not be seen as a weakness and threat to the economy but rather a strength and opportunity to turn around the misfortunes of the nation for a better future. As the informal economy engulfs almost everyone, any policy to address poverty in the informal economy may well address the poverty of the nation as a whole. The issue may not be so much to do with informality (de Soto 1989) but lack of or inadequate specific projects and programmes to address the ills of the informal economy. What policymakers see as a problem may well be a solution if they could just harness the informal economy by providing the necessary interventions, instead of hoping that it will one day dissolve or be immersed in the formal economy as the country achieves some level of economic development. This may not happen anyway.

As decent work is at the centre of the government's formalisation policy, steps should be taken to address the inherent problems with formalisation—such as bureaucracy. Anecdotal evidence suggests that some formal workers, especially those at the institution in charge of business registration, are the beneficiaries of a cumbersome process. As a consequence, any attempt to streamline the registration process is always sabotaged. Again, the formalisation policy of the government lacks a clear-cut definition. What constitutes formalisation presently is very ambiguous. In some sense, formalisation is concerned with informal workers registering their enterprises. On the contrary, others also emphasise the need to practice basic booking principles by recording all activities and the like. It is therefore suggested that the government must have a definitive meaning of formalisation. The advantage of this is that it will provide a means to evaluate the policy to find out whether it is worth pursuing it or if it is better to discard it in the interest of the nation.

Informal Workers and the Regulatory System

It has been established that informal work often occurs outside the regulatory ecosystem. However, according to Hart (2006), the regulatory system is offering some sort of partnership to informal operators in the name of formalisation. Formality is about conformity (Hart 2006) and thus formalising the informal economy will bring about conformity to certain behaviours that conform to rules and regulations. Institutions believe that formalisation will engender development, thus revisiting the modernist view of informal work in the twentieth century, which of course never materialised.

The point of departure between the modernists and neoliberals is that development is not only embedded in formalisation but also in making sure that the ecosystem encourages doing business formally at a reasonable cost. The evidence from the literature is that informal workers do so in opposition to the state as a result of overregulation. In contrast to the core beliefs of the neoliberals, which is opposition to state overregulation, the majority of informal activity is on a micro scale, which may not warrant the registration of such activity and therefore operators hardly attempt to register their businesses. For example, those selling sachet iced water (locally called "pure water"), mobile phone sim cards and top-up vouchers, shoeshine boys, match sellers and so on, may see it as bizarre to register such a business. Most of these informal activities are livelihood activities that help people to subsist and thus are not too much concerned about regulations. Nonetheless, these micro enterprises have their own associations that regulate members, building a shield to prevent more people entering into that particular segment in order to ensure such an activity remains worth doing. Notwithstanding this, there is a small proportion of informal participants who disregard the state because of the perceived overregulation and bureaucratic tendencies. These are the owners of small enterprises that often employ few people. They tend to be the opportunity-driven informal workers who have seen that informal work is more profitable than the formal and thus the informal economy becomes an alternative to the formal economy. Their motive is not to avoid paying tax (because, as highlighted, in Ghana informal workers do pay some form of tax whether registered or not) as the evidence of this chapter shows, and thus avoiding registration is not an incentive to evading tax. Although policymakers are often reluctant to admit that the system is infested with bribery and corruption, they do not depart from the fact that it is a bit cumbersome and therefore needs to be made more efficient to satisfy the needs of potential informal participants who willingly want to transition to formality. It is further argued that the modernists and/or neoliberals do not offer a "cure-all" solution to the problems of the informal economy. Neither do they propose a common relationship between the formal and informal economy for all participants. Different people and sectors may have different relationships. This therefore calls for different policy interventions for various dynamics of the informal economy ecosystem.

Conclusion

Formalisation of the informal economy has been debated for years but the question that remains unanswered is which aspects of the informal economy need to be formalised and how that could be implemented. For example, in 2007 the country (Ghana) director of the World Bank, Mats Karlson, made a strong statement about formalisation of the informal economy:

> What is left for Ghana to do is to begin to embark on action programmes that would lead to movement of Small and Medium Scale Enterprises (SMEs) from the informal sector to the formal sector in order for there to be more permanent jobs for the youth. That way, both the economic and social dimensions of development would have been properly taken care of and then we can talk of economic development.[1]

However, he did not indicate any policy direction for formalisation. It seems that the idea of formalisation is shrouded in some secrecy and until someone decodes it formalisation will remain merely rhetoric. Notwithstanding the formalisation agenda, the reality about the informal entrepreneurship is that it is increasing across every space and it is part and parcel of the economy. It is therefore incumbent on the government to formulate policies the will address the challenges of the informal economy to make it more vivacious and a key contributor of the economy. Government rhetoric about the private sector as the "engine of growth" is still ongoing. But the bad news for formalisation is that the private sector has few formal enterprises and they engage in informal entrepreneurship. Recently, foreigners, especially Chinese, have been participating in informal entrepreneurship and this has become a source of worry for all the participants in informal entrepreneurship because their resources are limited to compete with the "dragon".

It is the wish of many, including the government of Ghana, to ensure that there are sufficient decent jobs for the potential employees. However, it is not clear which institutions are there to ensure that formalisation of the informal economy becomes a reality and is not a mirage. Evidence available reveals that the TUC has been at the forefront of mobilising and organising informal workers. The ILO is also helping to bring about more decent work for informal workers. Until now, however, there is no government agency tasked to ensure the transition of informality to formality. Ministries such as the Employment and Labour Relations, Local Government and Rural Development, Trade and Industry just to mention but a few, have no clear policies on formalisation of the informal economy. The do nothing policy option has rather allowed informal entrepreneurship to flourish and more people are entering it every day. The deterrent approach by the city authorities has registered limited success and has increased the social cost.

If formalisation will ever see the light of day then government policy must be focused on deregulating the formal economy since, as de Soto (1989) puts it, the real issue is not so much informality but the over-regulation by formal institutions. The need to streamline bureaucratic processes is more urgent than ever before. Business registration processes must be updated to incentivise informal entrepreneurs to formalise their activities, rather than being punitive.

Formalising the informal economy is not a new concept but has attracted increased attention in recent times. Yet what constitutes formalisation is ambiguous. Institutions themselves work well with clear rules and regulations and thus they could play a vital role if the formalisation concept is to be understandable. Some believe the purpose of formalisation is to reduce decent work deficit but for others it is about increasing the tax morality of informal entrepreneurs (Williams and Shahid 2014). Whatever it is, this important policy must not be left to interpretations but rather conscious effort must be taken by the institutions to have a clear-cut policy trajectory to address the issue of formalising informal entrepreneurship.

Leaving formalisation to take a natural course may be a mirage and only a recipe for the further growth of informal entrepreneurship. Any attempt by the institutions to implement formalisation policy must be backed by effective public education so that sceptics will not distort the policy. After all, what constitutes formalisation is even unclear among the policymakers, let alone the ordinary informal entrepreneur with a low educational level. The cost of formalisation must not present any disincentive to informal entrepreneurs. Institutions such as TUC and ILO must work in concert with government agencies to ensure the realisation of the formalisation dream in the near future.

Note

1. (http: www.myjoyonline.com/archives/business/200702/2743.asp)

References

Adom, K. (2014). Beyond the marginalization thesis: An examination of the motivations of informal entrepreneurs in Sub-Saharan Africa: Insights from Ghana. *International Journal of Entrepreneurship and Innovation, 15*(2), 113–125.

Adom, K., & Williams, C. C. (2012). Evaluating the explanations for the informal economy in third world cities: Some evidence from Koforidua in the Eastern Region of Ghana. *International Entrepreneurship and Management Journal, 8*(3), 309–324.

Adu-Amankwah, K. (2015). Foreword. In J. Assens & E. Tabor (Eds.), *Paving the way for formalisation of the informal economy.* Copenhagen: LO/FTF Council.

Asamoah, K. (2015). Perspective and priorities for social dialogue with employers and government of Ghana. In J. Assens & E. Tabor (Eds.), *Paving the way for formalisation of the informal economy* (pp. 10–11). Copenhagen: LO/FTF Council.

De Soto, H. (1989). *The other path.* London: Harper and Row.

Croucher, R. (2007). Organising the Informal Economy: Results and Prospects – the Case of Ghana inComparative Perspective. In Wood, G and Chris, B., In Industrial Relations in Africa. Palgrave Macmillan ltd.

Debrah, Y. A. (2007). Promoting the informal sector as a source of gainful employment in developing countries: Insights from Ghana. *International Journal of Human Resource Management, 18*(6), 1063–1084.

Government of Ghana. (2015). *National employment policy.* Accra: Creative Alliance.

Hart, K. (2006). Bureaucratic form and the informal economy. In B. Guha-Khasnobis, R. Kanbur, & E. Ostrom (Eds.), *Linking the formal and informal economy concepts and policies* (pp. 21–34). Oxford: Oxford University Press.

Hawkes, C., & Popkin, B. M. (2015). Can the sustainable development goals reduce the burden of nutrition-related non-communicable diseases without truly addressing major food system reforms? *BMC Medicine, 13*(1), 143.

ILO. (2002a). *Effect to be given to resolutions adopted by the International Labour Conference at its 90th Session (2002), (b) Resolution concerning decent work and*

25 the informal economy; Governing Body, 285th Session, Seventh item on the agenda. Geneva, doc. GB.285/7/2.

ILO. (2002b). *Decent work and the informal economy*. Geneva: International Labour Organization.

ILO. (2009). *The informal economy in Africa: Promoting transition to formality: Challenges and strategies*. International Labour Organisation. Geneva: International Labour Office.

ILO. (2015). *Academy on formalisation of the informal economy*. International Labour Organisation. Geneva: ITC.

ILO. (2016). *Way out of informality: Facilitating fromalisation of informal economy in South Asia*. International Labour Organisation. Co-Dhaka, ILO Country Office.

Palmer, R. (2007). Skills for work?: From skills development to decent livelihoods in Ghana's rural informal economy. *International Journal of Educational Development, 27*(4), 397–420.

Portes, A. (1994). The informal economy and its paradoxes. In N. J. Smelser & R. Swedberg (Eds.), *The handbook of economic sociology*. Princeton: Princeton University Press.

Sauka, A., Schneider, F., & Williams, C. C. (Eds.). (2016). *Entrepreneurship and the shadow economy: A European perspective*. Cheltenham: Edward Elgar.

Small Business Council. (2004). *Small business in the informal economy: Making the transition to the formal economy*. London: Small Business Council.

United Nations. (2015). *Sustainable development goals*, Sixty-ninth Session. New York.

Williams, C. C. (2007). The nature of entrepreneurship in the informal sector: Evidence from England.*Journal of Developmental Entrepreneurship,* 12(02), 239–254

Williams, C. C. (2009a). The motives of off-the-books entrepreneurs: Necessity-or opportunity-driven? *International Entrepreneurship and Management Journal, 5*(2), 203–217.

Williams, C. C. (2009b). Beyond legitimate entrepreneurship: The prevalence of off-the-books entrepreneurs in Ukraine. *Journal of Small Business & Entrepreneurship, 22*(1), 55–68.

Williams, C. C. (2014). Tackling enterprises operating in the informal sector in developing and transition economies: A critical evaluation of the neo-liberal policy approach. *Journal of Global Entrepreneurship Research, 4*(1), 1–17.

Williams, C. C. (2015). Out of the margins: Classifying economies by the prevalence and character of employment in the informal economy. *International Labour Review, 154*(3), 331–352.

Williams, C. C., & Gurtoo, A. (Eds.). (2017). *Routledge handbook of entrepreneurship in developing economies*. London: Routledge.

Williams, C. C., & Horodnic, I. A. (2015). Self-employment, the informal economy and the marginalisation thesis: some evidence from the European Union. *International Journal of Entrepreneurial Behaviour and Research, 21*(2), 224–242.

Williams, C. C., & Horodnic, I. A. (2016). Cross-country variations in the participation of small businesses in the informal economy: an institutional asymmetry perspective. *Journal of Small Business and Enterprise Development, 23*(1), 3–24.

Williams, C. C., & Shahid, M. (2016). Informal entrepreneurship and institutional theory: explaining the varying degrees of (in)formalisation of entrepreneurs in Pakistan. *Entrepreneurship and Regional Development, 28*(1–2), 1–25.

Williams, C. C., & Windebank, J. (1998). *Informal employment in the advanced economies: Implications for work and welfare*. London: Routledge.

Williams, C. C., & Youssef, Y. (2015). Theorizing entrepreneurship in the informal sector in urban Brazil: A product of exclusion or exit? *Journal of Entrepreneurship, 24*(2), 148–168.

Williams, C. C., Shahid, M., & Martinez, A. (2016). Determinants of the level of informality of informal micro-enterprises: Some evidence from the city of Lahore, Pakistan. *World Development, 84*, 312–325.

Evidence on Corruption in Public Procurements in Healthcare and the Implications for Policy

Julia Schipperges, Milena Pavlova, Tetiana Stepurko, Paul Vincke, and Wim Groot

Introduction

The healthcare sector is one of the sectors most susceptible to informal practices and corruption. Healthcare fraud and corruption may also have more serious consequences than informal practices in other sectors as

J. Schipperges (✉)
Program Health Policy Innovation and Management, Faculty of Health, Medicine and Life Sciences, Maastricht University, Maastricht, The Netherlands

M. Pavlova
Department of Health Services Research, Faculty of Health, Medicine and Life Sciences, Maastricht University, Maastricht, The Netherlands

T. Stepurko
School of Public Health, National University of 'Kyiv-Mohyla Academy', Kiev, Ukraine

P. Vincke
EHFCN—European Healthcare Fraud & Corruption Network, Brussels, Belgium

W. Groot
Department of Health Services Research, Faculty of Health, Medicine and Life Sciences, Maastricht University, Maastricht, The Netherlands

A. Polese et al. (eds.), *The Informal Economy in Global Perspective*, International Political Economy Series,
DOI 10.1007/978-3-319-40931-3_16

they could threaten the patient's life and its quality, and may deteriorate healthcare service delivery (Mackey and Liang 2012). Vian (2008) describes seven areas or processes of corruption (informal practices) in the healthcare sector, for example education of healthcare professionals, medical research, purchase of equipment and supplies, including pharmaceuticals. In this chapter, we focus on public procurement and the informal practices and corruption linked to it. The European Commission (2013) has emphasized the far-reaching consequences of corruption in public procurements, like inefficient use of public resources, decrease in access to and quality of care.

Grødeland and Aasland (2007) suggest using the concept of "informal practices" rather than "corruption" because of its neutrality, and they argue that corruption is an informal practice with a clearly negative connotation. Informal practices are, however, constructed by country-specific contextual factors with their own historical, political and economic as well as socio-cultural peculiarities that provide specific motivations and expected benefits. Although there is a large grey area between informal practices and corruption, informal practices with clear negative effects are commonly seen as corruption. At the same time, tight connections (that are culturally predisposed), a culture of gift-giving and exchange of favors together with gaps in public service provision serve as a kind of crutch to the elements of the system (Polese 2008).

In this chapter, we study arrangements in public procurements from a normative perspective and we use the term *corruption* as we focus on those informal practices in public procurements that are seen as socially unacceptable, for example bribery and kickbacks, including the less tangible ones, such as collusion and favoritism. The most well-known and widely-used normative definitions of corruption is "the abuse of a public position of trust for private gain" (Girling 1997) or "misuse of entrusted power for private gain" (Vian 2008). However, Gardiner (2002) argues that corruption varies in meaning due to differences in national legislation and public opinion. As what is counted as corruption depends on the amount and content of legislation, corruption in Western and non-Western countries can be of a different nature. At the micro level, such as a patient–provider relation, the distinction between corruption and gratitude can be multifaceted, while at the healthcare system level, practices considered as corruption are more unambiguous. In the case of public procurements in healthcare, the abuse of power is committed by health professionals, policymakers, and hospital management who are involved and able to influence the procurement processes. Most of them have clear public roles and responsibilities (Gardiner 2002) and thus basic principles of conduct and good governance are violated when they abuse their power and engage in corruption. With abuse of power, we refer to forms of corruption such as bribery, kickbacks and favoritism amongst others. We call them corruption in this chapter.

Under public procurements, we understand there to be the procurement of medical devices and pharmaceutical products. The procurement process usually entails three phases: pre-bidding, bidding and post-bidding. The distinction between these phases is sometimes blurred and the procurement process is often seen as all steps from the contact with potential suppliers to the final purchasing agreement. Corruption in public procurement is seen as one of the weaknesses of the system of public procurement, next to fragmented procedures, lack of professional expertise and absence of openness and competitiveness (Jones 2007). In particular, corruptive practices and pre-negotiations deemed acceptable in a country may impose a barrier to firms from abroad, impeding openness and competition. Existing guidelines and regulations, such as the Anti-Corruption Ethics and Compliance Handbook for Business (OECD-UNODOC-World Bank 2013), are seldom enforced and prosecution is often difficult, hindered by more corruption and evidence that is hard to find. The report "Study on Corruption in the Healthcare Sector" by the European Commission (2013) states that, only about 30 % of EU member states have developed procurement guidelines at all.

Identifying corruption in healthcare will not only save money—it can save lives. As a result of corruption, the overall service costs might increase due to the prices agreed in the tendering contract and thus, money will be wasted instead of being invested in better quality of care (European Commission 2013). Even when corruption does not result in higher service costs, it might lead to less care or reduced quality of care if the quantity and quality of the purchased products are not taken into account. Well-known cases of corruption and bribery in public procurements are the Johnson & Johnson case, as well as the Philips Poland case (European Commission 2013). In both cases, healthcare personnel and public health officials were bribed in order to favor one company's medical products regardless of pricing and quality. Thereby, public money was wasted and not spent in the most efficient way. The money that was lost could have been used to finance other much-needed equipment and supply, or could be invested in new necessary treatments.

The topic of corruption in public procurements in healthcare is highly relevant but also rather sensitive. There have been several studies in different countries (e.g. Australia, EU member states) that find evidence for the existence of corruption in public procurements. It remains unclear, however, whether the forms of corruption and their causes are similar across the countries. Therefore, our study is a further step in providing insight on this topic by bringing together empirical evidence from different countries. The review is based on the method of document analysis. We review studies and reports collected by the European Healthcare Fraud and Corruption Network (EHFCN). The network was founded in 2004 as a result of the first pan-European conference on fraud and corruption in healthcare. It is a not-for-profit umbrella organization located in Brussels, which has members from various European countries, including government agencies and health insurers. The EHFCN members aim to improve Europe's healthcare systems and to reduce the waste of resources due to fraud and corruption.

The structure of the chapter is the following: after this introductory section, the chapter continues with theoretical deliberations on the concepts of corruption and public procurement. This is followed by the overview of the results. The subsequent discussion and interpretation of the results provide a base for policy recommendations and suggestions for further research.

Corruption and Public Procurements

Corruption may occur in any process involving a transaction between two actors. The two main actors in public procurements in healthcare are the buyers of medical devices and pharmaceutical products (e.g. healthcare providers and the government), and the sellers of these devices and products (e.g. producers and suppliers). We will hereon refer to them as buyers and sellers. Although corruption may lead to increased personal benefits of both buyers and sellers, the disadvantages and damage done by such practices are incurred by third parties (e.g. patients), which makes these practices problematic and socially undesirable (European Commission 2013).

Various forms of corruption can be associated with public procurements of medical devices and pharmaceutical products, including bribery, kickbacks, collusion, state capture, favoritism and nepotism (see Table 1). Each phase of the public procurement process may offer opportunities for corruption:

- In the pre-bidding phase, the needs assessment, tendering procedure and the tendering itself can be jeopardized due to corruption. For example, a tender can be written without an actual need, due to an agreement between the procurement official and

Table 1 Types of corruption

Type	*Definition and description*
Bribery	Bribery is the direct or indirect promise, offer or gift to a person, or another person or entity, that encourages this person to breach his/her duties and act or refrain from acting in a certain way. This can include monetary benefits, discounts, loans, donations, gifts, pieces of valuable information, preferential treatment and also offers of employment. Bribing is actually one of the easiest ways to engage in corruption, as it does not require much preparation or effort. It can consist of as little as referral or recommendation to another business partner, to large amounts of money changing hands, depending on the service expected in return. It often works as a kind of quid pro quo, expecting a service in return for a favor, a present or a payment. Bribery, can be initiated by all stakeholders involved in procurements. The role of the briber and bribed are often unclear. The sellers of medical devices and pharmaceuticals can initiate a bribe, but also the buyers procuring these goods can ask to be bribed in order to grant favors. Bribing occurs when the opportunity arises and one party approaches the other. Sometimes, the one initiating the bribe acts spontaneously but in most cases, bribers have been instructed to initiate a bribe. However, offering a bribe is not enough, there has to be someone willing on either side of the bargain
Kickbacks	Kickbacks are a more organized form of bribery. They are negotiated prior to a transaction and often involve services or goods, which are not needed or are of poor quality. The pre-action negotiations are done to ensure that the other party willingly enters the corruption scheme. A simple bribe is often negotiated much more spontaneously, while kickbacks are agreed upon ahead of time, negotiating the terms in detail
Collusion	In the case of collusion, the procurement departments tendering the bids are not involved in corruption, but the bidders try to restrict competition amongst each other. They do so by market division, engaging in bid-rigging and/or by fixing prices. Collusion is often seen as a phenomenon next to corruption. It only happens when two or more sellers agree to influence and alter processes in a way that maximizes their profits. Within collusion, the sellers can also agree to certain kickbacks amongst themselves, or bribe each other for agreeing to a collusion scheme. Therein, two or more sellers agree to either fix their prices, dividing the market amongst them to ensure maximum profit for all of them. Or they do bid-rigging, the most common form of collusion, which can occur in four different forms: bid suppression, complementary bidding, bid rotation or subcontracting. Each of these schemes are based on agreements between the sellers on either who wins the bid (bid rotation), who enters their bid or not (bid suppression), with what intention they enter the bidding (complementary bidding) or how more than one can directly profit from one of them winning the bid (subcontracting). In the end, all of them profit in one way or another

(*continued*)

Table 1 (continued)

Type	*Definition and description*
State capture	State capture is a more aggressive form of bribery, as it refers to the inappropriate use of influence and addresses high profile stakeholders involved, such as politicians and administrative heads. It occurs when a government official is approached by, for example, a person working for a pharmaceutical company. The official then might be offered certain advantages, or financial incentives for voting against certain legislation, or other favors that great an undue advantage for the pharmaceutical company. The government official's interest then slowly shifts from regulating the resources they are responsible for, and protecting the people's interests, to favoring/protecting the interests of the briber. State capture relies on the immense power, and sometimes even monopoly, of the government and its officials. Their inclination to make decisions based on the influence and power of the lobbies of producers are hardly matched by an opponent lobby of those who ultimately have to bear the consequences of those decisions
Favoritism and Nepotism	Favoritism and nepotism are based on the natural human behavior of officials in the public procurement sector to be inclined to award bids or make advantages available to persons they know (including friends and family) instead of other bidders they do not know personally. Nepotism thereby refers to such behavior with family members or relatives of any degree, and favoritism refers to such behavior with friends and acquaintances. For example, a procurement official chooses his brothers, nephews or sons companies' bid over others that might have been cheaper or better
Healthcare specific	Other forms of corruption in healthcare include unethical drug promotion, theft or diversion of medical goods, accepting informal payments from patients by medical doctors, or other healthcare personnel, and unnecessary referrals or treatments

Sources: European Commission (2013), OECD (2007), UNCAC; World Bank (2007), Vian (2008)

a certain supplier/producer. It is also possible that the tender is written in a way that would only fit, or exactly fit, the offer of a certain bidder. A procurement official could have been bribed to engage in such behavior, or the official can do this as a favor for a relative (nepotism).

- In the bidding phase, especially the bid evaluation can be prone to bribery and kickbacks as well as to favoritism and collusion. This means that a procurement official is approached with bribes by one of the bidders, or a kickback has been pre-negotiated to influence the decision-making process. It can also occur that in this phase the procurement official only has one bidder or other bids are not available or are too bad, or simply too expensive, due to collusion amongst the bidders. These practices actively manipulate the procurement official's choice for contract awarding.

- Even in the post-bidding phase, false invoicing and changes of contract agreements may occur as a result of corruption. The corruption here may also occur in the form of bribery, where a procurement official is bribed to alter the contracts retrospectively in favor of the supplier/producer.

In public procurements especially, it is important to first do a needs assessment. Also, a check whether the procurement process is properly regulated and follows specific, predetermined and verifiable protocols, and whether the conditions for fair competition are being met, is advisable. The chance of corruption may increase if a tender is not publicized or has a very short deadline to ensure that only those who know of it would be able to bid. Also, a lack of transparency and unified guidelines enables unjustified contract awarding and contract changes in hindsight. These corruptive activities abuse public resources allocated to procurements as a part of these resources are used for personal gains. In some instances, such practices may have far-reaching consequences.

Those consequences are usually financial losses and damages to social welfare, but can also affect patients' health. This could be the case, for example, with poorly tested or unsafe drugs, procured and prescribed by bribed health professionals, affecting the health of patients of all age groups, including infants and children (U4 2008). In a report by the U4 Anti-Corruption Resource Centre (2008), three main drivers for engaging in corruption in public procurements are mentioned: opportunity, environment and pressure. A procurement official needs to have the opportunity to act, or an environment where it seems legitimate to do something that could be considered as corruption. Or he/she feels pressured to do so, as it might be expected or be common practice in some institutions or even regions.

The reasons or drivers for this kind of behavior are assumed to be linked to the absence of good governance combined with the potential financial gain and a lack of effective and deterrent sanctions (European Commission 2013).

Buyer and Seller Informal Relationships and Corruption

In order to fully understand how corruption occurs in public procurements in healthcare, we need to assess the relationship between the buyer and the seller. The buyers, therein, can be procurement agents, officials on local or national level, committees organized to make procurement decisions or the government (which in this case can consist of expert consultants, medical doctors or other healthcare professionals). The sellers include all producers of medical devices and pharmaceutical products.

Vian (2008) presents a conceptual model on corruption in the healthcare sector. The model presents corruption from a government official's point of view, describing three main motivations behind corruptive behavior. These are: perceived (financial) pressure or pressure from clients directly, personal attitude and one's normative system, used to support or justify corruptive behavior to oneself, and the opportunity to abuse public power for personal gains. Perceived pressure can be a very dangerous motivator, as the person experiencing it sees himself/herself in a situation where he/she is left without a choice. It is either expected by superiors or simply regarded as a common practice in a certain business. This creates the environment for justification of the action and a feeling that there is no other choice, which makes the engagement in corruption easier. That is an issue of individual attitude, however. Some individuals have a stronger sense of justice while others do not want to get into trouble for speaking up against it. Some might have a high sense of integrity while others might grasp the opportunity, moral principles notwithstanding (European Commission 2013).

Vian (2008) presents six concepts that either enable corruption (monopoly, discretion, accountability), or help to prevent and counteract it (citizen voice, transparency, enforcement, accountability). Centralized procurement procedures can be added to the latter group. When the seller and/or buyer has the monopoly in the area of the procurement, they also have an amount of power to influence the procurement process, especially in the absence of clear and strict regulations and no monitoring system to detect corruption. This creates the environment that enables the buyer and seller to gain more by using less legitimate tactics than they properly should. Such tactics do not necessarily breach the rules and regulations, especially if these are vague or inexplicitly related to procurement procedures. In public procurements, pharmaceutical companies often have a monopoly due to patents. As no one else is able to produce and sell the same medication for as long as the patent holds, the company has considerable freedom to set the prices, as long as it falls within government regulations. With few clear guidelines and regulations on public procurement, the buyer/seller often has a great amount of freedom in what and how to purchase. Too much discretion, though, gives too much freedom combined with too little transparency, and presents an opportunity to engage in corruption (U4 2011).

To counteract this, governance of procurement needs to be well developed. This may involve other parties (e.g. citizens/patients) in the decision-making process concerning the procurements of new devices and pharmaceuticals. For this, transparency is essential. Only when the proceedings are transparent, they can be understood and re-enacted. However, full transparency may not always be achievable, for example when discounts on prices are being negotiated by the buyer that the seller does not want to become known to other buyers. To fully counteract corruption in public procurement, however, enforcement is essential. Only when real repercussions are feared, sellers/buyers will be deterred from taking the opportunity as it presents itself. In order to make this work, though, accountability is essential as only then can rules, regulation and punishments be enforced (UNDP 2011; U4 2011).

Figure 1 shows the relationship between buyer and seller, the two main stakeholders involved in procurements in healthcare. In the acquisition of goods (i.e. the transaction between sellers and buyers), many actions are not well regulated and this leaves a lot of space for both parties to act freely. Their cultural background can play an important role in the motivation for corruption, and the definition and understanding of it.In this model, we further highlight the relationship between the buyer and seller. Corruption can start with the buyer or the seller, it can also happen amongst sellers, which is then called collusion. The consequences will eventually always impact upon the patient since in case of corruption, the purchased goods are not necessarily up to quality standards or are simply too expensive.

Empirical Results

Our study features two separate document analyses: corruptive practices in public procurements in healthcare in general, and corruptive practices in public procurements across geographical regions. The analysis was carried out in May 2014. The 23 reports collected by the EHFCN were scanned for relevant information and categorized in either one or both document

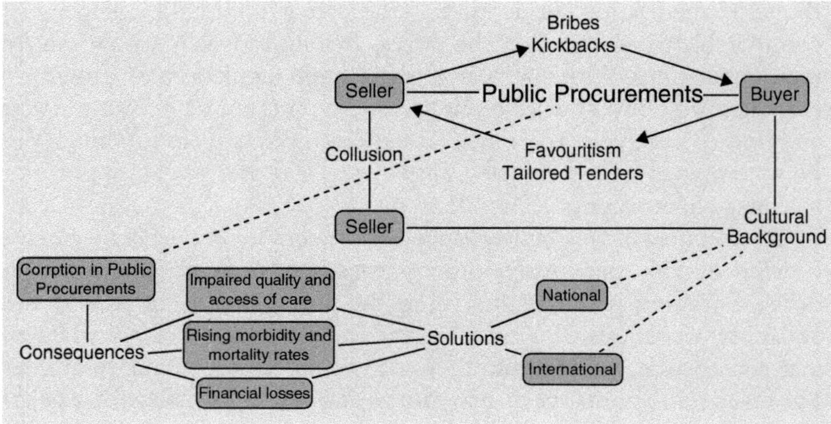

Fig. 1 Concept model of corruption in public procurements in healthcare (*Source*: The authors)

analysis categories specified above. Thereof, 19 reports were suitable for our analysis. Of those 19 reports, nine were put in the general document analysis, six were sorted into the country comparison documents analysis only, and four were used for both document analyses. Table 2 lists all reports analyzed. Table 3 and Table 4 summarize the key findings. The key findings are also presented narratively in the subsequent sections.

Types of Corruption

Almost all reports mention that public procurements are more susceptible to corruption than other healthcare activities, especially because of the frequently high amount of funds involved (UNDP 2011; World Bank 2007). While different types of corruption are mentioned in the reports, bribery is most often indicated as a form of corruption in public procurement. Different scenarios are described in this regard. Bribes are used to avoid government regulation on pharmaceuticals, to get a pharmaceutical approved faster or despite of research evidence indicating harmful effects, or despite the lack of sufficient research (e.g. U4 2011; Vian 2002). Sellers also use bribes to get on shortlists identifying them as approved suppliers. Bribery is also initiated by suppliers to influence the procurement officers to alter a tender or to retrospectively change a contract. But not only sellers initiate bribery, also procurement officials tend to initiate bribery.

Table 2 List of reports for the document analyses

Title	*Author*	*Year*
Accountability and health systems: Toward conceptual clarity and policy relevance	Binkerhoff, D. W.	2004
Addressing corruption in the health sector. Securing equitable healthcare for everyone	U4	2011
Annual report 2012	Transparency International	2013
Anti-corruption ethics and compliance handbook for business	OECD, UNODOC and World Bank	2013
Anti-corruption in the health sector: preventing drug diversion through supply chain management	U4	2006
Assessment of international assistance in the Serbian Health sector	ECORYS	2010
Corruption in the health sector	U4	2008
Deadly medicines and organized crimes	Peter Gotzsche	2013
EU Anti-corruption report	European Commission	2014
Fighting corruption in the health sector	UNDP	2011
Global corruption report 2006	Transparency International	2006
Measuring corruption in healthcare	EHFCN	2006
Medicine, the cashier	Martina Keller	2009
Review of corruption in the health sector: theory, methods and interventions	Taryn Vian	2008
Sectoral perspective on corruption. Corruption and the health sector	Taryn Vian	2002
Strengthening the corruption resistance of the NSW public health sector	ICAC	2005
Study on corruption in the healthcare sector	European Commission	2013
The anti-corruption catalyst: realizing the MDGs by 2015	Transparency International	2010
The many faces of corruption	World Bank	2007

Therefore, a call for more accountability is mentioned by several authors addressing this problem (e.g. Vian 2002).

Other forms of corruption, such as kickbacks and collusion, are also mentioned by at least five sources (e.g. Vian 2002, 2008). While kickbacks are seen as a more specific form of bribery, collusion is described as an informal corruptive relation established between the sellers only. In collusion, the sellers fix prices or restrict buyers' choices in other ways, so that only they benefit from the procurements.

Table 3 Findings of the general document analysis

Main findings		*Sources*
Types of corruption in public procurements in health-care	Bribery	U4 (2006, 2008, 2011), Transparency International (2006, 2010), OECD, World Bank and UNODC (2013), European Commission (2013, 2014), UNDP (2011), Vian (2002,2008), European Commission (2013), World Bank (2007)
	Collusion (bid rigging)	Vian (2002, 2008), European Commission (2013), EHFCN (2006), U4 (2008)
	Kickbacks	U4 (2006, 2008), Vian (2002, 2008),
	Fake and counterfeit drugs	World Bank (2007), Transparency International (2006), U4 (2006), Vian (2002)
	Altering of tenders and related	European Commission (2013), Transparency International (2006), Vian (2002)
	Funds diversion	U4 (2008, 2011)
	Diversion of drugs	U4 (2006)
	Favoritism	European Commission (2014)
	Extortion	Vian (2002)
Consequences/impact of corruption in public procurements in health care	Increase in morbidity and mortality rates	U4 (2006, 2008, 2011), Transparency International (2006, 2010), UNDP (2011), European Commission (2013)
	Hindered access to care and damages on equity	U4 (2006,2008), European Commission (2013), Transparency International (2010), UNDP (2011), European Commission (2013), World Bank (2007), Vian (2002, 2008)
	Financial damages	U4 (2008, 2011), European Commission(2014), Vian (2002, 2008), European Commission (2013, 2014), Transparency International (2006),
	Reduced quality of care and ineffectiveness	U4 (2008, 2011), Vian (2008), European Commission (2013), Transparency International (2006)

Problem-solving strategies related to corruption in public procurements	Strengthening/improving: transparency, accountability, governance, integrity, management	U4 (2006, 2011), Transparency International (2006, 2010), OECD, World Bank and UNODC (2013), European Commission (2014), EHFCN (2006), UNDP (2011), World Bank (2007), Vian (2002)
	E-procurement, online sources for sharing market intelligence	European Commission (2014), Transparency International (2006), Vian (2002)
	Reducing information asymmetry	U4 (2008, 2011), Vian (2008), Transparency International (2006)
	Budget and resource management systems	U4 (2011)
	Open to restricted tender process	Vian (2002)

Table 4 Main findings of the country comparison

Region	*Main Finding*	*Sources*
Europe	Eurobarometer Survey → 76 % have a negative perception on corruption, think it is widespread in their country, 26 % consider themselves personally affected in their daily lives	European Commission (2014)
	Almost all EU member states have reported or investigated cases of corruption regarding procurement of pharmaceuticals or medical devices	European Commission (2013)
	Bribery Enforcement is strongest in the USA and Germany for example, it is low in countries like Mexico, Luxemburg and Bulgaria and not at all it can be found in countries like Ireland, Greece, Poland and others.	Transparency International (2013)
	Bulgaria → governance, integrity and transparency	Transparen cy International (2006)
	Serbia → Interventions target is public procurements	ECORYS (2010)
	Kosovo →Tender for an overpriced treatment without adequate effectiveness for investment	Transparency International (2013)
North America	Producer provider relationship on a level where patient does not matter anymore. Drugs are prescribed easily and cause suicidal tendencies in young people	Gotzsche (2013)
	USA: Strong bribery enforcement	Transparency International (2013)
South America	Chile → electronic bidding system Costa Rica → corruption in medical device procurements	Transparency International (2006)
Africa	Uganda → Management and accountability as main reasons for failure/susceptibility to corruption	Brinkerhoff (2004)
	Nigeria → Strong leadership against counterfeit drugs	Transparency International (2006)
Asia	China → Huge problem with counterfeit and fake drugs entering other countries, even Europe China →192,000 people die of fake drugs	European Commission (2013), U4 (2011)
Australia	Procurement identified as vulnerable part of healthcare	ICAC (2005)

In addition, the reports mention another major problem in the healthcare sector, namely fake (not genuine) drugs and counterfeit (deliberately and fraudulently mislabeled) drugs. Fake and counterfeit drugs are a serious issue and several reports point to the severe health threats such drugs may cause. Patients treated with fake and counterfeit drugs can suffer immensely from not receiving adequate treatment. Such drugs seem to be equally damaging to patients and the whole healthcare system (U4 2011).

Consequences of Corruption

As discussed in the reports reviewed, the consequences of corruption in public procurements are not limited to financial losses. The most often named consequences are an increase in morbidity and mortality (especially infant mortality), and barriers to access to care, which are mentioned by eight sources (e.g. Transparency International 2010, 2006; U4 2008; World Bank 2007). Those two aspects directly affect patients, meaning life or death in extreme cases. Eight sources mention the concern of increased morbidity and mortality rates globally, including infant mortality (e.g. U4 2008, 2011), which shows the gravity of procurement corruption, impacting the weakest and most defenseless members of society. While the negative effect on morbidity and mortality is straightforward, the effect of procurement corruption on access to care is more indirect, but nevertheless harmful. The waste of scarce resources due to corruption might push medical doctors and other staff involved in care delivery to demand informal payments to make up for the lost funds and, thereby, people who cannot afford to pay extra and are not properly informed about their rights might have none or limited access to care (e.g. Stepurko et al. 2010; Transparency International 2006).

Financial losses and reduced quality of care are mentioned nearly as frequently. Both consequences have the potential to be as dangerous to people in need of care as the first two aspects mentioned. Especially, insufficient quality of care can seriously impact patients in a harmful way. By altering and influencing the procurement process, quality of care can be reduced. As indicated in several reports, quality and effectiveness of a device or drug may be disregarded in favor of accepting tenders offering newer but much more expensive products without proven additional value. At the same time, financial losses are also reported. Financial losses can result in reduced funding for acquiring other needed supplies and can indirectly make care less accessible for patients due to the impact on pricing of pharmaceuticals or medical services (e.g. Transparency International 2006; U4 2008). Such financial damages are mentioned by seven sources (e.g. European Commission 2013; Transparency International 2006; Vian 2002, 2008). In addition, the issue of corruption in the use of donor funding is mentioned. This type of funding is essential in some countries to keep the healthcare sector functioning. Nevertheless, if donor funds are diverted or misused, especially in care of public procurements, credibility and trust are lost, donor funds become delayed and partially unavailable (U4 2008). Therefore, the call for more transparency is emphasized in the reports.

Problem-Solving Strategies

Many of the reports reviewed suggest a strong link between good governance and a corruption-free procurement process (e.g. Vian 2002). Much stronger though appears the association between transparency and corruption-free procurement (e.g. UNDP 2011; World Bank 2007). Procurement processes are often obscure and do not follow strict guidelines. Therefore, accountability and integrity are recommended to make employees working with public money adhere to guidelines more strictly. An employee displaying a high level of integrity and feeling loyal to his employer is much less likely to engage in corruption (OECD, World Bank and UNODOC, 2013). Transparency, governance, integrity and accountability are mentioned by several sources as necessary problem-solving strategies.

Another important issue, not specifically concerning the seller, but the buyer and the patient most of all, is information asymmetry. While the buyer should be aware of actual prices and quality standards of the products to be acquired, the patient has a hard time accessing this information. The European Commission (2013) describes this as a vulnerability of the healthcare sector, partly due to the great number of actors and stakeholders involved. This information asymmetry is the reason for market failure in healthcare, making the sector vulnerable to corruption. This is viewed as an argument for greater patient involvement in decision-making processes, and their interests need to be represented better and more strongly. Vian (2002) describes this as citizen voice, one of the ways to counteract corruption mentioned above.

Furthermore, reports mention e-procurement (e.g. European Commission 2013, 2014; Transparency International 2013), a system that would make procurement easier, more transparent and less susceptible for corruption due to standardized processes. E-procurements are electronic bidding and tendering systems. They have the advantage that processes can be controlled and retraced and a single official can be held accountable. E-procurements are internet-based information technologies, relying on online listings of prices for medical supplies as a comparison, for employees to rely on as well as for patients to refer to. E-procurements are mentioned as a way to alleviate the burden of corruption and make people and organizations more aware of their healthcare spending.

Although transparency is the most often mentioned prerequisite essential to a corruption-free procurement system in healthcare, to be successful it should be accompanied with measures to enhance integrity, accountability and the reduction of information asymmetry to enable all actors to be on equal footing. Accountability will make it harder to get away penalty free, as people will have to bear the consequences of their actions. Clear guidelines on this, as well as in the regulation of the procurement process are essential in eliminating corruption in the procurement process.

Evidence from Europe

Within Europe, there are great differences reported, not only concerning the level of corruption generally, but also in the extent of enforcement of countermeasures. Many European countries have introduced myriad legislation and guidelines but are unable to enforce these. Only 30 % of the EU member states have procurement guidelines, at all (European Commission 2013). The Eurobarometer survey from 2013 found that 76 % of Europeans were convinced that corruption was widespread in their country, even though only 26 % considered themselves personally affected.

Countries in Western Europe usually have to deal with a moderate level of corruption in public procurements in healthcare, but not all present an equal or appropriate level in enforcement of anti-corruption measures. For example, in Austria, a producer/seller of prosthetic parts allegedly paid the management of a clinic for "proving" the benefits of his products. There was no prosecution though, as the money was returned and the case dropped (European Commission 2013). In 2013, in Finland, a case of nepotism was prosecuted. In this case, a hospital executive director was found guilty of favoring his son's companies, or the ones associated with him, over a period of eight years (2000–2008). A conflict of interest case in the Netherlands, from 2012, affected around 10,000 patients receiving questionable hip implants, even though doubts had been voiced as early as 2007. In this case, orthopedic surgeons entered consultancy contracts with companies producing these implants and, for personal gain, chose to use the implants of that seller. This case highlights the need for more transparency on how medical doctors interact with medical device and pharmaceuticals suppliers (for more examples of fraud and corruption in healthcare in the Netherlands see Groot and Maassen van den Brink 2014).

From 2009 to 2011, the purchase of influenza vaccines in three countries (Belgium, Finland and the Netherlands) got special attention. In all of these countries, a possible conflict of interest was suspected as normal tendering procedures were foregone. In Finland, it was argued that the purchase was necessary and could not be subjected to the normal time frame of a proper procurements procedure. Nevertheless, the direct purchase of the vaccines was highly suspicious, and the procuring public health organization was suspected of acting on a conflict of interest basis. In Belgium, there was also no tender organized, and a third of the experts consulted for this purchase had links to the company from which the vaccines were ordered. In the case of the Netherlands, the government chose an outside advisor who, it was found out later, had indirect relations and even financial ties to the sellers of the influenza vaccines.

A much higher level of corruption is reported in Central and Eastern Europe than in Western Europe, as well as a lower level of anti-corruption legislation enforcement (ECORYS 2010). Hungary, Slovakia and Poland are amongst the Central and Eastern European countries with the highest occurrence of bribery in healthcare reported. For example, from 2008 to 2011 only, there were three big corruption cases in the Czech Republic, all related to the procurement of medical devices. Only one of these cases was actually proven in court though. A case of possible conflict of interest concerning a tendering procedure for a vaccine in Slovenia made the news, as one of the medical doctors in this panel influenced the decision in favor of a company he worked for as a special consultant. The curious thing about the decision was that there were other bidders offering better and cheaper products, who were rejected. Although it was never proven, a pharmaceutical company in Poland allegedly paid government officials and cardiologists for positive recommendations to get a pharmaceutical on the refinanced list of the Polish Health Ministry (European Commission 2013).

A particularly bold case took place in Poland, Greece and Romania at the same time in 2006. A large multinational company did not just bribe procurement officials or high ranking hospital managers. They went and bribed all willing hospital employees, from medical staff (nurses to surgeons) to directors and managers, to favor their products and influence procurements that way. The expenses were covered up as trainings or consultations. The company also went as far as to bribe a high-ranking Polish official, who supposedly altered tenders to favor the company's medical supplies (European Commission 2013).

Evidence from North and South America

A shocking example of how little the patient matters in some instances is found in the study by Gotzsche (2013) in the USA. Although there is a strong enforcement of anti-bribery measures in the USA (Transparency International 2013), the big pharmaceutical companies still continuously appear in the media with scandal after scandal. Gotzsche (2013) presents case after case of corruption initiated by pharmaceutical companies and their recklessness in achieving what they set out to do. Large-scale cases and smaller issues alike are described by this author, as well as the techniques of covering these up, regardless of the consequences. The most dangerous instances in the USA seem to be concerning the mood-altering medications, like anti-depressants, which are prescribed to young adolescents. The sellers (large multinational pharmaceutical companies) sometimes go as far as to fake and manipulate the outcomes of studies on the effectiveness and safety of their pharmaceutical products. Thus, many pharmaceutical companies knowingly sell their medication without proven effects and safety on the market, using their money and influence, and completely disregarding the interests, health and safety of the people affected by their actions.

The South American countries show that, while many of them are still overwhelmed by corruption, there are some signs of improvement. In Chile, for example, an electronic bidding system was introduced and successfully tested (Transparency International 2006). However, in Costa Rica, one of the best-funded healthcare systems in the region, a scandal erupted when in 2004 several high ranking officials and managers of the organization responsible for healthcare coverage were accused of corruption. They allegedly bought unnecessary equipment and received commissions for this.

Evidence from Asia and Africa

In Asia, fake (not genuine) drugs and counterfeit (deliberately and fraudulently mislabeled) drugs are reported to be a huge problem, especially in China, where many people die as a consequence of this. But those fake or counterfeit drugs not only cause problems in China or Asia as such, they are also brought to the rest of the world. In 2007, three different counterfeit medicines from China entered the UK supply chain via Belgium, Hong Kong and Singapore. These drugs, used to treat serious conditions (prostate cancer, heart disease and schizophrenia), were entered by using fake packaging and barcodes with a supposedly French origin. After a thorough investigation the case was proven and five men were convicted (European Commission 2013). Transparency International reported in its 2006 Global Corruption Report that China has had approximately 500 illegal drug producers/sellers, and that about 192,000 people died of fake and counterfeit drugs in 2005.

In India, the health minister proposed the introduction of the death penalty as a punishment for manufacturing or selling counterfeit drugs, due to the serious harm done when taking these drugs. A very positive example is the one of a medical device manufacturer in India that openly advertises its anti-corruption stance, and does everything to remain corruption free—although they sometimes experience difficulties in doing business as not many others have followed their example so far (Transparency International 2006).

In Africa, corruption in procurements of pharmaceuticals has a huge impact on the population, limiting access to life-saving medications. Counterfeit or fake drugs in regions where a great part of the population is infected with HIV/AIDS have dire consequences, and most people are too poor to purchase them on the black market (Transparency International 2006). In Uganda, corruption in management and a lack of accountability in procurements significantly enhance the failure of the healthcare system (Brinkerhoff 2004).

Strong leadership in the Nigerian National Agency for Food and Drug Administration and Control (NAFDAC) has helped to lessen the impact of counterfeit drugs. Since drug distribution in Nigeria was denationalized, counterfeit drugs have been a huge problem. Only with the help of the NAFDAC, that approved and registered pharmaceuticals and identified counterfeit drugs, can this problem be reduced.

Discussion and Conclusions

Healthcare—in many parts of the world—is a highly economically important sector accounting for a substantial share in national income and of great importance to people's health and wellbeing. This emphasizes the need to ensure that the money allocated for healthcare is put to the best use and reaches those in need. Public procurement is where the public money is invested in medical supplies such as drugs and medical devices. At this point, however, some stakeholders involved sometimes see an opportunity to achieve personal gains, by engaging in corruptive activities that can severely affect patients. Pharmaceutical companies that sell products without proper testing knowingly endanger people in situations where they are at a disadvantaged position of already being sick. Medical devices of poor quality could malfunction and cause more damage than good. A false positive diagnosis can impact patients mentally and physically, as they suffer from unnecessary procedures and medications.

There are, however, cultural differences in corruptive practices and the perception of them. What is considered corruption in one country could be seen as rather normal and accepted behavior in another. Cultural differences are not to be disregarded when it comes to regional comparisons of corruption in public procurement. Based on our region-specific analysis, we observe a trend concerning the regional distribution of losses resulting from procurement corruption. While in richer regions damages are more frequently of a financial nature and only so often resulted in actual severe damages to patients, corruptive practices in poorer countries frequently lead to more direct harm to patients in addition to the financial losses because scarce public resources are wasted for personal gains. Within Europe, the Central and Eastern European countries display a high level of corruption, while in Western Europe, corruption is highly frowned upon and cases of fraud and corruption are a lot more likely to be prosecuted.

The wealthier and better-governed regions have established administrative tools (better sanction enforcement and prosecution) and thereby provide a more effective response to corruption. Taking into account our normative vision, it is expected that poorer regions will probably need support in designing and implementing policies which facilitate a more efficient use of resources. Anti-corruption policies are often seen as a part of this movement. Still, good practices of public procurements promoted by international agencies could demonstrate positive outcomes and sustainability only when local voices, culture and values are considered. For example, the implementation of procurement regulations and monitoring systems, even e-procurement and training of procurement officials, are well-known tools for improving transparency in Western settings, but it only works when context specificity is embedded. As shown in our review results, Chile, India and Nigeria have certain success in promoting and implementing good practices in this direction.

We do not, however, imply that poorer regions experience more corruption in public procurements in healthcare than wealthier regions. The corruptive behaviors differ as well as their consequences, as indicated above. While in poorer regions corruptive activities in the public procurement of drug supply are most often reported, in wealthier regions the problem is related to illegitimate actions in the public procurement of both drugs and medical devices. Nevertheless, all over the world countries are affected by corruption in public procurements in healthcare and this problem needs to be addressed on a global scale. Many of the stakeholders involved in public procurements are big multinational companies and getting them to agree to the terms of an integrity pact would set a good example.

Irrespective of the regional differences, the most frequent form of corruption in public procurement that we observed in the reports is, without a doubt, bribery. Ranging from small favor requests and rewards being offered to immense sums of money, from a simple procurement official to a high-ranking politician, bribery has many forms and stages of severity. The consequences can range from a simple gap in finances to severe consequences, such as direct or indirect harm to the patients. A medication or device not being available could prevent treatment or diagnosis and lessen the patient's chances of surviving a medical condition. The role of briber and bribed is not always clear, as the bribe can be initiated or demanded from both buyer and seller. As we explained at the outset of this chapter, the relationship between buyer and seller is complex. Drivers of corruption are varied, money undoubtedly being the single most attractive motivator for both sides (OECD 2007).

According to the reports reviewed, collusion is the second most frequent form of corruption in procurements. In case of collusion, sellers come to certain agreements or bribe each other, and influence the competition and the tendering of procurements for personal gains. In this case, the buyers are the first to be affected, as their choice of supplier becomes artificially limited and they are not able to get a fair price for the goods they need to purchase. Eventually, though, it is again the patients who suffer the consequences of corruption in public procurements (direct financial damage and indirect harm to patients) (European Commission 2014).

In the region-specific document analysis, we encountered another form of procurements corruption, namely conflict of interest. In the case of conflict of interest, medical doctors or other medical experts work for panels deciding on what should be procured with public money and from which supplier. Some of them, however, have consultancy contracts with potential supplier companies. That sparks the suspicion that their decisions might not be entirely neutral, but influenced by their consultant position. Whether they would receive certain bonuses after or incentives in advance of the decision-making is hardly provable (European Commission 2013).

Many reports that we reviewed describe ways, strategies and models to reduce corruption in healthcare in general and in public procurements in particular. A mix of transparency and accountability seems to be most useful, however. In order to apply these strategies, supporting techniques are necessary.

This is where e-procurement enters the picture. The OECD (2007) regards transparency in this context as the availability of information generally. Moreover, they regard transparency as a precondition for accountability and control in procurement. Given these conditions, e-procurement can be useful. Without transparency and accountability, it would only be half as effective. E-procurement generally offers electronic standardized catalogues. In addition, it can also feature classification systems and a prescribed list of "safe" providers. Thereby, corruption would become less attractive. In the end, it will also be useful for the enforcement of sanctions (OECD 2007).

Another solution proposed by Transparency International is the integrity pact. When buyers and sellers agree on an integrity pact, they willingly enter an agreement to not engage in any form of corruption between and amongst each other (bribery, collusion, bid-rigging or kickbacks, etc.). A third party should also be integrated to act as an unbiased and neutral observer.

As indicated by our analysis, many sources describe how and to what extent corruption in public procurements happens in healthcare all over the world. In this chapter, we aim at illustrating the perspective of the negative effects of the corruptive side of informal practices. We thus neglect the differences in functions and meanings of corruption in different contexts. In contrast to other chapters, our research approach is based on the normative vision of corruption and it is expected to supplement the picture of informal practices and to bring more details into the dialogue. Evidence is often hard to find, but working toward a more transparent procurement system will help to identify the most susceptible issues. Good governance, guiding those working in procurements and supporting them with guidelines, online sources and electronic bidding systems help to make the waste of public funds less appealing. Further research on the use of e-procurements and the sustainability of more transparent arrangements brought by international agencies in transition economies is still needed in order to achieve a better understanding of context-specific informal practices in health and its sub-sectors, including public procurements.

References

Brinkerhoff, D. W. (2004). Accountability and health systems: Toward conceptual clarity and policy relevance. *Health Policy and Planning, 19*, 371–379.

ECORYS. (2010). *Assessment of international assistance in the Serbian health sector*. Rotterdam: European Commission.

EHFCN. (2006). *Measuring corruption in healthcare*. Brussels: European Healthcare Fraud and Corruption Network.

European Commission. (2013). *Study on corruption in the healthcare sector*. Luxembourg: Publications Office of the European Union.

European Commission. (2014). *EU anti-corruption report*. Brussels: European Commission.

Gardiner, J. (2002). Defining corruption. *Political corruption: Concepts and contexts, 3*, 25–40.

Girling, J. (1997). *Corruption, capitalism and democracy*. London: Routledge.

Gotzsche, P. (2013). *Deadly medicines and organized crime*. Buckinghamshire: Radcliff Publishing Ltd..

Grødeland, Å. B., & Aasland, A. (2007). *Informality and Informal Practices in East Central and South East Europe* (Working Papers Series, 3). CERC (Contemporary Europe Research Centre, University of Melbourne).

Groot, W., & Maassen van den Brink, H. (2014). Oorzaken van fraude in de zorgsector. *Justitiele Verkenningen, 40*(3/14), 88–98.

ICAC. (2005). *Strenghtening the corruption resistance of the NSW public health sector*. Sydney: Independent Commission Against Corruption.

Jones, D. S. (2007). Public procurement in Southeast Asia: Challenge and reform. *Journal of public procurement, 7*(1), 3–33.

Keller, M. (2009). Medicine, the cashier. *Die Zeit*, 39.

Mackey, T. K., & Liang, B. A. (2012). Combating healthcare corruption and fraud with improved global health governance. *BMC International Health and Human Rights, 12*(1), 1.

OECD. (2007). *Bribery in public procurement. Methods, actors and countermeasures*. Paris: OECD Publishing.

OECD-UNODOC-World Bank. (2013). *Anti-corruption ethics and compliance handbook for business*. Paris: OECD, UNODOC and World Bank.

Polese, A. (2008). If i receive it, it is a gift; if i demand it, then it is a bribe' on the local meaning of economic transactions in post-Soviet Ukraine. *Anthropology in Action, 15*(3), 47–60.

Spelsberg, A., Martiny, A., & Schoenhoefer, P. S. (2009). Is disclosure of potential conflicts of interest in medicine and public health sufficient to increase transparency and decrease corruption? *Journal of Epidemiology and Community Health, 63*, 602–605.

Stepurko, T., Pavlova, M., Gryga, I., & Groot, W. (2010). Empirical studies on informal patient payments for health care services: A systematic and critical review of research methods and instruments. *BMC Health Services Research, 10*, 273.

Transparency International. (2006). *Global corruption report 2006.* London: Pluto Press.

Transparency International. (2010). *The anti-corruption catalyst: Realising the MDG's by 2015.* Berlin: Transparency International.

Transparency International. (2013). *Annual report 2012.* Berlin: Transparency International.

U4. (2006). *Anti-corruption in the health sector: Preventing drug diversion through supply chain management.* CMI/U4.

U4. (2008). *Corruption in the health sector.* U4 Anti-Corruption Resource Centre.

U4. (2011). *Addressing corruption in the health sector. Securing equitable access to health care for everyone.* CMI/U4.

UNDP. (2011). *Fighting corruption in the health sector.* New York: United Nations Development Programme.

Vian, T. (2002). *Sectoral perspective on corruption. Corruption and the health sector.*

Vian, T. (2008). Review of corruption in the health sector: Theory, methods and interventions. *Health Policy and Planning, 23*, 83–94.

World Bank. (2007). *The many faces of corruption.* Washington, DC: World Bank.

Index

Note: Page numbers followed by "n" denote footnotes.

A. Polese et al. (eds.), *The Informal Economy in Global Perspective*, International Political Economy Series,
DOI 10.1007/978-3-319-40931-3

CPI Antony Rowe
Chippenham, UK
2017-07-18 21:28